THE   STIRLING   REGION

THE

STIRLING REGION

Edited by

Duncan Timms
Professor of Sociology, University of Stirling

Stirling University for the Local Committee of
The British Association, 1974

First published in 1974 by the University of Stirling

Printed and bound in Scotland by Wm Culross and Son Ltd., Coupar Angus, Perthshire

ISBN   0   901636   03   7

ACKNOWLEDGEMENTS

The decision to produce a regional survey to accompany the 1974 Meeting of the British Association was not taken until May, 1973. As a result, it has been necessary to work to an exacting timetable. Without the co-operation of contributors and technical staff it would have been impossible to complete the task in the time available. Particular thanks are due to Ms Diane Evans and the Cartography Section, Department of Geography, University of Strathclyde, who prepared the maps and diagrams; to Dr G Farrow, Department of Geology, University of Glasgow, Dr J Proctor, Department of Biology, University of Stirling, and Dr G Gordon, Department of Geography, University of Strathclyde, who acted as sub-editors; to Ms Ida Stevenson, Composer Operator, University of Stirling, who prepared the typescript; and to Ms Jane Brook, Marion Govan and Pamela Drysdale who helped with the proof-reading. A grant towards the cost of illustrations from the Carnegie Trust for the Universities of Scotland is gratefully acknowledged.

CONTENTS

LIST OF FIGURES

LIST OF TABLES

x

INTRODUCTION — THE STIRLING REGION

It has become a convention that the Scientific Surveys produced to accompany the meetings of the British Association for the Advancement of Science begin with a lengthy introduction in which the host town or area are placed in the regional setting. We acknowledge the convention only to break it.

The key to an understanding of the Stirling Region is its diversity and its location on the periphery of more integrated regions to east and west. The area which forms the base for the survey is loosely modelled on that of the new local government area of the Central Region. In the report of the Royal Commission on Local Government in Scotland, under the chairmanship of Lord Wheatley, it is pointed out that 'the region is compact . . . . and its southern end is situated astride the corridor that connects the Clyde basin in the West region with the lower Forth and Lothians in the South East region. It has links with both these regions but it is in itself an area of potential growth of population and economic development which gives it an identity separate from both'. In accepting the Commission's proposals for the establishment of the Central Region, the Government White Paper, published in February 1971, concedes 'that of all the regions this one has at present the least degree of conscious identity'. In the search for such an identity the diversity of the Region may, paradoxically, prove its greatest asset.

Viewed from a satellite, the Stirling Region consists of two lowland basins, surrounded by highlands. The burgh of Stirling guards the gap which connects the upper and lower Forth basins and which provides a route through the barrier formed by the Ochil Hills in the east and the chain consisting of the Touch Hills, the Gargunnock Hills, and Fintry Hills and the Campsie Fells in the west. In the north the Region abuts Breadalbane, the southern edge of the Scottish Highlands, and includes, in the Braes of Balquhidder and the Trossachs, some of the most spectacular mountain scenery in Britain. The central lowlands include the flats of the Carse of Stirling, stretching from Aberfoyle and Gartmore in the west to Falkirk, Grangemouth and Alloa in the east, and the glacially-enlarged valleys of Loch Ard, Strath Gartney, Strathyre and Strath Allan. All drain to the Forth. In the south the regional boundary is formed by the Slamannan plateau and the edge of the Kilsyth Hills. In the west the boundary follows the watershed between the Forth and Loch Lomond. Only in the east is the Regional boundary indeterminate in physiographic terms, placing reliance instead on the administrative divisions between the old counties of Clackmannan, Kinross and Fife.

The division in terms of land form is repeated in terms of the differentiation of habitats. Plant and animal communities characteristic of Highland and Lowland come together in the Region producing a richness and diversity of flora and fauna which it had to match elsewhere

THE STIRLING REGION

in Scotland. The abundant surface water of the Region provides yet further biological diversity.

The effects of human activity have served largely to consolidate the physical and biological differentiation of the Stirling Region. The north and west of the Region are devoted to agriculture, forestry, and tourism; the south and east are more industrial. In the Highlands moor and forest vie for supremacy, Queen Elizabeth Forest Park alone extending to 45,000 acres. In the lowlands rich agricultural uses are intermingled with an industrial landscape, a landscape dominated by high technology petrochemical plants around the Forth and by obsolescent coal mines. Unlike the Strathclyde and Lothians Regions at the western and eastern extremities of central Scotland, the Stirling Region is not dominated by a single large urban centre. The industrial core of the Region is in the sprawling urban area centred on Falkirk and stretching between Denny and Dunipace in the west and Grangemouth in the east. Stirling is primarily a service centre, meeting the commercial and administrative needs of a large tributary area to the north and west and overlapping the hinterland of Alloa in the east. Not surprisingly for two towns which have figured so large in the history of Scotland, there is considerable rivalry between Stirling and Falkirk. Neither is able to exercise hegemony and the influence of both is widespread throughout the Region. It is perhaps only the 'accident' of the British Association meeting at the University of Stirling that justifies the use of the term 'Stirling Region' rather than a more general title which would include Falkirk.

PART ONE

THE PHYSICAL BACKGROUND

INTRODUCTION

THE PHYSICAL BACKGROUND – INTRODUCTION

The keynote to the physical background of the Stirling Region is variety. The Region lies at the meeting of the major north-south and east-west divisions of Scotland. To the north are the Trossachs and Breadalbane, the beginnings of the Highlands; to the south are the Central Lowlands and the Forth Estuary. To the west is the maritime influence of the Atlantic; to the east the continental influence of European air-masses. In few areas of Britain is it possible to trace so diverse an interaction between geology, geomorphology, climate and soils.

In chapters one and two the geology and geomorphology of the Stirling Region are out-lines by T Neville George. Much of the Region is underlain by Palaeozoic rocks, often greatly deformed. Major fault lines, notably the Highland Boundary Fault and the Ochils fault, help to define major unconformities in both geology and topography. Much of the topographic detail, however, as well as the patterning of the river systems, reflects the in-fluence of recent glaciation. As Professor George writes 'signs of the glaciation are ..., very fresh and impressive, and are seen in a great variety of features that much modify the pre-glacial landscape'.

The theme of diversity is joined, in chapter three, by that of transition. Writing on the climatology and hydrology of the Region, K Smith points out that airmasses from either west or east may temporarily prevail at any season while, from time to time, the more severe climatic conditions associated with the Highlands may also encroach. Seasonal fluctuations in precipitation and run-off are reflected in a marked seasonal variation in river flows, although these are, to some extent, damped by the natural storage provided by the numerous western lochs. Overall, the Region is a major source of surface water supplies.

The complex interplay between geology, climate, topography and biological action is nowhere better illustrated than in the distribution of soils. In chapter four B M Shipley provides a detailed mapping of the soil associations and soil series found in the Stirling Region. Not surprisingly, in view of the varied nature of the other environmental charac-teristics, the distribution of soil types proves highly complex.

CHAPTER 1

THE GEOLOGY OF THE STIRLING REGION

The geological environment

Stirling lies in the watergap of the River Forth between the Gargunnock and Touch Hills of Carboniferous volcanic lavas on one flank, and the Ochil Hills of Devonian volcanic on the other: its site is a textbook example of the close dependence of physical landscape on geological structure. To the north rocks of the Old Red Sandstone come to outcrop in the wide expanse of the Strathmore syncline in its western extension; and beyond them the ruggedly etched Highlands, abruptly emerging in a contrast of rock-type as the Highland Boundary fault is crossed, are eroded in deformed and metamorphosed grits and slates of the Dalradian suite. To the south and south-east, sharply defined in surface profile by the Ochil fault, the folded and fractured rocks of the Central Coalfield extend in lower ground to the Forth estuary and beyond.

The region lies along the northern flank of the Midland Valley of Scotland, a graben of broadly synclinal structure between the Highlands to the north and the Southern Uplands to the south. Palaeozoic rocks accumulated the great thickness, perhaps to 1500m (4900ft), in the graben, and in the region of its bordering massifs. They intermittently span Cambrian to Permian times, but their accumulation was periodically interrupted by earth-movements, sometimes intense, that resulted in folding and unconformity and in a broken rock succession. No 'solid' rocks of Mesozoic or Cenozoic age are known in the district, apart from a veneer of unconsolidated clays, sands, and gravels geologically of very recent Glacial and post-Glacial origin, that rest upon the deeply eroded Palaeozoic rocks beneath.

The geological history of the district may be summarised in alternating pulses of sedimentation and earth-movement (see Fig. 1.1):

8   Deposition of Quaternary boulder clays, morainic and periglacial sands and gravels, late-Glacial and post-Glacial raised beach deposits, and alluvium.

7   A long interval of Mesozoic and Tertiary times, spanning some 200 million years, of which there is no record in the Stirling district.

6   Strong earth-movements (the Hercynian erogeny) closing the period of Palaeozoic sedimentation and imposing the major structural form of the Midland Valley that continues to the present day.

5   Formation of the Upper Palaeozoic rocks:
    (c) Minor igneous activity seen in residual volcanic vents of late-Carboniferous and perhaps Permian age.

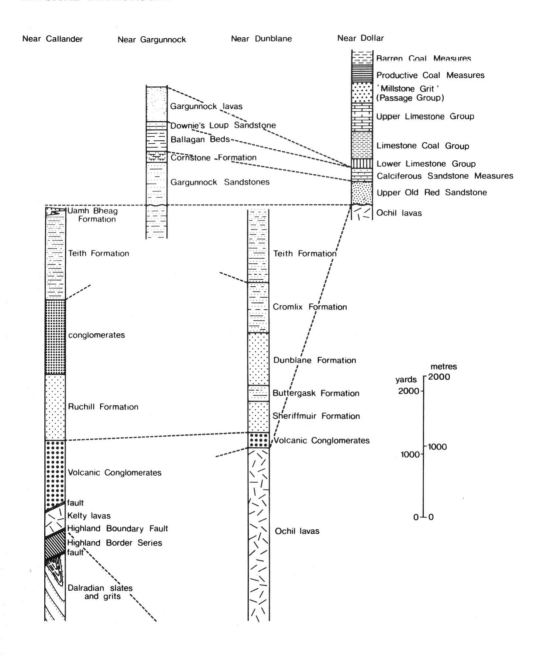

Near Callander   Near Gargunnock   Near Dunblane   Near Dollar

Barren Coal Measures
Productive Coal Measures
'Millstone Grit' (Passage Group)
Upper Limestone Group
Limestone Coal Group
Lower Limestone Group
Calciferous Sandstone Measures
Upper Old Red Sandstone
Ochil lavas

Gargunnock lavas
Downie's Loup Sandstone
Ballagan Beds
Cornstone Formation
Gargunnock Sandstones

Uamh Bheag Formation
Teith Formation
conglomerates
Ruchill Formation
Volcanic Conglomerates
fault
Kelty lavas
Highland Boundary Fault
Highland Border Series
fault
Dalradian slates and grits

Teith Formation
Cromlix Formation
Dunblane Formation
Buttergask Formation
Sheriffmuir Formation
Volcanic Conglomerates
Ochil lavas

metres
yards 2000
2000
1000
1000
0 0

Fig 1.1   COMPARATIVE COLUMNS IN THE SOLID GEOLOGY OF THE STIRLING REGION

There is no continuous succession to be seen at outcrop, the Lower Palaeozoic rocks and the Lower Old Red Sandstone being found only to the north of the Ochil fault, the Upper Old Red Sandstone only to the south.   In the older rocks the Callander sequence on the north-western flank of the Strathmore syncline is significantly different from the Dunblane sequence on the south-eastern;   and in the younger rocks notable differences between western outcrops near Gargunnock and eastern near Dollar include a thinning of the Upper Old Red Sandstone and the Lower Carboniferous rocks with a disappearance of the Clyde (Gargunnock) lavas.

(b) Carboniferous rocks:
Coal Measures, the older members (the Productive Measures) with many workable coal seams, the younger members (the Barren Measures) with few.
'Millstone Grits' (the Passage Group).
Carboniferous Limestone Series, in threefold division, the Limestone Coal Group separating the Lower Limestone Group from the Upper Limestone Group.
Calciferous Sandstone Measures, in which are interbedded the thick piles of the Clyde (Campsie) lavas to the west of Stirling.

(a) Old Red Sandstone, divided by strong late-Caledonian earth-movement and internal unconformity into Upper Red Sandstone and Lower Old Red Sandstone, the thick piles of the Ochil lavas being a prominent formation in the Lower Old Red Sandstone to the north-east of Stirling.

4 A long interval during which Silurian rocks, not seen in the Stirling district but probably lying at depth, were deposited and later deformed in a Caledonian orogenic episode the deformation subsuming an earlier Caledonian deformation of the Arenig rocks.

3 Deposition of the Highland Border Series, probably in older members of late-Cambrian or early-Ordovician (Arenig) age, in younger members of late-Ordovician (Caradoc) age.

2 Large-scale deformation of the Dalradian rocks, in overfolds and metamorphism, in a major episode of the Caledonian orogeny.

1 Sedimentation of the Dalradian rocks in Cambrian times.

The Dalradian rocks

The Dalradian rocks, their outcrop covering a large part of the southern Highlands between the Highland Boundary fault and the Great Glen, run in the Stirling district from Loch Lomond by Loch Katrine and Loch Lubnaig towards Loch Earn, in country abundantly exposed to reveal their nature and the complex deformation they have suffered (see Fig. 1.2). In greatest part they are terrigenous sediments whose members — grits, sandstones, siltstones, and shales — reach a thickness in the district (where only Upper Dalradian rocks come to outcrops) of perhaps 3500m (11500ft). The older units, the Pitlochry Schists and the Aberfoyle Slates, form the Pelitic Group, while the younger Leny and Ben Ledi Grits form the Psammitic Group.

Pitlochry Schists are mainly altered mudstones and siltstones with some grit bands upon which a schistose structure has been imposed by a metamorphism to chlorite grades. The Aberfoyle Slates are similar in original rock types, but the metamorphic changes they have suffered are less intense, the grade being chloritic, and in their structure a slaty cleavage is dominant, which allowed the beds formerly to be worked for roofing slates. Old quarries are conspicious notably near Aberfoyle, but the many intercalations in the slates of thin

N.W.   S.E.

? base of Upper O.R.S.

Near Crieff   Lower O.R.S.

Upper Old Red Sandstone

Lower Old Red Sandstone

Lavas (Ochil?) and conglomerates

Highland Border Series

Near Callander   ? base of Upper O.R.S.   ? base of Upper O.R.S.

? Lower O.R.S.

Serpentine

Dalradian grits

Aberfoyle synform

Aberfoyle Slates

? base of Upper O.R.S.

Near Balmaha   no Lower O.R.S.

0   1 mile

0   1 km

Highland Boundary
fault

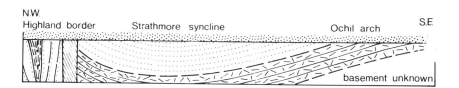

N.W.   S.E.
Highland border   Strathmore syncline   Ochil arch

basement unknown

Fig 1.2   COMPARATIVE SECTIONS ACROSS THE HIGHLAND BOUNDARY FAULT

Recognisable episodes in the evolution of the fault include:

(a)   early-Caledonian initiation of the fault in Ordovician times after the overfolding of the Tay nappe;

(b)   peneplanation in late-Silurian times of the foundation structures, and the deposition across the line of the fault from the Midland Valley into the Highlands of the Lower Old Red Sandstone (the Ochil lavas at the base), a relationship illustrated in the neighbourhood of Crieff;

(c)   late-Caledonian deformation of the Lower Old Red Sandstone by folding of the Strathmore syncline and by faulting with downthrow south along the Highland Boundary fault;

(d)   peneplanation in mid-Devonian times of the structures in the Lower Old Red Sandstone and the deposition across the line of the fault from the Midland Valley into the Highlands of the Upper Old Red Sandstone, a relationship illustrated in the neighbourhood of Balmaha;

(e)   anomalous post-Carboniferous (Hercynian) downthrow of the Upper Old Red Sandstone on the Highland flank of the Highland Boundary fault.   The three sections disclose at present erosional levels the variant structural expression along 30km of outcrop.

THE DEPOSITION OF THE UPPER OLD RED SANDSTONE

A diagrammatic reconstruction of the relationship between the Upper Old Red Sandstone and the underlying rocks between the Highland border (where all the Lower Old Red Sandstone may be missing) and the Ochil arch near Pool of Muckhart (where perhaps 4500m of the Lower Old Sandstone suite are overstepped) is an indication of the magnitude of the mid-Devonian earth-movements.

grits and siltstones and the consequent imperfections in the cleavage result in the manufactured slates being thick and heavy and demanding massive timbering in roof construction. The resources, although indefinitely extensive, are no longer exploited.

The Leny and Ben Ledi Grits display a proportionate increase in the number and thickness of the coarser bands, shales (slates) being subordinated to grits that are massive and form bold scarps and crags. The individual units commonly show wedge and graded bedding, and many of them appear to have originated as turbidites; the rhythmical alternation of coarse and fine layers (also to be seen in inverse proportion in the Aberfoyle Slates) suggests a 'geosynclinal' environment of sedimentation. Bands of calcareous shale intercalated in the Leny Grits constitute the Leny Limestone, a formation of importance in having yielded the only fossils of zonal significance known in the Dalradian sequence – pagetiid trilobites indicating an early mid-Cambrian age. It is to be presumed that much or all of the Dalradian (or at least of the Upper Dalradian) falls into the Middle and Lower Cambrian.

The structural complexities of the Dalradian rocks have not yet been completely resolved, especially the relations of the Aberfoyle Slates with the neighbouring grits. The Slates appear in elongate faulted outcrops in which the steep dips were formerly read as implying a place for the Slates either in a sandwich between grits below and grits above, or in the core of a locally acute anticline, the Ben Ledi Grits to the north being equated with the Leny Grits to the south as sediments of approximately the same age, the minor differences in detailed sequence across the anticline being interpreted as a reflection of lateral variation in lithology during time of deposition. Recently, however, widespread evidence mainly in graded bedding shows the grits repeatedly to be overturned; and in outcrops where there appears to be relatively gently dip and the succession to be little disturbed, the rocks are progressively older the higher they rise in the present-day sequence. The Slates are then truly in the core of an anticline, but the core closes as a downward-facing structure, deceptively appearing as a syncline (see Fig. 1.5 p.19).

When the evidence is extended northwards, the rocks, despite their low dips, are then recognised to be part of the flank of an enormous overfold and, in the so-called 'flat Belt', very well seen in the scarps forming the valley walls running north-westwards beyond Aberfoyle from Loch Ard and Loch Chon to Loch Katrine, the overturned limb of the fold (the Tay nappe) is all that remains of the original structure, the uninverted 'upper' limb having been almost completely eroded away. Only in the neighbourhood of the Highland border, where the nose of the fold has itself been down-turned by secondary folding superposed on the nappe and preserves the synformal 'outline' of the Aberfoyle Slates, can both limbs of the structure be seen (see Figs. 1.3, 1.5).

The acute folds of the Dalradian rocks extend over most of the Grampian Highlands. They are a sign of orogenic deformation of the first magnitude and characterise the southern part of the Caledonian fold belt, the northern part of which continues across the Great Glen into the Moinian terrain of the Northern Highlands.   A second sign of the tectonism to which the Dalradian rocks have been exposed lies in their metamorphic grade.   The overfolding, later in development than mid-Cambrian rocks caught in the structures, appears to be older than the Ordovician rocks against which they are faulted, and it is significant than an isotopic dating of the metamorphism give an age of about 470 million years, approximately early-Ordovician, and confirms the place of these structural effects in an early but powerful episode of the Caledonian earth-movements.

The Highland Border Series

Abruptly thrown against the Dalradian rocks in the Highland Boundary fault belt, the Highland Border Series occupies a narrow outcrop, rarely more that 1200m (3900ft), wide and sometimes reduced by strike faulting to nil, from Loch Lomond and Balmaha by Aberfoyle and Callander to Glen Artney (see Fig. 1.1). They appear to differ markedly in lithological type, degree of metamorphism, and structural pattern from the Aberfoyle Slates and the Leny Grits, and give the impression of being younger not only than the Dalradian sediments but also than the Tay nappe, and then to imply a major depositional and tectonic gap not spanned by any rocks in the Stirling district; but argument and some evidence have been offered for putting diminished emphasis on the contrasts and for regarding the Series to be not greatly different in age from the Leny Grits.

The rocks consist of a very mixed suite of black shales and cherts with some spilitic-lavas, sheared and broken by being wedged in the faulted strip between the Leny Grits and the Old Red Sandstone.   They contain a few poorly preserved fossils including inarticulate brachiopods, phyllocarid crustaceans and radiolarians, whose age cannot be closely determined but is certainly Lower Palaeozoic: not as old as the mid-Cambrian Leny Limestone and possibly Ordovician.   The rock-suite is remote from comparable rocks elsewhere in Scotland: in general facies it compares most closely with the Lower Ordovician rocks of Ballantraw, in which well-preserved graptolites prove an Arenig age, and in tentative lithological correlation the Highland Border Series may then also be regarded as Arenig.   A tongue of conglomerates and grits (the 'Margie Series') at Aberfoyle, resting on the black shales and cherts apparently with unconformity, has analogy with the rocks of Upper Ordovician (Caradoc) age near Girvan, and as at Girvan they may indicate a regional northward overstep implying strong mid-Ordovician tectonism.   Beneath the Upper Palaeozoic surface formations of the Stirling district there may thus be a foundation composed of variously folded and faulted rocks, Cambrian (Dalradian), Lower Ordovician, and Upper Ordovician in age, severly deformed and eroded in multiple stages.   The northern development of the foundation is exposed in the linear outcrops of rocks which by the chance of strike faulting, are brought to view along the Highland border but that would otherwise not be known, and in the more extensive outcrop of the Dalradian terrain.

Associated with the sediments of the Highland Border Series are major basic and ultra-basic igneous intrusions of which a carbonated serpentine, much altered to talc, forms the most conspicuous member.   The intrusions run intermittently for scores of miles along the Highland border, being well seen for some 20km (12miles) north-eastwards from Loch Lomond to Loch Venacher.   Present outcrops are narrow, contained and sometimes extinguished between branches of the Highland Boundary fault and the original form of the intrusions is uncertain, but the petrological and tectonic affinities, and the close parallelism in all the outcrops, of the serpentine and gabbro with the spilites of the Highland Border Series, suggest that all the rocks fall into a common igneous episode of Arenig age.   The contiguity of the serpentine belt with the fault, across Scotland into Ireland, very strongly suggests a tectonic community of origin of intrusion and fracture, and although the igneous rocks now occupy a comparatively small, even insignificant, area of outcrop, they are of the greatest importance in strengthening the conclusion that the Highland Boundary fault, and so part of the framework of the Midland Valley rift, were initiated in early Ordovician times.

Lower Old Red Sandstone

The Old Red Sandstone occupies the wide expanse of country between the Highland Boundary fault and the Ochil fault, as the next youngest group of formations after the Ordovician rocks in the sequence of outcrops as they are followed towards the south-east.   The absence of Silurian rocks, and the great contrast between the relatively simple structure in the Old Red Sandstone and the complex structures in the Highland Border Series and the Dalradian rocks, are a sign of a long geological interval for which no evidence remains in the Stirling district.   Correspondingly the Old Red Sandstone rests with strong unconformity on the older rocks, an unconformity seen in transgressive outliers overlying residual Dalradian rocks of the Tay nappe near Balmaha and again near Crieff, just beyond the conventional boundaries of the Stirling district.   It is clear that before Devonian sedimentation began the Highland Boundary fault as a major fracture defining the Midland Valley rift was fully established, and the Highlands as a horst-like massif became in due course a major control on contemporary geological processes (see Fig. 1.3).

The full thickness of the Old Red Sandstone is not known, the base not being appropriately seen, but it probably exceeds 6500m (21300ft).   None of the sediments accumulated in deep water and some of the volcanic piles of the lavas are so thick that they must have stood above depositional level as lava plateaus.   There can be little doubt, therefore, that the downthrown basin of the rift filled as it grew and there was very close correlation

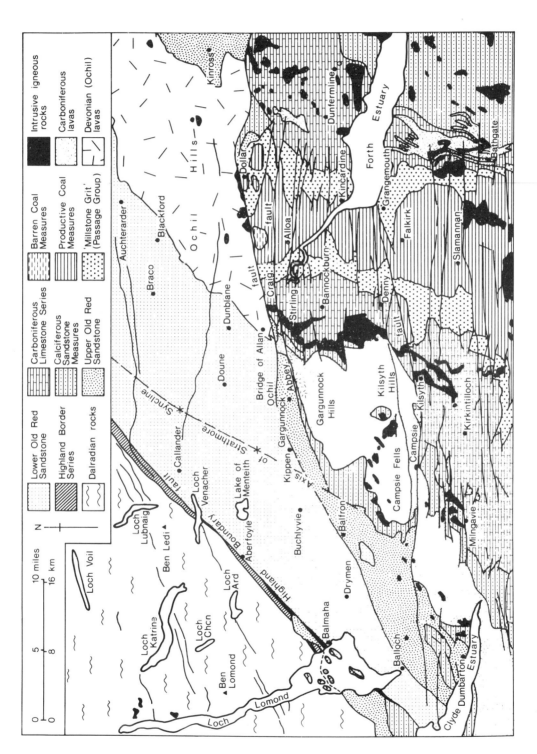

Fig 1.3   OUTLINE MAP OF THE SOLID GEOLOGY OF THE STIRLING REGION

The multiplicity of fractures in the brittle Carboniferous sediments to the south of the Ochil fault contrasts with the broad simplicity of the deeper structures in the Old Red Sandstone of the Strathmore syncline.   *After the maps of the Geological Survey.*

between structure and sedimentation, not least in the pulsed movement along the Highland Boundary fault in a complementary uprise of the Highland massif. A contemporary environment is thus to be reconstructed of intense erosion of terrain to the north, which was matched by a pouring of the eroded detritus into a trough (the 'Caledonian cuvette') to the south through the agency of powerful streams; in great part the lithology of the Old Red Sandstone confirms the reconstruction. The restlessness of the deforming crust was further increased by violent igneous activity during the earlier part of the period when the Ochil lavas were outpoured.

Locally, the oldest known members of the Old Red Sandstone suite are the lavas. In the scarp faces above Tillicoultry they are not less than 2500m (8200ft) and may be as much as 3000m (8750ft) thick (see Fig. 1.5). They are mainly basaltic and andesitic in composition, and occur as interfingering flows, any one flow not persisting beyond a few miles. Beds of tuff and agglomerate, interbedded with the basalts, record explosive events interrupting extrusive flow, but most of the rocks suggest fissure eruption and a gentle welling of magma to the surface. The detailed sequence is variable as it is traced laterally, and the contemporary geography of the volcanic terrain is not readily reconstructed in detail. Perhaps significance is to be read into a concentration of vents and fissures that can be identified along courses near the Ochil fault, the fault being interpreted as a fissure conduit from the lava reservoir; the fault (in its present features mainly post-Carboniferous) may, like the Highland Boundary fault, have thus been active in early Devonian times.

The sagging of the floor of the rift continued as rapidly as the lavas accumulated and during periods of igneous quiescence layers of water-carried volcanic debris were deposited to become interbedded in the lava sequence, sometimes not to be readily distinguished from true tuff. Such sediments become proportionately dominant towards the south-west of the main lava outcrops and in the neighbourhood of Bridge of Allan there are relatively few lava flows, the volcanic suite wedging out in diminishing tongues to final disappearance against the Ochil fault (see Fig. 1.4, p.15).

Along the Highland border, in Keltie Water near Callander on the north-western flank of the Strathmore syncline, volcanic rocks reappear in a narrow outcrop for some 2km; elsewhere they are downthrown to depth along the Highland Boundary fault. They are mainly basalt and andesite lavas analogous and probably equivalent to the Ochil lavas, and as in the Ochils they carry sedimentary intercalations of water-borne volcanic debris. Presumably they imply a widespread continuity of the lava series from east to west beneath the younger rocks of the syncline, fed from vents and fissures to the south-east of the fault (for there are no feeders cutting the Dalradian rocks immediately to the north). Similar lavas are well developed between Comrie and Crieff, a few kilometers to the north-east, where their base is seen to rest on an eroded floor of steeply dipping Dalradian slates and grits (see Fig. 1.3).

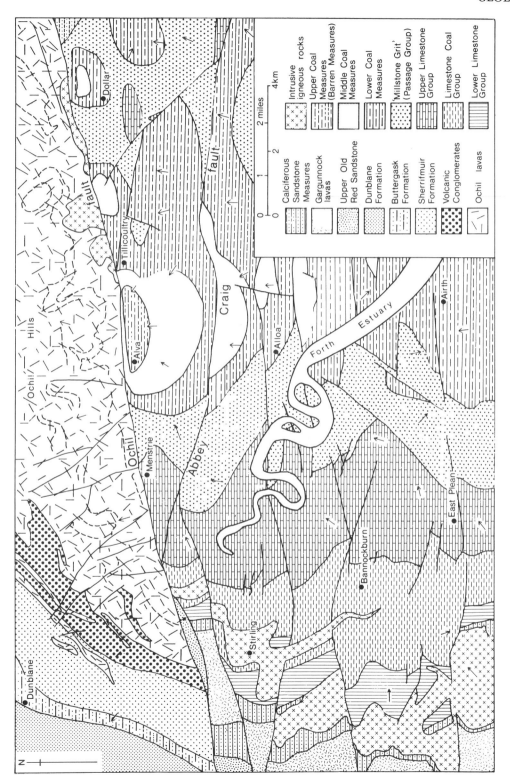

Fig 1.4   MAP OF THE SOLID GEOLOGY IN THE NEIGHBOURHOOD OF STIRLING   (slightly simplified)

Particular features are the packing of the minor folds along the Ochil fault from Dollar to Alva and Menstrie; the alinement of the fault in oblique transection of the strike of the beds in the Lower Old Red Sandstone; and the sharp changes in horizon of the Stirling sill. *After 1-inch map no. 39 of the Geological Survey.*

Igneous intrusions of several kinds are associated with the Ochil lavas and are presumably also early-Devonian in age.   Small stocks of diorite, perhaps converging into a larger mass at depth, emerge north of Tillicoultry; they sometimes give the impression of reconstituted lavas and commonly contain many xenoliths of country rock.   A number of dykes and a few sills of basalt or porphyrite, many not randomly orientated but suggesting an already-existent fracture pattern, also cut the lavas but do not continue into the overlying sediments of Old Red Sandstone.

The lavas of the Ochil Hills dip gently northwards under a great thickness, perhaps 3500m (11500ft), of sandy and pebbly sediments belonging to the Lower Old Red Sandstone (see Fig. 1.4).   The beds immediately overlying the lavas reflect the erosion that the uneven surface of the volcanic rocks underwent: they are coarse conglomerates, many with abundant well-rounded pebbles, whose lenticular beds suggest deposition in channels and hollows and delta spreads on the irregular floor.   At maximum the conglomerates may reach 250m (820ft), but their high irregularity is shown in their variable thickness which diminishes in places almost to nil and they mark an end to the major volcanic outbursts although they contain the occasional thin lava flow even at high horizons.

The conglomerates are overlain, northwards in outcrop succession, by characteristic brown and purple sandstones of great thickness showing only relatively minor changes in lithology.   They range in grain size from fine mudstones, silty shales, and siltstones to coarser grits, the variations allowing a broad division of the sequence into four of five main formations that may be followed along the strike for many miles and give an impression of much greater uniformity in the depositional environment than the underlying 'volcanic' conglomerates.

The Sheriffmuir Sandstones, immediately above the volcanic conglomerates, but with some thin interbedded lavas, is 300m (1000ft), to 500m (1600ft) thick.   It is relatively coarse, with some finer silt and shale bands, and some thin conglomerates with pebbles of igneous rock.   Calcareous concretions indicate temporary desiccation of some of the beds and contemporary erosion, and a calcareous cement is pervasive.   The formation is notable for having yielded the ostracoderms *Cephalaspis* and *Pteraspis* as proof of a Downtonian or Dittonian age.   The overlying strata of the Buttergask formation, mainly finer sandstones and siltstones about 300m (1000ft) thick, appear to be sediments deposited towards the quieter parts of the basin as flood-plain spreads transported by gentle currents, indicating only a subdued hinterlands of lava hills at a time when the irregularities of the contemporary Ochils had become much degraded or submerged under a cover of accumulating sediments.   The Dunblane formation, about 750m (2500ft) thick, is composed of massive cross-bedded sandstones, sometimes arkosic, mostly without lava fragments.   The matrix is usually calcitic and there are beds of cornstone and of fragmented mudstone with a calcareous bond, suggesting periodic desiccation. The succeeding Cromlix formation, 800m (2600ft) thick at maximum but thinning northwards to less than 300m (1000ft) is analogous to rocks of the Sheriffmuir formation in its fine-grained character of silty mudstones and fine siltstones, some of which, poorly bedded, tend to weather into cuboidal fragments. It emphasises a cyclical alternation in the Old Red Sandstone of rocks differing in grain size and colour, especially when it is followed by the Teith formation, coarser well-sorted and well-bedded sandstones, perhaps 1200m (3900ft) thick, like the rocks of the Dunblane formation.

On the north-west flank of the Strathmore syncline, towards the Highland border, the rocks are in general very much coarser, the well-defined formations of the south-eastern out-crops losing their uniformly sandy character with the development of thick wedges of con-glomerates and the formational sequence not being readily recognised over the whole area of the basin (see Fig. 1.1). The conglomerates of volcanic debris that (presumably) rest upon the Ochil lavas are as much as 100m thick, their upper members perhaps equating with the lower beds of the Sheriffmuir formation. They are followed by the Ruchill formation, mostly flagstones, fine sandstones, siltstones, mudstones and shales not unlike the sediments of the Sheriffmuir and Buttergask formations. The overlying thick conglomerates, variously named and together reaching 1000m (3300ft) probably pass laterally at depth in the heart of the basin into the Dunblane and Cromlix formation and tongues of conglomerates are deve-loped in and above the Teith formation. The pebbles in these conglomerates, except the volcanic conglomerates, are mostly of quartzite, schist, and other Highland metamorphic rocks, although lava pebbles may be admixed, and they give every sign of the intense erosion of a hinterland (reflected in the present Highland massif) that was repeatedly renewed by uplift, the erosion being the work of powerful streams descending into the basin and forming delta fans and spreads of gravel as 'the molasse of the Caledonian chain'. Traced laterally the conglomerates tend to be lenticular and especially towards the south-west to thin out and die away: the comparatively thin beds near Aberfoyle and towards Loch Lom-ond are quite overshadowed by the massive beds near Callander and by the great thicknesses towards Glen Artney where in hills above 630m (2070ft) they reach altitudes not much be-low the summits of the Ochils, but they nevertheless are locally prominent as in Beinn Dearg and the Menteith Hills and in Gualann and Conic Hill.

Upper Old Red Sandstone

The Upper Old Red Sandstone rests upon the Lower with great unconformity, no Middle Old Red Sandstone being known in the Stirling district (or anywhere in the Midland Valley). Overstep at the base of the formation is particularly well seen east of Dollar towards Kinross, where the Gargunnock Sandstones descend transgressively onto low horizons in the Ochil lavas, the equivalents of the thousands of metres – perhaps 3000m (10000ft) – of overlying Lower Old Red Sandstone being absent from the succession (see Fig. 1.2).

Along the Highland border evidence is fragmentary, but a few kilometres south-west of Aberfoyle towards Loch Lomond spectacular overstep by the Upper Old Red Sandstone across the Highland Boundary fault is seen in a descent of the formation onto the Highland Border Series and onto Dalradian grits, all the Lower Old Red Sandstone being absent although it is several thousand metres thick immediately to the south.   It is evident not only that folds of very large amplitude were imposed upon the Lower Old Red Sandstones before deposition of the Upper, but also that movement along the Highland Boundary fault in the same order of throw took place in mid-Devonian times in sustained development of the rift (see Fig. 1.3).

The Upper Old Red Sandstone is conveniently divided into two major lithological groups.   The lower group, the Gargunnock Sandstones, consists of mainly red and pink sandstones — the brightness of their red colour being a very convenient means of distinction from the darker brown and purple beds of the Lower Old Red Sandstone — with some finer beds of siltstone and mudstones.   Intercalated conglomerates contain abundant pebbles of vein quartz, quartzite, and schist derived from Highland sources (perhaps after reworking from Lower Old Red Sandstone), together with pebbles of lava and brown gritty sandstones directly derived from the Lower Old Red Sandstone.   Much of the cement is carbonate. Most of the sandstones are cross-bedded, the foresets repeatedly suggesting currents flowing from terrain, presumably Highland, to the north-west.   The formation is about 600m (2000ft) thick in western outcrops, but it thins to 350m (1150ft) towards Stirling before being cut out by the Ochil fault.   No fossils have been found in it.

The overlying Cornstones Beds are defined arbitrarily at the first appearance of a corn-stone layer.   Characteristically they are arenites deposited in marked rhythmic cycles of alternating pebbly sandstones and fine mudstones or silty shales.   Each sandstone, massive and thick-bedded, commonly has a bottom layer of pebbly or conglomeratic texture with an irregular base that scoops into the underlying bed and with cross-stratification the foresets of which, as in the Gargunnock Sandstones, suggest derivation from the north-west.   Usually the coarse sandstone becomes finer-grained upwards and passes without sharp contact into the silts and muds above.   Such cyclothemic deposits are widely developed in the Old Red Sandstone of other areas in Britain and are generally considered to be a product of flood-plain sedimentation in which fluctuations in river-flow, referable to a variety of factors (including hinterland revival), caused the rhythms.

The sandstones usually contain much carbonate cement and a feature of the formation, which gives the formational name, is the recurrence of cornstone bands, most of which are strongly dolomitic. The concretionary cornstones, sometimes massive, sometimes little more than scattered nodules, are usually found in the finer-grained upper members of the sand-stones with a rich calcareous cement to cornstones with an abundance of quartz grains.   The cornstones are analogous to kankar and caliche, seen in present day deposits as carbonate-

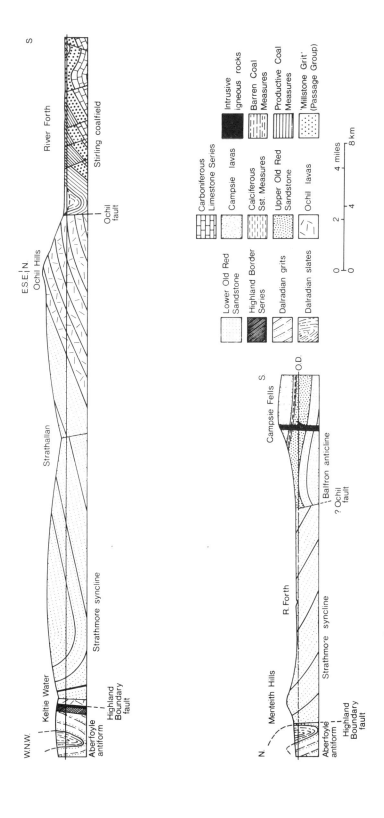

Fig 1.5   COMPARATIVE SECTIONS IN THE SOLID GEOLOGY OF THE STIRLING REGION

The sections illustrate the complexities along the Highland Border, the asymmetrical Strathmore syncline, the abrupt change in sequence and structure across the Ochil fault, the thick Carboniferous Clyde lavas of the Campsie Fells, and the thicker Devonian Ochil lavas of the eastern outcrops. *In part after the Geological Survey.*

enriched layers in a pedocal soil that originated mainly by leaching under semi-arid or desiccatory conditions, and they give signs of a Devonian environment in which intervals of terrigenous sedimentation by fairly powerful rivers in flood-plain spreads alternated with intervals of drying-out pools and dried-out flats; but there are no signs in the formation of brines and true evaporites.   A feature of the cornstones not easily explained is the dolomitic composition of the carbonate: this is presumably a secondary feature, most of the beds showing signs of recrystallisation.   Like the Gargunnock Sandstones the Cornstone Beds show progressive thinning eastwards from some 400m (1300ft) about Balfron and Kippen to little more thn 100m (330ft) east of Gargunnock.   The Cornstones have not as yet yielded any fossils: they are regarded as falling into the Upper Old Red Sandstone on the basis of their bright brick-red colour, their unconformable contact with the Lower Old Red Sandstones and their conformable transition into the Carboniferous Ballagan Beds above.

Calciferous Sandstone Measures

The earliest formation of the Carboniferous rocks, the Calciferous Sandstone Measures, enters above the Old Red Sandstone in a suite of shales, mudstones, thin sandstones and particularly dolomitic cementstones that are notably distinct from the red rocks beneath in their general grey or limonitic-brown colour.   At an arbitrary junction they are probably diachronous in their lowest layers in a lateral passage into uppermost Cornstone Beds and they do not indicate any great change in the environment of sedimentation except in their hints of a distant marine influence.   The first members of the suite (the Cementstones, locally called the Ballagan Beds) are followed by the Spout of Ballagan Sandstone and farther east the equivalent Downie's Loup Sandstones, rocks that in their strong development of cross-bedding and in the occurrence of conglomeratic layers imply a revival of hinterland erosion and an in-pouring of deltaic detritus.   The undersides of some of the beds carry load-casts and other signs of rapid sedimentation, and some of the upper surfaces show polygonal desiccation cracks occupied by sandstone wedges.   Fossils both in the Ballagan Beds and in the Sandstones are rare: they include ostracods and occasional fish scales, while scattered algal nodules (*Girvanella, Ortonella*) offer a hint of open-sea neritic conditions at no great distance.   The thickness of the two groups diminishes from 500m (1600ft) in western outcrops to 250m (800ft) in eastern perhaps in relation to an incipient growth of the Strathmore syncline.

During the period when the oil shales were accumulating not far away in the Lothians at horizons above the Downie's Loup Sandstones the environment was transformed in the Stirling district by volcanic out-pourings that complemented in the Carboniferous west the Devonian Ochil volcanics of the east.   They constitute a salient of the Clyde plateau lavas and are prominently exposed in the Campsie Fells and the Fintry and Gargunnock hills.   A few thin lava tongues are inter-layered with the uppermost members of the Downie's Loup

Sandstones, a prominent bed of tuff, the Slackgun interbasaltic bed, resting on the sandstones in the west but being separated from them by some 100m of lavas in the east (see Fig. 1.2.).

The rocks are dominantly basalts — Markle basalts with abundant large phenocrysts of plagioclase and Jedburgh basalts with smaller phenocrysts of plagioclase and olivine — in flows ranging up to 25m (82ft) thick, some of them being traceable for 5km (3miles). Some of the flows are composite with alternating Markle-type and Jedburgh-type bands. Many of the lavas display flow structure, there being repeated contrasts between slaggy and ropy flows, and a wedging of tongues of lava. The vesicular and slaggy upper surfaces of the flows are commonly decayed and leached by contemporaneous weathering into dark-red bole, the stepped erosion of which gives rise to the characteristic trap featuring of the hill profiles. Tuffs are comparatively rare, the only considerable development being the Slackgun, which in the Fintry Hills reaches 80m (260ft): the primary volcanic fragments may be admixed with much water-borne detritus, and may be decomposed into bole.

In the Campsie and Kilsyth hills a number of centralised pipes and necks penetrate the lavas and were conduits for volcanic flows: Dunfoyn and Dumgoyne, Barniemore and Dunmore are prominent examples. But farther east in the Fintry and Gargunnock hills the volcanic terrain is without such intrusions and in general form and range the lavas appear as sheet and flood basalts probably fed as fissure eruptions — again, like the Ochil lavas, hinting at fracturing at depth in an ancestral proto-Hercynian tectonic structure. Dykes of basaltic composition are common in the lava field and may have been feeders, but they do not occur in parallel swarms and do not bear any obvious systematic relationship to the major faults of the region.

The lavas and tuffs are thickest in the western outcrops, where in residual sequence (the uppermost layers of the Gargunnock suite not being preserved) they are about 350m (1150ft). They reach a similar thickness (but with some scores of metres of the uppermost lavas added) in the Gargunnock Hills, but farther east — the details lost because of faulting — they diminish rapidly, the last outcrops being seen near Stirling, and the Carboniferous outcrops near Dollar showing them to be absent (see Figs. 1.1, 1.4). How far northwestwards they originally continued is unknown, but there are no signs of correlated intrusions in the terrain of Old Red Sandstone, and it is not likely that they advanced more than a few kilometres beyond their present limits of outcrops. The thinning of the Clyde lavas to the east, matched by the earlier thinning (at outcrop) of the Ochil lavas to the west, and the consequent fall in altitude of their resistant hill summits in convergence, thus constitute the 'accidental' geological context of the site of the Forth watergap and the determinant of the site for Stirling.

The Clyde lavas, like the Devonian Ochil lavas, accumulated in thicknesses that took them well above contemparaneous depositional level (as the successive bole soils indicate), and while sediments of the oil shales were being laid down to the south-east the Stirling district remained as islands undergoing irregular degradation. The sedimentary rocks succeeding the lavas thus rest with unconformity on the igneous rocks, the time-span of the volcanic interval resulting in their being markedly different from the basal Carboniferous suite underlying the lavas. They continue to be regarded as part of the Calciferous Sandstone Measures, but they reflect a major subsidence of much of the Midland Valley beneath the sea, and as the Upper Sedimentary Group of the Measures they are dominantly marine in origin. The diachronous first rocks that overstep and overlap onto the lavas are coarse grits and conglomerates dominantly composed of detritus eroded from the volcanic rocks — the typical basal beds of a transgressive sea. They are very variable in thickness but may reach as much as 60m (200ft) and they rise in horizon almost to the Murrayshall Limestone as they are banked against the floor of lavas. The conglomerates lie in hollows on the eroded lava floor, They are followed by shales with calcareous bands as rows of calcareous nodules or as continuous limestone ribs, strata that are in places richly fossiliferous, notably with large productid brachiopods (*Gigantoproductus*), chonetids (*Tornquistia*), spirifers (notably *Crurithyris*), scallops, corals (*Lithostrotion*), and occasional goniatites (*Beyrichoceras*), the fossils proving the rocks to lie near the top of the Visiean (D_2) in Carboniferous (Dinantian) zonal terms. Some of the beds contain ironstone nodules, and there is an occasional rootlet bed, but there are no thick coals.

Carboniferous Limestone Series

The lithological justification for separating the Carboniferous Limestone Series from the Calciferous Sandstone Measures is arbitrary, the Murrayshall Limestone that defines its base being no more than a rather more widespread bed than any of the underlying limestones and (as the Hurlet Limestone) a useful marker over much of the Midland Valley. In general sequence the lowest formation of the Carboniferous Limestone Series, the Lower Limestone Group compares with the Upper Sedimentary Group in consisting of a series of mainly marine calcareous shales and thin limestone with some siltstones and fine sandstones, and with a few thin and unimportant coals and thin seat-earths. Fossiliferous layers are common and the limestones (of which the Shields, Fankerton, and Hosies are the chief) yield a number of species of brachiopods (productids, spirifers, athyrides), bivalves, gastopods, nautiloids, goniatites (*Beyrichoceras*), and rugose corals (*Lithostrotion*), the rocks falling into the upper (*Dibunophyllum* D_2) Zone of the P_2 goniatite zone of the Dinantian Series. The formation ranges from 100m (330ft) to 140m (460ft) thick, there being a significant increase and a corresponding sag of the floor eastwards into an incipient Kincardine depositional basin that became deepened in later Carboniferous times.

Above the topmost limestone (the Top Hosie) of the Lower Limestone Group there is a change to the Limestone Coal Group, a formation that, as its name suggests, is much less notably marine than the beds beneath.   The sequence of strata displays well-marked rhythms of sedimentation, in cyclothems each composed of shales followed by siltstones and sand-stones, seat-earth, and coal.   There are eight or ten such rhythms, more or less complete, to be recognised in the sequence, a number of the coals being sufficiently well developed to en-courage exploitation in former days (and so to anticipate the true Coal Measures in their stratigraphical appearance).   Some of the coarser beds are sheet-flood and channel sandstones indicating repeated revival of the hinterland.   There are very few truly marine beds, of which the Johnstone Shell Bed is the chief, but there are a number of mussel beds and some *Lingula* beds indicating a non-marine or brackish environment.   The few index fossils show that the formation (with the Top Hosie Limestone beneath) belongs to the Pendleian Stage (E_2) of the Namurian Series despite its being grouped in the Carboniferous Limestone Group. The formation increases in thickness eastwards from 200m (660ft) to 550m (1800ft), again with strong sign of the continuing growth of the contemporary Kincardine basin of deposition.

The interlude of coal-measures deposition was followed by a return to limestone-phase cyclothems in the Upper Limestone Group, in which there was less a radical change in sedi-mentary process than in marine emphasis, coals being relatively subordinate, limestones re-turning.   The bulk of the sediment is composed of shales and mudstones with clay-band ironstones and fine sandstones, the limestones being thin — a metre or two — and interleaved with terrigenes.   The Index Limestone, the basal member that introduces the formation, is characteristically marine with common fossils, and is followed at intervals by similar thin limestones of which the Lyoncross, Orchard, Calmy, Plean and Castlecary limestones are the chief.   They, and some of the associated mudstones, contain many kinds of fossils including brachiopods (notably *Gigantoproductus*), bryozoans, gastropods, bivalves (scallops, nuculids, *Edmondia*), and annelids.   There is no proof of the precise age of the formation in the Stirling district, but elsewhere in the Midland Valley goniatites have shown equivalent beds to belong to the Arnsbergian Stage (E_2) of the Namurian.   The formation is about 350m (1150ft) thick in the development around Plean south of Stirling, but in correlation with the growing Kin-cardine basin it increases rapidly towards the Forth estuary to 600m (2000ft).

'Millstone Grit' (the Passage Group) and Coal Measures

The 'Millstone Grit' as a lithological unit in Scotland forms a group of rocks transitional to the Coal Measures and, to avoid confusion with the more extended Millstone Grit of England, are best given the name of the Passage Group.   The group differs from the beds be-low in being mainly composed of grey and yellow sandstones, often felspathic, with beds of grit and conglomerate often resting on eroded surfaces beneath, the provenance of the deri-ved material being exposed terrain of Dalradian rocks to the north.   Coals are thin and lent ticular. Marine bands are recurrent, and although they are thin they are stratigraphically important in yielding goniatites that probably prove the Dabdenian (H) and Kinderscoutian (R) stages of the Namurian Series. There is, however, no evidence of higher Namurian Zones, which may well be represented in the lowest beds of the locally designated Coal Measures. The Passage Group is little more than 240m (800ft) near Alloa and Dollar, but it increases to 350m (1150ft) in the Kincardine basin to the south.

The difficulty of separating Westphalian from Namurian sediments is enhanced by the absence in the Stirling district of a recognisable *Gastruiceras subcrenatum* Marine Band — the horizon defining the base of the Coal Measures elsewhere in Britain — and there is only arbitrary distinction between the Passage Group and the Coal Measures, whose base is taken to be at the Lowestone Marine Band, doubtfully equivalent to the *subcrenatum* band.

The rocks fall into two lithnological divisions, the Productive Measures (Lower and Middle Coal Measures) below, with many seams of coal, and the Barren Measures (Upper Coal Measures) above with few workable seams: elsewhere in the Midland Valley the distinction between the two is placed at Skipsey's Marine Band (the Mansfield or Cefn Coed Band of England and Wales, the Aegir Band of the Continent), but the band is not known in the Stirling district. The Productive Measures consist mainly of non-marine alternations of mudstones, sandy shales, blue and black shales, fireclays and seat-earths, and coal seams, commonly in rhythmic sequence. Shale bands contain freshwater mussels, in some abundance, giving evidence of the *leniculcata, communis, modiolaris,* and *similispulchra* zones. The Queenslie Marine Band in the *modiolaris* Zone is exceptional in the occurrence of crinoids, productoid brachiopods, *Lingula,* sponge spicules, forminifers, and ostracods: it is the equivalent of the Amman or Clay Cross Bands of England and Wales, the Katharina Band of the Continent. The Productive Measures are 300m (1000ft) thick in the south-east, but, like the strata beneath, they thin significantly north-westwards. Over much of the district the coals are worked out, but resources are still considerable in the northern fault-blocks.

The Barren Measures, known at outcrop elsewhere in the Midland Valley, are not exposed, being hidden by superficial deposits in the Stirling district; but they are inferred to occur to a residual thickness of perhaps 210m (690ft) in the deep synclinal pocket immediately against the Ochil fault near Alva and Tillicoultry (see Figs. 1.4, 1.5).

Volcanic rocks interbedded with the Upper Carboniferous sediments are inconsiderably developed except around Bathgate in the south-east of the district, where recurrent basaltic flows span much of the interval of the Carboniferous Limestone Series; but intrusions of late-Carboniferous or Permian age are common and may be impressive — spectacularly so in the Stirling sill, reaching 90m (295ft) in thickness, which forms a series of prominent crags and scarps extending for some 20km (12miles) south from Abbey Craig and Stirling Castle.

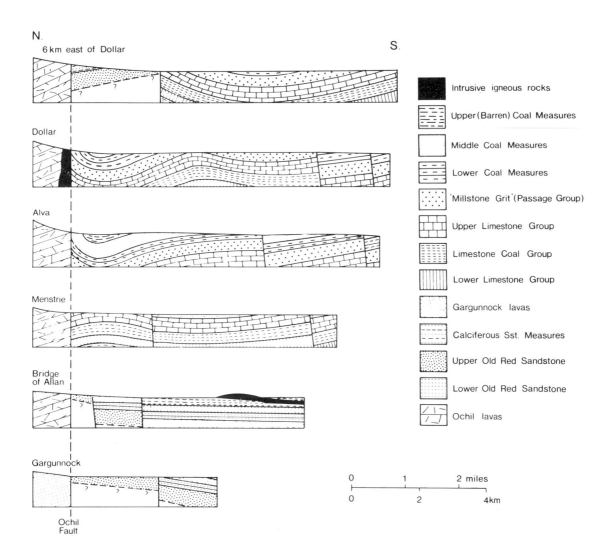

Fig 1.6   COMPARATIVE SECTIONS ACROSS THE OCHIL FAULT (slightly simplified)

The sections, in present outcrops show variation in the throw of the fault and in the structures on the downthrown (southern) flank, with the implication of strike-slip along the fault.

In lithology the sill is a quartz-dolorite, like a number of similar intrusions farther west.   It is not a constant horizon but is stepped, sometimes along pre-existing fracture planes, within the Lower Limestone and Limestone Coal groups (see Fig. 1.4).   It thins eastwards at depth and does not reappear on the east flank of the Clackmannan syncline.   Other intrusions of about the same age include widely scattered smaller sills and stocks of pod-like bodies of quartz-dolite intruded along the Ochil fault between Alva and Dollar, dykes in the Dalradian rocks and the Old Red Sandstone running for 25 to 39km (15 to 19miles) east from the Callander neighbourhood, and many east-and-west dykes cutting the Carboniferous rocks of the Stirling and Clackmannan coalfields, and of the terrain south of the Campsie and Kilsyth hills running towards Glasgow (see Fig. 1.2).

The mineral viens in the Ochil Hills are in great part also to be attributed to hydrothermal activity associated with the intrusions of quartz-dolerite; they follow fracture planes in which concentrates of copper and silver, with some iron, lead and arsenic were formerly exploited but which are now worked out or are too inconsiderable to be worth working.

Geological structure

The Stirling district is slashed by two major faults, the caledonoid Highland Boundary fault in the north-west, and the east-and-west Ochil fault running almost through Stirling itself.   The Dalradian rocks of the Highlands, greatly deformed in late-Cambrian or early-Ordovician times, were downthrown south-eastwards by thousands of metres along the Boundary fault before and during the deposition of the Lower Red Old Sandstone, in phases of the Caledonian orogeny that controlled the early evolution of the Midland Valley rift and that imposed upon southern Scotland a tectonic framework that for 400 million years has persisted to the present day (see Fig. 1.2).   The fault defines not only the 'Caledonian fold belt' to the north, but also the Strathmore syncline to the south — a region of relatively gently folded Old Red Sandstone in sharp tectonic contrast to the immediately contiguous overfolds and nappes of the Dalradian rocks.   There is evidence that the syncline had in incipient growth some control on thickness of the Old Red Sandstone.   The Lower Old Red Sandstone was notably downfolded before unconformably transgressive Upper Old Red Sandstone was deposited on it: the Teith Formation, high in the Lower sequence, is preserved in the heart of the syncline, while it and all older formations except the lavas are absent from parts of the Ochil sequence, notably in the ground about Kinross, east of Dollar; and all the Lower formation, lavas included, are absent between Aberfoyle and Loch Lomond, in rapid overstep by the Upper across a fold of amplitude of not less than 4000m (13100ft) (and across a revived Boundary fault of comparable throw) (see Fig. 1.3).

The Ochil fault as it is now seen is younger in origin than the Highland Boundary fault, perhaps only because no rocks older than Lower Old Red Sandstone are exposed along its length.   Like the Boundary fault it has a large downthrow to the south, probably of not less than 3000m (10000ft) near Tillicoultry, and it separates two regions of contrasted tectonic style.   To the north, the Strathmore syncline, in its present post-Carboniferous form, is a relatively gentle structure, asymmetrical as shown by the steep dips along its northern flanks, its axis running in oblique north-east and south-west (caledonoid) trend towards Buchlyvie, its elements perhaps in echelon.   To the south, the Clackmannan syncline expressed in the Carboniferous rocks is a fold much broken by faults, whose axis runs north-and-south and is abruptly terminated by the Ochil fault against which it directly impinges.   The fault, with variable effect, diminishes in throw westwards, older sediments down to and including Lower Old Red Sandstone progressively appearing on its southern face towards Kippen and Balfron, where it runs obliquely across the south-east flank and the axis of the Strathmore syncline, and where it is complemented by a minor (Balfron) anticline in the Upper Old Red Sandstone at the foot of the Campsie escarpment (see Fig. 1.6).

An incipient Kincardine basin is recognisable in the Upper Carboniferous rocks, but the later (Hercynian) imposition of the major downfold of the Clackmannan syncline a little to the west was not obviously controlled by the basin, and the axial form of the downfold, well brought out by the outcrops of the Coal Measures, is not easily understood in its tectonic context.   Southwards it continues into the Glasgow syncline and takes up a more 'Normal' south-westerly trend; and the local compressive stresses that gave it a southerly trend from Alva and Tillicoultry to Falkirk are not recognised immediately to the west where the Campsie-Gargunnock lavas consistently dip south-eastwards at a gentle angle.   Asymmetry in pressure-response to nodes of massive lavas in the older Ochils and the younger Gargunnock-Campsies, to a marginal Ochil fault, and to 'incompetent' Upper Carboniferous rocks, may partly explain the contrasts, but a full dynamical analysis has yet to be sought.

As a downfold the Clackmannan syncline is gentle and open, but it is broken by a great number of east-and-west normal faults (some of them paralleled by east-and-west dykes) that mostly have a downthrow south like the Ochil fault.   Amongst them the Abbey Craig fault is conspicious in its continuation from the core of the fold westwards beyond Stirling to Gargunnock, where it cuts into the outcrop of the Carboniferous rocks below the lavas.   Between it and the Ochil fault the youngest Palaeozoic rocks of the district are found in an outlier of Barren Coal Measures in the deepest pocket of the basin.   Between it and the Ochil fault, around Dollar, small periclinal folds with an anomalous east-and-west trend show displacement along both faults to be highly variable, and suggest locally resolved tectonic stress with some strike-slip; and there are geophysical signs of disturbance, perhaps by igneous intrusion, at depth near Tillicoultry.

REFERENCES

Bassett, D A   1958   'Geological excursion guide to the Glasgow district', *Geol Soc. Glasgow.*

Bluck, B J   1973   'Excursion guide to the geology of the Glasgow district', (editor)   *Geol Soc. Glasgow.*

Clough, C T and Others 1952   *The Geology of the Glasgow district.   Mem. Geol. Surv.* Scotland.

Francis, E H   1956   'The economic geology of the Stirling and Clackmannan Coalfield, Scotland: Area north of the River Forth'. *Coalfield Pap. Geol Surv. 1.*

Francis, E H and   1970   *The Geology of the Stirling district.   Mem. Geol. Surv.* Others   *G. B.*

Geological Survey   10-mile map, sheet 1; ¼-inch map, sheet 14; 1-inch map sheets 30, 31, 39.

George, T N   1958   'The geology and geomorphology of the Glasgow district', *In* R Miller & J Tivy (editors):   *The Glasgow Region.* pp. 17-61. Brit. Assoc. Adv. Sci.,   Glasgow.

George, T N   1960   'The stratigraphical evolution of the Midland Valley', *Trans. Geol Soc. Glasgow* 24: 32 – 107.

Johnstone, J S   1966   'British regional geology: The Grampian Highlands', *Inst. Geol. Sci.*

Macgregor, M and   1948   *British Regional Geology: The Midland Valley of Scotland.* MacGregor, A C   *2nd edition,*   H.M.S.O.

Muir, R O   1963   'Petrography and provenance of the Millstone Grit of Central Scotland', *Proc. Edinburgh Geol. Soc.* 19: 439 – 85.

Read, W A   1959   'The economic geology of the Stirling and Clackmannan coalfield, Scotland: Area south of the Forth', *Coalfield Pap. Geol. Surv. 2.*

Shackleton, R M   1958   'Downward-facing structures of the Highland border',
                                 Quart. J. Geol. Soc.   113:   361 – 91.

Whyte, F   1968   'Lower Carboniferous volcanic vents in the west of Scot-
                                 land', *Bull. Vulcanol.* 32:   253 – 68.

CHAPTER 2

THE GEOMORPHOLOGY OF THE STIRLING REGION

Rock outcrops and the physical landscape

A close relationship between kinds of rock, structural pattern, and geomorphic physique is manifest in the Stirling region.　In general terms a delineation of the outcrops of hard rock — metamorphics in the Highlands, igneous rocks and massive conglomerates farther south — is a delineation of hills from lowlands.　The Highland Boundary fault, etched along Glen Artney, eastern Loch Venacher, and the north-west face of the Menteith Hills by Aberfoyle to Conic Hill, separates a mountain mass, the southern Grampians, in which there are many summits approaching or exceeding 920m (3020ft), from the ground to the south, in which not many summits reach 615m (2020ft); the contrast receives part explanation when the northern area is recognised to have Dalradian rocks at the surface, the southern only Upper Palaeozoic.　Similarly, in the southern area the lavas of the Ochil Hills and the comparable lavas of the Campsie-Gargunnock Hills have withstood erosion more effectively than the sediments flanking them; within the sediments only the thick conglomerates of the Old Red Sandstone form hills of comparable altitude.

Moreover, the forms of the hills are closely adapted to structure, their profiles being correlated with dip, strike, and fracture.　This is clearly so in the Ochils, where the steep southern face is the degraded scarp of the Ochil fault — a towering scarp where the throw of the fault is greatest, about Dollar, Tillicoultry, and Alva, but a scarp diminishing in impressiveness westwards to Menstrie and Bridge of Allan as the throw diminishes.　Correspondingly, the north-westerly slopes of the hills, controlled by the dip of the lavas, are in asymmetry much more extensive than the fault-scarp face and, broken by the valley of the Devon, repeat in minor steps (the trap featuring) the general pattern of relief picked out by alternations of lavas and tuffs.

The Campsie and Gargunnock hills are slightly more complex in structure.　They are of mildly rippled synclinal form in the Clyde lavas, with a regional eastward plunge, the summits rising above 550m (1800ft) in Meikle Bin and Holehead near the heart of the outcrop.　The gentle southerly dip along the north face produces the bold scarp overlooking Gargunnock and Kippen and although the scarp is cut into deeply by the Endrick Water it is no less prominent on the flanks of the Fintry valley; it stands high above Killearn in Earl's Seat　at 583m (1913ft)　and it is almost as prominent in the Strathblane Hills.　Along the south face of the Campsie and Kilsyth hills the structure, in the development of the east-and-west Campsie fault, closely matches the south face of the Ochils, the fault scarp, not greatly degraded, looking over the low ground of Carboniferous sediments of the Glasgow syncline.　A particular feature of the Carboniferous igneous field is the manner in which the intrusions also impose physique on landscape on a smaller scale than the lavas in bulk but with no less precision: the scarp of the gently dipping Stirling sill, at Abbey Craig and the Wallace Monument, magnificently at Stirling Castle, at King's Park, at Touchadam Craig and at Sauchie Craig is the most extensive, but the volcanic necks in the western Campsies and in the Blane valley are in their resistance to erosion scarcely less impressive.

The Uamh Bheag range of hills east of Callander reflects the foundation of tough conglomerates of the Old Red Sandstone in which they are carved: with a south-easterly dip the multiple scarp overlooks the trench of Glen Artney and (in complement across the Strathmore syncline to the Ochil front) may be regarded as a fracture face much eroded and dissected along the Highland Boundary fault belt. The scarps of Beinn Dearg and the Menteith Hills, the Old Red Sandstone dipping at high angles, are in hog-back continuation to the south-west, Conic Hill above Balmaha being a last outpost along the line to Loch Lomond.

Such descriptive allusion to the effects of differential erosion on variously resistant rocks is however little more than tautologous and to add that the hill masses are flanked by low ground eroded in softer sediments of the Old Red Sandstone of the Strathmore syncline in the Forth and Allan valleys, and of the Carboniferous formations below the Ochil scarp, is but to repeat the correlation without extending the principle. A more refined analysis suggests that in evolutionary process the emergence of the present-day physical landscape was less simple than a distinction between hard and soft rocks implies.

Upland landform

The Dalradian rocks of the Highlands no doubt form rugged hills because they are an upfault massif, a horst, in relation to the Old Red Sandstone; but in regional landform they give the appearance of a dissected plateau whose residual summits may in accordant integration allow the plateau conceptually to be restored. The rocks in the Highlands are in detail very varied, with a strong caledonoid structural trend. The hill summits on the other hand are randomly scattered – those approaching or above 920m (3020ft) including Ben Ledi and Ben Vorlich on quartzites, Beinn Tulaichean, Beinn a'Chroin, Beinn Chabhair, and Ben Lomond on phyllites. The integrated plateau surface incorporating these high summits thus trangresses structure and implies a primary landform not simply 'explained' by reference to Dalradian outcrops.

The fragmentation of the surface by river valleys makes it difficult to reconstruct the continuity southwards. A number of summits in the neighbourhood of 620m (2035ft) on the flanks of Loch Katrine and Loch Venacher suggest a gradual fall, a regional tilt, of the surface, but beyond the Stirling district for many miles within the Highlands summits not widely departing from 620m (2035ft) lend themselves to integration into a surface not greatly warped or tilted; even within the Stirling district summits about 620m (2035ft) and about 920m (3020ft) are in close proximity, perhaps most notably in the trains of hills along Lomondside from Ben Lomond south-eastwards through Beinn Bhreac. It may well be that the plateau surface was originally stepped — or that gentle tilting was superposed on a stepped profile.

The Ochil Hills, structurally defined by the marginal fault, with regional back slope, have minor folds and faults not always reflected in the details of landscape, and although plateau form is not particularly impressive within the uplands it is noticeable that the high summits are in a variety of rocks — Blairdenon Hill in upper basalts, Bencleuch in lavas with a truncated dolerite intrusion, King's Seat in lower basalts than Bencleuch, Whitewisp Hill and Tarmangie Hill in still lower basalts, Innerdownie Hill in yet lower basalts — and are moreover areally and not linearly distributed. The summits are all a little over 620m (2035ft) in altitude, the coincidence perhaps being random but carrying the hint of collation with the similar heights of the summits in the marginal Dalradian terrain. It is then not irrelevant to note that the highest peaks in the Uamh Bheag range of conglomerates in the Old Red Sandstone, lying between the Ochils to the south and the Ben Vorlich mass to the north and isolated from one another by deep-cut river valleys, all a little exceed 620m (2035ft).

The Campsie Fells are perhaps even more revealing, their structural framework being relatively complex and yet having only modified effect on landform. Meikle Bin is eroded in a vent agglomerate, Holehead, Lecker Hill, and Cort-ma-Law are in upper lavas, Earl's Seat is in lower lavas. The heights of these high summits are of the order of 550m (1800ft) in a hill mass that in its isolation is clearly a dismembered remnant of a larger plateau area not very distant from the Ochils. Immediately to the east and north, in the Kilsyth, Fintry and Gargunnock hills, the scattered summits range about 460m (1500ft), at a significant step below the Campsie crests.

The great dissection of the whole district by rivers makes an imposed unifying coherence on the upland landscape more or less speculative. The massifs and 'islands' of high ground in their remnant plateau form encourages the inference that the plateau surface may have been tilted or undulating to give the outliers different altitudes, but no less it may have been stepped in a staircase of platforms each in succession notched into earlier and higher platforms. The conceptual plateau may then be regarded as a peneplain of uncertain origin, uplifted to heights above its original base-level and then dissected; or it may be regarded as a composite marine-planned bench, the suggested steps in its profile being attributable to successive stages of pulsed uplift. In either case the plateau is not greatly mutilated by recognisable folding (although it may well have been affected by repeated movement along the main faults) and presumably its surface, like the plateau surface elsewhere over much of Scotland, was not greatly modified by the mid-Tertiay deformation identified notably in

Hebridean terrain. That is, the plateau form, and its erosive destruction, are young (Neogene) in geological terms.

The river system

It is not easy to recognise a simple drainage pattern in a concentration of main tributaries on the Forth estuary and a brief analysis of present and former river courses reveals a trellised relationship of primary and 'subsequent' elements that is a consequence of piracy on the one hand and glacial diversion on the other (see Fig. 2.1). The geological grain of the country is dominantly caledonoid, but the principal rivers tend mainly to flow eastwards. Ancestral courses are not always or even often accordant with structure and only along short reaches are major parts of them adapted to tectonic lines. Like the Tummel and the Tay to the north, they found their headwaters in a divide far to the west; they crossed the line of Lomond trench before the trench had been gouged; and they crossed geological outcrops indifferently, often with revealing obliquity. They thus give very strong evidence of being superimposed onto the Palaeozoic foundation from a surface transgressively discordant and unaffected by the folds and faults in the Palaeozoic rocks. Such a surface has in the past been regarded as attributable to a former cover of Chalk, in only minor degree deformed after uplift, and gently falling with low dip eastwards to the synclinal basin of the North Sea; but such an attribution is certainly not applicable to other areas in Scotland where the rivers are similarly superimposed and it is no more than conjecture. In alternative hypothesis the high-level plateau remnants may be signs of the surface, and thus point to late (Neogene) initiation of the river system.

The pre-Glacial Balvag drains Loch Voil at the end of a reach having its sources almost as far west as Loch Lomond and crossing contorted Dalradian rocks from phyllites onto grits. At Kinghouse below Balquhidder it bends sharply southwards to Loch Lubnaig and the Pass of Leny, but in doing so it abandons an obvious almost rectilinear continuation by the Edinchip dry col into the Earn valley (and ultimately the Tay) and it is evident that the Lubnaig reach is a diversion brought about by capture to become a headwater of the Teith.

It is not certain that a second course of the Teith above Loch Katrine was fed by headwater flowing across the Lomond trench near Ardlui; but there is little doubt that a western source is to be identified in Inveruglas Water on the farther side of Loch Lomond, which before the glacial gouging of the Lomond trench flowed by Inversnaid and the Arklet gap into Loch Katrine. Downcourse, by the Glengyle Water, Loch Katrine, the Achray Water, and Loch Venechar, the river valley is grossly discordant in flowing from phyllites onto grits and the synformal Aberfoyle Slates before crossing the Highland Boundary fault and continuing on Old Red Sandstone. At Callander the Upper Teith makes a right-angle bend into the lower Teith and, like the Balva, gives a strong impression of piracy:

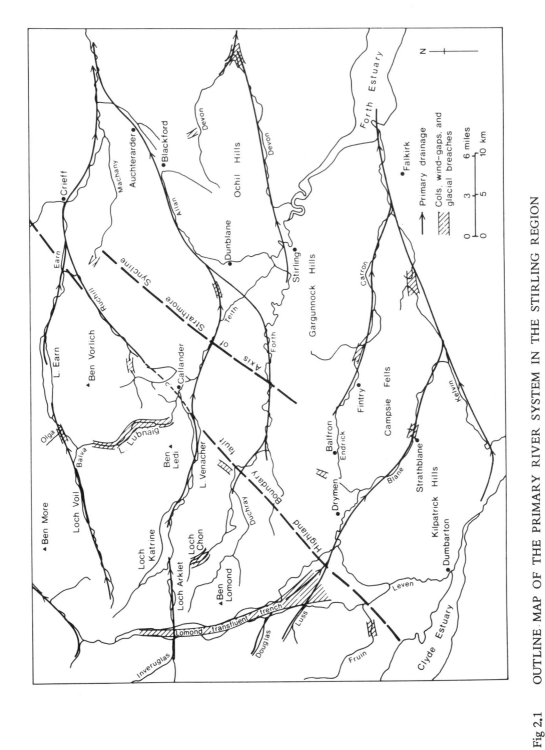

Fig 2.1   OUTLINE MAP OF THE PRIMARY RIVER SYSTEM IN THE STIRLING REGION

The dominant trend, indifferent to major structure, is manifestly superimposed. In secondary adjustment ancient 'subsequent' breaches, notably of the Forth through the Stirling gap and probably of the Ruchill along the Highland Boundary fault in Glen Artney, are accompanied by geologically recent diversions affected by glacial gouging, as in the Lomond and Lubnaig trenches, and glacial obstruction, as of the Devon at Crook of Devon, that have radically modified the river courses in many parts.

a system of cols to the north-east leads to Glen Artney and the Earn Valley and invites a re-construction as a former course of the Teith before capture.   Or conceivably it may have left the Highlands in a continuing course south-eastwards to the Doune-Dunblane gap, where in confluence with the Forth it fed a reversed Allan ultimately to flow through the Blackford-Auchterarder gap to the Ruthven Water, the Earn, and the Tay, on a line obliquely across the axis of the Strathmore syncline.

The source of the Forth is now in streams of the hills around Loch Ard, but the Gleann valley, a deep col at its head, may point to more distant tributaries on Lomondside.   The upper Forth now follows the depression in Old Red Sandstone between the Campsie-Gargunnock lava hills on one flank and the Beinn Dearg conglomerate range on the other, but to do so it is grossly transgressive in crossing almost at right angles the Highland Boundary fault a little below Loch Ard, from the mixed Dalradian rocks of the Ben Lomond–Ben Venue country.   In now flowing through the Stirling watergap it has abandoned the conjunction with the Teith near Doune and a route on the Old Red Sandstone through Strathallan to the Earn.   The watergap is then to be interpreted as a sign of major piracy, its position determined by the dying-away of Ochil lavas on one flank and Gargunnock lavas on the other, and by the effects of the Ochil and Abbey Craig faults.   With the diversion of the Teith and the upper Forth through the gap and the lowering of baselevel in the gap, the Allan was initiated as a reversed obsequent now flowing south-westwards from Blackford and contributing to the enlargement of the lower Forth.

Despite the reversal of flow of the Endrick and Blane streams, the regional relief on the flanks of the Campsies strongly suggests a comparable flow of headwaters rising on the west side of the Lomond trench and following south-eastwards along an early Strathblane into what is now a reversed Kelvin, and then continuing by the Kelvinhead gap above Kilsyth to a confluence with the Forth in the neighbourhood of Falkirk.   On a smaller scale, the upper-most Endrick is aligned south-eastwards, but is now diverted through an acute angle to feed the west-flowing reach that continues past Fintry and Balfron to Loch Lomond; the angle is a sharp elbow of capture; the west-flowing reach is a reversed obsequent; the uppermost reach is directed towards an abandoned gap by which, before the piracy, it fed the Carron; and the present Carron is a beheaded primary consequent.

Like the high-level Carron in terrain of Carboniferous lavas, the upper Devon on the lavas of the Old Red Sandstone flows eastwards to its acute elbow at Crook of Devon, beyond which is the low ground of Fossaway now without significant stream as the lower Devon, very much younger and discordant in origin, swings to the west by Tillicoultry to join the Forth at Cambus.

The Devon adds a further item to the regional pattern of east-flowing streams.   The pat-

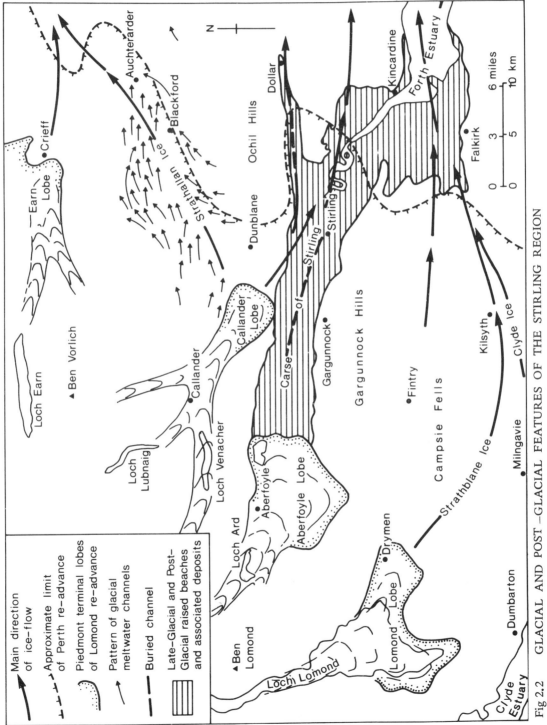

Fig 2.2   GLACIAL AND POST-GLACIAL FEATURES OF THE STIRLING REGION

The persistent streaming of the ice eastwards, including Clyde ice, Lomond-Strathblane ice, and Strathallan ice, and the relation of the piedmont Aberfoyle moraine at the Lomond re-advance to the late-Glacial and post-Glacial deposits of the Carse of Stirling and the Forth estuary are to be noted.

tern frame is clearly discernable, but in many details, and sometimes in large scale, it has been mutilated by river diversion brought about by several factors. Some of the principal instances of capture, by rejuvenation and differential down-cutting and an adjustment to the geological structure — notably in the evolution of the Stirling gap and in the reversal of the Allan drainage — were pre-Glacial, presumably Neogene, in origin, but others are to be ascribed to the effects of ice, both in the erosion of new channels of flow and in the blocking of old.

Glacial erosion

Together with the rest of Scotland (and most of Britain), the Stirling district was completely blanketed by ice during the Pleistocene period, the final melting and a last disappearance of the ice-sheet taking place only some 10,000 years ago. Signs of the glaciation are thus very fresh and impressive, and are seen in a great variety of features that much modify the pre-Glacial landscape. In general, the ice-flow inherited routeways already plotted by the antecedent valley system and thus was in a south-easterly and easterly direction, mainly from the Highlands towards the North-Sea basin. The mountains and mountain valleys suffered intense erosion and display a multiplicity of spectacular ice-moulded profiles. The low ground received thicknesses of ice-transported detritus, glacial drift, that veneered and obscured the foundation of 'solid' rock on which the drift came to rest.

Glacial erosion is best seen in the Highlands. Hollowed steep-walled corries, with ragged slopes and swathes of apron-scree, are not as common in the Stirling district as they are farther north and few of them occur in the full perfection of hemispherical form and central lochan; but good examples are to be seen on the flanks of Ben Vorlich, of Ben Ledi, of Stuc a' Chroin and of Beinn a' Chroin, and at the source of Glen Kendrum behind Lochearnhead. The heads of many valleys, on the other hand, are deep-scalloped, some with near-vertical walls, in incipient corrie development and in incongruous correlation with the small stream rising in them.

Corrie form in the hills south of the Highlands, at lower altitudes, is usually only allusively expressed even towards the summits of the Ochils; but it is notable that the steep north-facing scarp of the Campsie Fells has well-formed corries pocketed in it, including the Ballochleam corrie and the impressive Corrie of Balglass.

Deeply gouged over-deepened valleys, on the other hand, are to be seen in all the hilly country and are the major elements contributing to the rugged profile of the uplands. In their more extreme developments they bear witness to their glacial origin in the true rock-basins whose floors, scooped below regional base-level, are now occupied by elongated lochs: many of the Highland lochs are of this type, the depth of water in them bearing evidence of their origin — Katrine to 148.5m (487ft), Venacher to 33m (110ft), Ard to 32m (105ft),

Voil and Achray to 29m (95ft), Drunkie to 24m (80ft), and Chon to 22.5m (75ft).   An associated feature of the lochs is the deposition of alluvial deltas where inflowing streams are reduced in velocity on entering the still loch waters, the alluvial spreads sometimes extending for a distance upstream.

In lower ground the blanket of glacial drift obscures the form of the foundation on which it rests, but before it was deposited, when glacier movement was sustained, the ice thick, and abrasive down-cutting powerful, similar gouging of local rock basins is proved by soundings to have occurred both above and below the dolerite sill at Stirling.   The large Forth glacier, fed in its lower reaches by confluent ice-streams spilling through the Stirling gap from Forth, Teith, and Allan tributories, ploughed its way eastwards, and in the process excavated trenches to depths exceeding 100m (330ft) below present sea level near Thornhill to the west of Stirling and at Menstrie and Alva to the east and to more than 175m (575ft) in the main Forth channel at Bo'ness, although the trenches may never have been occupied by lochs if the thick drift left by the ice was deposited in them as the ice melted (see Fig. 2.2).

A comparable feature of glacial erosion was excavation by transfluent ice − the spilling across an ice-shed of ice congested in one valley and finding a lateral col into another.   The outstanding example, the Lomond trench, lies immediately west of the Stirling district; it serves as an illustration of the manner in which east-flowing pre-Glacial stream courses (the Inveruglas − Arklet − Katrine − Teith and the Douglas-Luss- Blane-Forth) were beheaded by a diversionary break-through of a part of a massive ice-flow (the Falloch-Dochart glacier) to the north and its bull-dozing of all obstructions as it made its way southwards to the Clyde .   The Lomond trench is a true rock basin of exceptional depth, its floor descending to 200m (650ft) below present sea level.

Similar basins within the Stirling district are not so spectacular, but they probably include the valley of the Balvag in its course by Strathyre and Loch Lubnaig to the Pass of Leny and Callander, the abandonment by Voil Waters of the Edinchip gap to the Earn then being (in geological terms) very recent, post-Glacial (as Loch Lomond is post-Glacial), although no doubt the diversion and the ensuing excavation of the Lubnaig rock basin were facilitated by a pre-Glacial col at the head of short tributories one flowing northwards by Strathyre, and the other flowing southwards along the east flank of Ben Ledi.

Farther east, there is weaker evidence of transfluence on the flanks of Glen Artney, notably in the interrupted spillway from the Findhu Glen into the Knaik valley and, farther south, transfluence from the Endrick valley eastwards into the Carron.   In the Ochils, the deep Glen Eagles probably carried a diffluent from the Annan glacier that was thrust southwards as far as Glenhead, without perhaps clearing the col into the Devon valley.

Landforms in glacial drifts

The ice, moving regionally from the west and north-west, was at maximum very thick, forming an ice-sheet that overtopped much if not all of the Ochils and the Campsie uplands and as a multiple piedmont glacier flowed into the North Sea. At the close of the Ice Age it melted first in the lower ground, its front receding, and being broken into many valley tongues, towards the upper reaches of the valleys. As it became sluggish and relatively static, and its bulk diminished, it deposited vast quantities of morainic material, boulder clay and water-mixed sand and gravel, in places over a hundred metres thick. Its meltwaters, sometimes in great floods, redistributed the morainic detritus in outwash plains that reached the contemporary coast and merged with beach deposits. The lateral passage and the interfingering of one kind of sediment into another and their fluctuating distribution give rise to a great variety of landforms in the Stirling district — a great variety whose relations are not always clear and whose interpretation remains in many places a matter of uncertainty and controversy.

There was sustained glaciation, complicated by climatic oscillations, in Scotland for much of Pleistocene times, but all the glacial deposits in the district appear to belong to the last of the major glacial stages, the Weichsel, there being no recognisable development of warm-climate interglacial deposits separating the Weichsel sediments from any older. There are, however, signs of pulsed glacier movements in the closing episode of ice retreat: an earlier, a less surely identified 'Perth' readvance, when glacial flow many have descended as far as Stirling, and a later, a much more positively recognisable 'Lomond' readvance, when ice descended into the upper Forth valley (see Fig. 2.3).

Boulder clay and glacial sands cover all the lower ground of the district, in very wide expanses in the Teith valley below Callander, in Strath Allan eastwards to Crieff and Auchterarder, in the Forth valley from the western mountains to the Firth. They are found fingering along the upland valleys, notably the Ochils, and they veneer upland plateau surfaces, notably in the Campsie-Gargunnock country. The deposits are very varied both in their nature and in their relief. They are clays or silts or sands with scattered or concentrated boulders derived from distant or local courses — schistose grits from the Highlands, sandstones from the Old Red Sandstone, lavas from the Ochil and Clyde suites. The erratic train of pebbles of the readily identifiable essexite, derived from a small intrusion near Lennoxtown on the south face of the Campsies, is traceable as a narrow band for some 30km (18.6miles) eastwards along the Kelvin valley to Grangemouth and beyond in significant comment on ice-movement.

Much of the surfaces of the boulder clay is gently rolling without notable features, but in places — near Dunblane, east of Doune, between Alloa and Dollar, along the foot of the Gargunnock Hills — drumlins, or hills with drumloidal profile, are moulded with axes aligned

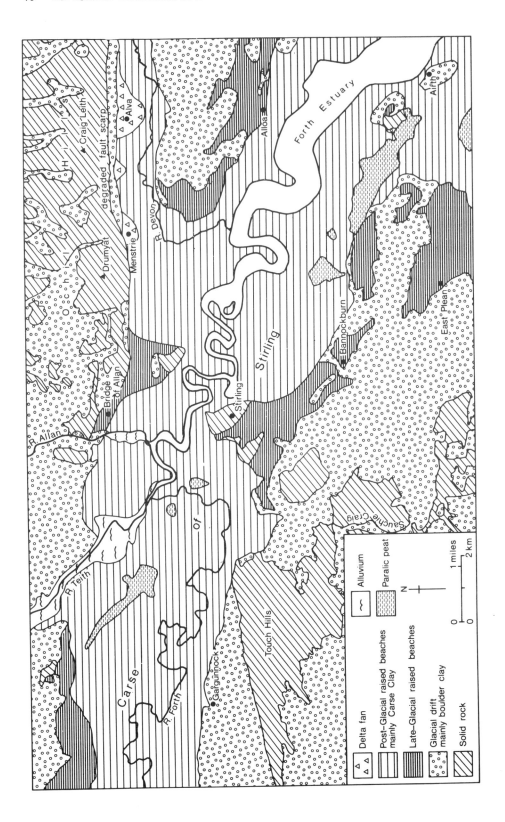

Fig 2.3   SUPERFICIAL DEPOSITS IN THE NEIGHBOURHOOD OF STIRLING (slightly simplified)

After the 1-inch map no. 39 of the Geological Survey.

in the direction of ice-flow. Elsewhere, moundy drift, often with intercalated strings and len-ticles of incorporated meltwater sediments, is a characteristic ablation deposit of dead ice in the latest stages of ice-front retreat; it commonly carries kettle-holes some of which, if local groundwater control is appropriate, may now be ponded.

Meltwater sands and gravels, sometimes poorly sorted but usually well if irregularly stratified in lenticular beds, take on a variety of forms. The Kame terraces, sometimes stepped, define in wide outcrops the successive stages of waning ice in Strathallan and the Teith valley,where they merge into and were in part contemporaneous with moundy moraine. Kame mounds are widely scattered in the spread of glacial gravels. Well-marked eskers of subglacial formation may be seen trailing more or less in direction of ice-flow notably at the mouth of Glen Eagles, at Callander (the Roman Camp esker), and near Doune (the Argaty esker).

The subglacial and emergent meltwater channels followed what courses they could on the irregular surface of the drift beneath, constrained in part by accidents of drift topography, in part by residual ice masses whose changing margins directed temporary flow. A great number, some of them several miles long, are identifiable in the Teith and Allan valleys, all directed eastwards or north-eastwards, implying an outlet by the Blackford – Auchterarder route to the Earn at times when the Stirling outlet to the Forth was congested or blocked. These channels are analogous to glacial overflow channels caused by an ice-barrier diversion of preglacial rivers, as of the Calair Burn at Balquhidder, the Ample west of Ben Vorlich, and the reversed Devon through the Glenhead gap to Glen Eagles.

The final pulses of glacial rejuvenation, seen in the Perth and Lomond end-moraines, are represented by drift that briefly advanced over late-Glacial outwash plains of sands and silts. The Perth episode, of about 13,000 years ago, is imperfectly defined in the Stirling district, not being conspicious in drift mounds or ridges or certainly known to rest on older fluviatile deposits, but it has been discerned in its relationship to the many meltwater channels in Strathallan as rising to heights of 350m (1150ft) near Doune and 275m (900ft) near Braco. Contemporaneous ice-flows may have spread, perhaps only as meltwater and outwash gravel, one through the Stirling gap into the plain to the south and east as far as Kincardine, another eastwards along the Kilsyth route on the south flank of the Campsies as far as Larbert.

The Lomond readvance of about 11,000 years ago is much more surely recognised. Named from the glacier along the Lomond trench that deposited a terminal moraine beyond Balloch in the Leven valley and as far as Drymen in the Endrick valley, it had its counter-part in a glacier in the neighbouring Laggan valley that splayed around the nose of the Men-teith Hills into the Forth valley beyond Aberfoyle. The limits of flow are recognised in

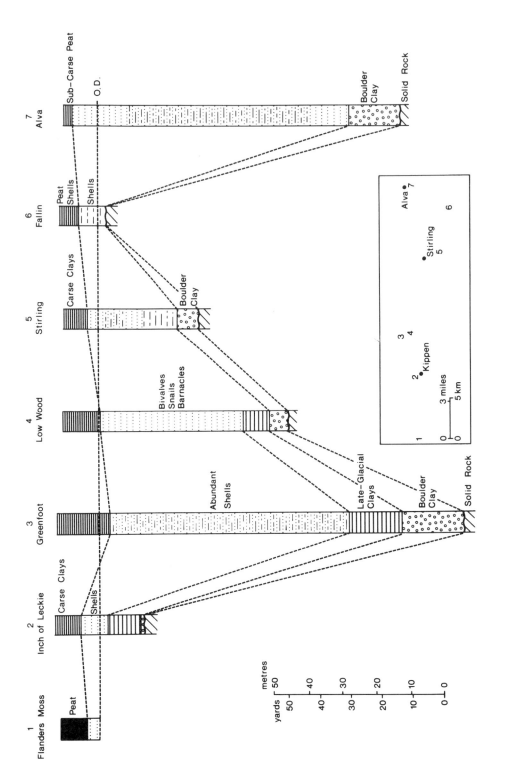

Fig 2.4   COLUMNS IN THE SUPERFICIAL DEPOSITS OF THE CARSE OF STIRLING

The columns illustrate the sequence of deposition and the wide variability in the thickness of the late-Glacial sands and silts beneath the Carse Clays – the deep buried channel of the Forth west of Stirling being illustrated in the Greenfoot column, and of the Devon in the Alva column. *After the Geological Survey.*

moundy drift running from Buchlyvie to Arnprior and Port of Menteith: inside the limits are the prominent morainic ridges, over 30m (100ft) in height, that rise towards Aberfoyle and form a broken barrier to the Laggan valley. In the mounds and ridges the Lake of Menteith occupies what may be looked on as a very large kettle-hole. The corresponding Lomond readvance in the Teith valley may have extended beyond Callander towards Doune as fresh moundy drift indicates, but there is no well-defined terminal moraine. On a small scale late tongues of ice descended the valleys of the Highland border and some of the corries, including the Uamh Bheag and Campsie-Gargunnock corries, were retouched.

Late-Glacial and post-Glacial lowlands

The deep, probably greatly over-deepened, valley of the Forth, a product of river erosion and glacial gouging, formed an arm of the sea during late-Glacial times as the ice melted and the ice-front retreated when the (local) Ice Age came to an end. The meltwater pouring from the Forth glacier carried large quantities of gravels, sands, silts, and muds into the enlarging estuary to deposit them as fluviatile and marine sediments to thicknesses in places of 100m (330ft). In lateral transition the coarser accumulations lay upstream, and in the wide spreads of outwash of the material that reached the sea it was sorted out as fine sand, silt or clay. The sediments deposited above tide level have a relatively steeper gradient of fall but the truly estuarine deposits redistributed under a marine regime have a surface nearly horizontal or with very slight fall seawards. Otherwise, the downstream limits of fluviatile outwash are not readily distinguished from marine sediments, except that fossils, especially planktonic forms including foraminifers, may be found in the marine beds.

Perhaps during, certainly shortly after, the mixed suite of late-Glacial aqueous deposits was laid down (from about 11,000 years ago) there was a regional fall in sea level to be ascribed in part to isostatic rebound as the ice-load melted away and the estuarine flats and delta gravels became elevated to heights approaching or exceeding 30m above present sea level to form the colloquially named '100-foot raised beach'. It is not a unitary beach and grew in stages – locally it may be as high as 40m (131ft), descending in steps to 13m (43ft). Its flat surface is now dissected by minor stream erosion into isolated fragments, notably in the neighbourhood of St Ninian's, Bannockburn, East Plean, and Falkirk, between Tullibody, Alloa, and Clackmannan, and in the Airthrey grounds of the University campus.

With the fall in sea level and the emergence of some of the flat-lying sediments as land, a cover of peat (with reeds in the lower part, woodland tree debris in the upper) grew extensively but to no great thickness over much of the area: it is rarely seen at the surface, being hidden beneath younger deposits, but it has been proved in borings to be widespread in the Forth valley. Palynological evidence shows the peat to be of the order of 8500 years old, Pre-Boreal in the Pleistocene-Holocene sequence. Sands perhaps of about the same age, or a little older, have yielded barnacles, periwinkles, and other marine shells in the sediments for some miles west of Stirling (see Fig. 2.4).

Stages in the replacement of glacial by fluviatile, estuarine, and marine deposits were doubtless interrupted by the Perth readvance of the ice, certainly by the Lomond readvance in the Laggan valley, for the Menteith moraine contains incorporated silty material with marine shells; and the 'cold' climatic fluctuation is represented stratigraphically in the Menteith neighbourhood by Lomond glacial drift overlying late-Glacial peat and silts, which in turn overlie main glacial drift.

With the final melting of the ice, perhaps 10,000 years ago, there was a transformation in the geomorphic environment and the late-Glacial sands and silts of the Forth valley, uplifted though they were by isostatic rebound to heights of over 30m (100ft) as the ice-front retreated, became submerged again in a post-Glacial drowning of coastal lands by a release of meltwaters into the oceans.   The Forth valley (like other valleys) was inundated by the sea and a younger (Flanderian) suite of post-Glacial sediments was deposited on the varied foundation of peat, estuarine and marine late-Glacial 'raised beach' muds and silts, outwash sands and silts, morainic gravel, boulder clay and solid rock.   These sediments constitute the true Carse Clays.   They form the impressive flats extending as a belt of rich agricultural land from Gartmore in the west to Falkirk and Kincardine in the east, their gently tilted surface falling from 14.5m (47ft) to 12.5m (41ft) above mean sea level in a distance of 40km (24miles). The Clays are usually laminated and fine-grained, but they contain layers, often in long lenticles, of silt and fine sand.   In them disturbance of the bedding by burrowing is common and they yield many kinds of marine shells including whelks, periwinkles, turret-shells, mussels, scallops, oysters and barnacles, together with the bones of stranded seals and whales. They have the general appearance of present-day tidal-flat deposits.   They are not always readily distinguished from underlying late-Glacial silts and sands, especially when the intervening (sub-Carse) peat is not to be recognised.

The Carse Clays, transgressively overlapping onto a varied floor, are variable in thickness, but may locally exceed 12m (38ft).   On the other hand, the growth of peat in Flanders Moss began perhaps in latest Glacial times, certainly not later than very early post-Glacial times: it appears to have kept pace with surrounding Carse Clay deposition (and so gives sign of the very shallow water in which the Clays accumulated) and there was continuous peat formation, as the palynological evidence shows, from Pre-Boreal to Sub-Atlantic times, at least from about 8500 to 2000 years ago; in places the Flanders peat (to a thickness of 8m) appears to rest directly upon the bed of sub-Carse peat in unbroken growth from early Pre-Boreal times.   In further evidence of age the Carse Clays have yielded artefacts of worked antlers indicating a contemporary Mesolithic culture and formerly they would have been regarded as representing in part the 'Neolithic' raised beach.   In detail, lines of low cliff, a metre of two in height, indicate successive 'coastlines' in a fall to the level of the present-day alluvium, and the Carse surface is multiple.

REFERENCES

Bremner, A   1942   'The origin of the Scottish river system', *Scott. Geogr. Mag.* 58: 54 — 59.

Cadell, H M   1913   *The story of the Forth.*   Glasgow.

Charlesworth, J K   1956   'The late-Glacial history of the Highlands and Islands of Scotland', *Trans. Roy. Soc. Edinburgh,* 62: 769 — 928.

Linton, D L   1940   'Some aspects of the evolution of the rivers Earn and Tay', *Scott. Geogr. Mag.* 58: 1 — 11, 61 — 79.

Geological Survey   v.d.   1-inch map, sheets 30, 31, 39 (drift).

Linton, D L   1949   'Watershed breaching by ice in Scotland', *Trans. Inst. Brit. Geogr.* 15: 1 — 15.

Linton, D L   1951   'Problems of Scottish scenery', *Scott. Geogr. Mag.* 67: 65 — 85.

Linton, D L and Moisley, H A   1960   'The origin of Loch Lomond', *Scott. Geogr. Mag.* 76: 26 — 37.

Newey, W W   1966   'Pollen analysis of Sub-Carse Peat in the Forth valley', *Trans. Inst. Brit. Geogr.* 39: 53 — 60.

Ordnance Survey   v.d.   ¼-inch map, sheet 3.
½-inch map (seventh series), sheets 53, 54, 55, 60 and 61.

Simpson, J B   1933   'The late-Glacial readvance moraines of the Highland Border west of the River Tay', *Trans. Roy. Soc. Edinburgh.* 57: 633 — 45.

Sissons, J B   1963   'Scottish raised shore line heights with particular reference to the Forth valley', *Geogr. Annalr.* 40: 180 – 5.

Sissons, J B   1963,1964   'The Perth readvance in Central Scotland', *Scott. Geogr. Mag.* 79: 151 – 63; 80: 28 – 63.

Sissons, J B   1966   'Relative sea-level changes between 10,300 and 8,300 B.P. in part of the Carse of Stirling', *Trans. Inst. Brit. Geogr,* 13: 19 – 29.

Sissons, J B   1967   *Scotland's structure and scenery.*   Edinburgh.

Sissons, J B and   1965   'Peat bogs in a post-Glacial sea and a buried raised beach in
Smith, D E   the western part of the Carse of Stirling',   *Scott. J. Geol.* 1: 247 – 55.

Soons, J M   1958   'Landscape evolution in the Ochil Hills',   *Scott. Geogr. Mag.* 74: 86 – 97.

Soons, J M   1960   'The sub-drift surface of the Lower Devon valley',   *Trans. Geol. Soc. Glasgow.*   24: 1 – 7.

CHAPTER 3

CLIMATOLOGY AND HYDROLOGY

Introduction

The Stirling Region comprises one of the most varied tracts of country in Britain. Unfortunately, however, it suffers from both a dearth of satisfactory records and a not-unrelated absence of previous investigation. The lack of data is particularly marked in the case of climatological observations and reflects, on a more local scale, the general deficiency of information which was noted for Scotland as a whole by Halstead (1956) and, more recently, by the Scottish Development Department (1971). At the present time no public body in Scotland is charged with a statutory duty to record climatic data. This contrasts with the situation in England and Wales where, as a result of a clause providing for the measurement of evaporation, the Water Resources Act 1963 has stimulated the establishment of a significant number of additional climatic stations during the past decade.

Ideally, the regional climatologist requires access to continuously recorded, long-term data for a number of representative locations. In the case of the Stirling Region, however, the nearest synoptic stations operated by the Meteorological Office lie well outside the area at Glasgow and Edinburgh airports. According to the Meteorological Office (1973), the former co-operating station at Sauchie House in Stirling, which closed down at the end of 1969, is the only site for which reasonably complete records of temperature are available for the standard 30-year period from 1931 to 1960 and there are no complete data runs for other weather elements such as wind or sunshine. Consequently, many of the long-period averages discussed in this chapter are estimates based on shorter term, and possibly discontinuous observations, made at either the station in question or at a comparable site. Some dependence has also had to be placed on measurements obtained from outside the strictly-defined Stirling Region. Despite the fact that several new climatological stations have begun operating within recent years, the period of record is, in most cases, too short to permit the derivation of long-term values for these stations from analogous sites.

The poor network of recording poses special difficulties in the Stirling Region in view of the complex nature of the topography, which in terms of altitude alone, range from 1174m (3843ft) on the summit of Ben More in the north-west down to sea level along the shores of the Forth estuary. Essentially, the area corresponds to the upper drainage basin of the eastward-flowing river Forth, although in the south-west the valley of the Endrick Water provides a river outlet to the Atlantic via Loch Lomond. The core of the region is composed of the broad, partially land-locked area of the Forth lowlands which lie to the east of the Lake of Menteith and Loch Venacher. Most of this gently sloping area is less than

30m (100ft) in height, even 22km (14 miles) upstream of Stirling, and is at its widest at both the eastern and western extremities so that there is a conspicious narrowing at the Stirling gap. To the south, the area is clearly defined by the escarpments of the Campsies, Fintry and Gargunnock Hills, whilst to the north and west the more extensive upland of the Highland Edge is deeply dissected by the often loch-filled valleys of the upper Forth and its major tributaries — the Teith to the north-west, the Allan Water to the north and north-east and the Devon to the east. Much of this elevated area lies over 305m (1000ft) above sea level with several peaks exceeding 914m (3000ft). To the north-east, between the Allan Water and the river Devon, the Ochil Hills form another broad area of upland which rises abruptly from the Forth valley.

In a region of such complicated terrain, which presents an almost limitless permutation of altitude, aspect, exposure and land use, the basic keynote of the climate must be diversity. Nevertheless, as a whole, the Stirling area can be regarded as transitional in a Scottish context, and on average a balance is maintained between the mild, west climate characteristic of so much of western Scotland and the drier, more 'continental' conditions of the coastal lowlands to the east. The surrounding uplands make their own climate and also provide some shelter for the central area, but the main WNW — ESE trend of the Forth lowlands, together with the ill-defined watershed between the Clyde and the Forth, ensures that strong airmass influences from either west or east may temporarily prevail at any season. Less frequently, the severe climate of the Highlands may also encroach, especially in that part of Strathallan lying to the north of the Ochils. As far as the hydrology is concerned, the high rainfall afforded by all the upland areas, but notably in the Trossachs, together with the natural water storage provided by the numerous lochs, has stimulated the exploitation of surface water resources on a large scale.

Wind

As elsewhere in Britain, the direction and speed of the prevailing wind is largely controlled by the changing pressure patterns associated with the travelling, synoptic-scale weather systems, but certain characteristic annual and seasonal features emerge and have regional significance. Fig 3.1 indicates the annual percentage frequency of the geostrophic wind at a height of 457 - 607m (1500 - 2000ft) above Cumbernauld and it can be seen that, in an average year, over 55 per cent of the airflow has some westerly component with approximately 25 per cent of the winds coming from the south-west. These south-westerlies are chiefly dominant during the autumn (September, October, November) when the region is strongly influenced by the passage of well-developed Atlantic depressions. However, in common with other areas lying fairly near to the eastern coast of Scotland, the late winter and spring periods bring an appreciable increase in the frequency of northerly and easterly winds and, in any one year, the frequency of easterly winds in spring (March, April, May) could well be higher than that for winds from any other direction. Near ground level the airflow becomes progressively modified by the surface geometry of the land, and the surface wind roses for Stirling, shown in Fig 3.2, reveal that at all seasons there is a clear east-west canalisation of winds through the Stirling gap between the Fintry and Ochil Hills.   As a result, winds from due west rather than south-west predominate through the year and, even during an average spring, the Forth estuary permits the penetration of easterlies to the extent that they are virtually as common as winds from the west.   Also during spring, the increased frequency of cold north easterly winds finds access to the central Stirling area by way of Strathallan.

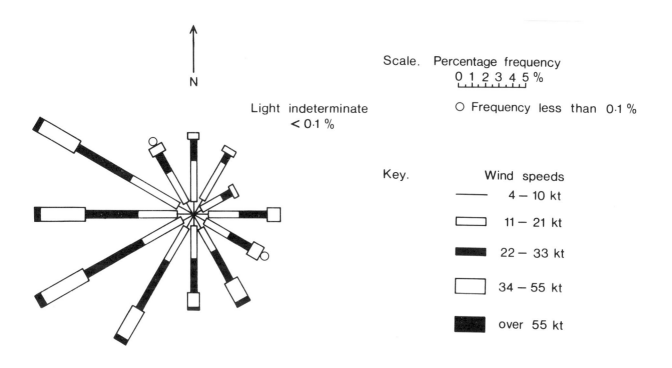

Fig 3.1   ANNUAL PERCENTAGE FREQUENCY OF GEOSTROPHIC WIND VELOCITIES OVER CUMBERNAULD

Observations taken at 00, 06, 12, 18hr. G M T, September 1962 — August 1965   *After Dight*

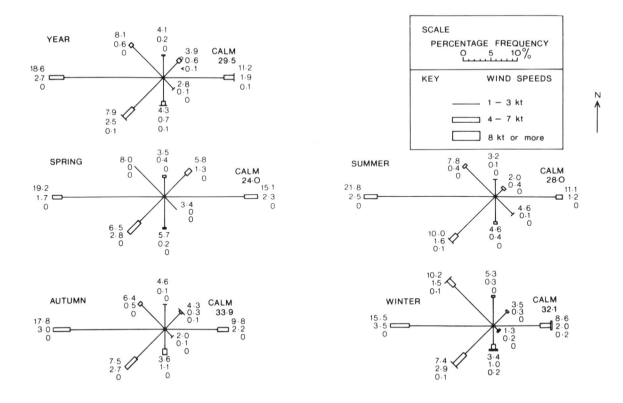

Fig 3.2   ANNUAL AND SEASONAL PERCENTAGE FREQUENCY OF WIND VELOCITIES AT STIRLING

Observations taken at 09hr G M T 1956 − 1965.   *After Dight*

Ground level wind velocities are significantly lower than those aloft (cf Figs 3.1 and 3.2). The strongest winds are, with few exceptions, from a westerly direction but, despite the funnelling which undoubtedly occurs in the Forth valley, the Stirling record suggests an average of only three days of gale-force winds per year, with an estimated value of five days for a more open exposure.   These are relatively low expectancies when compared with, for example, the average of twelve days recorded at Turnhouse (Edinburgh) airport (Plant, 1969). The gales are concentrated in winter (December, January, February), but although the summer season is normally gale-free, it should be noted that westerly winds blowing on sunny days at this season are often characterised by a marked gustiness.   This turbulance is due to the development of a steep lapse rate in the lowest atmospheric layers during the early and middle part of the afternoon.   In addition, it must be appreciated that the 0900 GMT observations depicted in Fig 3.2 are taken at a time when local winds are not well established and, therefore, such records will contain an excessive number of calms.

The varied, rugged nature of much of the topography will undoubtedly produce a wide range of local air circulations although, in the absence of instrumental observations, their presence can only be inferred. Thus, local wind accelerations will certainly be found above hills or ridges and when air currents are channelled through valleys. Similar increases in speed will occur over the relatively smooth loch surfaces, as demonstrated at Loch Leven some 13km (8miles) to the east of our area by Smith (1974), and also over the Forth estuary where, during the severe gale of 14 - 15 January 1968 the maximum gust exceeded that at Turnhouse airport, which lies 35m (114ft) above sea level, and the anemograph at Grangemouth went off the top of the chart at 47m/s (106mph). Equally, other areas experience shelter and parts of the Endrick valley enjoy such protection from the Campsies. In the dissected country to the north and west individual valley circulations must develop with katabatic drainage occuring on anticyclonic nights, whilst there is some evidence to suggest that, under the appropriate synoptic conditions, well-developed lee waves exist quite frequently on the downwind side of the major upland areas. For example, Fyfe (1952) has described the effect of standing wave airflow on glider flight immediately to the south of the Ochils. In this instance it was found that, although the height differential between the summit of the Ochils and the Earn-Allan lowlands to the north is only about 240m (800ft), the downwind oscillation extended to at least 3000m (10000ft) in the atmosphere. Strong surface heating of the lowlands around the Forth estuary in summer will lead to a diurnally-reversing sea breeze.

Temperature

Bearing in mind the relatively northerly latitude and the inland location, mean annual temperatures are remarkably high over the Stirling area. During the standard 1931 - 60 period, Stirling itself recorded an overall mean value of 9.0°C. Comparative data show that only four other stations out of a total of 43 representative Scottish sites recorded higher values in this period: all the warmer sites lay either on or near to the west coast and, with the exception of Tiree, all lay to the south of our area. This thermal advantage is due to a combination of factors operating at different seasons. Thus, conditions in winter are ameliorated by both the intrusion of maritime influences from the west and the shelter provided by the Ochils barrier against the incursion of arctic and polar continental airmasses from the north and east. During the summer months, on the other hand, the enclosed lowlands warm up quickly to produce high maximum temperatures. This can be illustrated by reference to Table 3.1 which lists mean annual and monthly temperature values for six stations in the area. It can be seen that between January and July the mean monthly maximum temperature at both Stirling and Falkirk, which are representative of the lower Forth valley, rises by some 14°C; this rate of warming is at least as rapid as that experienced anywhere in Scotland. On the other hand, especially under winter anticyclonic conditions, the broad lowlands are subject to cold air drainage and the resulting low night minima produce quite a large range of temperature, both seasonally and diurnally. From Table 3.1 it would appear that on average the seasonal temperature range is rather greater at Falkirk than at Stirling but, in terms of absolute extremities, Stirling has recorded the higher maximum (30.6°C) and has also reported an absolute minimum of −14.4°C on more occasions than Falkirk. The diurnal range of temperature tends to be highest during summer anticyclones. Extreme maxima have exceeded 26.5°C in each of May, June, July and August; during the same months, especially May and June, absolute minima have approached the freezing point. According to Dight (1969), air frosts at Stirling normally occur during the six-month period between 24 October and 20 April, but have been recorded as early as 6 September and as late as 31 May.

TABLE 3.1

Mean temperature at selected stations 1931 - 1960
in degrees Centigrade

a) Mean Maximum;   b) Mean Minimum;   c) Mean

Station		Jan.	Feb.	March	April	May	June	July	Aug.	Sep.	Oct.	Nov.	Dec.	Year
Stirling	a)	5.6	6.6	8.9	12.2	15.5	19.5	19.5	18.9	16.3	12.3	8.9	6.9	12.5
Alt. 46m	b)	0.3	0.8	2.3	4.0	6.3	9.4	11.3	11.1	9.1	6.4	3.2	1.8	5.5
	c)	2.9	3.7	5.6	8.1	10.9	13.8	15.4	15.0	12.7	9.4	6.0	4.3	9.0
Falkirk	a)	5.8	6.7	9.1	12.2	15.6	18.6	19.8	19.3	16.9	13.0	9.1	7.0	12.8
Alt. 30m	b)	-0.3	0.3	1.7	3.6	5.7	8.8	10.9	10.7	8.6	5.8	2.8	1.3	5.0
	c)	2.8	3.5	5.4	7.9	10.7	13.7	15.4	15.0	12.7	9.4	5.9	4.2	8.9
Earl's Hill	a)	2.3	3.5	6.2	9.5	13.1	15.7	16.7	16.3	14.0	10.0	6.3	4.1	9.8
Alt. 335m	b)	-1.2	-1.4	0.5	1.8	4.0	6.9	8.7	8.7	7.1	4.7	2.1	-0.1	3.5
	c)	0.5	1.1	3.3	5.7	8.5	11.3	12.7	12.5	10.5	7.3	4.2	2.0	6.6
Balfron	a)	5.5	6.1	8.1	11.4	15.1	17.4	18.9	18.2	15.7	12.0	8.9	6.7	12.0
Alt. 104m	b)	-0.8	-0.3	1.2	2.6	4.9	8.0	10.2	9.8	7.9	5.4	2.4	1.0	4.4
	c)	2.3	2.9	4.7	7.0	10.0	12.7	14.5	14.0	11.8	8.7	5.7	3.9	8.2
Ardtalnaig	a)	5.1	6.0	8.3	11.6	15.4	18.3	19.2	18.3	16.1	12.0	8.3	6.5	12.1
Alt. 130m	b)	0.0	0.1	1.2	2.7	5.1	8.3	10.3	9.8	7.7	5.5	2.8	1.7	4.6
	c)	2.5	3.1	4.7	7.1	10.3	13.3	14.7	14.1	11.9	8.7	5.5	4.1	8.3
Gleneagles	a)	5.0	5.7	7.9	11.2	14.7	17.7	18.9	17.9	15.9	12.0	8.2	6.4	11.8
Alt. 152m	b)	-1.7	-1.5	-0.2	1.5	3.9	6.9	8.9	8.5	6.5	4.4	1.5	0.2	3.2
	c)	1.7	2.1	3.9	6.3	9.3	12.3	13.9	13.2	11.2	8.2	4.9	3.3	7.5

In the hills and valleys surrounding the Forth lowlands, the temperature conditions are greatly modified by relief.   The lapse rate brought about by altitude is clearly shown by the figures for Earl's Hill at 335m (1100ft) where the greatest contrast with the Stirling record lies in the depression of summer maxima which, in turn, is caused by more persistent cloud cover and higher windspeeds.   Bleak conditions are also apparent even at relatively low elevations in the western foothills.   For example, it has been estimated that the number of days per year when the air temperature never rises above 0°C throughout the 24 hours shows a 50 per cent increase from twelve days at Stirling to eighteen days in the upper Teith valley. This indicates a much more severe winter climate.   The station at Balfron situated at 103m (338ft) above O.D. in the valley of the Endrick is reasonably representative of the smaller western valleys.   Table 3.1 shows that despite the shelter afforded by the Campsie Fells the mean temperatures are fairly low; the main reason for this is probably a frost hollow effect near the valley bottom.   Although the discontinuous nature of the Balfron record makes direct comparisons invalid, the evidence suggests that Balfron has an average of about 70 air frosts per year compared with only 56 at Stirling, with a significantly higher frequency during the critical spring growing period in April and May.   Of course, such valley sites have very variable temperature characteristics but Dight (1967) has drawn attention to a consistent and surprisingly large diurnal range of temperature in several Scottish glens and, with an absolute minimum of −16.7°C recorded at Balfron in January 1940, there appears no reason to regard the Endrick valley as in any way exceptional in terms of this general feature.

Unfortunately, no data are available for valley bottom sites adjacent to large lochs in the Trossachs area but the Ardtalnaig record, although lying well to the north of the Stirling area on the southern bank of Loch Tay, provides some guide to loch-side stations which are situated near to much higher ground.   Despite the fact that Ardtalnaig is almost 30m (100ft) higher than Balfron and lies further north, Table 3.1 shows that it is, if anything, slightly warmer throughout the year.   It is tempting, if possibly unjustified, to ascribe this relative warmth to the local heat storage created by the thermal capacity of Loch Tay.

A special mention must be made of the Strathallan area lying to the north of the Ochils and represented in Table 3.1 by the Gleneagles site.   Here the open exposure to northerly and easterly influences helps to create a particularly harsh winter climate which is more characteristic of districts further east or north so that, although the station altitude is broadly comparable with that at Ardtalnaig, there are large differences in minimum temperatures.   Since the main slopes in the Gleneagles locality are basically all north-facing it seems likely that the low temperatures are partly explained by the unfavourable orientation of the site with respect to incoming solar radiation.

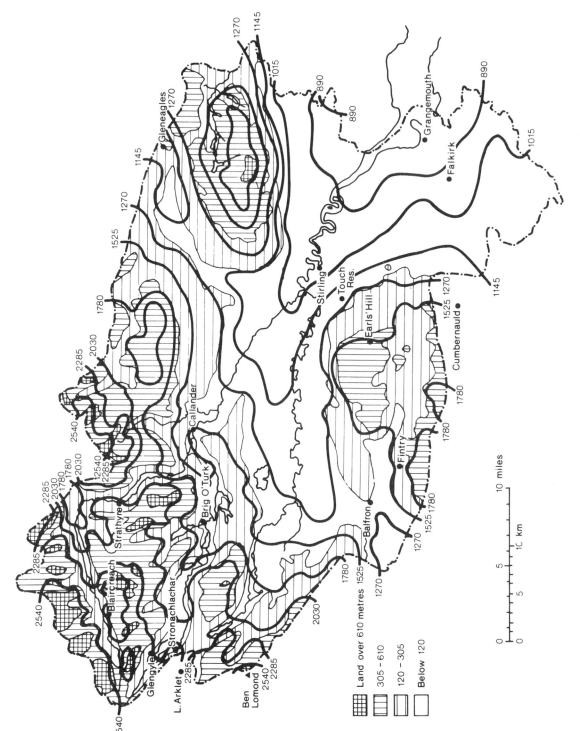

Fig 3.3   THE DISTRIBUTION OF MEAN ANNUAL PRECIPITATION IN THE STIRLING REGION 1916 – 1950.

Isohyets are rounded to the nearest 5mm.   Placenames indicate sites referred to in the text.

Precipitation

As shown in Fig 3.3, the major precipitation gradient over the region lies in the WNW — ESE direction. There is a considerable spatial variation of mean annual rainfall. The wettest area, with annual totals in excess of 2500mm (100in) lies in the mountains to the north of Loch Katrine whilst along the estuary near Grangemouth values decline to less than 890mm (35in). This overall pattern is modified to some extent by the intrusion of the highland flanks to the north and south, and the south-facing escarpment of the Ochils produces one of the steepest gradients in the region. As in other areas of Britain, individual annual totals may depart appreciably from the long-term mean and at Callander, for example, values during the standard 1915 - 50 rainfall period have ranged between 968mm (38.2in) in 1941 and 2114mm (83.1in) in 1928.

Table 3.2 lists the mean monthly rainfall for two stations representative of the extreme ends of the rainfall spectrum, and it can be seen that the seasonal incidence of precipitation is comparable over the whole area. Indeed, at virtually all stations January is the wettest month although there is usually a build-up of heavy rainfall during the late summer to produce a secondary peak in October. Conversely, the driest season is spring and early summer from April to June.

The pattern of mean annual rainfall is reflected to some extent in the distribution of extreme rainfalls which, for a variety of reasons, are relatively infrequent in the Forth lowlands compared with the surrounding hills and valleys. Generally speaking, heavy rain over periods up to 24 hours in length tends to occur as a result of either vigorous winter depressions or short-lived summer thunderstorms and, although intense storms occur anywhere over the region, the frequency of prolonged, heavy falls of rain is normally appreciably higher in localities with a large mean annual rainfall. Thus, at Stronachlachar with an annual mean 2379mm (93.6in) a fall of 25mm (4in) in 16 hours is experienced, on average on almost 15 days per year compared with an incidence of less than three days per year at Cumbernauld which has an annual mean 1147mm (45.2in) (Plant, 1971). Such heavy daily falls arise mainly from frontal precipitation, especially during winter, and in most cases the meteorological processes are reinforced by orographic influences. Such a reinforcement was responsible for the highest recorded daily fall in the region when 113mm (4.4in) fell in the Duchray valley on 20th December, 1916. In comparison, most of the intense falls which last for 2 hours or less originate from thundery activity in summer and, despite the fact that warm, relatively stagnant air in the Stirling basin will be inherently unstable at this season, the evidence available suggests that such storms only produce excessive rainfalls when additional uplift is provided by the surrounding hills. The flanks of the Ochils and the Campsies seem particularly favourable for this type of development and Table 3.3 which summarises the cumulative frequencies of daily rainfall at Touch reservoir located at a height of 231mm (758ft) some 6km (4miles) from Stirling, suggests a peak occurrence of intense falls during August.

TABLE 3.2

Monthly and annual averages of rainfall at
two selected stations 1916 - 1950 in millimetres

a) Rainfall;   b) Percentage of Annual Total

Station		Jan.	Feb.	March	April	May	June	July	Aug.	Sep.	Oct.	Nov.	Dec.	Year
Blaircreach	a)	317	224	168	157	142	134	168	193	211	301	263	299	2577
Alt. 140m	b)	12.3	8.7	6.5	6.1	5.5	5.2	6.5	7.5	8.2	11.7	10.2	11.6	100.0
Falkirk (Kerse)	a)	93	62	54	47	62	52	77	84	75	90	82	75	853
Alt. 6m	b)	10.9	7.3	6.3	5.5	7.3	6.1	9.0	9.8	8.8	10.6	9.6	8.8	100.0

TABLE 3.3

Accumulated frequencies of daily rainfall, in millimetres,
over the 1916 - 1950 period at Touch Reservoir No. 3 (Old Site)

Daily Totals	Jan.	Feb.	March	April	May	June	July	Aug.	Sep.	Oct.	Nov.	Dec.	All Months
75mm								2					2
60mm								2					2
55mm								2	1			1	4
50mm						2	1	2	2	2		1	8
45mm	1			1		3	1	2	3	1	2	2	16
40mm	1	1		2		3	1	4	4	2	3	3	24
35mm	5	3		2		4	2	7	7	11	7	5	53
30mm	12	6	3	4	1	6	6	11	14	17	15	11	106
25mm	30	15	7	14	6	10	14	19	23	25	27	21	213
20mm	63	31	20	26	20	19	27	39	45	58	55	53	456
15mm	121	63	40	40	46	30	52	69	68	104	98	97	828
10mm	218	113	92	88	90	69	112	140	135	193	171	178	1599
5mm	373	261	219	175	204	175	231	259	264	316	283	325	3085
0.1mm	322	372	476	477	510	477	447	422	414	373	349	344	4983
Total number of days	1085	989	1085	1050	1085	1050	1085	1085	1050	1085	1050	1085	12784

According to McNaughton (1963), the heaviest recorded falls of rain for periods up to two hours in duration for Stirlingshire between 1860 and 1953 were 16mm (0.63in) in ten minutes and 35mm (1.4in) in one hour. It was further estimated that in the mountains near the northern end of Loch Lomond really intense falls in excess of 63mm (2.5in) per day occurred on average about twice per year; falls more than 89mm (35in), once.   Such extreme falls probably have a random distribution and it is difficult to place much reliance on frequency estimations or to define areas of preferred occurrance.   It is noteworthy however that the two most intense, short-duration falls recorded between 1922 and 1957 were both on the northern edge of the Campsies: at Fintry (12mm in six minutes) and at Balfron (17mm in 20 minutes).

Strictly speaking, it is possible for thunder to be heard in any month of the year but the main thunder season lasts from May through to September with a peak in July. The average number of days per year with thunder heard shows a slight increase towards the west, from four to five days at Stirling to six or more at Balfron, probably reflecting the tendency for unstable air to become trapped in the western valleys.   Hail is observed to fall on rather fewer days during the year than thunder is heard and also has a different seasonal distribution with most falls coming in the spring months of March and April.

Snow is a highly variable aspect of the precipitation regime throughout the area. It is generally considered that the number of days with snow falling and, more especially, the number of mornings with snow lying, provides a useful guide to the severity of winter climate. Table 3.4, which lists these data for two representative valley stations in the Trossachs, indicates the large fluctuations which have occurred recently in individual years. Other things being equal, altitude will markedly increase the duration of snow-lying through the winter and Fig. 3.4 illustrates this effect for the mountainous district around the head of Loch Lomond.   It can be seen that prolongation of wintry conditions at the higher levels is achieved not only by the fact that the mountain snows have a more extended seasonal duration but is also due to the much greater persistence of snow on the ground during even the coldest months such as January and February. In contrast, the Stirling lowlands enjoy a good deal of protection from the northerly and north-easterly snow-bearing winds. This protection may be largely attributed to the Ochil Hills; the efficiency of this barrier has been partially demonstrated by Dight (1969) who estimated that, at an altitude of 457m (1500ft) the Ochils would have about 55 - 60 days per year with snow lying compared with only 45 - 50 days each year at an equivalent height in the Fintry Hills to the south. In the lowlands very little snow is observed before November or after the end of March with the main concentration in January and February. During the 11-year period from 1956-7 to 1966-7, snow lay for an average of 16 days per year at Stirling and, somewhat surprisingly, this mean value increases to only 19 days per year at Strathyre situated at an altitude of 130m (426ft) in the upper Teith valley (Dunsire 1971).   However, an examination of the actual depth of snow recorded reveals that much heavier falls occurred at Strathyre where only half the falls were less than 3cm (1.2in) deep compared with over three-quarters of the falls in Stirling.

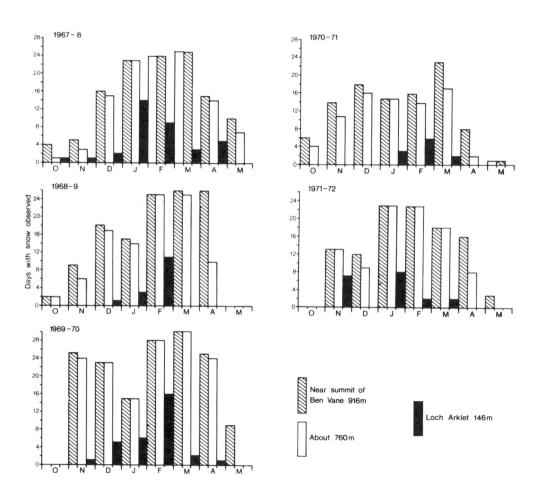

Fig 3.4   THE EFFECT OF ALTITUDE ON THE NUMBER OF DAYS WITH SNOW LYING

The number of days with snow lying at three different altitudes in the upland area around Loch Lomond, October to May, 1967 – 1972.

Fig 3.5   DAYS AND DEPTH OF SNOW LYING AT STIRLING AND STRATHYRE
1956 − 7 to 1966 − 7.

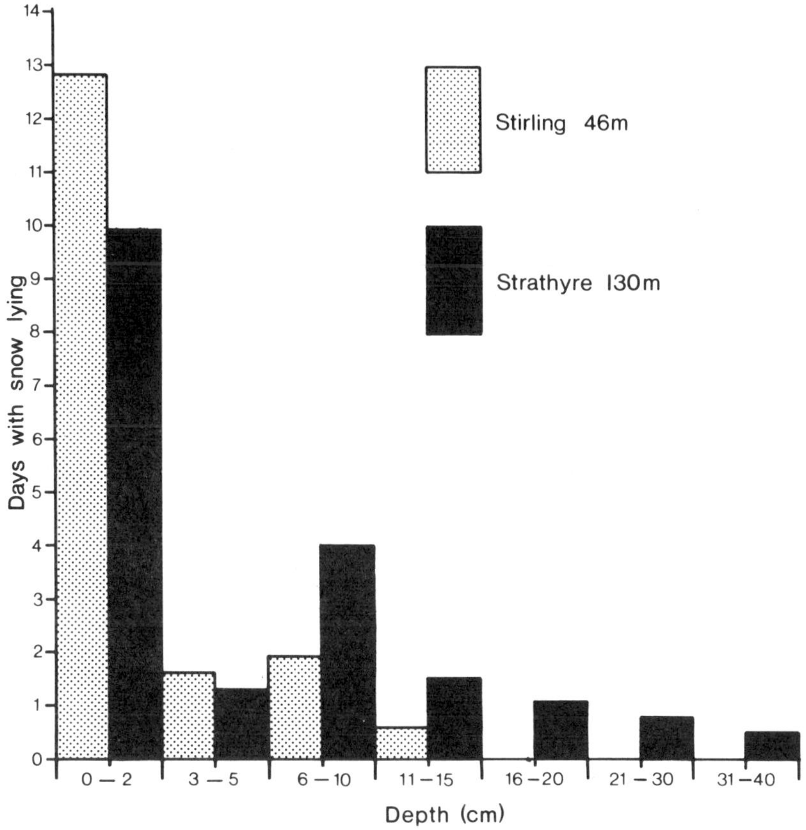

TABLE 3.4

Number of days per year with (a) snow falling
and (b) snow lying at two stations in the Trossachs
1955 - 6 to 1971 - 2

Station	1965 - 6 (a) (b)		1966 - 7 (a) (b)		1967 - 8 (a) (b)		1968 - 9 (a) (b)		1969 -70 (a) (b)		1970 - 1 (a) (b)		1971 - 2 (a) (b)	
Glengyle Alt. 116m	34	42	18	6	34	54	34	29	79	32	7	12	18	15
Brig-O-Turk Alt. 84m	14	33	10	10	23	35	15	20	20	35	7	7	17	17

Sunshine and Visibility

Sunshine and the clarity of the atmosphere make an important impression on subjective assessments of a climate, and estimated average monthly and annual sunshine durations in hours are given for three locations within the Stirling area in Table 3.5. If allowance is made for the northerly latitude, there is no doubt that the flatter eastern part of the region, exemplified by Stirling with a mean daily sunshine duration of 3.72 hours, enjoys a tolerably good sunshine record.   As might be expected, there is a well-defined seasonal cycle of incidence with minimum receipts in December and maximum durations in May or June. In practice, rather more than half of the annual total is recorded during the first six months of the calendar year.   Whilst stations nearer to the east coast are more favoured in terms of the duration of bright sunshine, Table 3.5 confirms the advantage experienced by Stirling when compared with other inland locations.   The record for Gleneagles, with a mean daily duration of 3.56 hours, suggests a rapid deterioration towards the north and there is, of course, a progressive decline to the west which is partly due to the effects of increasing altitude as shown by Earl's Hill.   Although most of the westward decline may be attributed to the higher frequency of cloud cover over the hills, many of the deeper valleys in the Trossachs area are likely to suffer some additional obstruction of sunshine by the hills themselves.   At this latitude the maximum altitude attained by the sun above the horizon at noon on 22 December is only $10\frac{1}{2}°$ so that, during midwinter, a hill lying to the south with a height equivalent to more than $10\frac{1}{2}°$ will effectively shield all the incoming sunshine.

TABLE 3.5

Estimated monthly and annual averages of bright sunshine
duration in hours (1931 - 60) at the locations specified

Station	Jan.	Feb.	March	April	May	June	July	Aug.	Sep.	Oct.	Nov.	Dec.	Year
Stirling	50	79	105	147	195	190	174	137	120	81	49	30	1357
Earl's Hill	54	81	106	144	179	185	154	133	111	77	55	46	1323
Gleneagles	42	75	99	139	174	187	159	137	119	84	48	35	1298

To some extent, the duration of sunshine will also be restricted by fog formation and the enclosed, damp Stirling lowlands will be a preferred area for the development of radiation fog during the winter months.   Indeed, at Stirling itself fog is recorded on an average of 30 days every year and 90 per cent of the occurrences are confined to the six winter months.   Such fogs tend to be shallow, with a majority probably extending less than 150m (500ft) from the surface.

In this situation, the surrounding hill slopes may well be fog-free and at Balfron, for example, with 12 days of fog per year the average incidence is less than half that at Stirling although the Balfron site is only 57m (180ft) higher.

During late spring and early summer, visibility is often reduced by advection fog moving inland from off the North Sea.   At this season the characteristic build-up of high pressure over Scandinavia produces a light easterly airflow which, after being cooled and moistened by its marine passage, brings low stratus cloud and sea fog to the lower Forth estuary.   This low-level condensation, collectively known as 'haar', is often burned off inland during the middle of the day by solar heating but, in an appropriate synoptic situation, the poor visibility often persists throughout the 24 hours near the coast and does much to lower both sunshine duration and maximum temperatures at this time of year.   To some extent poor visibility will also be associated with light south-easterly winds at all seasons due to the downwind transfer of atmospheric pollutants originating in the industrial district around Grangemouth.

Hydrology

Even the most superficial examination of the hydrology of the Stirling region reveals appreciable spatial differences in the availability of water.   These differences are dominated by the overall precipitation gradient illustrated in Fig 3.3 and, over much of the upland area to the north and west, there is a surplus of rainfall over evaporative needs in every month of the year.   Whilst this surplus is largely due to the increase in rainfall with height, it should also be noted that evaporation undergoes a slight reduction at the higher elevation which will contribute further to the water surplus.   Thus, from Table 3.6 it can be seen that at an elevation of 165m (540ft), which is the average height of the County of Stirling, the mean annual potential evapotranspiration is 443mm (17.4in) compared with 458mm (18.0in) at a height of 100m (330ft), which represents the average county height below 305m (100ft) above sea level.   In general, the potential evaporation demand is estimated to drop by 6mm

TABLE 3.6

Mean monthly and annual values of potential
evapotranspiration in Stirlingshire (mm)

a) at 100m (average height below 305m)
b) at 165m (average height of County)

	Height	Jan.	Feb.	March	April	May	June	July	Aug.	Sep.	Oct.	Nov.	Dec.	Year
a)	100m	0	8	28	50	81	88	82	63	39	19	1	-1	458
b)	165m	1	8	27	48	79	86	81	61	36	16	3	-1	443

(0.24in) for every 30m (100ft) during the summer months and by 3mm per 30m in the winter, leading to an annual reduction of 9mm per 30m (Smith, 1967). The highest values of potential evapotranspiration are recorded near the coast where the relative absence of cloud and haze allows greater receipts of incident radiation. Around the lower Forth estuary it is likely that the annual evaporative demand reaches 500mm (19.7in). Over 85 per cent of evaporation occurs during the six summer months with a peak in June, which is one of the driest months of the year. This means that, in the eastern lowlands, a soil moisture deficit approaching 50mm (2in) will be built up by early July and, despite its progressive elimination during the wetter summer months, this deficit can create considerable problems for agriculture (O'Riordan, 1963).

Virtually all water supplies in the Stirling area are derived from surface sources, due largely to the predominance of relatively impermeable rocks. It is the seasonal river regime, therefore, which is effectively responsible for the availability of supplies and Table 3.7 depicts the variation in mean monthly rainfall and runoff for the Teith catchment above Bridge of Teith. In general, the river flows show a marked seasonal pattern with maximum discharges

TABLE 3.7

Mean monthly and annual values of rainfall and
runoff for the river Teith at Bridge of Teith
from October, 1957 to September, 1965 in millimetres

a) rainfall;   b) runoff

		Jan.	Feb.	March	April	May	June	July	Aug.	Sep.	Oct.	Nov.	Dec.	Year
a)	rainfall	222	30	121	130	125	203	118	174	210	103	180	255	1871
b)	runoff	238	68	109	110	93	152	51	125	184	94	156	205	1585

in December and January and low flows during late spring or early summer, but in the higher parts of all catchments there is likely to be a minor seasonal peak in March or April which may be attributed to spring snow-melt. The combination of fairly hard rocks, steep slopes and high rainfall tends to give most rivers a flashy pattern of short-term behaviour although, on the Teith itself, this feature will be balanced to some extent by the smoothing effect exerted by both natural loch storage and the artificial regulation achieved by the statutory discharge of compensation water from Loch Venacher. On the other hand, many of the smaller rivers are not subject to these smoothing influences and Fig 3.6 illustrates the sensitive response of the Endrick Water to an isolated summer storm. The Endrick Water has a catchment area of 220km^2 (85 square miles) and, before entering Loch Lomond, drains a large area of the Campsie

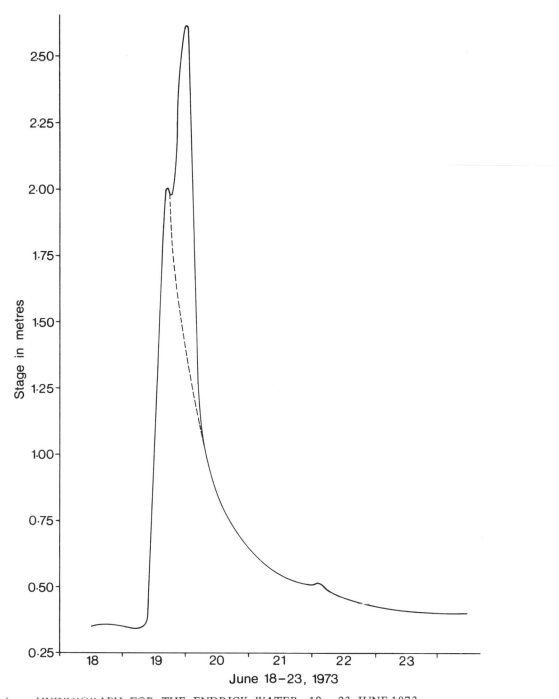

Fig 3.6   HYDROGRAPH FOR THE ENDRICK WATER, 18 – 23 JUNE 1973

This is a typical flood hydrograph for the Endrick Water, showing separate run-off contributions from the Endrick and the Blane.

Fells by means of two large tributaries — the river Endrick to the north and the River Blane to the south. Both of these streams appear to have a similar time of concentration which means that, after an intense rainfall over the Campsies, the flood pulses from the streams tend to coincide near the gauging station to produce the steeply rising hydrograph shown in the figure. Indeed, this particular hydrograph shows a clear step on the rising link due to the arrival of the second flood a short time after the river has started to rise.

The general abundance of surface water in the Trossachs and other upland areas has led to a long history of resource development. In the first instance, development on a fairly small scale was undertaken to provide water power for local industry, as described by Turner (1958), but since the mid-nineteenth century the major factor has been the impounding programme necessitated by increasing water demands in the Glasgow area (Crabb and Douglas, 1970). For some time, one of the main roles of the area has been that of an exporter of water supplies southwards to the central industrial belt of Scotland. In recent years increases in water demand have occurred within the region itself, in the drier parts of the Forth lowlands and, in particular, in the concentration of large water-consuming industries which has grown up around Grangemouth. Local sources are inadequate to satisfy these requirements and the area is heavily dependent on water from the Loch Turret scheme, which lies on a tributory of the river Tay some 48kn (30miles) to the north. According to the Scottish Development Department (1973), there are plans to increase water supplies to the Stirling region from indigenous sources, but it seems likely that deficiencies in the south-eastern area will have to be met increasingly in the long-term by means of large-scale inter-regional transfers of water from either the Tay basin to the north or the Loch Lomond scheme to the west.

REFERENCES

Crabb, P and Douglas, I   1970   'Water resources management in south-west Perthshire', *Scott. Geogrl. Mag* 86: 203 — 207.

Dight, F H   1967   'The diurnal range of temperature in Scottish glens', *Met. Mag.* 96: 327 — 334.

Dight, F H   1969   *The Climate of North Stirlingshire, South Perthshire and Clackmannanshire.   Climatological Memorandum No. 63.* Meteorological Office, Edinburgh and Bracknell.   11 pp.

Dunsire, A   1971   *Frequencies of Snow Depths and Days with Snow Lying at Stations in Scotland for Periods Ending Winter 1970 — 71.   Climatological Memorandum No. 70.*   Meteorological Office, Edinburgh and Bracknell.   100 pp.

Fyfe, A J	1953	'Lee-waves of the Ochils', *Weather* 7: 137 – 139.
Halstead, C A	1956	'Climatic observations in Scotland', *Scott. Geogrl. Mag.* 72: 21 – 23.
McNaughton, D	1963	'Heavy falls of rain in short periods in the counties around Glasgow', *Memorandum No. 1.* Glasgow Weather Centre. September, 3 pp typescript.
Meteorological Office	1973	Private Communication.
O'Riordan, T	1963	'Spray irrigation and water supply in East Lothian', *Scott. Geogrl. Mag.* 79: 170 – 173.
Plant, J A	1969	*The Climate of West Lothian. Climatological Memorandum No. 59A.* Meteorological Office, Edinburgh and Bracknell. 78 pp.
Plant, J A	1971	*A Study of Intensities of Rainfall Recorded at Places in Scotland. Hydrological Memorandum No. 40.* Meteorological Office, Edinburgh and Bracknell. 63 pp.
Scottish Development Department	1971	*An Investigation into the Requirements for Climatological Data in Scotland.* Report of a Working Party appointed by the Secretary of the Scottish Development Department, 22 pp.
Scottish Development Department	1973	*A Measure of Plenty: Water Resources in Scotland – A General Survey.* H.M.S.O. Edinburgh. 100 pp.
Smith, I R	1973	'The assessment of winds at Loch Leven, Kinross', *Weather* 28: 202 – 210.
Smith, L P	1967	*Potential Transpiration. Technical Bulletin No. 16.* Ministry of Agriculture, Fisheries and Food. H.M.S.O. London 77 pp.
Turner, W H K	1958	'The significance of water power in industrial location: some Perthshire examples', *Scott. Geogrl. Mag.* 74: 98 – 115.

CHAPTER 4

SOILS

Introduction

The character of the soil in any place results from the interaction of six factors: climate, parent material, relief, vegetation, man, and time. These factors operate gradually and continually, and their influence is reflected in the different morphological characteristics and other properties of soils. It is difficult to assess the effect of any one of these factors in isolation, but before going on to describe these end results it is necessary to underline their relative importance in determining the variability of soils in the Stirling Region.

Several climatic factors are involved in the development of soil types. An important element in Central Scotland is the high average rainfall. Although the Stirling region extends into the east-coast lower rainfall belt, the presence of hill masses to the north and north-east attracts rain from both east and west, so that most of the region receives a fairly high rainfall. In the far south-east of the region average annual rainfall is as low as 800mm (31in), but for the other lowlands it is between 800 and 1100mm (43in), while for the foothills and hill areas at least 1250mm (49in) of rain falls per annum. In the highland part of the region, above 500m (1640ft), more than 1500mm (60in) falls in an average year, with extremes greater than 2500mm (98in) at altitudes above 900m (1950ft) in the north and north-west around Ben Vorlich and Ben Lomond. The high rainfall, coupled with a high proportion of fine-textured parent materials and the tendency of coarse-textured parent materials to have an indurated horizon which impedes soil drainage, has produced an extensive development of surface-water gley soils and gleyed brown forest soils. A further effect of the high rainfall is the tendency for active accumulation of surface organic matter and blanket peat occurs at the relatively low altitude of 200m (650ft). Above this altitude the peaty podzol and peaty gley soil groups dominate the soils and peat is widespread on the gentler hill slopes and rounded summits.

The strong south-westerly, westerly and north-westerly winds, in combination with the pattern of high ground in the region, results in most of the farmland suffering from exposure to some degree. In addition, the low-lying Carse of Stirling and the contiguous till plains suffer occasionally in most seasons of the year from east coast haar, the presence of which effectively excludes sunshine and reduces the temperature (Dight, 1969).

Whilst climate is an important regional factor in explaining broad differences in soil properties within the Stirling region, the effects of parent material and topography are locally very important. The varied geological formations making up the terrain of the region have been glaciated, often severely. This has resulted in the development of many distinctive soil parent materials, including glacial tills, moraines and fluvioglacial deposits. Post-glacial fluctuations in sea-level have caused the formation of extensive raised-beach deposits and spreads of marine alluvium; extensive accumulations of basin peat also occur.

As well as the general and indirect influence of altitude on climate, relief also exerts an important influence on soil at the local scale. A well defined hydrologic sequence of profiles on slopes can be generally observed over most of the region, but especially in the upland areas. Freely-draining profiles occupy slope flanks, with imperfectly-drained soils occurring on the lower slopes. Freely or imperfectly-draining soils occur on the interfluves, with poorly-draining soils occurring in the topographic hollows. This sequence is frequently modified in drumlin topography, where the soils are usually developed on fine-textured parent material with poorly-drained soils occurring on the gentler slopes of the summits of the drumlins and in the hollows, while the drumlin flanks are occupied by imperfectly-drained soils. Extensive flat areas with high water table are usually occupied by poorly-drained soils whether on coarse or fine-textured parent materials.

The majority of the soils in the lowland areas of the Stirling region have been cultivated and man's influence as a soil forming factor has been strong. Most soils have, as a result of ploughing, a dark grey-brown surface horizon about 10cm (8in) in depth). Artificial drainage has frequently improved the soil drainage status while the nutrient status has been improved by the addition of fertilizers and by liming. In several localities coalmining operations have affected pedogenesis, and even in the uplands the anthropogenic factor is not entirely absent, although its influence decreases with increasing altitude.

Soil Types

The distribution of the major soil groups in the Stirling region is illustrated in Fig 4.1.

The primary unit of soil mapping is the 'soil series', which comprises those soils with similar type and arrangements of horizons developed on similar parent material. In order to relate them to their environment, and particularly to geology, soil series are grouped into a larger unit, the 'soil association'. A soil association comprises soil series developed on parent materials derived from similar rocks, but varying in profile morphology, mainly because of differences in hydrological conditions. The usefulness of the association is in grouping together series which occur in a related pattern in a landscape, and which are developed on parent materials with related total mineral content.

Twenty soil associations, comprising almost 80 soil series, have been mapped in the Stirling region. Many of these have been recognised in other regions of Scotland. The

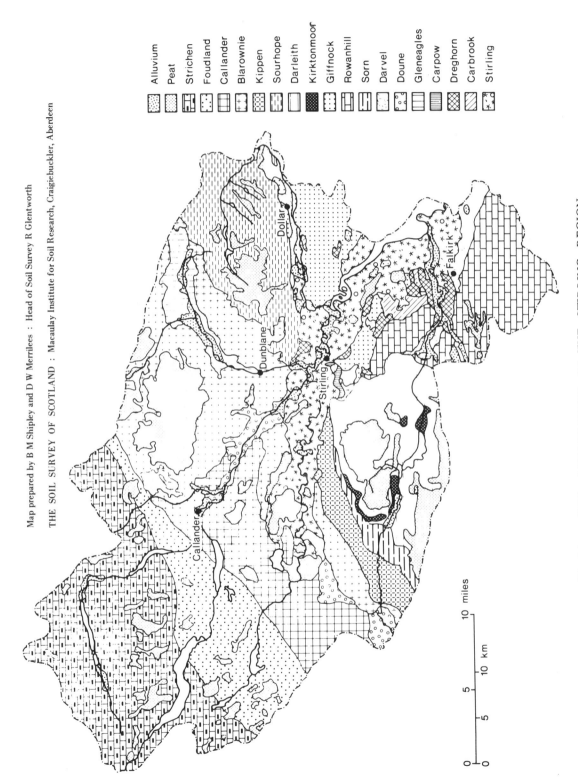

Map prepared by B M Shipley and D W Merrilees : Head of Soil Survey R Glentworth

THE SOIL SURVEY OF SCOTLAND : Macaulay Institute for Soil Research, Craigiebuckler, Aberdeen

Alluvium
Peat
Strichen
Foudland
Callander
Blarownie
Kippen
Sourhope
Darleith
Kirktonmoor
Giffnock
Rowanhill
Sorn
Darvel
Doune
Gleneagles
Carpow
Dreghorn
Carbrook
Stirling

Fig 4.1   SOIL ASSOCIATIONS IN THE STIRLING REGION

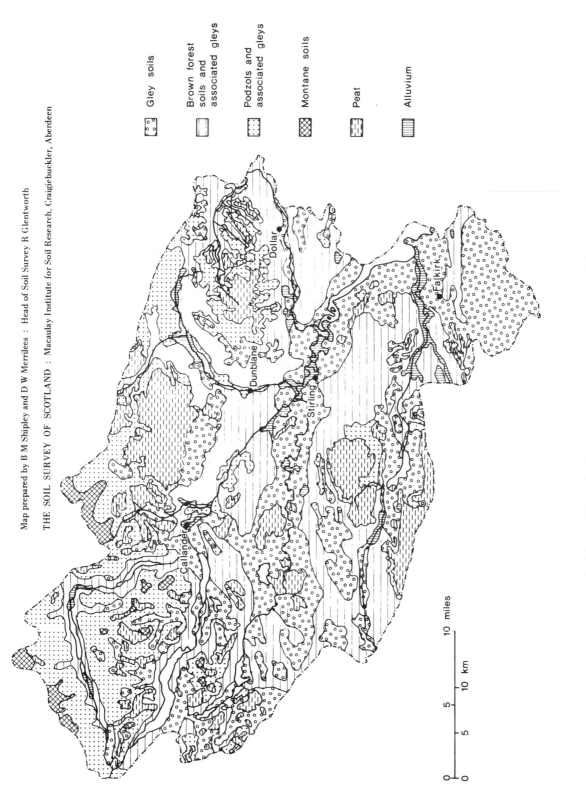

Map prepared by B M Shipley and D W Merrilees : Head of Soil Survey R Glentworth

THE SOIL SURVEY OF SCOTLAND : Macaulay Institute for Soil Research, Craigiebuckler, Aberdeen

Gley soils

Brown forest
soils and
associated gleys

Podzols and
associated gleys

Montane soils

Peat

Alluvium

Dollar

Falkirk

Dunblane

Stirling

Callander

10 miles

0   5   5   10 km

Fig 4.2   SOIL GROUPS IN THE STIRLING REGION

following associations are distinguished in the accompanying map (fig. 4.2).

Association	Parent Material
Strichen	Till derived from acid schists and schistose grits of the Dalradian Series of Highland Schists.
Foudland	Till derived from slates and agrillaceous schists of the Dalradian Series of Highland Schists.
Callander	Till derived from an intermixture of Dalradian Series rocks and Lower Old Red Sandstone sediments.
Balrownie	Till derived from Lower Old Red Sandstone sediments – sandstones, flags and mudstones – with some Highland Schist erratics.
Kippen	Till derived from Upper Old Red Sandstone sediments – red and yellow sandstones – with some Highland Schist erratics.
Sourhope	Till derived from andesitic and basaltic lavas, tuffs and agglomerates of Lower Old Red Sandstone age.
Darleith	Till derived from basaltic lavas and intrusions of Carboniferous and Permo-Carboniferous age.
Kirktonmoor	Morainic debris derived from basaltic lavas and ashes of Carboniferous age.
Giffnock	Till derived principally from sandstones of Carboniferous age with some shales, coals and limestones.
Rowanhill	Till derived from shales and sandstones of Carboniferous age with some coals and limestones.
Sorn	Till derived from an intermixture of Lower Carboniferous and Upper Old Red Sandstone sediments and lavas.
Darvel	Fluvioglacial sands and gravels derived from Carboniferous igneous and sedimentary rocks with some Lower Old Red Sandstone and Highland Schist rocks.
Doune	Fluvioglacial sands and gravels derived from Highland Schists and Lower Old Red Sandstone sediments and lavas.
Gleneagles	Fluvioglacial sands and gravels and moraine derived from Lower Old Red Sandstone sediments and lavas with some Highland Schist rocks.
Carpow	Terrace and raised-beach sands and gravels derived principally from Old Red Sandstone sediments and intermediate lavas.
Dreghorn	Raised-beach sands and gravels derived principally from Carboniferous sediments and basic lavas.
Carbrook	Estuarine High Raised Beach silts and clays (reddish colour).
Stirling	Estuarine Low raised Beach silts and clays (greyish colour).

The map also shows the distribution of the alluvium and peat. The alluvium category consists of recent alluvial deposits along rivers, alluvial fans, alluvial deposits intermixed with peat, and marine alluvium (saltongs). The peat category contains raised moss and low moor stages of Basin Peat, with Hill Peat and Flush Peat of Blanket Peat deposits.

As has been pointed out in chapter two, although the topography of the Region has been considerably modified by glaciation, relief is to a large extent determined by the solid geology. The resultant topography effectively sub-divides the Stirling region into seven natural landform units, each with its characteristic soil pattern. These are as follows:-

1) The Highlands
2) The Highland Border Zone and Old Red Sandstone Uplands
3) The Old Red Sandstone Lowlands
4) The Carse of Stirling and Flanders Moss
5) The Volcanic Hills
6) Carboniferous Lowlands
7) The Slamannan Plateau

We shall describe the soil patterns of each in turn.

1) *The Highlands*

The highest ground in the region is formed by the more resistant, metamorphosed Dalradian Series of Highland Schists which occur north-west of the Highland Boundary Fault. The extreme north and west of the region is occupied by acid schists, schistose grits and coarse grits of the Ben Ledi Grit group (Francis, et al., 1970) from which the till which forms the parent material of the Strichen Association is derived. The contiguous argillaceous schists and slates of the Aberfoyle Slate group, occurring further to the south-east, adjacent to the fault, form the parent material of the Foudland Association.

The valley floors are occupied by immature alluvial soils, frequently subjected to seasonal flooding, and are usually imperfectly or poorly-drained as a result of the high water table. Contiguous with the alluvial soils, free-drainage soils developed from moundy moraine or fluvioglacial gravel occupy the lowest slopes of the valley sides. The steep lower slopes of the hills, which often support deciduous woodland, usually have free-draining brown forest soil of low base status, developed on this stony till or directly from weathering rocks. At altitudes above 300m (1000ft) the soils become more leached and podzolic in character, and above 400m (1300ft) pass into well developed podzols. On gentler slopes and rounded summits at these high levels peaty podzols and peat are often present, while in the hollows and broad depressions poorly-drained peaty gley soils and blanket bog occur. The mountain tops above 800m (2600ft) consist of shallow peaty lithosols and podzolic lithosols among bare rocks, with scree and patches of montane humus soils on the more stable slopes and montane podzols on the stable level sites.

Soils of the Strichen and Foudland Association have similar broad characteristics, but there are important differences.   Strichen soils are usually more acid, with coarse gritty texture and many unweathered stones throughout the profile, whereas their Foudland counterparts are smooth and fine-textured with fewer stones, most of which are weathered to some degree.

2)   *The Highland Border Zone and Old Red Sandstone Uplands*

The southern fringe of the highland area is underlain by a complex sequence of rocks, within the fault zone, known as the Highland Border Series and, immediately to the south-east of the fault, by conglomerates and sandstones of the Lower Old Red Sandstone formation.   The latter dip very steeply parallel to the fault and at some points are overturned or vertical.   They are relatively resistant to erosion and form many of the foothills of the highland fringe.   The till derived from an intermixture of these rocks with the Dalradian Schists forms the parent material of soils of the Callander Association.

The parent material is variable in characteristics and there is a gradual transition from the low-nutrient, stony, acid soils of the highest ground, to the richer deeper soils of the adjoining lowlands to the south and east.   There are two extremes: on the more rugged country, adjacent to the Highland Boundary Fault, free-to imperfectly-drained, leached, podzolic and brown forest soils of low base status, often with indurated sub-soil horizons, and developed on shallow, stony, coarse-textured tills; in the hollows and depressions and on the less rugged topography contiguous with the lowlands area, imperfectly and poorly-drained, gleyed, fine-textured soils are found.

The soils of the Callander Association are generally low in nutrients and tend to be deficient in some trace elements, notably cobalt and copper, except when they are developed on the deeper, fine-textured till.   Their reclamation and improvement require very careful planning and management.

3)   *The Old Red Sandstone Lowlands*

This lowland area of the region extends in a broad, almost crescent shaped, belt from Blackford in Strathallan in the east across and up the Forth Valley to Balfron in the west. It can be conveniently subdivided into two parts, one north and the other south of the River Forth, and includes some very productive agricultural soils.

South of the Forth the grey sandstones of the Lower Old Red Sandstone which contribute to the development of the soils of the Callander Association, give way to a sequence of red sandstones and dark-red and purple sandstones and mudstones , which form the parent rocks for soils of the Balrownie Association.   Soils developed on the fine-textured sandy-clay loam derived from these rocks are among the most productive in the region, but because of their high silt and fine-sand content, require careful management, especially in periods of wet weather.   The dominant soils are freely and imperfectly-drained brown forest soils of moderate base status which respond well to fertilizer treatment.   The better drained soils usually occur on the steepest hill slopes and on the flanks of the frequent drumlins, while the imperfectly-drained soils occur on the gentler slopes and summits of some drumlins.   On the higher ground, around Buchlyvie Muir, podzols and peaty podzols occur on the better drained sites, while peat and peaty gley soils occupy many of the hollows.

To the south-east of Arnprior the Lower Old Red Sandstone rocks are succeeded unconformably by brick-red coarse sandstones and reddish-yellow finer-grained sandstones of Upper Old Red Sandstone age, which give rise to a bright-red, moderately fine-textured till, on which soils of the Kippen Association are developed.   The dominant soil is a brown forest soil of low base status and imperfect drainage, with consequent slight gleying. Although not naturally endowed with plant nutrients these soils respond fairly well to generous fertilizer treatment.   Towards the west the high rainfall becomes a problem and careful management is necessary to get the best results.   The higher ground around Kippen Muir, and similar terrain further west, has imperfectly drained podzolic soils on the ridges and poorly drained peaty gleys and peat on the hollows and broad depressions, while the better drained gentler slopes are occupied by peaty podzolic soils with and without iron pans. In the wetter extreme west, peaty and gleyed soils are more widespread in the soil pattern.

The Upper Old Red Sandstone rocks are succeeded conformably by grey, brown and yellow sandstones and cementstones of the Calciferous Sandstone Measure of Lower Carboniferous age.   The fine-textured silty clay till developed from an intermixture of these rocks forms the parent material of the Sorn Association, of which the dominant soil is a well developed surface-water gley with a tendency to form an organic surface horizon.   These properties make it a difficult soil to farm, but with very careful management it can be utilized for good quality grassland.   On the flanks of the drumlins, and on steeper slopes, a better drained variant is more easily farmed and can, under suitable management, be utilized as a good arable soil.

On the lowest ground, between Buchlyvie and Killearn, there is a spread of gravelly moraine and fluviological sand and gravel which forms part of the terminal morainic deposits of the last readvance of the Highland ice-sheets.   Soils developed on these deposits are included in the Doune Association, whose dominant series is a freely-drained brown forest soil of low base status.   The moundy topography occasionally causes cultivation problems, but the soils, although not inherently rich in plant nutrients, respond to generous fertilizer treatment; they may also occasionally suffer from minor trace element deficiencies.

North of the Forth, in the Teith Valley, the till intermixture of Highland Border Series and Lower Old Red Sandstone rocks extends in a broad lobe spreading out from the Leny Gap north-west of Callander south-eastwards almost to Doune and Thornhill.   The dominant soil is the Callander series of the Callander Association, a brown forest soil of low base status and imperfect drainage, which occupies the gentler slopes of the drumlinoid topography.   The steeper slopes have freely-drained soils of brown forest type, while the semi-natural sites around Lennieston Muir and Torrie Forest are occupied by podzols, peaty podzols and peaty gleys.

The Lower Teith Valley and Strathallan are underlain by red and purple sandstones, mudstones and siltstones of Lower Old Red Sandstone age, and soils of the Balrownie Association occur extensively.   The dominant soil of the interfluve between the River Teith and the Allan Water, and along the northern side of Strathallan between Dunblane and Blackford, is the freely-drained Dunblane series.   This is a brown forest soil of moderate base status developed on till with a high proportion of mudstone and siltstone as its main rock component.   It is a productive soil, because of its high silt and fine-sand fraction, requires careful management under grassland or arable conditions to prevent poaching, capping, loss of aggregation or more severe structural damange in very wet weather.

The dominant soils of the south side of Strathallan are imperfectly-drained associates of those of the north side.   The Kippendavie series, occurring between Dunblane and Sheriffmuir, is derived mainly from the mudstone and siltstone components of the till, while the Balrownie series, derived mainly from the sandstone component, occupies the remainder of the valley side north-eastwards of Blackford.   The exposed moorland areas of the Braes of Doune, Sheriffmuir, Tullibardine Muir, Braco Muir and Coire Odhar are dominated by podzolic and peaty gley soils of imperfect or poor drainage.

The lowest part of the Teith Valley is occupied by moundy fluvioglacial sand and gravel deposits, the outwash from the Highland glaciers.   The deposits consist largely of rocks of Highland origin, but also contain some local Lower Old Red Sandstone material.   The dominant soil developed on them is the freely-drained Doune Series, a brown forest soil of low to moderate base status included in the Doune Association.   Soils of the Doune Association are also present in association with the prominent system of glacial melt-water channels which occurs on the lower and middle slopes of the Braes of Doune.   The mainly moundy topography frequently causes cultivation problems and many of these soils remain under grass for long periods.

The lowest part of Strathallan is also occupied by moundy fluvioglacial sand and gravel deposits formed by local outwash from the complex system of glacial melt-water channels which are evident on both sides of the strath, and also by the major outwash northwards from the Ochil Hills which forms the local watershed between Blackford and Gleneagles. The dominant soil is the Gleneagles series, a cultivated podzol developed on gravels composed mainly of Lower Old Red Sandstone sedimentary and igneous rocks included in the Gleneagles Association. The moundy topography again causes cultivation problems and the very stony soils are severe on implements. Nevertheless, except in very dry season, the Gleneagles soils respond fairly well to generous application of fertilizer.

4) *The Carse of Stirling and Flanders Moss*

The raised-beach deposits of the Forth Valley constitute some very important soil parent materials. Most significant are the deposits of the Low Raised Beach, occurring at altitudes between 3 and 15m (10 – 50ft) above sea level, and locally known as the Carse Clays. These make up the almost flat Carse of Stirling and extend from beyond Flanders Moss in the west, in a tract from two to six km (1.25 – 3.7miles) wide, to beyond Grangemouth in the east. The deposits form the parent material of soils of the Stirling Association which includes some of the most productive agricultural land in the region.

Two hundred years ago most of the flat area adjacent to the River Forth was covered with thick deposits of peat. In the late eighteenth and early nineteenth centuries much of the peat was cleared off and floated down the Forth, and the land claimed for agriculture. Now, only remnants of the peat remain, notably at East and West Flanders Moss, Gattrennich, Ochtertyre, Dunmore and Letham, and several other smaller mosses. Letham moss is worked for horticultural peat and the others are areas of rough grazing and birch scrub, or are being developed for forestry. Complete clearance of the peat deposits to provide more land for agriculture is an expensive undertaking in modern times.

The parent material of soils of the Stirling Association is very fine-textured and varies between a silty clay and a clay-silt. The proportion of coarse sand present is usually less than 10 percent, while the clay content can be sometimes as high as 70 percent or the silt as much as 60 percent. It has been found that, as a general guide, the percentage of clay present is highest in the western areas, while the percentage of silt present becomes highest towards the east. The dominant Stirling series is a well developed poorly-drained ground-water gley soil, which has many of the characteristics of a surface-water gley. When wet the soil is massive, sticky and structureless, but on drying, it shrinks into large almost perfect prismatic structural units which become very hard. The soils are responsive to fertilizer treatment, but are difficult to cultivate unless at the correct "tid" or moisture content, and require very careful management.

Several low-lying areas bordering the lower reaches of the Forth have in the past been reclaimed by the building of embankments to keep out tidal flood waters. Through time, soils similar to those of the Stirling series have developed, but in the past two decades some of these areas have suffered as a result of the neglect of sluices and the failure to repair flood damage, and spreading patches of saltings have resulted.

The High Raised Beach deposits are of two types, silts and clays, and sands and gravels, both occurring at altitudes between 25 and 40m (22 – 131ft) above sea level. The silts and clays occur at approximately 25m altitude up-slope from the carse deposits, notably round Bannockburn, Plean and Larbert in the lower Forth, farther west near Arnprior, and also between Tillicoultry and Dollar in the Devon Valley; they form the parent material of soils of the Carbrook Association. The dominant soil is a surface-water gley which poses some management problems as a result of the high silt and clay content, but which will grow high quality grass and a restricted range of cereals if managed carefully. The sands and gravels are conveniently separated into two parent materials. Those derived principally from Old Red Sandstone sediments and intermediate lavas form the parent material of the Carpow Association, which occurs intermittently on both sides of the Forth from Stirling to as far west as Arnprior. The dominant soil is a free-draining brown forest soil of low base status, which responds well to cultural treatment and becomes a good arable soil. The sands and gravels derived from Carboniferous sediments and basic lavas form the parent materials of the Dreghorn Association which occurs more extensively east of Stirling, notably at Sauchenford, Cowie, around Larbert, near Alloa and at the university site at Airthrey Castle. The dominant soil is also a brown forest soil, with slightly better base status, which responds well to good management and forms a good arable soil.

5) *The Volcanic Hills*

The soils developed on the lavas of the volcanic hills provide a striking contrast to those of the Carse of Stirling. The volcanic hills of the region can be conveniently separated into two groups: the smaller group comprises the western part of the Ochil Hills; the more extensive group includes the Fintry, Gargunnock and Touch Hills and the northern slopes of the Kilsyth Hills and Campsie Fells.

That part of the Ochil Hills within the region consists of deep valleys and long ridges leading up to broad summit areas at an altitude of over 600m (2000ft). The vast thickness of andesitic and basaltic lavas and tuffs of Lower Old Red Sandstone age give rise to the parent material of the Sourhope Association, first mapped in the Cheviot Hills (Muir 1956). There are two forms of this till parent material, one, the most widespread, is a freely-drained gritty loam; the other is poorly-drained and fine-textured, and usually confined to the valley bottoms. Above these, slope and climate play a dominant role in soil formation, a common upward sequence being; on the lower and steepest slopes brown forest soils of low base status, passing up through more acid and podzolic variants, to podzols and peaty podzols above 300m (1000ft). On the shoulders of hills a structureless peat often occurs, which has apparently been washed from the ridge tops and summits where deep peat or montane humus soils are found. The steep scarp face of the Ochil Hills is drift-free, with abundant rock outcrops and scree; the more mature soils are usually shallow free-drainage brown forest soils or brown lithosols. On the lowest flanks of the major valleys, such as Glen Devon, Glen Sherrup and Glen Quey, moundy deposits of sand and gravel occur, on which have developed soils of the Gleneagles Association. There is evidence that many of the soils have formerly been cultivated, but at the present time they support only rough grazing.

The Campsie Fell hill area and its associated foothills consist of a thick sequence of basic lavas, mainly basaltic, of Lower Carboniferous ages. These rocks also give rise to a fairly-uniform soil parent material on which are developed soils of the Dalreith Association, first mapped in Ayrshire (Mitchell and Jarvis 1956). There are two forms of this till parent material: one, the most widespread, is stony, often indurated and moderately fine-textured; the other, a fine-textured clay loam variant, is usually confined to the broad hollows of the higher ground, and occupies much of the low ground adjacent to the Carboniferous Lowlands.

The dominant soil on the lower ground, especially on the very steep slopes, is a freely-draining stony, brown forest soil of low base status. Many of the hill farms have no field drains and poorly-drained gley soils are frequent in hollows or on gentle slopes below spring lines. The slow permeability of the clayey varient of the till which often occurs in the situations, in combination with the high rainfall, worsens the drainage problems.

On the higher slopes of the hills above 300m (1000ft), where the topography is frequently a series of shallow step-like levels — each step a lava flow — the soil pattern is one of peaty podzols with iron pan, or peaty brown soils on the steeper slopes, under heather or mat grass respectively, with peaty gley soils on the wet, rushy gentler slopes, and peat widespread on the shelves. The edges of each lava scarp have frequently rock outcrops around which are developed brown and podzolic lithosols. The northern extremity of these volcanic hills consists of a high rocky scarp of several lava flows, with an apron of bare scree and shallow colluvium below.

There are several narrow tracts of hummocky moraine in the broad valleys and on the flanks of the volcanic hills. They consist largely of angular fragments of lava and tuff left by the last ice sheet and form the parent material of soils of the Kirktonmoor Association. In the Carron and Endrick Valleys the dominant soil is a free-draining brown forest soil of low base status which, when well managed, will support good quality grassland.

Associated with the moraines are mounds of fluvioglacial sand and gravel consisting mainly of rounded water-worn fragments of lava with small proportions of material of High-land origin.   Soils developed on this parent material have been included in the Darvel Assoc-iation in which the dominant soil is also a free-draining brown forest soil of low base status.

6)   *The Carboniferous Lowlands*

This lowland area is approximately bisected by the River Forth into the Clackmannan drift plain to the north and the Stirlingshire drift plain to the south.

The Clackmannan drift plain is underlain by Carboniferous sediments of variable litho-logy, but with a high proportion of sandstones in the succession.   The moderately fine-textured till derived from these rocks the parent material of the Giffnock Association. The dominant soil around Alloa is the Aberdona Series, a brown forest soil with gleying, while between Coalsnaughton and Dollar the dominant soil is the Giffnock series, a poorly-drained surface-water gley.   In the relatively drift-free area between Forest Mill and Devilla the cultivated soils are brown forest soils while those under woodland are humus iron pod-zols, both developed directly on the underlying coarse-grained sandstone.   The Aberdona and Forest Mill series are well suited to arable agriculture, but the Giffnock Series is best utilized for grassland with occasional arable cropping.

The Stirlingshire drift plain extends south from Stirling to Denny, Bonnybridge and Falkirk, and includes the eastern end of the Kelvin-Bonny Corridor, as well as the lower Carron Avon Valley.   Almost all the ground is mantled by drift deposits derived from the underlying Carboniferous sediments.   The till immediately south of Stirling is derived mainly from arenaceous rocks, with some intermixed shales and coals, and soils developed on it are included in the Giffnock Association.   The till occurring around Plean, Denny, Bonnybridge and Falkirk is derived from shales and sandstones, with some inter-mixed coals, and gives rise to soils of the Rowanhill Association.

The dominant soil of the Giffnock Association in this part of Stirlingshire is the Aber-dona series, an imperfectly-drained brown forest soil with gleying, of moderate base status developed on a moderately fine-textured till.   It usually occurs on low rounded drumlins of moderate dimensions and forms a good agricultural soil for grass and arable crops.

The dominant soils of the Rowanhill Association in the area are the imperfectly-drained Caprington series, a brown forest soil with gleying, and the poorly-drained Rowanhill series, a surface-water gley soil, both developed on clayey till.   The imperfectly-drained soils tend to occur on drumlins, while the poorly-drained gleys occupy the broader depressions between them or the almost level summits of low ridges which are interspersed among the drumlins. The better-drained soils are suitable for both arable and grass crops, while the poorly-drained ones, although they can sometimes be cropped, are best utilized for grass.

The lower ground, adjacent to the principal drainage channels of the Bonny Water and the Rivers Carron and Avon, is occupied by coarser-textured, often water-modified, soil parent materials. Soils developed on water-modified till are included in both the Giffnock and Rowanhill Associations. They have coarser-textured topsoils and subsoils overlying sandier tills, which merge downwards into unaffected clayey tills below. The more open structure makes them better arable soils than their normal counterparts.

The gravel soils which are associated with them are included in the Darvel Association, the parent material of which includes water-worn fragments of lava and other basic igneous rocks, local Carboniferous sediments and some Highland Schist rocks. The dominant soil is a free-drainage brown forest soil of low to moderate base status, which responds well to fertilizer treatment. The moundy topography occasionally causes cultivation hazards, but the majority of these soils are very productive for arable agriculture.

7) *The Slamannan Plateau*

The Carboniferous sediments extend southward from the Bonnybridge/Falkirk area to underlie the upland plateau (214m) named after the village of Slamannan located there. The sequence of drift-covered east-west aligned ridges and depressions, becomes progressively higher and correspondingly wetter towards the regional boundary to the south.

The grey-coloured till parent material of the Rowanhill Association is thick and extensive. The dominant soil is a poorly-grained, well developed surface-water gley, which occurs almost everywhere. Peat deposits and peaty gley soils occur in some depressions or on the higher exposed broad summit ridges, and on steeper slopes there are limited areas of imperfectly-drained brown forest soils.

The increased rainfall and lower evapotranspiration, and consequent greater wetness of these soils, results in their being more difficult to manage than their lowland counterparts. Surface organic horizons tend to develop, especially if the fertility level falls, and all soils of the area are difficult to drain. Excess surface-water is a major problem and many areas of the upland are infested with rushes. Few fields have effective drainage systems, but recent experimental work carried out in the district has indicated that more drainage may be successful in overcoming this problem. If drained and well-managed, the soils can support good quality grass crops. Once the drainage problem is solved the Slamannan Plateau could become an important area for grassland production.

Land Use Capability of the Soils

In order to present the results of soil surveys in a form useful to agricultural advisers, farmer, planners and other land users, the Soil Survey of Scotland, in conjunction with the Soil Survey of England and Wales, has prepared a Land Users Capability Classification for the soils of Britain (Bibby and Mackeny 1969). This is a development of the system used by the Soil Conservation Service of the United States Department of Agriculture, with modifications appropriate to British conditions. It assesses land capability from known relationships between the growth and management of crops and physical factors of soil, site and climate. Land is graded according to its potentialities and the severity of its limitations for crop growth. Land suited to arable cultivation and other uses is included in classes 1 – 4, and land not generally suitable for cultivation and of only limited use for other purposes is included in classes 5 – 7. Class 1 land has a wide range of use with few minor limitations, while the remaining six classes suffer increasingly severe limitations and are progressively more restricted in their uses. The seven capability classes are listed below.

Class 1	Land with very minor or no physical limitations to use.
Class 2	Land with minor limitations that reduce the choice of crops and interfere with cultivation.
Class 3	Land with moderate limitations that restrict the choice of crops and/or demand careful management.
Class 4	Land with moderately severe limitations that restrict the choice of crops and/or require careful management practices.
Class 5	Land with severe limitations that restrict its use to pasture, forestry and recreation.
Class 6	Land with very severe limitations that restrict use to rough grazing, forestry and recreation.
Class 7	Land with extremely severe limitations that cannot be rectified.

Each capability class from 2 – 7 may be sub-divided into five sub-classes as indicated by the use of the letter notation, w,s,g,c, or e attached to the relevant class number e.g. 3s or 4w. Each letter indicates the *kind* of limitation affecting land use, while the class indicates *degree* of limitation. Letter 'w' indicates wetness, 's' refers to soil limitations, 'g' to gradient and soil pattern limitations, 'c' to climatic factors, and 'e' to liability to erosion. Where more than one limitation affects land use capability a combination of letters is used e.g. 3ws or 4sg. Because soil, site and climate are involved in complex interactions affecting land use, the separation of dominant limiting factors is seen as a necessary, if arbitrary, simplification.

Although there are considerable expanses of good agricultural land throughout the Stirling region, there are no areas which can be included in Class 1 and only very limited areas which can be included in Class 2. These are confined to the coarser-textured soils of the sandy raised-beaches near Plean, Larbert and Clackmannan. The majority of the productive arable soils of the region are included in Class 3.

The most productive soils of the Stirling Association in the Carse of Stirling are included in Class 3ws, largely because of the difficulty of producing a seed-bed for crops in this fine-textured soil in the predominantly-wet climatic regime of the district. These problems of cultivation preclude the growing of root crops on a large scale, even in the drier eastern part of the Carse. Further west, around Flanders Moss and beyond, many of the soils are included in Class 4 because of the increased rainfall and the lack of fall for natural drainage. It must be emphasised, however, that the Carse soils are good agricultural soils, although they do require careful management for their successful cultivations.

The most productive soils of the Old Red Sandstone Lowlands in the Callander, Balrownie and Kippen Associations have been included in Class 3sg because of the care needed to retain good topsoil structure in arable cultivation and the tendency for soils under grass to poach in very wet weather. These soil limitations are sometimes aggravated in wet weather by tractor wheel-slip on the steeper gradients of the drumlinoid topography common to the area.

The most productive soils of the Carboniferous Lowlands, the imperfectly-drained series of the Giffnock and Rowanhill Associations, have been included in Class 3ws because of the wetness of these soils at critical times of the year, for example, at sowing and harvest. Careful management is needed to ensure minimum damage to soil structure by working these soils only when conditions are suitable. The finer texture, and consequent longer periods of wetness, of the poorly-drained soils of these associations, makes successful cultivation very difficult and these soils are included in Class 4w.

The gravelly soils of the lowlands (Doune, Darvel and Gleneagles Associations) are usually coarse-textured and stony, with steep slopes included in the moundy topography associated with them. In the drier east, these soils are limited by their low moisture-holding capacity, while in the wetter west, the uneven topography and steep slopes can cause cultivation difficulties in wet weather. These soils are mainly included in Class 3sg, but in the wetter areas they are included in Class 4sg.

Above altitudes of about 150m (500ft) on south and west facing slopes, and 120m (400ft) on north and east facing slopes, climatic effects become more pronounced. Consequently soil and site limitations become more severe, and soils occurring above these levels are usually included in Class 4. At altitudes above about 180m (600ft) topographic and climatic limitations can be severe and soils are generally included in Class 5. The organic soils of the lowland peat mosses are also included in this class because, although at present supporting rough grazing, they are capable of improving to better pasture.

In the uplands, at altitudes from about 180m (600ft) to about 500m (1600ft), the slopes are too steep and too elevated for arable cultivation, but are suitable for permanent pasture. Most soils are included in Class 5, provided the rainfall is less than 1500mm (60in) per annum. At higher altitudes, severe exposure, excessive rainfall and restricted growing season, limit the shallow peaty soils and blanket peat deposits to Class 6. The hill and mountain tops above an altitude of about 700m (2300ft), and other areas of scree and rock outcrop at lower altitudes such as the Ochil and Campsie scarp features, are included in Class 7.

The wide range of soils which occupy the region has a marked influence on the variety of agricultural activities which are carried out. The land use capability of the arable soils reflects the high agricultural potential of the Stirling region, while the extensive areas in classes 5, 6 and 7 reflects both the continued arability of grazing and forestry and the attractiveness of the region for tourism.

REFERENCES

Bibby, J S and D Mackney   1969   *Land Use Capability Classification.* Technical Monograph No. 1, The Soil Survey of Great Britain, HMSO, Edinburgh.

Dight, F H   1969   *The Climate of North Stirlingshire, South Perthshire and Clackmannan.* Climatological Memorandum No. 63, Meteorological Office Climatological Services, Edinburgh.

Francis, E H and I H Forsyth   1970   *The Geology of the Stirling District.* Memoirs of the Geological Survey of Great Britain (Scotland) HMSO, Edinburgh.

Glentworth, R   1954   *The Soils of the Country round Banff, Huntly and Turiff.* Memoirs of the Soil Survey of Great Britain (Scotland) HMSO, Edinburgh.

Mitchell, B D   1956   *The Soils of the Country round Kilmarnock.* Memoirs of the Soil Survey of Great Britain (Scotland), HMSO, Edinburgh.

Muir, J W   1956   *The Soils of the Country round Jedburgh and Morebattle.* Memoirs of the Soil Survey of Great Britain (Scotland), HMSO, Edinburgh.

PART TWO

THE BIOLOGICAL ENVIRONMENT

INTRODUCTION

THE BIOLOGICAL ENVIRONMENT — INTRODUCTION

The transitional nature of the Stirling Region is nowhere more apparent than in its vegetation and wildlife. The diversity of habitats to be found within the region allows a complex intermingling of species otherwise characteristic of distinct northern and southern, highland and lowland realms. Many species are at the limits of their environmental ranges and the region is the scene of many critical ecological relationships in which human influence plays a critical role.

The diversity of habitats in the Stirling Region is highlighted in the discussion by J Proctor and P Bannister, in Chapter 5, on the vegetation and flora of the area. Eight main habitat types are distinguished, each with sub-types: woodland, grassland, heathland, rivers and lochs, bogs and mires, salt marsh, submontane rock outcrops, and montane vegetation. Each has characteristic plant communities and each displays the effects of human intervention.

The theme of human intervention is taken up again in Chapter 6 in which J Proctor provides a short guide to the mammals found in the Region. Several species have become extinct in relatively recent times while pollution in the Forth has had severe effects on the marine mammals which seem once to have been much more frequent visitors to the area. The point is made yet again that there is a great shortage of recent records for the Region.

Chapters 7 and 8 are concerned with birds and with freshwater fish. Human fascination with both has resulted in rather better records being available than is the case for most other forms of wildlife. D M Bryant provides information on the wide spectrum of birds — over 120 breeding species — which are recorded in the Stirling Region. He points out that the influence of human activity has been both positive and negative, leading to increases in the number of some species but being fatal to others. Distinct bird communities are found in the various habitats of the Region and in some cases there have been dramatic recent changes in status. R J Roberts and D Johnston report similar dramatic changes in their account of the freshwater fish of the Region. To anglers, the streams of Central Scotland mean trout and salmon. Salmon are confined to the tributaries of the Forth and have been badly-affected by pullution. Brown and rainbow trout are more widely-distributed and for many years have been carefully nurtured in local fish-farms. The influence of man has again been both beneficient and malevolent.

In view of the diversity of habitats in the Stirling Region and the critical nature of many of the ecological relationships which characterize the area there is a powerful case to be made for conservation and study. The peripheral location of the region between the major population concentrations of Strathclyde and the Lothians, seems, however, to have resulted in its relative neglect. Moreover, as J Procter and D Bryant have pointed out (pers. comm.)

the level of conservation activity in the area is relatively low.

The Nature Conservancy Council has offices at Balloch, by Loch Lomond, dealing with Stirlingshire, and in Edinburgh, dealing with the counties of Perth and Clackmannan. The only National Nature Reserve in the vicinity of Stirling is in the National Trust for Scotland property at Ben Lawers, the highest mountain in Perthshire at 3984ft (1214m). This is outside the area agreed for the Survey but falls within the local government Central Region. The National Trust, the Nature Conservancy and the Countryside Commission for Scotland have co-operated in the establishment both of the nature reserve and of a series of visitor facilities designed to illustrate, in particular, the rich Alpine flora of the area.   Elsewhere, there are a series of 'Sites of Special Scientific Interest', which have been notified by the Nature Conservancy to the local planning authorities.   As is usual in such cases the precise locations are not publicly advertised.   No Local Nature Reserves are currently in existence although one is prepared for Gartmorn Dam, a major location for waterfowl. The Scottish Wildlife Trust, a registered charity, has one reserve in the region, near Thornhill in the south-eastern corner of Flanders Moss, a raised bog with a wide variety of ericaceous and other plants.   Admission is by permit, obtainable from the Trust's headquarters in Edinburgh.

Nature reserves are created primarily to ensure the protection of threatened habitats and species. In addition to the sites already mentioned there are several other areas in which the critical nature of the present ecological situation would seem to justify quick action: the remaining oak-forests in the area of the Queen Elizabeth Forest Park, the estuarine habitats at Skinflats, the rest of the relatively undisturbed positions of Flanders Moss, the Lake of Menteith, Carsebreck, and the riverside marshes along the lower Forth.   In most cases it should prove possible to extend protection without denying controlled human access.

The balance of 'conservation' and 'development' is difficult and controversial. The Stirling Region has a great opportunity to capitalize on the diversity of its habitats and to pioneer in the combination of agricultural, forestry, wildlife, sporting and tourist activities. The Region enjoys a relatively low 'people pressure' and may thus be able to ensure a localization of human intrusion. The 'urban lake' created by the Carron Dam at Stenhouse-muir could well provide an object-lesson in the performance of the dual roles of wildlife sanctuary and human leisure-time centre.   A similar possibility exists at Airthrey Loch, in the University campus.   The establishment of a flourishing local branch of the National Conservation Corps, with an office in Doune, is an encouraging sign for the awakening of an enlightened attitude towards the wild-life of the Stirling region.   The reorganization of local government in the area provides an opportunity for the new Regional and District authorities to demonstrate their concern with the natural heritage.   The diversity of the Region is, perhaps, its most valuable characteristic.   A combination of conservation and development will ensure that it remains so.

CHAPTER   5

VEGETATION   AND   FLORA

Introduction

The Stirling Region comprises large parts of the Watsonian vice-counties, Stirling-shire, West Perthshire (with Clackmannan) and Mid Perthshire (V.C.'s 86 – 88).

A flora of these vice-counties is unlikely to be published for a number of years although records are currently being collected for V.C. 86 by Mr B Ribbons[*] and for V.C.'s 87 and 88 by Mr A W Robson[+].   Seventy years ago however, due to the efforts of skilled amateur botanists, such as Robert Kidston of Stirling and Francis Buchanan W White of Perth, the area was as well surveyed floristically as any in Scotland.

Kidston is renowned throughout the world for his work on the fossil flora of the Rhynie Chert.   Much of his earlier work was concerned with the fossil plants of the rocks of the Carboniferous period which are well represented around Stirling.   Colonel Stirling of Gargunnock collaborated with Kidston to produce a meticulously compiled Flora of Stirling-shire which was published in the Transactions of the Stirling Natural History and Archaeo-logical Society between 1891 and 1900.   The area north of the Forth is included in the Flora of Perthshire edited by J W H Traill from Buchanan White's manuscript after his death in 1898.

Since these works were published several additions to the species lists have been repor-ted in the transactions of local natural history societies.   However, the most accessible sour-ces of recent information on the flora of the area are the species distribution maps in the "Atlas of the British Flora" (Perring and Walters, 1962).

Herbarium collections of local plants exist in Glasgow University, The Smith Institute and Museum in Stirling, and in the Perth Museum and Art Gallery.

The total number of native vascular plants recorded from the Stirling area appears to be quite high, a reflection of the diversity of habitat types.   These include lowland salt marshes, farmland, raised bogs and woodlands, upland grassland, heath and blanket bog and high mon-tane vegetation.   *The Vegetation of Scotland* (Burnett, 1964) provides a background to the vegetation of these habitats although it contains few references to sites specifically in the area.

*Department of Botany, The University, Glasgow, G12 8QQ.
+Towerview, Dunning, Perthshire, PH2 0RY.

This survey considers the vegetation of the most important habitats around Stirling and is followed by some notes on the flora of the region.

History of the vegetation since the ice age

Following the withdrawal of the main ice sheets there began a period of more settled conditions which allowed the development of lake sediments and peat. In these deposits is preserved a record of the vegetation of the area since they contain preserved and still identifiable pollen grains. The changes that have occurred in the vegetation can be deduced from the examination of pollen that is preserved at different levels in the sediments.

From such work it is clear that sparse vegetation, consisting mainly of grasses, sedges and a few dwarf shrubs with mosses followed in the wake of ice. Much rock debris would have been exposed, and continually disturbed by frost action, at this time. The developing vegetation cover increased to a closed tundra but even after several thousand years by about 9000 B.C. there were still few or no trees. Donner (1957) and Vasari and Vasari (1968) examined the pollen deposits at a small reservoir about four miles north of Drymen. The site is just outside the survey area but is the nearest example with very early, "late-Glacial" remains. The tree pollen was only a low percentage of the total and it was considered to have been blown in from distant sites. Many species apart from grasses, sedges and heaths have been recorded from these early sediments including "weeds" such as *Rumex* * spp. (Docks and Sorrels) and *Epilobium* spp. (Willow herbs) and aquatic species *Typha latifolia* ('Great Reedmace') and *Myriophyllum alterniflorum* ('Alternate-flowered Water-milfoil'). Most of the species were recorded in more recent sediments but two genera, *Thalictrum* (Meadow Rue) and *Helianthemum* (Rockrose) were not. These are light demanding species of base rich soils which can be interpreted as having disappeared on the face of competition from other species and as a result of progressive soil leaching.

The climate became colder again for 500 years or so and there was a return to much frost movement of the soil and extremely open vegetation. This period ended 10,300 years ago and was followed by a rapid amelioration of the climate and marked change in vegetation.

There are a number of pollen samples within the area for this later, "post-Glacial", period. Those of Dunro (1956) at Flanders East Moss and Darnrigg Moss cover the longest continuous time and show a rapid invasion of trees following the climatic amelioration. Birch was dominant, together with some Scots Pine and sporadic occurrence of Alder. Around 7000B.C. there was a great increase in Hazel; Oak and Elm increased to some ex-

---

* *Higher plant nomenclature follows that of Clapham et al, (1962). Some plants have no English names in this source and hence are given Latin names only here.*

tent but less than in England and Wales.   Around 5500B.C. there was a rapid increase in Alder and a decrease in Birch and Scots Pine.   For the next 2000 years forest was at its greatest extent; in low lying areas on good soils there was forest of Oak, Ash, Elm and Alder with varying proportions of Birch; on the lower and middle slopes of the hills there were Birch, Alder, Aspen, Rowen, Willow and Hazel with probably a zone of Birch and Willow at higher altitude.   The amount of Scots Pine in these forests was probably greatest on the poorer soils and this species would have been most common in the north and west of the region. The altitude limit of trees at this time was certainly much higher than at present and was about 1000m. In the few areas above tree line there may have been a zone of heath and above this, montaine grassland communities. The only lowland areas without forest would have been developing raised bogs and salt marshes

There was a sudden decline in Elm pollen around 3000B.C. which may have been connected with the first influence of man, since there is evidence that Elm was selectively used as a fodder plant (Pennington, 1969). Man's impact was relatively slight until Roman times and was probably restricted to a clearing, for pasture, of the forest from hill land in the Bronze Age. However, some detailed pollen analyses from Flanders Moss (Turner, 1965) indicate that, about 2000 years ago, there was an extensive clearance of forest.

This extensive clearance was followed by a period in which the lowland forest largely recovered although a climatic deterioration beginning about 500B.C. had probably favoured the replacement of upland forest of flat areas by blanket peat. However, an exploitation of primeval forest that was to end in its almost total destruction began early in the medieval period.   During the 12th and 13th centuries there is evidence that many trees were felled to provide fuel for the making of salt. At this time in Scotland "The greatest concentration of salt-works was on the carses bordering the River Forth from Kalentyre (Callander) up to Stirling" (Anderson, 1967a).   With the destruction of wolves, deer preservation became increasingly popular and sheep farming expanded enormously, no doubt at the expense of the remaining high level forest.   Deliberate clearance of the lowlands for timber and farming also continued.   In the 17th and 18th century much of the remaining forest was probably totally removed for charcoal for iron smelting. Man's influence is shown quite clearly in the pollen diagram of Durno (1957) by the decrease in the proportion of tree pollen and the corresponding increase of that of heath and herbaceous species.

Besides forest, man has influenced every other habitat. Much of the raised bog was reclaimed in the late 18th and early 19th century by the activities of Lord Kames (Cadell, 1913); sheep grazing and fires have modified all the habitats above the primeval timberland with the possible exception of the very highest mountain vegetation, and even the salt marshes have been subjected to severe grazing pressures.

The area has a long history of tree planting which has offset the general woodland decline to some extent.   Planting on a small scale began over 500 years ago, there was an orchard at Dunmore in 1438 (Anderson, 1967a), and by the end of that century there are references to planting of trees other than fruit trees.   In February 1501, 15 shillings were paid to George Campbell, gardner of Stirling, to buy sauchs (willows) and to set them (Anderson, 1967a).   Tree planting on private estates reached a maximum between 1750 and 1850.   The plantations varied in size from large forests to belts planted for ornament and shelter.   For example, the New Statistical Account (1845) mentioned luxuriant plantations totalling over 1800 acres in the Parish of Falkirk.   Many details about plantations in Stirlingshire are given in Graham (1812).

Since the nineteen twenties the rate of planting has been greatly accelerated, especially by the Forestry Commission, and introduced conifers are now a striking component of the vegetation.

In brief, the present vegetation of the Stirling region is similar to all other areas in Britain in that it reflects the overriding influence of man.

Present day vegetation

1   *Woodland*

There are very many woodlands from tiny copses to forests of several hundred hectares, which are always a conspicuous part of the lowland landscape.   In the west are the woodlands of the Trossachs country, a mixture of old coppiced Oaks and recent conifer plantations.   Many private estates have good woodlands such as those of Airthrey, Leny, Lanrick Castle, Doune Lodge, Blair Drummond, Keir, Touch, and Callander near Falkirk.   There are several large Forestry Commission plantations particularly those in the Queen Elizabeth Forest Park, Strathyre and Carron Valley.   In addition there are many smaller plantations around mansions, home farms and for shelter belts.   A very valuable source of information on the woodlands of the survey area is the two volume work *A History of Scottish Forestry* (Anderson, 1967a and b).   There are also useful descriptions in *Forests of Central and Southern Scotland* (Edlin, 1969).

(a)   *Pinewood*

It is not certain if Scots Pine occurs as a native remnant of the ancient forests or whether all trees of this species have been planted.   The best candidates for native status are:

i   The scattered trees on rocky knolls above the oakwoods at the east end of Loch Katrine.

ii A small group of trees in Strathyre, cited as possibly native in Traill (1898) and still persisting (A W Robson pers. comm).

iii The Pinewood near Braco Castle.

This last wood has a ground flora modified by grazing but nevertheless contains species characteristic of Pinewoods elsewhere. The following higher plants have been recorded by Mr A W Robson, who brought the wood to our attention:

Calluna vulgaris	(Ling or Heather)
Chrysosplenium oppositifolium	('Opposite-leaved Golden Saxifrage')
Erica cinerea	(Bell-heather)
Galium saxatile	('Heath Bedstraw')
Juniperus communis	(Juniper)
Molinia caerulea	('Purple moor-grass')
Prunus avium	(Gean or Wild Cherry)
Salix cinerea ssp. atrocinerea	(Common Swallow)
Sorbus aucuparia	(Rowan or Mountain Ash)
Vaccinium myrtillus	(Blaeberry, Bilberry, Whortleberry or Huckleberry)

(b) *Conifer plantations*

The first conifers planted were native Scots Pine although the greatest area of plantation is now occupied by introduced species. Introduced conifers have been planted here for at least 250 years and there are good examples on many private estates. The largest areas have been planted within the last 50 years by the Forestry Commission which now possess a number of sizable forests, e.g.:

i *Queen Elizabeth Forest Park*
Most of Loch Ard Forest (9,517 hectares) and the whole of Achray Forest (3,588 hectares) lie within the survey area. The forests were begun in 1929 and since then have been planted mainly with Sitka and Norway Spruce, some Scots Pine and Japanese Larch and small quantities of Douglas Fir, Western Hemlock, Silver Fir and broadleaved trees. Further information about these Forests is given in the *Queen Elizabeth Forest Park Guide* (Edlin ed. 1973).

ii *Strathyre Forest*
Planting was started here in 1930 and there are about 2,000 hectares of trees with plantations going up to 1800ft, amongst the highest in Scotland. The main species are Sitka and Norway Spruce, some Scots Pine and smaller quantities of European and Japanese Larch.

iii *Carron Valley Forest*
Planting here began in 1937 and now the main part of the forest around Carron Valley Lake occupies about 3000 hectares. The main species are Sitka and Norway Spruce with a little Lodgepole Pine and Larch.

In addition there are many more conifer plantations, some owned by the Forestry Commission, whilst others are in private ownership. These forests of introduced conifers are an important addition to the vegetation of the region. They are often of very limited interest to the botanist, however, because of their uniformity and the suppression of the ground flora.

(c) *Deciduous woodlands*

The deciduous woods of the area have nearly all been planted, or at least much influenced, by man. Apart from the planting of Oak, Elm, Ash, Beech, nearly all possibly relict native forest has been greatly altered by activities such as felling, coppicing, stripping of bark for tanning and selective removal of some species. This "unnatural" state of the deciduous woodlands is highlighted by the *New Statistical Account of Scotland* of 1845. Nearly every parish is said to have plantations and it is obvious that any remaining primeval woodland was of very local distribution. The description for the parish of Alloa succintly expresses the situation. "In this, and in most of the lower districts of Scotland, few remains of her ancient sylvan vegetation present themselves, and these confined chiefly to ravines and narrow glens, where they are generally intermingled with planted trees". An example of a surviving, little modified, woodland is that in the upper part of Arnprior Glen*. Although there are a few introduced Sycamores the woodland is dominated by Wych Elm, Ash and Oak with a shrub layer of Hazel and *Prunus padus*, (Bird-Cherry). The ground flora here is notable in having extensive sheets of *Chrysosplenium alternifolium* ('Alternate-leaved Golden Saxifrage') mixed with some *C. oppositifolium* ('Opposite-leaved Golden Saxifrage'); There are also stands of *Mercurialis perennis* ('Dogs Mercury') and *Allium ursinum* (Ramsons) and also grass communities with *Milium effusum* ('Wood Millet') and *Zerna ramosa* ('Hairy Brome'). There are small but pure stands of *Melica uniflora* (Wood Melick) on the dry ledges underneath the overhanging Red Sandstone cliffs. *Thelypteris dryopteris* (Oak Fern) occurs commonly on damp slopes where humus has accumulated.

The planted and much modified deciduous woodlands are of many types and are of prime importance for wildlife in the region. We have selected two examples, one on acid soils around Loch Katrine and the other on more base-rich soils at Kippenrait Glen near Bridge of Allan, to illustrate some of the features of these woods.

i *Oakwood at the eastern end of Loch Katrine*

The woods are of a distinctive type and, although they have a long history of management, they represent the largest area, in the survey region, that has been continuously wooded. They occur mainly in slopes and are dominated,

* *Mr E T Idle provided the notes for this description*

often exclusively, by Oak. This high stocking of Oak is unnatural and is a product of intensive coppice management; other woody species (except Hazel) have been deliberately eliminated. There are very few large standard Oaks. The species of Oak is somewhat indeterminate and the population is dominated by intermediates between *Quercus robur and Q. petraea* (Cousens, 1963). (Some of the purest *Q. petraea* collected by Cousins in Scotland was from Menstrie Glen in the Ochils). Apart from the Oaks there is a small amount of Birch *(Betulapubescens ssp odorata)* and Mountain Ash or Rowan *(Sorbus aucuparia)*.

The ground flora is a species characteristic of acid soils and the following are all commonly encountered.

Argostis tenius	('Common Bent-grass')
Blechnum spicant	(Hard-fern)
Calluna vulgaris	(Ling or Heather)
Deschampsia flexuosa	('Wavy hair-grass')
Erica cinerea	(Bell-heather)
Vaccinium myrtillus	(Bilberry, Blaeberry, Whortleberry or Huckleberry)
V. vitis-idaea	(Cowberry or Red Whortleberry)

and among the mosses *Sphagnum* spp., *Hylocomium splendens* and *Pleurozium schreberi* are common.

In some places Bracken *(Pteridium aquilinum)* is very abundant and dominates the ground flora.

ii *Mixed deciduous woodland in Kippenrait Glen*
The part most thoroughly investigated by us is on a north west facing slope. There is much evidence of planting and other types of interference. There are large specimens of Beech, Wych Elm, Ash, Sycamore, and Oak although most of the wood is of Birch of no great age. Hazel is abundant and in some local patches, dominant.

The ground flora is rich and varies in different parts of the wood. The following species are amongst those present:

Ferns and Horsetails

Athyrium filix-femina	(Lady-fern)
Blechnum spicant	(Hard-fern)
Dryopteris filix·mas	(Male-fern)
D. dilatata	('Broad Bucklet-fern')
Equisetum sylvaticum	('Wood Horsetail')
Phyllitis scolopendrium	(Hart's-tongue fern)
Polypodium vulgare agg	('Polypody')
Polystichum aculeatum	('Hard shield-fern')
Pteridium aquilinum	(Bracken)
Thelypteris phegopteris	(Beech fern)

Higher Plants

Ajuga reptans	(Bugle)
Allium ursinum	(Ramsons)
Anemone nemorosa	('Wood Anemone')
Brachypodium sylvaticum	('Slender False-brome')
Campanula latifolia	('Large campanula')
Chrysosplenium oppositifolium	('Opposite-leaved Golden Saxifrage')
Dactylorchis fuchsii	(Common Spotted Orchid)
D. maculata ssp. ericetorum	(Moorland Spotted Orchid)
Deschampsia cespitosa	('Tufted hair-grass')
Digitalis purpurea	(Foxglove)
Endymion non-scriptus	(Bluebell or Wild Hyacinth)
Epipactis helleborine	('Broad Helleborine')
Festuca gigantea	('Tall Brome')
Galium odoratum	(Sweet Woodruff)
Geramium robertianum	(Herb Robert)
Geum rivale	(Water Avens)
G. Urbanum	(Herb Bennet or Wood Avenue)
G. rivale x urbanum	hybrids
Glechoma hederacea	(Ground Ivy)
Hedera helix	(Ivy)
Heracleum sphondylium	(Hogweed, Cow Parsnip or Keck)
Hypericum hirsutum	('Hairy St. John's Wort')
Luzula sylvatica	(Greater Woodrush)
Mercurialis perennis	(Dog's Mercury)
Neottia nidus-avis	(Bird's-nest Orchid)
Oxalis acetosella	(Wood-sorrel)
Poa nemoralis	('Wood Poa')
Primula vulgaris	(Primrose)
Pyrola minor	('Common Wintergreen)
Ranunculus ficaria	(Lesser Celandine or Pilewort)
Sanicula europea	(Sanicle)
Teucrium scorodonia	(Wood Sage)
Veronica montana	('Wood Speedwell')
Vicia sylvatica	('Wood Vetch')
Viola riviniana	('Common Violet')
Zerna ramosa	('Hairy Brome')

The bryophyte ground flora is luxuriant and many of the species present are especially characteristic of upland deciduous woodland.

e.g.   *Dicranum majus*
Hookeria lucens
Hylocomium splendens
Isothecium myosuroides
Nowellia curvifolia
Plagiochila asplenioides var. major

Plagiothecium undulatum
Rhytidiadelphus triquetrus

The epiphytic bryophyte flora is also very rich. *Ulota crispa, Frullania tamarisci* and *Metzgeria furcata* are very common, especially on Hazel branches. There are good foliose and fruticose lichens also.

2   *Cultivated land and grassland*

Much of the survey area is farmland and is discussed in detail in chapter 12. Very briefly, the best agricultural land, such as the Stirling carse land, is arable and Oats, Wheat, Barley, Potatoes and Turnips are grown. Hay, in which Timothy (*Phleum pratense*) predominates is another important crop of the better land. These arable lands are important for the botanist because they provide a reservoir, albeit a diminishing one, of agricultural weeds. Weeds are of course a common component of gardens. The following weed species have been recorded from Dunblane and this list includes many of the common weeds of the area.

(a)   *In cultivated ground*

Alliaria petiolata	(Garlic Mustard, Jack-in-the-Hedge or Hedge Garlic)
Arabidopsis thaliana	(Thale Cress or 'Common Wall Cress')
Barbarea vulgaris	('Winter Cress' or 'Yellow Rocket')
Capsella bursa-pastoris	(Shepherd's Purse)
Cardamine hirsuta	('Hairy Bitter-cress')
Chamaenerion angustifolium	(Rosebay Willow-herb or Fireweed)
Epilobium montanum	('Broad-leaved Willow-herb')
E. nerteroides	
E. obscurum	
Equisetum arvense	('Common Horsetail')
Euphorbia helioscopia	('Sun Spurge')
E. peplus	('Petty Spurge')
Fumaria muralis ssp. boraei	
F. officinalis	('Common Fumitory')
Gnaphalium uliginosum	('March Cudweed')
Lamium purpureum	(Red Dead-nettle)
Matricaria matricarioides	(Pineapple Weed or 'Rayless Mayweed')
Papaver rhoeas	('Field Poppy')
Poa annua	('Annual Poa')
Polygonum aviculare	(Knotgrass)
Ranunculus repens	('Creeping Buttercup')
Rumex acetosella	(Sheep's Sorrel)
R. obtusifolius	('Broad-leaved Dock')
Senecio vulgaris	(Groundsel)
Spergula arvensis	(Corn Spurrey)
Stellaria media	(Chickweed)

Tripleurosplermum maritimum
    ssp. inodorum   (Scentless Mayweed)
Veronica agrestis   ('Field Speedwell')
V. persica   ('Buxbaum's Speedwell')
Viola arvensis   ('Field Pansy')

(b)   *In lawns*

Bellis perennis   (Daisy)
Hypochaeris radicata   (Cat's Ear)
Plantago lanceolata   (Ribwort)
P. major   ('Great Plantain')
Prunella vulgaris   (Self-heal)
Taraxacum officinale   (Common Dandelion)
Trifolium repens   (White Clover or Dutch Clover)

(c)   *On waste-ground*

Aegopodium podagraria   (Ground Elder, Herb Gerard, Goutweed or Bishop's Weed)
Agropyron repens   (Couch-grass)
Dactylis glomerata   (Cock's-foot)
Heracleum sphondylium   (Hogweed, Cow Parsnip or Keck)
Poa pratensis   (Meador-grass)
Symphytum officinale   (Comfrey)
S. tuberosum   ('Tuberous Comfrey')
Urtica dioica   (Stinging Nettle)

An important habitat, often very rich in the same weedy species found in cultivated ground and waste places, is roadside verges.

Also among the common plants of this habitat are the legumes *Lathyrus pratensis* ('Meadow Vetchling'), *Lotus corniculatus* (Birdsfoot trefoil or Bacon and Eggs), *Vicia cracca* (Tufted Vetch), *V. hirsuta* (Hairy Tare) and *V. sepium* ('Bush Vetch') and the umbellifer *Anthriscus sylvestris* (Cow Parsley or Keck). A delightful plant which appears restricted to roadsides in the region is *Myrrhis odorata* (Sweet Cicely). This may be an old introduction and it is certainly commoner on verges near houses. Its leaves smell very strongly of aniseed and it may have had an ancient culinary use.

On many farms on flatter areas there are grass fields which are ploughed every 7 - 10 years. Usually a crop is then taken off and they are reseeded for grassland. In addition there is much permanent grassland on less easily worked, sloping and rocky ground. The species composition of permanent grasslands is closely correlated with soil type (King and Nicholson, 1964). On the better brown earth soils *Argostis tenius* ('Common Bent-grass') and *Festuca ovina* agg. (Sheep's Fescue) are characteristic and are accompanied by such species as *Festuca rubra* ('Creeping Fescue'), *Plantago lanceolata* (Ribwort), *Thymus drucei* (Thyme) and *Trifolium repens* (White Clover or Dutch Clover).   *Argostis canina* ('Brown Bent-grass'), *Anthoxanthum odoratum* ('Sweet Verbal-grass'), *Galium saxatile* ('Heath Bedstraw') and *Potentilla erecta* (Common Tormentil) occur also and are increasingly common in the grassland of more acid brown earth soils.

These grasslands on brown earths are found mainly at lower altitudes and grade into grassland types of poorer soils.   Such soils are often strongly leached and acid and may have a thick layer of mor humus which grades into peat.   *Argostis tenius* and *Festuca ovina* agg. usually persists on these soils, and are frequently replaced as dominant species by less palatable grasses such as *Deschampsia flexusa* ('Wavy hair-grass'), *Molinia caerulea* ('Purple moor-grass') and, in particular, *Nardus stricta* (Mat-grass). Other characteristic higher plant species in these poor grasslands are *Vaccinium myrtillus* (Blaeberry, Bilberry, Whortleberry or Huckleberry), *Argostis canina*, *Anthoxanthum odoratum*, *Carex binervis* ('Ribbed Sedge'), *Juncus squarrosus* ('Heath Rush'), *Gallium saxatile* and *Potentilla erecta*.

Large areas of former grassland have been invaded by *Pteridium aquilinum* (Bracken), as a result of neglect over the last hundred years (e.g. on the southern slopes of the Ochils).   Bracken is a serious weed since it tends to occupy the better grassland soils, often to the exclusion of all other species.   It is virtually inedible (except for the very young fronds), and poisonous to stock.   Recent chemical methods of Bracken eradication combined with the stimulus from increasing food shortages may result in the clearance of this species within the next few years.   *Ulex europaeus* (Furze, Gorse or Whin) and *Sarothamnus scoparius* (Broom) are also common plants of neglected pastures on better soils.

3   *Heathland*

Extensive areas of Heather moor, dominated by *Calluna vulgaris*, so characteristic of hillsides in many parts of eastern Scotland are not a conspicuous feature of the survey region.   *Calluna* heath was probably much more widespread than it is now, particularly immediately after the initial forest clearances.   It seems likely that heath has much diminished under the influence of grazing and excessive burning and has been replaced by various types of grassland (and more recently reafforested).

An illustration of the influence of management on the abundance of Heather is provided by the dramatic differences that occur in a few places across field boundaries. On one side is grassland grazed by sheep, on the other Heather moor managed for grouse. Good discussions of the dynamics of the replacement of Heather moor are given by

King and Nicholson (1964) and Gimingham (1964).   Pollen analyses (Durno 1956) shows no fall in Heather pollen.   They include, however, the contribution from Heather which has expanded greatly on bogs which have been drained by man.   The Heather dominated communities of bog sites are dealt with in section 5.

Areas of heathland in the area include sites north of the Highland Boundary Fault, such as on the eastern slopes of Meall Mor (which has been recently planted with trees) and on the opposite side of the valley on Ben Each.

Scattered areas of heathland occur south of the Highland Boundary Fault in the Menteith Hills, on the northern and western slopes of the Ochils, and to a lesser extent on the Gargunnock and Fintry Hills.   In several places there is a 'Vaccinium edge' (Gimingham, 1964; Pearsall, 1950), e.g. on Callander Craig, of *Calluna vulgaris* and *Vaccinium myrtillus* (Bilberry, Blaeberry, Whortleberry or Huckleberry) with *Empetrum nigrum* (Crowberry) and *Erica cinerea* (Bell-heather).

Heathland in the southern hills is illustrated by a stand, burned for sheep and grouse, from Black Hill in the Ochils.

The dominant species is *Calluna vulgaris* although there are scattered individuals of *Vaccinium myrtillus, Erica cinerea, Carex binervis* ('Ribbed Sedge') and *Potentilla erecta* (Common Tormentil).   *Hypnum cupressiforme* is the dominant moss.   Grasses are relatively abundant and are often dominant in depressions in the microtopography. They include *Argiotis canina* ('Brown Bent-grass'), *A. tenuis* ('Common Bent-grass') *Deschampsia flexuosa* ('Wavy hair-grass').   *Festuca ovina* agg.   (Sheep's Fescue), *Nardus stricta* (Mat-grass), and *Molinia caerulea* ('Purple moor-grass').   *Erica tetralix* (Cross-leaved Heath or Bog Heather), *Juncus squarrosus* ('Heath Rush'), *Molinia caerulea* and the moss *Polytrichum commune* become more abundant in the wetter areas.   The many grasses suggest the gradual replacement of the heathland by grassland which is the dominant vegetation of these hills.

4   *Lochs, fens and rivers* [*]
Only a little information is available on the vegetation of these habitats in the survey region and this is clearly a field ripe for investigation.   There is a large variety of lochs varying from lowland lakes (e.g. the Lake of Menteith) to lochs more characteristic of the Highland zone (e.g. Loch Voil).   Some are reservoirs with an artifically raised water level (e.g. Loch Katrine), other reservoirs are almost completely artificial.

* *Mrs B. Ottley provided much of the information for this section.*

An example of a lowland reservoir is that at Pendreich near Bridge of Allan. The following submerged and floating species have been recorded there: *Potamogeton natans* ('Broad-leaved Pondweed'), *P. alpinus* ('Reddish Pondweed'), *Ranunculus aquatilis, Littorella uniflora* (Shore-weed) and *Polygonum amphibium* ('Amphibious Bistort').

Vegetation types, transitional between open water and dry land, are associated with the margins of lochs. Their status is somewhat controversial and we have adopted the terminology of Ratcliffe (1964) and called them fens. They are well developed where the sides of the loch are not very steep and where there has been deposition of silt.

Around the margins of Pendreich Reservoir the following species have been recorded: *Achillea ptarmica* (Sneezewort), *Caltha palustris* (Kingcup, Marsh Marigold or May Blobs), *Dactylorchis maculata* ssp. *ericetorum* (Moorland Spotted Orchid), *Equisetum palustre* ('Marsh Horsetail'), *Juncus effusus* (Soft Rush), *Lychnis flos-cuculi* (Ragged Robin), *Myosotis secunda* ('Water Forget-me-not'), *Ranunculus flammula* (Lesser Spearwort) and *Rhinanthus minor* (Yellow Rattle).

A rich fen occurs at the head of Loch Lubnaig and Mr A. W. Robson has provided the following details about this. *Nymphaea alba* (White Water-Lily) is conspicuous in the deeper water, which in some places is fringed by large colonies of *Scirpus lacustris* (Bulrush). In shallower waters there is an extensive sedge bed. The sedges forming distinct zones are *Carex lasiocarpa* ('Slender Sedge'), *C. rostrata* ('Bottle Sedge' or 'Beaked Sedge'), *C. vesicaria* ('Bladder sedge') and *C. aquatilis*. In progressively drier ground occur *Carex curta* ('White Sedge'), *C. nigra* ('Common Sedge') and *C. ovalis* ('Oval Sedge'). *Littorella uniflora* (Shore-weed) occurs in suitable places. There are some very attractive wet ground species in this locality such as *Scutellaria galericulata* (Skull-cap), *Myosotis scorpioides* ('Water Forget-me-not'), *Dactylorchis purpurella* ('Northern Fen Orchid'), *Platanthera chlorantha* (Greater Butterfly Orchid), *P. bifolia* (Lesser Butterfly Orchid), *Dactylorchis incarnata* (Meadow Orchid) and *Lythrum salicaria* (Purple Loosestrife). The wet ground grades into meadows through which the river, with Alders lining its banks, flows.

The rivers vary from fast flowing mountain streams to wide, slower-flowing, meanders (e.g. the Forth above Stirling).

The Allan Water at Dunblane is a good example of a rocky fast flowing stream in which the current is too swift to allow the establishment of completely submerged vascular plants. The mosses *Fontinalis antipyretica, F. squamosa, Eurhynchium riparioides* and *Cinclidotus fontinaloides* are common submerged species together with filamentous algae and diatoms.   A channel, from the jute mill, where the water is almost still has much *Potamogeton obtusifolius* ('Grassy Pondweed').   On the river margins or on rocks which are occasionally submerged the following are encountered: *Epilobium nerterioides, Festuca arundinacea* ('Tall Fescue'), *Mimulus guttatus* (Monkey-flower), *Montia sibirica, Myosotis scorpioides* ('Water Forget-me-not'), *Phalaris arundinacea* (Reed-grass), *Rorippa nasturtium-aquaticum* (Watercress), and *Veronica beccabunga* (Brookline).   *Heracleum mantegazzianum* is a common and increasing plant of the river banks here.

The Teith at Callander is an example of less turbulent though still fast flowing river.   Here there are the more aquatic higher plants.   *Myriophyllum alterniflorum* ('Alternate-flowered Water-milfoil') is frequent and also present are *Littorella uniflora* (Shore-weed), *Apium inundatum* and *Callitriche intermedia*.   *Lythrum salicaria* (Purple Loosestrife) is an attractive member of the river bank flora.

There are extensive beds of *Phragmites communis* (Reed) which fringe the Forth between Stirling and Alloa.

5   *Bogs and Mires*

The terminology used here is that of Ratcliffe (1964).   Although mires and bogs intergrade the following situations can be distinguished:

(a)   Bogs occur on flat ground and their high water table is maintained by a combination of high rainfall and low evaporation rate.   The water supply is derived almost entirely from the atmosphere rather than from drainage water seepage from adjacent ground.   These bogs are frequently referred to as "ombrogenous" and have a low nutrient status because virtually all the nutrients are derived from rainwater.   Bogs occur as "Raised bogs" on lowland sites where the living surface has grown above the influence of drainage water and "Blanket bogs" on flat or gently contoured uplands.   Both situations are well represented in the Stirling region.

Raised bogs formerly covered much of the carse land around the Forth. They were extensively drained and literally washed down the river by the late 18th and early 19th century reclamation initiated by Lord Kames (Cadell, 1913). Nevertheless the series of raised bogs, collectively known as Flanders Moss, in the upper part of the Forth Valley is still the most extensive area of raised bog in Britain.   West Flanders Moss has recently been afforested but East Flanders Moss still provides an extensive area of less disturbed continuous raised bog of about 10km^2.   This is substantially intact albeit much altered by drainage and burning.

The south west parts of the bogs to the west of High Moss Pow are the least disturbed and consist of a carpet of *Sphagnum* spp. A rather open growth of *Calluna vulgaris* (Ling or Heather) *Erica tetralix* (Cross-leaved Heath or Bog Heather), *Eriophorum vaginatum* (Cotton-grass or Hare's tail), *E. angustifolium* ('Common Cotton-grass'), *Narthecium ossifragum* (Bog Asphodel), *Drosera rotundifolia* (Sundew) and *Rhyncospora alba* ('White Beak-sedge') is associated with the *Sphagnum*. *Andromeda polifolia* ('Marsh Andromeda') and *Vaccinium oxycoccus* (Cranberry) are plentiful and very characteristic of the more southerly Scottish raised bogs. *Andromeda polifolia* is at its northern limit in Britain in this area.

Ledum groenlandicum is an intriguing species, of Flanders Moss, which occurs in small quantity with the species just listed. *Ledum* is discussed further on page 111.

There is much Birch on the south margin of Flanders East Moss and also Birch of varying density throughout the moss, a sure sign of disturbance. The part of the moss owned by the Scottish Wildlife Trust is at the south-east corner and is drier and dominated by *Calluna*. Attempts are being made to increase the height of the water table by blocking drainage channels in order to promote the growth of more interesting bog plants.

Smaller raised bogs, variously disturbed, occur for example at:

(i) Dunmore Moss; a severely disturbed bog but noteworthy for harbouring a large population of *Ledum groenlandicum* on the afforested part.

(ii) Shirrgaton Moss; this has been subject to some drainage but is relatively intact. It does have *Rhyncospora alba* in one locality.

(iii) Killorn Moss; is much modified by drainage yet still harbours a large range of raised bog communities. It also has *Rhyncospora alba*.

Blanket bog tends to be developed on all flat or gently sloping land above about 800ft in this region. Large areas of this bog occur on the plateaux of the Fintry and Gargunnock Hills, the Ochils and to the north and east of Callander. The present vegetation is probably derived from a much less disturbed bog dominated by *Sphagnum* which accumulated on the site of former woodland. Remains of trees at the base of the peat have been seen in a number of places. The change from woodland to bog was brought about by a combination of prehistoric clearances and climatic deterioration.

The typical blanket bog community is now dominated by *Calluna* and *Trichophorum cespitosum* (Deer-grass) with varying proportions of *Sphagnum* spp.

In general they are very species poor and apart from the two dominants, the only common higher plants are *Erica tetralix*, *Eriophorum angustifolium* and locally *Narthecium ossifragum*. The blanket bogs are regularly burned. Excessive burning and grazing tend to eliminate *Calluna* and the community becomes dominated by *Trichophorum*.

In several places there is severe erosion or "Hagging" of the peat, presumably another symptom of excessive disturbance.

Rubus chamaemorus (Cloudberry) is notably abundant in blanket bog on the Campsies and occurs there in drier situations also.

(b) Mires occur where the wetness of the ground is maintained by lateral seepage of ground water. They are common in hill country, in channels and hollows or where slopes flatten out, especially in valley floors. Ecologists often refer to mires as "soligenous" since the water table is maintained by a flow of water through the adjacent soil. The nutrient status of mires depends on the mineral content of the soil through which the water has flowed.

Soligenous mires occur in suitable situations throughout the survey area.

Nutrient-poor mires are usually dominated by *Juncus effusus* (Soft rush) or *J. acutiflorus* ('Sharp-flowered Rush') and the mosses *Sphagnum* spp. and *Polytrichum commune* and usually have *Carex nigra* ('Common Sedge'), *Galium saxatile* ('Heath Bedstraw'), and *Potentilla erecta* (Common Tormentil) as associated higher plants. Mires dominated by *Molinia caerulea* ('Purple moor-grass') and *Myrica gale* (Bog Myrtle or Sweet Gale) occur locally in the western parts of the region, e.g. by the road from Loch Katrine to Aberfoyle.

In mires of higher nutrient status the dominant plants are *Juncus acutiflorus* and bryophytes of which *Acrocladium cuspidatum* is a constant. There are usually associated characteristic species such as *Holcus lanatus* (Yorkshire Fog), *Carex panicea* (Carnation-grass), *Achillea ptarmica* (Sneezewort), *Crepis paludosa* ('Marsh Hawk's beard'), *Epilogium palustre* ('Marsh Willow-herb'), *Prunella vulgaris* (Self-heal), *Ranunculus acris* ('Meadow Buttercup') and the mosses *Bryum pseudotriquetrum* and *Sphagnum* ssp. of more nutrient rich situations.

6 *Maritime vegetation*

There are no shingle beaches, sand dunes or maritime cliffs in the survey area and the only vegetation that is directly influenced by the sea is salt marsh. This is best developed on the south side of the Forth estuary below Stirling, although it is not species rich and lacks plants of more southern affinities e.g. *Spartina* (Cord-grass) and *Limonium* spp. (Sea Lavender).

The salt marsh vegetation is developed on silty material deposited by the river. Often large expanses of this silt are scarcely colonised by plants and extensive "mud flats" occur e.g. around Grangemouth.   Salt marsh brown sea weeds are very little in evidence.

An easily accessible part of salt marsh is that near Kincardine Bridge. Here, in the lower parts *Puccinellia maritima* ('Sea Poa') together with *Triglochin maritima* ('Sea Arrow-grass') and *Aster tripolium* ('Sea Aster') are always important. A small quantity of *Salicornia* sp. (Glasswort or Marsh Samphire) is present but it never appears as a dominant pioneer. *Plantago maritima* ('Sea Plantain') together with *Spergularia media* are more abundant higher up the marsh; *Armeria maritima* (Thrift or Sea Pink) is infrequent.   Towards the top of the marsh *Puccinellia* is replaced as the dominant grass by *Argostis stolonifera* (Fiorin) and *Festuca rubra* ('Creeping Fescue') and *Juncus gerardii* ('Mud Rush') is abundant.   Other characteristic salt marsh plants recorded include *Cochlearia officinalis* (Scurvy-grass), *Glaux maritima* ('Sea Milkwort' or 'Black Saltwort') and *Atriplex littoralis* ('Shore Orache').

7   *Sub-montane rock outcrops**
At Lime Hill, in Loch Ard Forest, there occurs an exposure of serpentine rock which is not grazed by sheep and is noteworthy for the occurrence of calcicolous species. There is some severely deer-browsed *Juniperus communis* (Juniper), the local fern *Asplenium viride* ('Green Spleenwort') and bryophytes such as *Tortella tortuosa*, *Neckera crispa*, *Ctenidium molluscum* and *Preissia quadrata*. *Asplenium cunifolium*, a very local fern, recently recognised as a British species, occurs there also.

There are conspicuous cliffs and rock outcrops on the Campsie/Fintry Hills. Characteristic species of these sites are mostly not restricted there but are often characteristic of other habitats. The rocky outcrops provide a suitably diverse environment in which plants of differing requirements grow in close proximity.

Ferns are abundant in places and include *Asplenium trichomanes* ('Maidenhair Spleenwort'), *Athyrium filix-femina* (Lady-fern), *Cryptogramma crispa* (Parsley Fern), *Cystopteris fragilis* ('Brittle Bladder-fern'), *Dryopteris borreri*, *D. filix-Mas* (Male Fern) *Polypodium vulgare* ('Polypody'), *Polystichum aculeatum* ('Hard Shield-fern'),

* *Most of the information in this section is from notes made by Mr John Mitchell and Mr A McG Stirling.*

Thelypteris dryopteris (Oak Fern) and *T. limbosperma* ('Mountain Fern').

The fern allies *Lycopodium selago* ('Fir Clubmoss') and *Selaginella selaginoides* ('Lesser Clubmoss') occur also. Higher plants include woodland herbs e.g. *Geranium robertianum* (Herb Robert), *Mercurialis perennis* (Dog's Mercury), *Oxalis acetosella* (Wood-sorrel), *Urtica dioica* (Stinging Nettle) and *Viola riviniana* ('Common Violet'). Other species are characteristic of wet places e.g. *Cardamine pratensis* (Cuckoo Flower or Lady's Smock), *Carex demissa*, *Filipendula ulmaria* (Meadow-sweet), *Geum rivale* (Water Avens), and *Pinguicula vulgaris* (Common Butterwort). Other ecological groups of species as well as plants from the surrounding grasslands, can be recognised also in these habitats.

A few localities harbour more local plants, some of which are very scarce indeed in the survey region.

Examples of such species are:

Anthyllis vulneraria	(Kidney-vetch or Ladies' Fingers)
Arabis hirsuta	('Hairy Rock-cress')
Asplendium viride	('Green Spleenwort')
Botrychium lunaria	(Moonwort)
Coeloglossum viride	(Frog Orchid)
Epilobium alsinifolium	('Chickweed Willow-herb')
Galium boreale	('Northern Bedstraw')
G. sterneri ssp. *sterneri*	
Geranium lucidum	('Shining Cranesbill')
Minuartia verna	('Vernal Sandwort')
Pimpinella saxifraga	('Burnet Saxifrage')
Potentilla tabernaemontani	('Spring Cinquefoil')
Sagina subulata	('Awl-leaved Pearlwort')
Sedum rosea	(Rose-root or Midsummer-men)
S. villosum	('Hairy Stonecrop')

Some localities have noteworthy bryophytes and *Bazzania tricrenata*, *Herberta hutchinsiae*, *Orthothecium rufescens*, *Rhytidium rugosum*, *and Scaponia aspera* are amongst those recorded.

The Ochil Hills also have a number of cliffs and rock outcrops. We have less information about these although it is clear that they have many characteristic species in common with those of similar localities in the Campsie/Fintry Hills. Particularly noteworthy and restricted, in the survey region, to the cliffs of the Ochils, is *Lychnis viscaria* ('Red German Catchfly'). This rare species is one of the botanical treasures of the area and is a beautiful sight, in flower, in late spring or early summer.

8   *Montane vegetation*

The survey area contains land over 2000ft in the Ochils and in the region beyond the Highland Boundary Fault.

Although they have some impressive cliffs and crags at lower altitudes the highest parts of the Ochils are on relatively gently sloping ground and are continuously vegetated.   The vegetation is not of a distinctly montane type but rather a continuation of the blanket bog and grassland that occur at lower altitudes.

On extreme northern edge of the survey area there are several peaks over 920m (3020ft) including Ben Vorlich, Stuc a' Chroin and Stob Coire an Lochan.   The highest point, right on the northern boundary, is the peak of Stob Binnein at 1165m (3821ft).   Montane vegetation does occur in these areas and there are topographic features which are typical of mountains such as steep slopes, scree, cliffs, corries and peaks.   However, there have been very few studies of the vegetation of these mountains because they lack extensive areas of calcareous rock and they are floristically impoverished compared with the species-rich calcareous mica schist areas on and around the internationally famous Ben Lawers.   Even so, many of the scarcer mountain plants have been recorded, albeit in small numbers

Much of the mountain slopes are covered with a montane heath or grassland type vegetation in which *Vaccinium myrtillus* is often abundant.   Sheep grazing has probably favoured the dominance of *Vaccinium*.   The following species were noted in a sheep-grazed stand near the summit 879m (2883ft) of Ben Ledi.

Argostis tenuis	('Common Bent-grass')
Deschampsia flexuosa	('Wavy hair-grass')
Empetrum hermaphroditum	(Crowberry)
Festuca ovina agg.	(Sheep's Fescue)
Galium saxatile	('Heath Bedstraw')
Lycopodium selago	('Fir Clubmoss')
Rubus chamaemorus	(Cloudberry)
Vaccinium myrtillus	(Bilberry, Blaeberry, Whortleberry or Huckleberry)
V. votos-idaea	(Cowberry or Red Whortleberry)

also the mosses *Andreaea rupestris*, *Hylocomium splendens*, *Pleurozium schreberi* and *Sphagnum* spp. and the lichens *Cetraria islandica* and *Cladonia* spp.

At higher altitudes lichens and mosses often become an increasingly important part of the vegetation e.g. in the community near the summit of Ben Vorlich 985m (3231ft).

In suitable situations there are high altitude mires and bogs in which *Eriophorum* spp. (Cotton-grass) are striking components.

A most characteristic mountain vegetation (although isolated examples occur at lower altitudes) is associated with springs and flushes, which are soligenous and similar to mires, but with a more localised and rapid flow of water so that they usually cover a smaller area. Springs are typically canalised into small rills whilst in flushes the irrigation water spreads out, giving a more diffuse flow. There is intergraduation between springs and flushes and mires. A common spring vegetation is dominated by the moss. *Philonotis fontana* associated with *Dicranella palustris* and *Saxifraga stellaris* ('Starry Saxifrage'). *Saxifraga aizoides* ('Yellow Mountain-Saxifrage') is a characteristic plant under slightly more base rich conditions when spring and flush vegetation is often floristically rich as in one spring on Ben Ledi where *S. aizoides* was associated with *Silene acaulis* (Moss Campion), *Thalictrum alpinum* ('Alpine Meadow Rue') and *Polygonum viviparum*.

There are two base rich mountain areas which just fall within the survey region and which have a flora of comparable richness to that of the more famous mountains to the north.

(a)   The calcareous mica schist on the south east slopes of Stob Garb. Roger (1961) noted the following species:

Armeria maritima	(Thrift or Sea Pink)
Carex vaginata	
Crepis paludosa	('Marsh Hawk's-beard')
Cystopteris fragilis	('Brittle Bladder-fern')
Draba incana	('Hoary Whitlow Grass')
Galium boreale	('Northern Bedstraw')
Juncus triglumis	('Three-flowered Rush')
Juniperus communis	(Juniper)
Luzula spicata	('Spiked Woodrush')
Polystichum lonchitis	(Holly fern)
Salix arbuscula	
Saussurea aplina	('Alpine Saussurea')
Saxifraga oppositifolia	('Purple Saxifrage')
Selaginella selaginoides	('Lesser Clubmoss')
Sibbaldia procumbens	
Silene acaulis	(Moss Campion)
Tofieldia pusilla	('Scottish Asphodel')
Trollius europaeus	('Globe Flower')

(b)   High-level outcrops of the Loch Tay limestone in the Braes of Balquhidder.

Here the following species have been recorded by Mr A. McG. Stirling.

Alchemilla alpina	('Alpine Lady's-Mantle')
A. glabra	
Antennaria dioica	(Cat's-foot)
Anthyllis vulneraria	(Kidney-vetch or Ladies' Fingers)
Arabis hirsuta	('Hairy Rock-cress')
Asplenium ruta-muraria	(Wall-Rue)
A. trichomanes	('Maidenhair Spleenwort')
A. viride	('Green Spleenwort')
Botrychium lunaria	(Moonwort)
Carex dioica	('Dioecious Sedge')
Cystopteris fragilis	('Brittle Bladder-fern')
Draba incana	('Hoary Whitlow Grass')
Epilobium anagallidifolium	('Alpine Willow-herb')
Equisetum palustre	('Marsh Horsetail')
Galium boreale	('Northern Bedstraw')
Geranium sylvaticum	('Wood Cranesbill')
Heracleum sphondylium	(Hogweed, Cow Parsnip or Keck)
Helictotrichon pratense	('Meadow Oat')
Juncus triglumis	('Three-flowered Rush')
Linum catharticum	('Purging Flax')
Lotus corniculatus	(Birdsfoot-trefoil or Bacon and Eggs)
Orchis mascula	(Early Purple Orchid or Blue Butcher)
Parnassia palustris	(Grass of Parnassus
Potentilla crantzii	('Alpine Cinquefoil')
Rosa villosa	
Rubus saxatilis	('Stone Bramble')
Saxifraga aizoides	('Yellow Mountain-Saxifrage')
S. hypnoides	(Dovedale Moss)
S. oppositifolia	('Purple saxifrage')
Salix arbuscula	
S. myrsinites	
Sedum rosea	(Rose-root or Midsummer-men)
Selaginella selaginoides	('Lesser Clubmoss')
Thalictrum alpinum	('Alpine Meadow Rue')
Tofieldia pusilla	('Scottish Asphidel')
Triglochin palustris	('Marsh Arrow-grass')
Veronica fruticans	('Rock Speedwell')

Notes on the Flora

The flora is difficult to assess accurately because the boundaries neither coincide exactly with those of the Watsonian vice counties nor with the 10km squares of the

Atlas of the British Flora and there is a lack of recent published data. Consequently, a few species may have been wrongly included or excluded from the following discussion.

Matthews (1955) divided the British Flora into 16 groups on the basis of the world distribution patterns shown by the species and thus provided a means of a rapid characterisation of any local flora in Britain.   Three of his groups — the "Wide Element", the "Eurasian Element" and the "European Element" contain plants of a very wide European distribution and in the survey area.   Three other groups the "Alpine Element", the "American Element" and the "Endemic Element" are not represented at all in this area.   The remaining ten groups are a useful starting point for discussion and their representation here can be compared with those published in past B.A. surveys.   The proportions of species occurring in these groups is summarised in Table 5.1

TABLE   5.1

MATTHEWS' ELEMENTS IN THE STIRLING REGION

Element	Total number of species in Britain	Approximate number of species native in the Stirling region*	Representation is Stirling region
			%
Mediterranean	38	1	2.6
Oceanic Southern	82	11	13.4
Continental Southern	127	13	10.24
Oceanic West European	87	21	24.1
Continental	88	16	18.2
Continental Northern	97	58	59.8
Northern Montane	31	12	38.7
Oceanic Northern	23	9	39.1
Sub-Arctic	28	7	25.0
Arctic Alpine	76	38	50.0

*Includes possibly extinct species

Three of Matthews' groups include species with a mainly southern distribution in Europe, i.e. the "Mediterranean", "Oceanic Southern" and "Continental Southern" Elements.   The first group is represented merely by *Fumaria bastardii* in a single locality.   The "Oceanic Southern" has about eleven species although most of these have very few localities and only *Ilex aquifolium* (Holly) of this group is at all common.   The "Continental Southern Element" has only two widespread species, *Lotus pedunculatus* ('Large Birdsfoot-trefoil') and *Myrrhis odorata* (Sweet Cicely).

The "Oceanic West European Element" is better represented and has about twenty one species, many of them occurring in many localities e.g. *Cares binervis*, ('Ribbed Sedge') *Corydalis claviculata* ('White Climbing Fumitory'), *Conopodium majus* (Earthnut or Pignut),

Endymion non-scriptus (Bluebell or Wild Hyacinth), *Erica cinerea* (Bell-heather), *E. tetralix* (Cross-leaved Heath or Bog Heather), *Salix cinerea* ssp. *atrocinerea*(Common Sallow) and *Ulex europaeus* (Gorse, Furze or Whin).

The "Continental Element", a group of central European affinities, has only two widespread species in the Stirling region, *Quercus petraea* (Durmast Oak or 'Sessile Oak') and *Q. robur* (Common Oak or 'Pedunculate Oak').

The remaining five groups constitute a mainly northern component and in general are better represented in the area. There are many common species in the "Continental Northern Element" e.g. *Alchemilla glabra, Angelica sylvestris* (Wild Angelica), *Betula pubescens* (Birch), *Eriophorum angustifolium* ('Common Cotton-grass'), *E. vaginatum* (Cotton-grass or Hare's-tail), *Trichophorum cespitosum* (Deer-grass), and *Vaccinium myrtillus* (Bilberry, Blaeberry, Whortleberry or Huckleberry). The "Northern Montane Element" are mainly very local plants, the most common being *Saxifraga hypnoides* (Dovedale Moss) and *Trollius europaeus* ('Globe Flower'). The "Oceanic Northern Element" includes some common plants e.g. *Narthecium ossifragum* (Bog Ashpodel), *Thymus drucei* (Thyme) and, particularly in the west of the area, *Myrica gale* (Bog Myrtle or Sweet Gale). The "Sub-Arctic Elements" are all local plants; *Rubus chamaemorus* (Cloudberry) is the most frequently encountered. The "Arctic Alpine Element" is well represented although some are rare plants e.g. *Veronica fruticans* ('Rock Speedwell') and, perhaps surprisingly in view of its abundance in other parts of Scotland, *Arctostaphylos uva-ursi* (Bearberry). More common plants included in this group are *Vaccinium vitis-idaea* (Cowberry or Red Whortleberry) and *Empetrum nigrum* (Crowberry).

Recent changes in the flora

Additions. There are very many records of alien species, from one or a few localities, which have never spread or have died out after a few years. Nevertheless a few aliens have established themselves and can be regarded as flourishing permanent additions to the flora. Examples of such species are:

Acer pseudoplatanus	(Sycamore)
Cymbalaria muralis	(Ivy-leaved Toadflax)
Epilobium nerteroides	
Heracleum mantegezzianum	
Juncus tenuis	
Matricaria matricarioides	(Pineapple Weed or 'Rayless Mayweed')
Montia sibirica	
Mimulus guttatus	(Monkey-flower)
Polygonum cuspidatum	
Rhododendron ponticum	
Veronica filiformis	

Plants not recorded recently

A list of species that are probably native, but which have not been recorded since 1930 at the latest, has been compiled (Table 5.2) from the *Atlas of the British Flora* and after consultation with local botanists. Most of these species have always been rare in the area. If they are now extinct this has been caused largely by a combination of overcollecting by botanists and the destruction of the habitat by man.

TABLE 5.2

Plants not recorded since 1930 from the Stirling area (in alphabetical order).

Species	English Name
Agrimonia odorata	('Fragrant Agrimony')
Agropyron junceiforme	('Sand Couch-grass')
Alopecurus myosuroides	(Black Twitch)
Anagallis minima	(Chaffweed)
Anthemis arvensis	(Corn Chamomile)
Anthriscus caucalis	('Bur Chervil')
Apium graveolens	(Wild Celery)
Artemisia absinthium	(Wormwood)
Astragalus glycyphyllos	(Milk-vetch)
Baldellia ranunculoides	('Lesser Water-Plantain')
Ballota nigra	(Black Horehound)
Bidens cernua	('Nodding Bur-Marigold')
B. tripartita	('Tripartite Bur-Marigold')
Callitriche hermaphroditica	('Autumn Starwort')
Cardus nutans	('Musk Thistle')
Carduus tenuiflorus	('Slender Thistle')
Carex laevigata	('Smooth Sedge')
Carex riparia	('Great Pond-sedge')
Catabrosa aquatica	('Water Whorl-grass')
Ceratophyllum submersum	
Cochlearia danica	('Danish Scurvy-grass')
Corallorhiza trifida	(Coral-root)
Crepis mollis	('Soft Hawk's-beard')
Drosera anglica	('Great Sundew')
Elatine hexandra	
Epipactis palustris	('Marsh Helleborine')
Equisetum hyemale	(Dutch Rush)
E. pratense	('Shady Horsetail')
Eriophorum latifolium	('Broad-leaved Cotton-grass')
Eryngium matitimum	(Sea Holly)
Filago germanica	(Cudweed)
Fumaria micrantha	
Gagea lutea	('Yellow Star-of-Bethlehem')
Galium mollugo	('Great Hedge Bedstraw')

Genista anglica	(Needle Furze, Petty Whin)
Geranium sanguineum	('Bloody Cranesbill')
Hammarbya paludosa	(Bog Orchid)
Hordeum marinum	('Squirrel-tail Grass')
Hordeum secalinum	('Meadow Barley')
Hymenophyllum tunbrigense	('Tunbridge Filmy Fern')
Hypochaeris glabra	('Smooth Cat's Ear')
Juncus castaneus	('Chestnut Rush')
Lamium molucellifolum	('Intermediate Dead-nettle')
Ledum palustre	
Lepidium latifolium	(Dittander, 'Broad-leaved Pepperwort')
Lysimachia thyrsifolia	('Tufted Loosestrife')
Mercurialis annua	('Annual Mercury')
Nuphar pumila	('Least Yellow Water-lily')
Ononis spinosa	(Restharrow)
*Paris quadrifolia**	(Herb Paris)
Polygonum minus	
P. nodosum	
Polygonum raii	('Ray's Knotgrass')
Potentilla argentea	('Hoary Cinquefoil')
Pyrola media	('Intermediate Wintergreen')
P. rotundifolia	('Larger Wintergreen')
Radiola linoides	(All-seed)
Ranunculus arvensis	('Corn Crowfoot')
R. circinatus	
R. lingua	(Great Spearwort)
R. sardous	('Hairy Buttercup')
Rorippa sylvestris	('Creeping Yellow-cress')
Sagina maritima	('Sea Pearlwort')
Salix nigricans	('Dark-leaved Willow')
Salsola kali	(Saltwort)
Salvia horminoides	(Wild Clary)
Saxifrage cernua	('Drooping Saxifrage')
S. hirculus	('Yellow Marsh Saxifrage')
Silene noctiflora	('Night-flowering Campion')
Sium latifolium	(Water Parsnip)
Stellaria palustris	('Marsh Stitchwort')
Valeriana dioica	('Marsh Valerian')
Vicia orobus	('Bitter Vetch')

The most celebrated plant in Table 2 is undoubtedly *Ledum palustre*. This species is described by Clapham et al. (1962) as "Possibly native in bogs near Bridge of Allan (Stirling and Perth), a rare escape elsewhere". It is almost certain, however, that *L. palustre* became extinct in the area sometime between 1915, when the last collection was made, and 1930, when an intensive search failed to locate it (Morris, 1931).

*Rediscovered in Bridge of Allan by Mr T Ottley in June, 1974.

The closely related *L. groenlandicum* still occurs in the area in a few places e.g. in a well-known locality on Flanders Moss and on Dunmore Moss. *L. groenlandicum* has never been regarded as a native plant and there is some evidence it may have been planted as a cover for game.

The taxonomic differences between *L. palustre* and *L. groenlandicum* are difficult to apply and have been a source of confusion. However, Mr John Deans, an Edinburgh University student has examined specimens of *Ledum* from Lecropt Moss which were deposited in the Herbarium of the Royal Botanic Gardens, Edinburgh, between 1830 and 1915. He considers (pers. comm) that at least some of them have the narrow leaves and ten stamens, typical of *L. palustre*. It therefore seems likely that both species of *Ledum* have occurred in the area; *L. groenlandicum* persists as an escape from cultivation while *L. palustre* is probably extinct. It is impossible to determine if *L. palustre* was native unless some sub-fossil remains can be found.

ACKNOWLEDGEMENTS

We would like to express thanks to Mr E T Idle, Mr J Mitchell, Maggi O'Brien, Mrs B Ottley, Mr A W Robson and Mr A McG Stirling for their data.

The above also, together with Dr C J Henty and Dr R Sexton provided very useful comments on the manuscript. Dr J H Dickson is thanked for his help with the section on the history of the vegetation.

REFERENCES

Anderson, M L	1967a	*A History of Scottish Forestry, 1.* Edinburgh: Nelson.
Anderson, M L	1967b	*A History of Scottish Forestry 2.* Edinburgh: Nelson.
Burnett, J H (ed)	1964	*The Vegetation of Scotland.* Edinburgh: Oliver and Boyd.
Cadell, H M	1913	*The Story of the Forth.* Glasgow: Maclehose.
Clapham, A R Tutin, T G and Warburg, E F	1962	*Flora of the British Isles.* Cambridge: Cambridge University Press.

Cousens, J E   1963   'Variation of some diagnostic characters of the sessile and pedunculate oaks and their hybrids in Scotland', *Watsonia*, 5: 273 – 286.

Donner, J J   1957   'The geology and vegetation of late glacial retreat stages in Scotland', *Trans. Roy. Soc. Edinburgh*, 63: 221 – 264.

Durno, S E   1956   'Pollen analysis of peat deposits in Scotland', *Scot Geoge Mag.* 72: 178 – 187.

Edlin, H L   1969   *Forests of Central and Southern Scotland. Forestry Commission Booklet No 25.* Edinburgh: HMSO.

Wdlin, H L (ed)   1974   *Queen Elizabeth Forest Park.* Forestry Commission Guide. Edinburgh: HMSO.

Gimingham, C H   1964   'Dwarf shrub heaths', (In Burnett (ed)): 232 – 282.

Graham, P   1812   *General view of the Agriculture of Stirlingshire.* Edinburgh.

King, J and Nicholson, I A   1964   'Grasslands of the Forest and Sub-alpine zones', (In Burnett (ed)): 168 – 231.

Matthews, J R   1955   *Origin and Distribution of the British Flora.* London: Hutchinson.

Morris, D B   1931   'Ledum palustre (Labrador tea)', *Trans. Stirling Natural History and ARcheological Society* 53: 129 – 139.

The New Statistical Account of Scotland
      1845   8: *Dunbarton – Stirling – Clackmannan.* Edinburgh: Blackwood.

The New Statistical Account of Scotland
      1845   10: Perth. Edinburgh: Blackwood.

Pearsall, W H   1950   *Mountains and Moorlands:* London: Collins

Pennington, W   1969   *The History of British Vegetation.* London: English University Press.

Perring, F H and Walters, S M (ed)   1962   *Atlas of the British Flora.*   London: Nelson.

Ratcliffe, D A   1964   'Mires and bogs', (In Burnett (ed)):   426 – 478.

Roger, J G   1961   'Report of the Alpine Section, 1960', meeting centred at Garth Memorial Hostel, Perthshire (18th and 19th June, 1960).   *Trans. Edinburgh Bot. Soc. 39:*   239 – 240.

Stirling Col and Kidston, R   1891   'Notes on the flora of the north-western portion of Stirlingshire', *Trans. Stirling Natural History and Archeological Society.*   13: 88 – 102.

Stirling, Col and Kidston, R   1892   'Notes on the flora of Stirlingshire with short geological sketch of the ground', *Trans. Stirling Natural History and Archeological Society,*   14:   74 – 102.

*Stirling, Col and Kidston, R   1893 et seq   'Notes on the flora of Stirlingshire', *Trans. Stirling Natural History and Archeological Society.*   15 et seq.

Traill, J W H (ed)   1898   *Flora of Perthshire.*   Edinburgh: Blackwood.

Vasari, Y and Vasari, A   1968   'Late and post-glacial macrophytic vegetation of the lochs of northern Scotland', *Acta botanica fennica.* 80:   1 – 116.

* *Note:*   *Col Stirling and R Kidston produced a series of articles on the flora of Stirlingshire between 1893 and 1900.   All are published in the Transactions of the Stirling Natural History and Archeological Society.*

CHAPTER 6

MAMMALS

Introduction

The Stirling Region is rich in habitat types and a substantial proportion of the terrestial British mammals dwell here. There have also been many marine mammals recorded from the upper Forth, although most of these have been merely visitors and are not truly resident.

The area was last surveyed in *A Vertebrate Fauna of Forth* by Rintoul and Baxter in 1935. The following account draws heavily on this source which includes many very old records. There is a great shortage of recent data on the Stirling Region. A general impression of the distribution of mammalian fauna in Britain can be gained from Corbet (1971), whilst much background information is included in Matthews (1952), Southern (1964) and the excellent, although unfortunately incomplete, work by Barret-Hamilton and Hinton (1910 – 1921).

Species no longer found in the Region

Some animals are known only from fossils and have not occurred here for many thousands of years. Some, such as the Mammoth (*Elephas primigenius*) and the Urus or Giant Ox (*Bas tourus primigenius*), are now totally extinct, whilst others, such as the Elk (*Alces alces*), the Reindeer (*Rangifer tarandus*) and the Lemming, are still found elsewhere in Europe.

Other species have died out more recently. Apparently no written record remains of the Wild Boar (*Sus scrofa*) in the region although several place names indicate that the species occurred around Aberfoyle and Muckhart. Wild Boar is still widespread in Continental Europe. Wolves (*Canis lupus*) were hunted in the neighbourhood of Stirling in the early days of the seventeenth century and possibly persisted a little longer in the more remote parts of the area. Wolves are now rare in Europe as a whole. Wild White Cattle (*Bos tourus tourus*) were probably not extinct here until after the sixteenth century. Bishop Leslie in 1578 wrote (from a translation by Dalrymple) of this species: "Now consumed through the gluttonie of men only in thrie places is left, in the Park of Strivling, the Wod of Cummirnalde and of Kinkairne". These cattle were probably similar to those now preserved in a semi-wild state, for example at Chillingham in Northumberland.

A number of species disappeared from the region during the nineteenth century. The Black Rat (*Rattus rattus*), an accidentally introduced species known from Scotland since at least the sixteenth century, was commonly but apparently gradually replaced by the more recently introduced (also inadvertently) Brown Rat (*Rattus norbegicus*).   The *New Statistical Account* of 1845 records some late survivors e.g. "very seldom seen in Alloa", and "to occur" at St Ninians.   The last record appears to be of one killed near Stirling in 1886 (Sword, 1908).   Black Rats occur in Glasgow and other parts in Britain.

Some species became extinct as a result of persecution by gamekeepers.   The Pine Martin (*Martes martes*) used to be fairly common although, when extirpated as a resident, occasional wandering individuals were still observed.   One was seen at Callander in 1879 whilst the last record of one killed is at Balquhidder in 1880.   The species is apparently increasing in some parts of Scotland and may return to the region with the increase in afforestation and diminished persecution.   The Polecat (*Putorius putorius*) also was once common, but had probably disappeared from most of the area by 1860.   The last known record is a report of a sighting on Ben Ledi in 1894.   The species still occurs in parts of Wales.   The Wild Cat (*Felis catus*) disappeared from most of the region before 1850.   One was seen at Cromlix in the Braes of Doune in 1857 or 1858 whilst there is a suggestion that they lingered on in the Balquhidder area for a few more years.   It is pleasing to report that there is one recent record from Stirlingshire and in view of the recovery this species has made in the Highlands it seems probable that it may become more widespread here.

A welcome extinction has been that of the Muskrat (*Ondatra zibetnica*).   Six pairs were brought from Canada to found a fur farm near Braco in 1927.   Five of the pairs escaped, multiplied enormously and spread over a considerable area.   The species is very destructive and had already caused considerable damage to the banks of the loch at Carsebreck (M'Naughton, 1931) when it was subject to an intensive eradication campaign by the Department of Agriculture for Scotland.   The campaign was successful and the Muskrat has not been seen in the region for many years.

Species currently found in the Region

Five members of the Order Insectivora (*Hedgehogs, moles and shrews*) occur within the region.   Hedgehogs (*Erinaceus eiropaeus*) are common in most areas of open country with cover for nests and shelter.   There is evidence that this species increased greatly in the first part of the nineteenth century since early records suggest its distribution was much more local.   In the *New Statistical Account* of 1845, Hedgehogs are mentioned from many places and the species has apparently maintained a fairly common status since then.   This is in spite of its frequent appearance as a road casualty.   The Mole (*Talpa europea*) is generally distributed throughout the area and occurs up to 1700ft in the Ochils.   It is noticeably absent from the poorer soils where its prey, mainly earthworms, do not occur.   The Common Shrew (*Sorex araneus*) is generally very common and occurs up to 3000ft.   It is most abundant in dense, low herbage. The Pygmy Shrew (*Sorex minutus*) is less common but is much more abundant in moorland than woodland. The Water Shrew (*Neomys fodiens*) is a more local species, although perhaps commoner than the few published records indicate. It is typically found by clear streams and has an affinity for watercress beds.

Of the Order Chiroptera (bats) four species are known to occur. The first certain record in Scotland of Natterer's Bat (*Selysius nattereri*) was made at Aberfoyle (Placido, 1972) when four hibernating specimens were found in an underground roost. Daubenton's Bat (*Leucanoe daubentanii*) has also been recorded in the Aberfoyle district and is possibly more widespread than the few records suggest. This species hunts commonly over water. The Pipistrelle (*Pipistrellus pipistrellus*) is the commonest bat in the area and is very generally distributed with roosts of 200 or more being found in many villages and towns. The Long-eared Bat (*Plecotus ouritus*) is less abundant although there are scattered records from all parts of the region.

In the Order Lagomerpha (Rabbits and Hares) the Rabbit (*Orcytolagus cunicuius*) is a good example of a well established but introduced species, it was probably originally native only in the Iberian peninsula and southern France, (Brink, 1967). Rabbits certainly occurred within the region at the time of the *Old Statistical Account* of 1795 and may have been established several centuries before that. There are records of rabbit warrens at Crail in Fife in 1264. At the present time numbers in any one locality fluctuate greatly under the influence of the disease myxomatosis, which arrived in Britain in 1953. The native Brown Hare (*Lepus capensis*) is common and occurs throughout the whole of the low ground areas and on the hills up to 2000ft. It is less frequent on the hills where the Blue or Scottish Mountain Hare (*Lepus timidus*) occurs. This species is typically found in the northern parts of the region above 1000ft and the southern limits of its natural range in the east of Scotland occur within the area. Dr C J Henty has recently noted that on the Ochils this species is particularly common on the heather hags and that up to 40 have been seen at a time. Small colonies occur on most of the rock scars and screes whilst on the grassland the species is widely but sparsely distributed. Occasionally the Scottish Mountain Hare has been seen on the southern scarp of the Ochils down to the tree line at 500ft whilst on the gentler northern slopes it overlaps widely with the Rabbit between 700 and 1000ft. The species is usually on Heather (*Calluna vulgaris*) which forms the bulk of its diet. There is a feeling that the Scottish Mountain Hare has decreased in numbers in recent years although evidence is lacking.

There are several members of the Order Rodentia (Rodents) in the region. The Red Squirrel (*Sciurus vulgaris*) is thought to have become extinct here, probably because of forest felling (Gabourt, 1750), and there is good evidence of a large spread after reintroductions at the end of the eighteenth century (Harvie Brown, 1878). The Red Squirrel population has undergone a considerable decline this century and there are no records for much of the region during the last few years. There have been a number of recent sightings, however, near Bridge of Allan and Doune and in Strathyre. It is not certain how the decline in the Red Squirrel population is related to the spread of the Grey Squirrel (*Sciurus carolimensis*), a native of North America. Diseased and dying Red Squirrels have been observed at a site in England where Grey Squirrels had recently arrived (Goldsmith, 1971), supporting the suggestion that Grey Squirrels carry a virus to which they are tolerant but which is highly virulent in the Red Squirrel. This may be the cause of the disappearance of the Red Squirrel from many of its localities in the region. The Grey Squirrel has been introduced in various parts of the area and has spread out from these centres. Perhaps the first specimen recorded from the area was one trapped at Touch, near Stirling in 1923 (M'Naughton, 1923). At present the Grey Squirrel appears to occur most abundantly in the West of the region although C J Henty has noted that it is common in the woodlands at the base of the south slope of the Ochils.

The Bank Vole (*Clethrionomys glareolus*) is common wherever suitable cover of woodland, hedgerow and bracken is present. The Short-tailed Vole (*Microtus agrestis*) is also common and tends to occur in more open grassy places than the previous species. In the early 1950's there was a dramatic plague of this species in the Carron Valley (Charles, 1956) which may have been caused by the enclosure of previously grazed land for afforestation. The removal of sheep and cattle from these areas was thought to have provided a habitat for the Vole free from competition with any other herbivorous mammal. At the peak of the plague the numbers must have exceeded 400 Voles per acre in the most badly affected parts. The Voles caused considerable damage to trees and marked changes in the grassland vegetation. The plague lasted about 18 months and the numbers declined slowly back to more usual levels of around 80 Voles per acre. Similar plagues have been reported from the Border Country, the English Lake District and the Welsh Mountains. The Water Vole (*Arvicola amphibius*) is usually found near water as its name suggests. There are records from a few scattered localities in the region but it is believed to be rather more widespread than these indicate.

The Wood Mouse (*Apodemus sylvaticus*) is probably ubiquitous wherever tree or shrub cover occurs and is also found above the tree line at high altitudes. This species frequently survives on or, at least, supplements its diet from domestic larders and is a common victim of the mousetrap and domestic cat. The true House Mouse (*Mus musculus*), a long standing, accidentally introduced species, was reported as very common by Rintoul and Baxter in 1935, but has a less well-known distribution today. There are surprisingly few recent records and it is probably currently under-recorded. It certainly occurs at Muckhart and also near the University campus. The Brown Rat (*Rattus norgegicus*), an inadvertant introduction from the Continent in the eighteenth century, has become very common and is abundant all over the area. It is largely dependent on man and usually dwells near or within buildings.

In the Order Carnivora (meat eating mammals) the Fox (*Vulpes vulpes*) is a common and widespread species in the region. The Badger (*Meles meles*) has decreased since the beginning of the nineteenth century and is reported by Rintoul and Baxter as "Formerly common, now scarce and local". Its present distribution is not clear but there are indications that it is fairly widespread, if local, in the region. It is known to be totally extinct in Clackmannanshire but there is a recent record from near Stirling University Campus. The Stoat (*Mustela erminea*) and the Weasel (*Mustela nivalis*) are also both widespread. There is some evidence that the Stoat has declined in numbers since the advent of myxomatosis affected its major food source. The Weasel feeds on Voles and Mice and is found wherever these occur. A recent arrival is the Mink (*Mustela vision*) whose origin and present distribution in Scotland is well discussed by Cuthbert (1973). This American species was introduced in 1929 to establish a fur farming industry. The first Mink farms in this region were set up after the war and a thriving feral population has become established from a few escapes. Mink are widespread in the central part of the region and typically found near rivers or streams. It appears that fish — salmonids and eels — form the staple diet at all seasons and that animals and bird prey are of lesser importance. Earlier scares of the damage to wildlife that the animals might cause appear to a large extent unfounded and there is no doubt that the feral Mink are established as permanent members of our fauna.

The Otter (*Lutra lutra*) has been reduced in numbers since the beginning of the last century by persecution and, more recently by, pollution in lowland waters. Nevertheless there are recent records available from several places within the region.

Four species of hoofed mammals of the Order Artioductyla are recorded for the area. Wild Goats *(Capra hircus)* occur in a few places in the mountains of the north and west of the region. Their origin and present population size have been discussed in detail by Gibson (1972). It is clear that they have occurred constantly in the area since, at latest 1819 (on Ben Venue near Loch Katrine). Although originally descended from escaped domestic stock they are clearly now permanently established. The Fallow Deer (*Dama dama*) is a very old introduction and there are records dating back to 1283 of this species being kept in the Royal Park at Stirling. Feral populations now occur on both the western and eastern fringes of the region. The native Red Deer (*Cervus elaphus*) is found in the Highland parts of the region. Large numbers of Red Deer occur in the mountainous areas to the northwest and east of Strathyre (D MacCaskill, pers comm). The native Roe Deer (*Capreolus capreolus*) was driven from most of the region, except the mountains of the north-west, by the spread of man. The species recovered during the nineteenth century, probably because of the great increase in reafforestation. At present it is fairly well distributed throughout the region.

Several marine mammals have been recorded in the Upper part of the Forth estuary. In 1933 a young Grey Seal (*Halichoerus grypus*) was taken alive near Alloa and there are more recent records of this species (Corbet, 1971). The Common Seal (*Phoca vitulina*) still occurs frequently and D M Bryant recently observed several individuals at Alloa feeding on flatfish. Two Harp Seals (*Phoca groenlandica*) were captured at Grangemouth in 1903.

There are many reports of fossil whales in the peat of the Carse of Stirling. In 1819 the skeleton of a Blue Whale (*Sibbaldus musculus*), seventy-two feet long, was found on the Airthrey Estate, the site of Stirling University. There are also numerous reports of whales stranded in the upper Forth: Common Roqual (*Balaenoptera physalus*) near Alloa in 1808; Lesser Roqual (*Balaenoptera acutorostrata*) at Alloa, and a Bottle-nosed Whale (*Hyperoodon ampullatus*) at Grangemouth in 1894 and also "nearly as far up as Stirling". In 1932 a young male Beluga or White Whale (*Delphinapteras leucas*) was shot near the Cruive Dykes, Kildean, Stirling.

Porpoises (*Phocoena phocoena*) are recorded as going up "the whole of the tidal part of the Forth" and as being a "familiar sight in all parts of the estuary". There is a shortage of recent observations in the upper part of the Forth, but they are still seen lower down the estuary. A female Killer Whale (*Orcinus orca*) was captured at Alloa in 1932 and there are a number of earlier records. There are also records of Risso's Dolphin (*Grampus griseus*) at Kincardine-on-Forth in 1904 and in 1919 at Alloa, and the White-beaked Dolphin *(Legenorhynchus albirostris)* at Alloa in 1923 and 1933.

Sightings of all marine mammals have apparently become fewer in recent years, almost certainly reflecting the increase in pollution in the upper Forth. Happily the sources of much of this pollution have now been controlled but it is still too early for the river to be fully clean since a backlog of sediments results in a continuation of a low oxygen concentration. Over the next decade a considerable improvement in water purity may be anticipated and, in consequence upon the return of more fish, more large marine mammals are likely to be seen.

Future Work

It is inevitable that this account will be found to contain inaccuracies because there is a great shortage of recent records for many species. Such a dearth is by no means peculiar to the Stirling Region and the accurate recording of the distribution of mammals in this country is one of the aims of the Mammal Society of Great Britain. Some progress has been made in recent years towards the production of maps representing distributions of the 10km square.   For anyone with an interest in the study of mammals this scheme offers an outlet for any observations made in the field.   Record cards and details can be obtained from the Biological Records Centre, Monks Wood Experimental Station, Abbots Ripton, Huntingdon, and provisional distribution maps are already available.   Useful handbooks for mammal study are the works by Brink (1967) and Lawrence and Brown (1973).

ACKNOWLEDGEMENTS

I am indebted to Mr Carmen Placido for providing a number of recent records. Mr John Mitchell is especially thanked for much helpful advice and Dr D Bryant, Sue Fogden and Dr C J Henty for their helpful comments on the manuscript.   Dr D S McCluskey provided basic information on marine mammals.

REFERENCES

Barrett-Hamilton, G E H and Hinton, MAC   1910-1921   *A History of British Mammals,* London: Gurney and Jackson.   (Incomplete: Carnivora, Cetacea and Artiodactyla are missing).

Brink, van den F H   1967   *A Field Guide to the Mammals of Britain and Europe,* London: Collins.

Charles, W N   1956   'Effects of a vole plague in the Carron Valley, Stirlingshire'. *Scot. Forestry, 10,* 201 – 204.

Corbet, G B   1971   'Provisional distribution maps of British mammals'. *Mammal Rev., 1:* 95 – 142.

Cuthbert, J H   1973   'The origin and distribution of feral mink in Scotland'. *Mammal Rev., 3:* 97 – 103.

Gibson, J A   1972   'The Goats of the Clyde Area'. *Western Nat., 1:* 6 – 25.

Goldsmith, J G (ed)   1971   'Classified Notes'.   *Norfolk Bird and Mammal Report.* Norfolk Naturalists Trust and the Norfolk and Norwich Naturalists Society.

Harvie Brown, J A   1878   'The squirrel in Stirlingshire'.   *Trans. Stirling Natural History and Archeological Society, I,* 11 – 13.

Lawrence, M J and   1973   *Mammals of Britain.   Their Tracks, Trails and Signs.*
Brown, R W   London: Blandford Press.

M'Naughton, J   1923   'Notes on recent additions to the Smith Institute Collection'.   *Trans. Stirling Natural History and Archeological Society, 45,* 103.

M'Naughton, J   1931   'Musquash or Muskrat (*Fiber zibethicus*) in Strathallan'.   *Trans. Stirling Natural History and Archeological Society, 53,* 152 – 153.

Matthews, J H   1952   *British Mammals,* London: Collins.

The New Statistical Account of Scotland
                                        1795   Edinburgh: W Blackwood and Sons.

The New Statistical Account of Scotland
                                        1845   Edinburgh: W Blackwood and Sons.

Placido, C   1972   'New Records of Natterer's Bat (*Myotis nattereri*) in Scotland'.   *Western Nat. 1,* 59 – 62.

Rintoul, L J and   1935   *A Vertebrate Fauna of Forth.* Edinburgh and London:
Baxter, E V   Oliver and Boyd.

Southern, H N   1964   *The Handbook of British Mammals,* London: Blackwell.

Sword, J   1908   'The vertebrate fauna of King's Park'.   *Trans. Stirling Natural History and Archeological Society, 30,* 123 – 152.

CHAPTER 7

BIRDS OF THE STIRLING REGION

Introduction

The Stirling Region is situated largely within the central lowlands of Scotland, though a sector in the northwest lies beyond the Highland Boundary Fault. This high ground is essentially peripheral to the highland massif and the bird fauna is without a number of typical montane species. Similarly, many species of birds found in southern Britain are either absent or only occur thinly in the lowland areas of the Region. The bird communities are therefore rather depauperate representatives of highland and lowland bird communities developed more fully towards the north and south of Britain respectively. However not only does this situation encourage a wide spectrum of species which includes over 120 that breed, but also means that the northerly limit of the distribution of many southern species, and the southern limit of some northerly species occur within the region. This confers a special interest on the status of such species and the changes in status which have been observed.

The River Forth and its tributaries dominate the area and provide waterfowl habitats ranging from upland streams to a muddy estuary. The agricultural lands of the valleys are a wintering ground for large numbers of grey geese, while the woodlands on the adjacent hillsides provide opportunities for productive breeding populations of many common birds and some relatively healthy predator populations. The uplands include the Ochil Hills and Campsie Fells and the high mountains and moorlands in the north west. In all these areas lochs are frequent and often provide a focus for bird life, either as breeding sites or as wintering or roosting areas. The birds of the Region will be described in relation to the six broad habitat types of Rivers and Estuaries, Lochs, Farmland, Woodland, Mountains and Moorland, and the Environs of Human Dwellings and Industrial Sites. The account will describe the most important changes in status of bird species since satisfactory records became available, though will concentrate on changes which have occurred since the publication of the major work on the birds of the region, Rintoul and Baxter's *Vertebrate Fauna of Forth* (1935). Also current status will be described and in order to give this a quantitative element when appropriate, the abundance of breeding species will be described by their percentage occurrence within the 10km squares in the Region. For this purpose entries in both columns 2 and 3 of the British Trust for Ornithology Atlas Survey, 1968 to 1972, indicating both probable and proven breeding, will be presented as a percentage of the total 22 squares which lie substantially (> 50%) in the Stirling Region Survey Area.

Rivers and Estuaries

The principle states of river development are all present in the Stirling Region and hold characteristic bird communities.   The swift-flowing upper reaches mostly lie in the north-west, though both the River Devon and Allan Water rise in the Ochil Hills and a few minor streams come from the Campsie Fells.   These streams hold Dipper, Pied and Grey Wagtails, and Common Sandpiper in summer with pairs of Mallard and some Teal in the marshy fringes.   The highest densities of Dippers and Wagtails occur in the middle reaches, for example on the Devon between Glendevon and Dollar.   Laying begins earlier in the Dipper on lower ground and is usually more successful, though late layings close, to towns have low success rate due to the depredations of egg collectors (G Shaw, pers. comm.).   Less frequent species include the Goosander which now breeds in 41% of the 10km squares of the Region and is no longer confined to south Perthshire as was the case early in the century.   Herons fish in the shallows while Sand Martins may nest where suitable sandy banks occur.   The Kingfisher has been proved to breed in only one area since the harsh winter of 1962-63, however summering records are becoming more frequent and if the current series of mild winters continues, a more widespread recolonisation must soon occur.   The pattern of colonisation and extinction of the Kingfisher over the last hundred years is typical of a species at the fringe of its range where adverse weather conditions can drastically influence populations.

Downstream the rivers widen and their waters become turbid, and are used mostly by waterfowl and gulls.   Flocks of Goldeneye can be seen in winter with smaller numbers of Goosander, Merganser and Cormorant.

Mallard and Teal, particularly concentrate during harsh winter weather on riverside pools where moving water keeps them free of ice.   The scrubby river fringes hold Sedge Warblers and Reed Buntings which are more restricted in the Region to their typical habitats than is now the case elsewhere in Britain.

Near Stirling the Forth is considered estuarine though the tidal changes involve a back-up of fresh water rather than an inflow of saline water.   Close to the town the banks are steep and little used by birds.   However, Whooper Swans roost on the river in the winter and up to 70 Mute Swans reside at Cambus, as the only substantial and regular remnant of the wildfowl flocks that used to be attracted to the distillery outfall (Thom, 1969).   In November 1962 peaks of 1554 Mallard and 4390 Teal were attracted to this supply of waste grain.   The duck evidently dispersed after the discharge was stopped in 1963 to prevent the deoxygenation of downstream waters in summer.   Recent observations have shown that Teal flocks may occasionally still reach 1000 though they do not persist, probably due to the heavy and often indiscriminate shooting.   Common and particularly Black Headed Gulls haunt the river outside the breeding season.   The Shelduck regularly feeds and also breeds in notably high numbers as far inland as Cambus, which is the upper limit of the inflow of saline waters.   Spring counts indicate breeding concentrations of national importance (Jenkins, 1972) and a clarification of the actual breeding population is required.

The river banks are fringed in places by reed beds and abandoned grazing marshes between Stirling and Kincardine Bridge.   Neither habitat holds the size of bird populations that their structure would encourage one to believe.   The former are probably unsuitable because of the deep litter layer covering both small pools and mud, and through their regular flooding.   The grazing marshes usually have a few Lapwing and Mallard and some Short Eared Owls in winter.   The occasional Yellow Wagtail still nests near Grangemouth though records indicate that the decline of this species was already well under way by the 1920's (Rintoul and Baxter, 1935).   However, there are two areas beside the lower Forth where birds may gather in large numbers, namely by the Black Devon mouth near Alloa and on the pools behind the seawall at Skinflats.   The value of both these sites derives ultimately from the productivity of the mudflats between Kincardine and Grangemouth.   Therefore they hold rather few birds at low tide, though waders generally associated with freshwater may remain, such as the Sandpiper.   At high tide many birds gather to feed and roost when they have been forced from more favoured areas by the rising tide.   In addition to the regular waders, Little Stint, Curlew, Sandpiper, Spotted Redshank, Greenshank and Ruff appear in small numbers and Green and Wood Sandpipers have occurred in most recent years.   There have been occasional records of Nearctic Waders such as Pectoral Sandpiper and the scarcer Palaearctic waders such as Red Necked Phalarope and Temminck's Stint.   The marsh at the Black Devon Mouth held a Common Sandpiper in January 1972 in a year when they were unusually abundant as wintering birds in the south of Britain (Prater, 1971) though this was the first Scottish record in winter.

There is a large area of estuarine mud at Skinflats, and several bird species occur in numbers which make them of regional or in some cases national or international significance Bryant (1974).   The flocks of Knot may exceed 20,000 in winter comprising more that 5% of the British population   (Ballantyne, 1973, also Grieve, 1972).   Shelduck exceeded 2,000 in the Grangemouth area (including mud immediately to the east of the Docks) on a recent midwinter count, making a substantial contribution to northwest European stocks.   Pintail are only regular on the Forth Estuary or in the Stirling Region at Skinflats with peak flocks of 100 to 150 birds.   Dunlin reach 8000 and substantial numbers of Golden and Grey Plover, Curlew, Redshank, Black Headed Gulls and Mallard use the area.   A small flock of Black Tailed Godwits is also probably resident in autumn and most winters.   These flocks of feeding and roosting waders attract predators in winter, Merlin, Sparrowhawk, Peregrine as well as Kestrels, Barn and Short-eared Owls hunt these flocks or those of passerines feeding on the saltings.   Twite, Linnet and some Snow Buntings are joined by Greenfinch, Chaffinch and House Sparrow along the tidal strand-line.   Breeding passerines are not abundant, however Meadow Pipit and Reed Bunting are the commonest species.   Mallard, Shelduck, Lapwing, Ringed Plover and Redshank largely complete the list of breeders.

The open river near Kincardine Bridge is notable in two respects.   Firstly the area is attractive to true seabirds and secondly, it provides a refuge for diving duck when their favoured freshwater haunts freeze.   Thus Fulmars and Kittiwakes (up to 500) are recorded and the regular Cormorants (up to 150) and Mergansers (up to 500) may be jointed byTufted Duck which reached totals of 2,300 off Kennet Pans in the harsh February of 1963. Pochard and Goldeneye also regularly exceed 200 in winter and Scaup occur.   In autumn Sandwich and Common Terns are present with attendant Arctic Skuas and sometimes a few Great Skuas.   Occasionally Pomarine Skua, Little Gull, Roseate, Little and Black Terns are seen and there is a single record of Gull Billed Tern.   There was a recent extraordinary record of four White Pelicans, though their wild origin must be in doubt.   Finally mention should be made of visitors which have occurred once or in small numbers mostly in winter such as Avocet, Sanderling, Common Scoter, Smew, Shag, Red Throated Diver and Black Necked Grebe.   The Slavonian Grebe is no longer recorded frequently near Alloa (Rintoul and Baxter, 1935) but is now confined to the outer Firth.

Lochs

The diversity and abundances of waterfowl on the lochs of the Region is related to their situation and successional maturity.   The principal hill lochs and reservoirs of Voil, Lubnaig, Katrine, Carron Valley and Vennacher generally hold rather few birds and these mostly concentrate by the inlets of shoreline.   In contrast the eutrophic lowland waters of Menteith, Carsebreck and Gartmorn Dam provide rich food supplies and also lie by major river valleys, the traditional routes of wildfowl movements, and consequently hold substantial waterfowl populations.

In winter the larger upland lochs have Mallard, Teal, Wigeon, Pochard, Tufted Duck and Goldeneye with some Goosander and Red Breasted Merganser, although the maximum count of any species will only be numbered in tens.   Graylag Geese and Whooper Swans also use these lochs in small numbers.   Some of the smaller hill lochs have fringing and emergent vegetation, such as Loch Mahaich, and they may hold over a hundred Mallard, Teal and Coot, according to season, as well as a variety of other species.   High counts on some waters such as the North Third Reservoir, may partly reflect their use as roosting sites for duck feeding in the Forth Valley, rather than their quality as a food source, and at times Mallard and Teal may be numbered in hundreds.

Breeding waterfowl are similarly scarce on the higher lochs, though this has evidently not always been the case.   Before the partial drainage of Loch Mahaick after the Second World War, Pintail, Pochard and Shoveler bred regularly (Rintoul and Baxter, 1935, Atkinson Willes, 1963).   Now they are scarce anywhere in the Region let alone in that loch. However, the Canada Goose bred at Mahaick in 1971 apparently for the first time in the Stirling Region and the Red Breasted Merganser nests by the large hill lochs of the north west such as Lubnaig and Voil (32% occurrence as a breeding bird in 10km squares). The Achray Reserve of the Wildfowlers Association of Great Britain and Ireland at Loch Vennachar is reported as a good breeding centre (W.A.G.B.I. Annual Report, 1971). Although the situation is confused by artificial introductions, current breeders include Pochard, Widgeon and Grelag Geese. The attempts to introduce Barnacle Geese and European White-fronted Geese at the reserve must be questioned on ecological grounds, as these species hardly nest in the wild state south of the Arctic Circle. It would be useful to clarify whether such introductions are intended to be ornamental or whether they are to provide sport for fowlers in the future. If the latter is the case, a more substantial contribution to conservation of wildfowl stocks could be achieved by concentrating on native Greylags. Also, if other breeding aliens such as Canada and Egyptian Geese are a guide, the Greylag would provide better sport.

The Dabchick has been noted in spring up to 850ft in the Trossachs and breeds widely. A Slavonian Grebe was reported on Loch Voil in early spring 1969. The main established range of the Red Throated Diver extends to within about twenty miles of the north of the Region. However a pair has attempted to breed in the northwest although success has not occurred due to disturbance by fishermen. Breeding gulls include four species though it is remarkable that the now widespread Common Gull was unknown as a breeding species up to at least the mid 1930's, (Rintoul and Baxter, 1935). The inland breeding of Lesser Black Backed and Herring Gulls on Flanders Moss is notable. Both breeding colonies have increased and the Lesser Black Backed Gull colony held about 1500 pairs in 1971 (C Henty, pers. comm.) in contrast to a few hundred in the early 1930's (Rintoul and Baxter, 1935). The Black Headed Gull has some large colonies such as that by Loch Mahaick and this species also has increased in recent years. The increase of all these gulls can probably be attributed to improved overwinter survival arising from the exploitation of food supplies associated with man's activities.

The lowland Lochs hold large numbers of duck, Coot and roosting geese and some swans. The highest waterfowl count anywhere in the region may usually be made in autumn at Carsebreck where more than 3000 of both Pinkfooted and Greylag Geese roost on the loch complex in company with hundreds each of Mallard, Widgeon and Coot. Gartmorn Dam and Airthrey Loch between them hold most of the Tufted Duck in midwinter, sometimes totalling over 1000 birds. On Airthrey Loch a sudden freeze will cause Tufted Duck numbers to drop from 200-400 to 10 overnight, although the Mallard will remain roosting on the ice. The return to the loch after a freeze in 1973 followed on the second day after a quick thaw, indicating the high mobility of these duck flocks and suggesting a nearby hard weather refuge which could be the Forth near Kincardine. However now that the grain supply from Cambus has ceased, movement may be further down the estuary which would account for the absence of observations of large Tufted Duck flocks off Kennet Pans in the last few years. Mallard and Teal generally favour Gartmorn Dam, while Widgeon concentrate at Carsebreck by the Allan Water. Pochard and Goldeneye are often abundant on Menteith and Gartmorn, and Goosander turn up widely in small numbers mostly at the more westerly lochs. Less common species such as Gadwall and Pintail probably occur on fresh-water sites most frequently at Carsebreck in ones and twos though they are seen elsewhere. Rintoul and Baxter (1935) refer to parties of up to thirty Gladwall on Carsebreck but such numbers have not been recorded in recent years. In early 1973 both Smew and American Widgeon occurred, the former being irregular but the latter was the first record for the Region. The Shoveler is most frequent on passage especially in spring and occurs only rarely in winter inland. There are a few inland records of Long Tailed Duck.

Mallard, Teal and Tufted Duck all breed on the lowland waters, most commonly on the lochs that support the most wildfowl in winter. Several lochs hold single pairs of Widgeon although Gladwall and Shoveler have recently been proved to breed only at single sites. The Pintail must now be classed only as a probable breeding species. The Tufted Duck (64% occurrence) and Pochard (14% occurrence) both colonised the region in the 1870's though the former is now much more numerous as a breeding bird. Possibly the shortage of waters with a wide *Phragmites* fringe makes the area unsuitable for nesting Pochard or possibly submerged macrophyte growth is inadequate. The Shelduck has been recorded in spring at the Lake of Menteith and this may reflect the national trend of colonisation of inland waters (Parslow, 1967). Gartmorn Dam is the most productive duck breeding site and also has several pairs of Great Crested Grebe, though they mostly leave the lake in winter and move to inshore waters. Colonisation of the Forth valley occurred in 1880 with a pair breeding on Loch Coulter, although this site is no longer occupied. The northwestern limit of the breeding range in Britain is roughly coincident in the west with the Highland Boundary Fault, with breeding on the Lake of Menteith though nowhere to the northwest but widely to the south where suitable habitats occur, especially south of the Forth. The distribution limit now appears stable and may represent an ecological limitation imposed by habitat and food supply. The Dabchick is common and is especially abundant on Airthrey Loch. The Black Necked Grebe has been observed at a suitable breeding site in the breeding season though was not subsequently known to breed. On the lowland lochs the Coot shares with the Moorhen the status of the most abundant breeding species. A study carried out on Airthrey Loch in 1971 revealed that 16 pairs were present and that chick mortality was one important factor in determining the autumn Coot population (Downie 1972). This mortality was closely linked with the weight of eggs at laying such that the heavier clutches enjoyed a better survival.

The Water Rail is now very scarce although Rintoul and Baxter (1935) reported breeding in south west Perthshire. No evidence of nesting was obtained during the B.T.O. Atlas survey, though a few birds have been seen recently both within and outside the breeding season. Cormorants occur regularly in winter. Herons breed at several colonies and one of the largest heronries in Scotland is established near the Lake of Menteith and has about 30 pairs

(J Mitchell, pers. comm.).   They may often be seen fishing the loch fringes and when these freeze Herons may move to the fast running streams on high ground or to the coast to find open water.   The most notable breeding species is a recolonist, after persecution and disturbance drove it out of the Region by the 1840's.   In 1972 a pair of Ospreys attempted to breed and in the following year three young were successfully reared.   This breeding is the first to occur south of the Highland Boundary Fault in the recent phase of recolonisation, and is thus a particularly significant consolidation of the Scottish population.

The loch fringes are often used by feeding and bathing waders.   Usually these will be local breeding birds such as Lapwing, Oystercatcher and Redshank.   In autumn their numbers rise and species such as Snipe become more frequent especially when water levels are low.   Generally the closer to the Forth Estuary the more the lochs are visited by migrant waders.   Wood and Green Sandpipers are occasionally recorded though surprisingly the Common Sandpiper is conspicuous by its scarcity.   Widespread as a breeding bird, it infrequently visits loch shores on passage, presumably because the area is not in the catchment area for Scandanavian immigrants, and most of the Scottish birds move along rivers and coast.

The remaining birds associated with freshwater lochs include the aerial feeding Swift, Swallow and Martins.   They are most conspicuous on spring and autumn passage, though they may feed over water at any time during the breeding season especially during inclement weather.

Farmland

The rich land of the Carse of Stirling and of the Allan Water and Devon Valleys has encouraged the clearance of woodlands for agriculture.   These areas are therefore of an open aspect with a large proportion given to the production of cereals.   In contrast the wooded terrain of the foothills is devoted mostly to mixed farming or entirely to livestock.

The distribution of wintering Geese and Swans is a close reflection of the distribution of these agricultural practices.   The primary food source utilised by geese and swans on arrival in autumn is spilled grain on the stubble fields.   Thus they are found on the arable land of the Forth and Allan Water Valleys particularly associated with Carsebreck, the Carse of Stirling and the Flanders Moss area.   When the stubbles are ploughed or the waste grain depleted the geese concentrate in the west of the Region and Greylag particularly take to grass.   Pinkfeet and Whooper Swan mainly feed on unlifted potatoes if they remain in the eastern sector.   In harsh snowy weather both species may resort to turnips where, in a situation of conflict with agricultural interests, they can be seen in mixed flocks with sheep. In late winter and spring both geese and the swans feed on grass or winter sown cereals.   The pattern of food utilisation therefore broadly resembles that described by Newton and Campbell (1974) for geese feeding in the Loch Leven area. The Bean Goose appears in small numbers every few years. The largest herds of Whooper Swans occur around Stirling, peaking in recent years at over 100 birds, though smaller groups are seen throughout the Region feeding on wet meadows and roosting on rivers or lochs.

The most conspicuous species of the fields in the winter are Black Headed and Common Gulls, Starlings, Wood Pigeons, Lapwings, Rooks and Jackdaws. A roost of about 10,000 Rooks and Jackdaws has been reported from Muiravonside (Munro, 1971). The Black Headed Gull is a bird of the ploughlands, while the Common Gull usually feeds on grassland as elsewhere in Britain (Vernon, 1970). Redwings and Fieldfares also feed on grass especially in late winter. Finch flocks comprised of more than 100 birds are usually of Chaffinch, Greenfinch and Linnet. In favoured localities Tree Sparrows can occur in similar numbers though the species was not proved to breed in Clackmannanshire until 1968. There has been a substantial local increase over the last thirty years and nesting now occurs in 73% of the 10km squares of the Region, with land over 100ft being avoided. The House Sparrow is very common on farmland, while the Goldfinch is sparsely distributed. The conspicuous appearance of Goldfinches in spring suggests that the species is a partial migrant in the area as it is elsewhere in Britain (Newton, 1970), though birds are certainly present in winter, occasionally even on high ground such as in Gleneagles. The Brambling is most often recorded feeding in mixed flocks with Chaffinches in stubble or kale fields.

The Crow family has two species of local interest in farmland areas. In winter small numbers of Hooded Crows (and Carrion x Hooded hybrids) haunt a few favoured lowland sites, though they are but a remnant of the large flocks of the 19th Century. Hybrid crows have been seen in circumstances which suggested breeding on the Ochils and to the south where Hooded Crows do not normally breed. The magpie is mainly a bird of the towns, although tall hedgerows and copses outside towns in remarkably discrete and constant localities. The species has certainly increased recently and although it remains rather scarce away from the town fringes, it can no longer be described as extinct or on the verge of extinction as a breeder in Clackmannanshire (Rintoul and Baxter, 1935).

The Stock Dove is regular in agricultural areas in winter and as a breeding bird but has possibly declined recently. Pheasants are common and often augmented by hand reared birds for shooting purposes. The Partridge maintains higher spring population densities than in some intensively farmed southern counties. The Yellowhammer is common on farmland and on hillslopes and is conspicuous at all seasons sometimes gathering in large flocks. In contrast the Corn Bunting is most prominent in the breeding season. The difference in summer populations between the Carse of Stirling and the environs of Loch Leven only 20 miles to the east is striking. In the latter area males may be perched on fence posts every few hundred yards along the roadside, though nearer Stirling rarely more than a few are seen during the course of a journey through the area. Winter flocking does occur in some areas, illustrated by an observation of over 60 birds near Grangemouth. This reflects a large but local breeding population south of the River Forth.

The Stirling Region is one of a few areas of mainland Britain where the Corncrake is still established. It is most abundant in the Forth Valley to the west of Stirling, although it still breeds sporadically to the east of the town. It suffers from the influence of grass cutting machinery in many of its usual habitats, so that any attempt to breed in fields used for silage preparation are rapidly eliminated. In contrast breeding in fields of hay may be successful or partially successful (Gilmour, 1972). There is a tradition of growing Timothy hay for seed on the Carse of Stirling and as this is cut late in the year it may be this feature which has allowed the species to persist in the area. A more remarkable aspect of these Corncrake populations has been the occurrence of calling birds in fields of winter sown cereals in at least two recent years. If these crops provide conditions suitable for successful breeding, therein lies an opportunity for the continued survival and possible spread of the Corncrake in the face of modern farm practices.

The breeding bird community on farm land in the Region has a rather low diversity when compared with published records from some southern farms. Typical southern species such as the Nightingale and Lesser Whitethroat are naturally absent, although near Doune the Red Legged Partridge has shown signs of persisting after introduction. However several species which could be expected in small numbers such as the Blackcap are only present in presumed optimal woodland habitats and not in the marginal sites which occur on farmland. The absence of the Blackcap from these sites must reflect its current low population in an area towards the northern perimeter of the species range. The rather low diversity of passerine breeding birds contrasts with the high densities of breeding wading birds. The Lapwing is the commonest species, while the Oystercatcher is widespread in river valleys and in places occurs right up to the edge of the sheep walks more than a mile from the nearest river. The occurrences of inland nesting is a recent phenomenon in many areas (Buxton, 1961; Heppleston, 1972) though it was already widespread as in inland breeder in the Stirling area more than forty years ago (Rintoul and Baxter, 1935). The Curlew breeds on grassland and the Redshank may be represented by several pairs even on a wet corner of a pasture. Similarly the Snipe takes to isolated damp areas in otherwise arable areas as well as the more usual habitat of extensive wet meadows.

The predatory birds of farmland are numerically dominated by the Kestrel though in late summer many of these birds move to the moors to exploit peak vole populations. In winter the Merlin is regular over agricultural country with peaks in observation frequency occurring in October and February suggesting movement through the Region. The Sparrowhawk can often be seen, most commonly in the more wooded country of the upper Forth and Teith and around the fringes of upland areas, with an expected peak in observations after the breeding season in September and October. Indeed in wooded country the frequency of sightings of Kestrel and Sparrowhawk in winter may be equal. The Buzzard hunts over the more wooded farmland in winter particularly where the area is adjacent to a forest. The Peregrine is not infrequent though it is unfortunate that this habit of feeding in farmland areas brings it into contact with prey potentially carrying high loads of agrochemical pollutants. It is probably no coincidence that a Peregrine which was observed near Dunblane to mistime a stoop and crash fatally into a tree was subsequently found to be carrying considerable organochlorine, polychlorinated biphenyl and mercury residues (Ratcliffe, 1972). The Hen Harrier is commoner on the rougher farmland in the west, being seen only rarely to the east of Stirling on low ground. Among these raptors only the Kestrel and Sparrowhawk breed in truly farmland habitats though to these must be added the widespread Barn and Tawny Owls, the former breeding in 65% of the 10km squares in the Region and the latter in 90% in the recent BTO Atlas survey.

In addition the following species also occur on farmland, Mallard, Feral Pigeon, Skylark, Meadow Pipit, Pied Wagtail, Dunnock, Wren, Swallow and Martins Blackbird, Mistle and Song Thrush, Whinchat, Robin, Great, Coal and Long Tailed Tit, Reed Bunting, Redpoll, Bullfinch, Sedge and Grasshopper Warbler and Whitethroat. The last species has been scarce since 1968 though is currently showing signs of recovery, particularly in optimal sites.

The visible passage of migrant birds is not an outstanding feature of the Stirling Region with the exception of Thrush and wildfowl movements. Redwings and Fieldfares fill many of the berry-laden hedgerow hawthorns in the space of a few days in October and then equally suddenly move on westwards. Visible movements of geese largely involve flights in the daily routine, though movements observed from the mountains in the north in spring and autumn are probably of more extensive migrations. Meadow Pipit, Skylark, Starling, Stock Dove, Wood Pigeon, Swift, Swallow, Martins, and Chaffinch are the only other species regularly seen flying in a manner which suggests long distance movement with the bulk of these occurring in autumn and early winter, although the Lapwing will also move in response to prevailing conditions.

A recent observation of 20 Willow Warblers in September by the River Teith feeding in a manner strongly recalling that of known migrants at east-coast observatories perhaps suggests that there may be important channels of migratory movements for other species along major river valleys or through the mountain passes of Strathyre and Gleneagles. Harvie Brown and Brickley (1892) felt assured that there was a regular flight line between the Firths of Forth and Clyde and mentioned Whimbrel and Cormorants in this context. (See also Clark 1912). Occasionally the peripheral effects of seabirds wrecks are felt in the autumn 1969 when a few dead Gullimotes were found inland near Drymen (Stewart, 1970).

Woodland

For the purpose of this section woodland will include the woodland edge, forestry plantation at all growth stages, scattered hillside and parkland trees, extensive scrubland areas and felled woodland among other trees, as well as the typical woodland habitat.

Some fine oakwoods occur in the Aberfoyle area and in Strathyre while some woods in the Stirling area have a high proportion of oaks.   The western oakwood bird communities are similar to some of those on Loch Lomond side described by Williamson (1974).   The Chaffinch is the dominant species with Wren, Robin and Willow Warbler subdominant.   The Blue and Great Tits and the Wood Warbler are in a lower order of abundance while Redstart and Tree Pipit are well represented.   The last two species breed in 82% and 95% respectively of the 10km squares in the Region, though outside the oakwoods the Redstart in particular is absent from many apparently suitable habitats.   In recent years the Pied Flycatcher has occasionally bred (Campbell, 1965) and may be further encouraged by the provision of nest-boxes in the older woods.   The first recorded breeding in Clackmannanshire was in 1957.

Most of the deciduous woodland in the region includes not only Oak but Sycamore, Beech and Ash and some have a well developed shrub layer including Rhododendron.   In these woods Chaffinch, Wren, Blue Tit, and Blackbird each account for 10% of the community while Willow Warbler, Robin, and Dunnock each make up 5% of the community (Henty, unpubl.).   Surprisingly the Coal Tit is slightly more frequent than the Great Tit, although the current sequence of abundance of the three commonest tits in mixed deciduous woodland, Blue, Coal and Great, is the same as that implied by Rintoul and Baxter (1935) for early this century.   The Willow Warbler is the only common summer migrant in these woodlands, the Blackcap and Garden Warbler being confined in woods to those with a rich shrub layer, such as Hermitage wood on the Airthrey Estate.   The Garden Warbler however can be quite common in scrubland areas even where there are no mature trees and thus was recorded in 68% of the 10km squares as a breeding bird, while the Blackcap was only reported in 55% of the squares in the region.   The Spotted Flycatcher occurs in most woods (100% occurrence in 10km squares) and is the only one of the less common summer visitors to appear every year in the valley oakwoods of the southern Ochils, in spite of a wealth of old trees.   Rintoul and Baxter (1935) also recorded the Wood Warbler in these glens but now this species is to be found only rarely though the occasional Pied Flycatcher is a new-comer (Campbell, 1965).   The Wood Warbler and Chiffchaff are ecologically segregated such that the former selects stands of large beech without ground cover while the latter prefers woods with rhododendron (see Meiklejohn, 1953).   The Starling is a common hole nesting species though usually it feeds on open ground outside the woods.   The Bullfinch and Long-tailed Tit are birds of the woodland edge and scrubland during the breeding season and only afterwards move into the mature woods.   All three species of Woodpecker have been recorded in the Stirling Region though the occurrence of the Lesser Spotted Woodpecker in the Aberfoyle area in 1968 was the first accepted record for Scotland (Mitchell, 1970).   It has been tentatively suggested that these (and subsequent) observations may have referred to immigrant birds from Scandanavia rather than northward moving British stock.

The Great Spotted Woodpecker reappeared as a breeding bird in 1906. The species is now widespread in the area (77% breeding occurrence) particularly in birch woods and parkland though also in conifer woods. There is an undated and possibly doubtful record of the Green Woodpecker in Tor Wood, Dunipace before 1934 (Rintoul and Baxter, 1935) which may have heralded the subsequent colonisation. Breeding was proven in Stirlingshire for the first time in 1960 and in Clackmannanshire in 1965 (Fisher, 1967). This Woodpecker is now as common along the south Ochil scarp as in many of its traditional habitats in southern Britain. At least 6 pairs were established between Dollar Glen and Wood Hill, Tillicoultry in 1968. The species now breeds in 59% of the 10km squares in the Region, however in the west several sites which were formally tenanted no longer hold breeding birds even while others further to the north are being colonised (Mitchell, in press). This rolling pattern of colonisation and extinction results in the range but not the total populations increasingly in the west, in contrast to the apparently stable population in the east of the Region. The Hawfinch was recorded occasionally in the 1920's in spring on the Touch and Blairdrummond estates near Stirling and on a few occasions recently. However it was certainly a surprise when a pair nested successfully near Bridge of Allan in 1973. The species also nests very sparsely just beyond the northern boundary of the Region. The fortunes of the Willow Tit contrasts with these increasing populations. It bred in many places in the west up to the late 19th Century (Rintoul and Baxter, 1935), though it is now apparently absent. Other southern species such as Marsh Tit, Nightingale, Nuthatch and Lesser Whitethroat have occurred once or twice and the pair of Golden Orioles which settled for a short time near Airth in 1969 will probably remain an exceptional record, though singles have occurred previously. In the last two years in late autumn Rooks, with some Jackdaws and even the occassional Black Headed Gull have been observed taking acorns from the tops of Oaks near Stirling and Dollar. (See Holyoak 1972, and Vernon 1972).

The greater proportion of woodland in the region is coniferous. The major forests of the Carron Valley, Achray, Loch Ard and Strathyre now have a wide age range of stands each with characteristic bird communities. The initial heath phase holds the dominant Meadow Pipit and Red Grouse where planting has been on heather moorland. The Grouse increase after planting due to the luxuriant heather growth, though after about 8 years this species is eliminated. The phase when trees pass from the heath to the scrub and early woodland phase comprise the most favourable nesting conditions for the Hen Harrier. The recolonisation of mainland Britain by this predator is an example of one of a very few predatory birds with a dynamic and expanding population. Initial colonisation occurred at the time of the last war probably aided by the concurrent relaxation of gamekeeping and the provision of secure breeding sites in the Trossachs forests. At the present time the breeding range extends north and eastwards from the Aberfoyle area and birds have been observed in the Ochil and Campsie Fells in summer. Of the 10km squares with much of their area over 500 feet, 50% are occupied by breeding Hen Harriers. The Short-eared Owl also breeds widely in young conifer plantations (73% occurrence in 10km squares) and has increased with the spread of forestry.   When voles were particularly abundant in the Carron Valley, 30 to 40 pairs bred in an area of 3500 acres (Locke, 1955).   The maturing plantations pass through a scrub stage which is favourable for Willow Warbler, Redpoll, Thrushes and Yellow-hammer.   Thereafter species such as Stonechat which are found in the plantations in the west are eliminated and Bullfinch, Linnet, and Whitethroat decline.   At the final woodland stage the Chaffinch is dominant along with Tits of three species though only the Coal Tit is abundant.   The Goldcrest is frequent while the Wren occurs commonly at most stages. The Jay is widespread in the west though generally sparse to the south and east of Stirling. The Long-eared Owl is scarce, breeding in 18% of the 10km squares.   The Sparrowhawk makes use of the mature conifers for nesting especially selecting Larch for the nest site. Among the Accipitridae the Sparrowhawk (82%) is second to the Kestrel (95%) in the frequency of breeding in the 10km squares of the region.   Superficially the Sparrowhawk appeared to decline little during the last fifteen years when populations in south eastern Britain declined so dramatically (Newton, 1972b).   However regular counts of nesting pairs in Loch Ard Forest showed that a decline took place from the level of 8 or 9 breeding pairs up to the late 1950's (R Rose, unpubl.).   The crash occurred about 1960 and within two years the Sparrowhawk had almost gone and no birds nested up to 1970.   These observations are difficult to reconcile with the widespread breeding records in the B.T.O. Atlas survey (1968 and 1972) and the regular observations away from the nest in the late 1960's. However on examination of the Atlas data for the Region revealed that only 20% of the Sparrowhawk breeding records involved evidence of young being present in the nest whereas the equivalent figure for the Kestrel was 60%.   While such an analysis is open to bias it provides suggestive evidence that observations of Sparrowhawks may have been of non-breeding or unsuccessful breeding, or winter visiting individuals.   Thus even though the fall in breeding success was insufficient to eliminate the species, there is evidence that a fall in breeding success occurred though rather later than elsewhere in Britain.   Since 1970 there has been a partial recovery in breeding performance.   The Buzzard enjoys a widespread distribution in the area, breeding in 77% of the 10km squares.   However, fluctuations occur almost annually and the three to four pairs reported in Clackmannan in 1968, have been reduced to a single possible breeder in 1973, possibly partly associated with a keeper being employed on the Estate holding the most regular nesting pair.

The Buzzard requires mature trees or cliff sites for nesting and mostly breeds in hillside woods and copses and hunts over moorlands and plantations.   The species has increased markedly since the last war.   Formerly the Buzzard was uncommon in the valleys of Loch Voil, Lubnaig and Katrine (J Mitchell, pers. comm.) though now it is widespread there. This appears to again be mainly due to the relaxation of persecution by gamekeepers, however it must be noted that the plantations have encouraged population increases of voles which probably provide a more abundant food supply than when these areas were under sheep and these may in turn have facilitated the Buzzard population expansion.   In autumn and winter the Buzzard can be seen soaring over lowland areas and a particularly favoured site lies immediately to the west of Stirling. At this site and on the south western sector of the Ochils where breeding Buzzards are scarce or absent, a regular pattern of sightings is apparent. The months of August to November usually produce many records with up to six birds together. They then become increasingly difficult to see until February, after which a slight further peak occurs in April. This pattern could reflect an autumn passage with subsequent return in spring, however Buzzards in Britain rarely move far (Mead, 1973). The mid winter decline probably reflects mortality which even now is caused partly by keepering activities. This is illustrated by the receipt by the Police of six Buzzard, and single Sparrowhawk and Hen Harrier carcasses from the Cromlix Estate near Dunblane in late 1972. The Buzzards concerned in the incident all contained sufficiently high gut concentrations of Phosdrin to cause death. (Nature Concervancy, 1973, unpubl. report). This demonstrates a common method of eliminating birds of prey, by the application of poison to rabbit carcasses and putting them out as carrion. Combined with the similarly illegal pole trap and shooting these causes of death constitute a substantial threat to predator populations. The increase in sightings in spring probably reflect the movements of young birds as they seek suitable nesting sites. The Crossbill is represented in Scotland by two races, favouring mature Scots Pine, and the European race often feeding in Larch in irruption years. The continuing maturation and planting of conifers should in theory ensure that suitable habitats are available in the future even though breeding is as yet unproven, though birds probably of the European race have recently been seen in the larches of Achray Forest in March. Whether these populations will persist in the face of extensive plantings of Sitka and Norway Spruce rather than Larch is a matter for conjecture. The Siskin continues to nest widely in the region where the habitat is suitable and has probably increased with the spread of conifer plantations and now occurs in 23% of the 10km squares, mostly in the west. The Capercaillie spread into the region in the 1840's after introduction just outside its boundaries. Further introductions were made later in the century at sites in the eastern and southern sectors of the Region but these are no longer tenanted. Now breeding occurs widely in the west and possibly still irregularly to the east of Stirling (36% occurrence of breeding birds in B.T.O. survey in 10km squares). The Black Grouse is widespread and breeds in all areas of the Region, except on the low ground within five miles of the Forth Estuary. A well-known lek is situated close by the Memorial to the Battle of Sheriffmuir.

Nightjars occur at a few sites in the west and at a single site in the south east. The species is evidently at a low ebb both locally and nationally though it would be a mistake to assume that this is entirely a recent phenomenon in the Region, because Rintoul and Baxter (1935) noted a decline earlier this century at several sites. Of two other species which may frequent recently felled or newly planted woodland, the Woodcock and Grasshopper Warbler, the latter has increased reflecting a national trend.

The bird communities of extensive scrubland areas include elements of both woodland and Farmland communities. Often the densities of birds are at their highest in these habitats particularly in the case of the Willow Warbler and species which are common in gardens.

Mountain and Moorland

Several peaks reach over 1000m (3000ft) in the Region, with Stob Binnein the highest at 1165m (3821ft).   The southern limit of the Ptarmigan in Britain occurs on Ben Lomond where the population in recent years has been of the order of a few pairs.   Elsewhere the Ptarmigan is restricted to the highest mountains.   Occasionally other montane species occur in summer such as Dotterel and Snow Bunting.   Only the Dotterel has possibly remained to breed and then as long ago as the mid nineteenth century on Stob Binnein itself (Rintoul and Baxter, 1935).   However the Snow Bunting does flock on the hills in winter.   Wheatears can be seen in summer on the grassy slopes or among the rocky outcrops on the peaks, while a Golden Eagle, Peregrine or Kestrel may fly past.   In 1972 three or four pairs of Golden Eagles were established in the Region.   A census in 1971 revealed that of seven known Peregrine territories in the west Stirling Region, six were occupied and of these four pairs successfully reared young   (J Mitchell, pers. comm.).   Peregrine populations in the Region up to 1971 had apparently been rather less affected by pesticides than more coastal or southerly populations even though analysis of eggs has revealed substantial levels or organochlorine residues (Ratcliffe, 1972).   However the recent discovery of the highest recorded British levels of Dieldrin in the liver tissue of two dead Peregrines from West Stirlingshire (Bogan and Mitchell, 1973) emphasises the precarious nature of populations of this species and may itself be associated with a reduced breeding success in the last two years.   The Corvids are represented by Raven, Carrion, and Hooded Crows and Jackdaws though all of these species nest in trees and on cliff faces at lower altitudes.   The first recorded breeding of the Raven in Clackmannanshire was not until 1968, even though it was evidently a common visitor to the country in the 19th Century (Statistical Account, 1845).   The Carrion Crow and Hooded Crow hybrid zone passes through the north west part of the Region and is probably slowly moving northwards.   This zone lies between 5 and 10 miles to the north of the Highland Boundary Fault and thus approximately equal numbers of Carrion and Hooded Crows occur in the area of the Braes of Balquhidder.   Choughs dwelt on the northern slopes of the Campsie Fells and on the crags above Alva up to the early nineteenth century though none have been recorded since then.   Ring Ouzels are patchily distributed throughout the region (59% occurrence in 10km squares as a breeding bird), for example being easy to find on the scree slopes of Gleneagles though only being traced after much effort on the apparently suitable terrain of Dumyat in the Ochil range.   The characteristic breeding birds of the heather moors are Meadow Pipit and Red Grouse while Golden Plover and Snipe nest with a few Curlew on the high bogs.   Twite still breed on the slopes to the east of Ben Lomond and sparingly on the Campsie Fells though they have not been recorded from the Braes of Balquhidder where they were reported by Rintoul and Baxter (1935).

A considerable proportion of the moorland in the region lies between 300m (1000ft) and 600m (2000ft) and consists of grassland which may be relieved by Gorse, Bracken and Heather with damp bottomed valleys with Rushes.   Birds are usually rather scarce in the more open areas, though where the moorland joins marginal agricultural land or where rocks and shrubs introduce a structural diversity to the terrain a wide variety of birds occur. Wading birds are abundant including the dominant Lapwing with Redshank, Curlew and Snipe occurring widely, and Dunlin possibly breeding in one area. The Whinchat nests particularly where bracken provided a look-out position and the Stonechat is now increasing after disappearing from many marginal habitats after the severe winter of 1962-63. It formerly occurred up to 100ft on Kinlochard though no longer nests in that immediate area let alone at that latitude, though a pair did nest in the Ochils at 700ft in 1973.

Singletons and parties of Black Grouse (up to 38 have been observed) wander over the moorlands, and leks are widespread. Partridges too breed at over 500ft in the Ochils and have been seen at 1700ft in winter. The abundance of Cuckoos in summer is of note, being regularly distributed over the lower elevations and using mainly Meadow Pipits as hosts. The Short-eared Owl, Hen Harrier and Kestrel all hunt over the moors, and occasionally single Golden Eagles are recorded in early winter over the Ochil Hills. The Merlin nests sparingly in the west of the region and although observed in summer has not recently been proved to breed in the Ochil or Campsie Hills and the Kite has been recorded on only one occasion since it was extinguished as a breeding species at the end of the 19th Century.

A striking feature of the moors is their attraction for aerial feeding Swifts and House Martins. On sunny days loose flocks exceeding one hundred birds may feed over the leeward hill slopes where insects have been caught up in wind eddies or above sunny slopes where thermals have carried insects aloft.

Green Woodpeckers may search for ants on the moors outside the breeding season or the occasional Fulmar may prospect the cliffs of the Ochil Hills. In winter though, apart from the hunting raptors, Crows and Grouse are the most conspicuous birds of the moorland scene. Other birds occurring on the moorlands include a wide spectrum of passerines where scrub and trees occur which were discussed in broad terms in the Woodland and Farmland sections.

Environs of Human dwellings and Industrial sites

In general the birds of the towns, gardens, farmsteads and industrial sites could be found anywhere in Britain. However a few species display interesting features.

The Collared Dove arrived in the region in the late 1950's and became established where spilt grain was freely available such as at the Distillery at Cambus. Today there is a major population focus in this area but generally the distribution remains patchy. For example along the south scarp of the Ochil Hills it occurs in Bridge of Allan and Dollar, though not in Menstrie, Alva or Muckhart and sparsely in Tillicoultry. The sites are presumably occupied in a sequence of favourability, though causal qualitative differences are not immediately apparent. If the population increase continues it is to be expected that other suitable localities will in time be tenanted.

A feature of the industrialised eastern parts of the Region are the coal mine spoil heaps. These are usually barren of vegetation though act as foci for aggregations of Corvids particularly Rooks and Jackdaws which engage in aerial manoeuvres above the highest points. This usually occurs from mid-summer to early winter when similar gatherings collect near the prominent peaks of the south Ochil scarp.

Somewhat unexpectedly for an inland town such as Stirling, the Herring Gull can often be seen perched on a chimney pot above the town centre. However such an event can be readily explained when it is considered that the estuarine conditions of the Forth extend up to Stirling Bridge. The Black Headed and Common Gulls may also be seen snatching food from the roadside in many of the towns in the area.

The Siskin has recently become increasingly common as a bird-table visitor in Britain (Spencer, 1972) though up until 1971 only a single occurrence had been reported in Scotland and that in Aberdeenshire. In spring 1972 several birds came to feed on suspended peanuts in Stirling illustrating the continued spread of the habit.

The House Martin is often a rapid colonist of the wide eaves of houses on new estates, and the Swift is common in Stirling and Bridge of Allan where old houses provide secure nesting sites. The Thrushes are regular garden birds though the Song Thrush in winter vacates gardens on high ground. These birds move to the coast and ringing has shown that at least some move to N. Ireland. The Waxwing can be quite common in irruption years, the most recent of which was 1970-71 when the last bird recorded in Scotland that winter was seen in Bridge of Allan as late as the 2nd May (Lyster, 1972).

Discussion

Since Rintoul and Baxter's account (1935) of the Birds of the Forth area some species have shown dramatic changes in status. Seven species have bred for the first time, three have at least attempted to breed and one species had bred after introduction. The Common Gull, Green Woodpecker and Collared Dove are now well established residents, and in the last case at least is showing a continuing increase. The Montagu's Harrier settled for a few years in the 1950's when the total British population was probably at a peak, though breeding has not taken place since. The Canada Goose bred first in 1971 and the Hawfinch for the first time in 1973 while the Pied Flycatcher now probably breeds in small numbers most years. The Red Throated Diver has only probably bred in the west of the region. Mention should also be made of a singing Redwing in 1972 and the Redwing which was observed carrying food in the breeding season of 1973, and Crossbills which were seen in the Queen Elizabeth Forest Park in March, 1972. These last three species may have already to be added to the new breeding species of the area but confirmation must still be obtained. The Greylag Goose has also bred after artificial introduction. One species, the Willow Tit has ceased to breed, though the current breeding range extends to within a small distance of the Region's boundaries. It could therefore return at any time and then fall into the same category as the only recolonist, the Osprey.

Sixteen or more species have simply occurred in the region for the first time since 1935 excluding the Collared Dove. Most of these newcomers are waterside species which have been observed in spring and autumn on the Forth near Kincardine Bridge partly as a result of intensive observer coverage of the Skinflats area. A few however may have appeared in the Region because of the increasing numbers occurring in Britain, such as the Little Gull.

The balance sheet of species which have changed quantitatively in status favours the increasing category. Apart from new breeders and lost breeders a total of 25 species have increased in abundance, or frequency of occurrence, while 23 species have decreased. Details are given in the list at the end of the chapter.

Total increases involve 36 species while decreased have affected only 24 species. Among the increasing species, 3 are winter visiting wildfowl, the Pink-footed, Graylag and Barnacle Geese. The increase of the first two species is widespread while the last may only involve displaced birds from other areas as no more than a score occur at any one site (Boyd and Ogilvie, 1969; Atkinson-Willes, 1973). Two visitors which have certainly increased, in reality as opposed to being recorded more frequently because of increased observer activity, are the Fulmar which occurs mostly on the Forth in autumn, though there are some inland records from the Hillfoots and Falkirk which suggest that breeding may take place in the future, and the Great Black Backed Gull. The remaining 20 species are all breeders and all are undergoing national increases in abundance or range, though the gulls in addition show increased winter populations (Parslow, 1969).   Similarly many of the species showing declines are reflecting national trends and nearly all are breeding species. This latter group however, includes two species which although they have exhibited an over-all decline, are now spreading after the last hard winter, the Stonechat and Kingfisher.   However the loss of habitat for the Kingfisher, brought about partly by pollution of rivers such as the Carron, will prevent this species ever regaining its former status while the rivers remain polluted.   The example of the Kingfisher illustrates how status changes may be attributed to factors both under and beyond the control of man.   Climatic amelioration in Britain (Johnson, 1969) could be partly responsible for increases in the southern species such as Chiff-chaff and Hawfinch and other species sensitive to the occurrence of harsh winters such as the Long Tailed Tit.   However, this proposition is difficult to reconcile with the concurrent establishment and southerly spread of the Redwing in Scotland now possibly just being re-flected in the Region and certainly so, less than 20 miles to the north.   Most of the other changes appear to be due to man's activities such as the reduction in gamekeeping in the west which has allowed the spread of the Buzzard and Hen Harrier since the last war.   Also, the incidental provision of winter food supplies at rubbish dumps has probably encouraged an increase of the Common and Black Headed Gulls and locally of Great Black Backed and Herring Gulls.   Maybe the decline of bird catching has allowed the Goldfinch to again be widespread locally though it is certain that in that county of bird fanciers, Clackmannanshire, the practice continues in spite of it illegality.   However, the most important changes are probably those in agricultural practice, which have helped the increase of the wintering geese and possibly the Tree Sparrow, although they have had an adverse effect on the densities of many farmland birds, and decreased the area of damp pasture, the breeding habitat of some wading birds, and seriously jeopardized bird of prey populations (Shrub, 1970).

The realisation of the proposals put forward in the note on conservation in the introduction to Part 2 of the Survey (p85) would do much to encourage the continuation of the important bird communities of the area for the pleasure of the local human population and visitors.   Their value as an amenity and as a source of aesthetic and scientific interest must not be underestimated.

Principal status changes which have occurred in the Stirling Region since 1935.

A   *Species which have bred for the first time*

Canada Goose	Hawfinch
Montagus Harrier	Red Throated Diver (Probable breeder)
Common Gull	Redwing (Probable breeder)
Green Woodpecker	Crossbill (Probable breeder)
Collared Dove	Greylag Goose (Introduced)
Pied Flycatcher	

(Total 8 species proven, and 3 more unconfirmed)

B   *Species which have recolonised*

   Osprey

   (Total 1 species)

C   *Species which have ceased to breed*

   Willow Tit

   (Total 1 species)

D   *Species which have increased,* though the bracketed species are those for which substantial evidence for an increase is lacking.   Status changes refer to breeding birds except those marked * which are non-breeding visitors and those marked + which have increased both as visitors and as breeding birds.

*	Fulmar	+	Black Headed Gull
	Tufted Duck		Short-eared Owl
	Goosander		Blackcap
	Red Breasted Merganiser		Chiffchaff
*	Barnacle Goose		Garden Warbler
*	Greylag Goose		(Grasshopper Warbler)
*	Pink-footed Goose		(Long-tailed Tit)
	Hen Harrier		Goldfinch
	Buzzard		(Siskin)
	Great Spotted Woodpecker		Tree Sparrow
*	Great Black Backed Gull		Magpie
+	Lesser Black Backed Gull		Jay
+	Herring Gull		

   (Total 25 species)

Plus new breeding species (except the introduced Greylag Goose) and the recolonist

   (10 + 1)

   (Total — 36)

E   *Species which have decreased.*   Refers to breeding birds except those marked *.

*	(Slavonian Grebe)	Corncrake
	Pintail	Nightjar
	Shoveler	(Cuckoo)
*	Brent Goose	Kingfisher
	Merlin	Stonechat
	Stock Dove	Redstart
	Dunlin	(Tree Pipit)
	Caperaillie	Yellow Wagtail
*	Quail	Whitethroat

Barn Owl   (Corn Bunting)
Long-eared Owl   (Hooded Crow)
Water Rail

(Total 23 species)

Plus lost breeding species (1)
(Total — 24)

F   *Species recorded for the first time* (excluding new breeding species) Probably incomplete.

Little Egret	Gull Billed Tern
American Widgeon	Little Cull
Pectoral Sandpiper	Pomarine Skua
Avocet	Little Auk
Red Necked Phalarope	Lesser Spotted Woodpecker
Temminck's Stint	Lesser Whitethroat
Spotted Redshank	Lapland Bunting
Wood Sandpiper	Yellow Bowed Warbler
Roseate Tern	Little Owl (Unconfirmed)

ACKNOWLEDGEMENTS

I would like to extend particular thanks to Dr C Henty, Mr J Mitchell and Mr G Shaw for allowing me access to a considerable amount of their original data on the birds of the Region. I am also gratful to these people for reading an early draft of the manuscript and to Mr D Merrie, Dr J Proctor and Mr H Robb for their very helpful comments on the whole, or part of the text.

REFERENCES

Atkinson-Willes, G L   1963   *Wildfowl in Great Britain.* Nature Conservancy Monographs No. 3. London: HMSO.

Atkinson-Willes, G L   1972   'Greylag Goose populations in Britain', *Wildfowl, 23.*

Ballantyne, J   1973   *Report on Estuary bird counts in Firth of Forth between October, 1972 and March, 1973.*

Baxter, E V and Rintoul, L J   1953   *The Birds of Scotland.* Edinburgh: Oliver and Boyd.

Bogan, J A and Mitchell, J   1973   'Continuing dangers to Peregrines from dieldrin', *Brit. Birds,* 66: 437 – 439.

Boyd, H and Ogilvie, M A   1969   'Changes in the British-wintering population of the Pink-footed Goose from 1950 to 1975', *Wildfowl,* 20: 33 – 46.

Harvie-Brown, J A and Buckley, T E   1892   *A Vertebrate Fauna of Argyll and the Inner Hebrides,* Edinburgh, Constable.

Bryant, D M   1974   *A preliminary report on estuarine wader populations, their feeding zones and roosts in the upper Firth of Forth.* Duplicated report, 32pp.

Buxton, E J M   1961   'The inland breeding of the Oystercatcher in Great Britain, 1958 – 1959', *Bird Study,* 8: 194 – 209.

Campbell, B   1965   'The British breeding distribution of the Pied Flycatcher, 1953 – 61', *Bird Study,* 12: 305 – 318.

Eagle-Clark, W   1912   *Studies in Bird Migration. Vol. 1.* London and Edinburgh.

Fisher, J   1967   *Thornburn's Birds.* London: Edbury.

Downie, A J   1972   *The biology of the nidifugous young of the Coot and the Quail.* Unpubl. Hons. Thesis, University of Stirling. 67pp.

Gilmore, J G   1972   'Corncrakes breeding in Stirlingshire', *Scot. Birds.* 7: 52.

Greenwood, J J D; Donally, R J; Feare, C J; Gordon, N J and Waterson, G   1971   'A massive wreck of oiled birds: northeast Britain, winter 1970', *Scot Birds.* 6: 235 – 250.

Grieve, A   1972   *Report on counts made on the Firth of Forth 1971 – 1972.* Duplicated report, 13pp.

Keppleston, P B   1972   'The comparative breeding ecology of Oystercatchers (Haematopus ostralegus, L.) in inland and coastal habitats', *J. Anim. Ecol.* 41: 23 – 52.

Holyoak, D   1972   'Food of the Rook in Britain', *Bird Study,* 19: 59 – 68.

Jenkins, D — 1972 'The status of Shelduck in the Forth area', *Scot. Birds*, 7: 183 – 210.

Johnstone, C G and Smith, L P — 1965 'The biological significance of climatical changes in Britain', *Institute of Biology Symposium, 14*. London: Academic Press.

Lockie, J D — 1955 'The breeding habits and food of Short-eared Owls after a vole plague', *Bird Study*, 2: 53 – 69.

Lyster, I H J — 1972 'Waxwings in Scotland, 1970 – 71', *Scot. Birds*, 6: 420 – 438.

Mead, C J — 1973 'Movements of British Raptors', *Bird Study*, 20: 259 – 286.

Meikeljohn, M F M — 1952 'Habitat of Chiffchaff in Scotland', *Scot. Nat.*, 64: 114 – 116.

Mitchell, J — 1970 'Lesser Spotted Woodpeckers in Scotland', *Scot. Birds*, 6: 210 – 211.

Mitchell, J (In press) — 'The Green Woodpecker in the Glasgow area', *Glas. Naturalist*.

Munro, J K B — 1971 'Scottish winter Rook roost survey – southern Scotland', *Scot. Birds*, 6: 438 – 443.

Newton, I — 1972a 'Finches', *New Naturalist* 55, London: Collins.

Newton, I — 1972b 'Birds of prey in Scotland: some conservation problems', *Scot Birds*, 7: 5 – 23.

Newton, I and Campbell, C R G — 1973 'Feeding of geese on farmland in East-central Scotland', *J. appl. Ecol.*, 10: 781 – 802.

Parslow, J — 1967 *Breeding Birds of Britain and Ireland, a Historical survey*, Berkhamstead: Poyser.

Prater, A — 1972 *Birds of Estuaries Enquiry. Report for 1971 – 72*. Published by B.T.O., R.S.P.B. and Wildfowl Trust, 33pp.

Ratcliffe, D A   1972   'The Peregrine population of Great Britain in 1971', *Bird Study*,   19: 117 — 156.

Rintoul, L J and   1935   *A Vertebrate Fauna of Forth*. Edinburgh: Oliver and Boyd.
Baxter, E V

Shrubb, M   1970   'Birds and farming today', *Bird Study*, 17: 123 — 144.

Spenser, R and   1973   'Siskin feeding in gardens', *Brit. Birds*, 66: 91 — 99.
Gush, G M

Stewart, A G   1970   'The seabird wreck — autumn 1969', *Scot. Birds*, 6: 142 — 149.

Thom, V M   1969   'Wintering duck in Scotland 1962 — 68', *Scot. Birds*, 5: 417 — 466.

Vernon, J D R   1970   'Feeding habitats and food of the Black-headed and Common Gulls. Part I — feeding and habitats', *Bird Study*, 17: 287 — 296.

Vernon, J D R   1972   'Feeding habitats and food of the Blackheaded and Common Gulls. Part II — food', *Bird Study*, 19: 173 — 186.

Williamson, K   1974   'Oak wood breeding bird communities in the Lock Lomond National Nature Reserves', *Q. J. For.* 68: 9 — 28.

CHAPTER 8

FRESHWATER FISH

Any general study of the freshwater fishes of Scotland is bound to be dominated by the salmonid fishes: the Atlantic salmon (*Salmo salar*), the sea trout and brown trout (*Salmo trutta*) and the rainbow trout (*S. gairdneri*). Apart from their inherent biological interest and relative abundance, they are also of such major economic significance that their presence controls the way in which other species are distributed. Predatory fish which threaten a valuable trout fishery are not likely to be tolerated.

The waters of the higher parts of the area are generally oligotrophic, and cooled in winter and spring by melting snow. This is reflected in the relative lack of diversity of their species. Salmon and brown trout predominate, with eels (*Anguilla anguilla*) and lampreys (*Lampetra fluviatilis*). In one or two of the higher lochs, especially in the Callander area, breeding populations of Arctic char (*Salvelinus alpinus*) are said to occur, but no direct recent evidence is available.

The lower lying water in the richer farming areas and the lower reaches of the main drainage river, the Forth, are mainly eutrophic and there is some enrichment in the fauna, with pike (*Esox lucius*), perch (*Perca fluviatilis*), roach (*Rutilis rutilis*) and three-spined sticklebacks (*Gasterosteus aculeatus*). The minnow (*Phoxinus phoxinus*) and the flounder (*Platichthyes flesus*) also occur more spasmodically.

The two anadromous species in the area, the salmon and the sea trout, are only found within the Forth system. This comprises three major tributaries: (a) The Upper Forth, draining the Carse of Stirling, the richest agricultural area of the watershed, and hence showing the greatest faunal diversity; (b) The Teith, which drains the Braes of Balquhidder, the Trossachs Lochs of Lubnaig, Venacher, Voil and Katrine and the scenic Callander area, a rugged sheep farming water table with relatively little agricultural fertilization; and (c) The Allan, the northernmost and smallest of the three major tributaries. These three join almost simultaneously to form the Forth proper, just outside Stirling, and suffer a degree of pollution, both organic and inorganic from there to the estuary.

The Forth estuary itself is quite highly polluted and this is considered by many to be a major reason for the poor salmon fishing of the Forth system compared with its northern neighbours, although the record rod-caught fish, a salmon of 45lbs, is by no means poor. However, this is no new phenomenon. Grimble, in his classical if somewhat sycophantic volume on the salmon rivers of Scotland, wrote in 1899 that there was 'a good deal of pollution below Stirling' and that 'the shores are very severely harried by bag and stake nets', and he considered the only useful salmon river to be the Teith tributary, although even that suffered severely from the depredations of the netsman below. He reserved his most severe criticism, however, for the river Allan '. . . . a considerable stream up which a few fish poke their way in autumn and down which a very few ever return . . . . . . It is not worth mentioning as an angling river and it would be just as well for the fish if they were barred from ever entering it'.

Fortunately the netting cruives and hang nets which Grimble so disliked have long since been banned and new controls over the years have regulated the net fishery. But still the salmon productivity of the Forth system is poor by comparison with many shorter rivers. Sea trout are even poorer in both quality and quantity and this appears to be a more recent phenomenon, with older anglers and netsmen recalling much better average runs than those experienced in recent years. The Forth estuary is highly industrialized and the effluvia of factories, mines, refineries and large cities does not render it ideal for the coastal feeding of the sea trout. It has been suggested that this may be a major factor in the recent demise of the fish.

Brown trout and rainbow trout are well distributed throughout the area. There are many good wild brown trout lochs, but in most of the waters the stocks are now maintained by stocking with fish from hatcheries and trout farms. Brown trout, the indigenous species, is much sought after by the angler, but its slow growth rate and its greater water requirements have made it more expensive to produce for restocking purposes and the faster growing and cheaper rainbow trout are often preferred. A major disadvantage of rainbow trout is their tendency to seek an exit from a loch and move down a river and be lost to the fishery, but they present problems also from their short survival time compared with brown trout and their reluctance to breed naturally in British waters.

The most famous brown trout fishery of all, the Loch Leven fishery, is just outwith the area covered by this survey, but another famous trout fishery, at the Lake of Menteith, Scotland's only lake, lies almost in the centre of the survey area, in the angle between the Teith and the Forth. This fishery was recently rehabilitated, with the assistance of the Freshwater Fisheries Laboratory. The major problem encountered was the very large number of pike, perch and roach which had to be reduced by every possible means prior to restocking with rainbow trout and brown trout in 1968. Since that date the fishery has continued to improve and an interesting observation is the claim by the late Dr T A Stewart, senior biologist on the rehabilitation programme, that rainbow trout were breeding naturally in the spawning streams, a most unusual occurrence in Scotland.

Another well-known trout fishery in the area is Airthrey Loch. This small artificially created loch forms the centre point of the Campus of the University of Stirling, but long before the University was established in 1966, the loch was well-known for the size and fighting qualities of its brown trout. The loch was originally created by one of the Haldane lairds of Airthrey.   It is said to have been created because Mr Haldane was a keen trout angler and was so fond of fishing Loch Leven that he resolved to create a similar facility on his own estate.   The low lying land was dug out, and a dam constructed to allow an average depth similar to that of Loch Leven.   Trout of Loch Leven origin formed the foundation stock and a very good fishery resulted.   The fishery was severely affected by the depradations of poachers during the first phase of the building of the University, but now an active restocking policy by the University Angling Club is enabling it to regain some of its former esteem.

Another feature of Airthrey Loch is its use as a base for the fish-tracking research of the University Biology Department.   This method of sonor tracking allows the movements of even small fish to be monitored continuously and a fascinating insight into the private life of the trout to be obtained.

No discussion of the game fish of the Stirling area would be complete without a reference to the Howietoun Fisheries.   This most famous of fish farms was established at Sauchieburn, just south of Stirling, by Sir James Maitland, Bart. in 1873.   The purpose which guided Sir James in his work was the proof 'by actual experience that the culture of *Salmonidae* can be made commercially a success if set about in a business-like manner'.   Unlike most present-day fish farms, which produce table fish or large stock fish for immediate recapture, Sir James aimed to produce 'ova and young fish for stocking and replenishing of barren or depleted waters at home and abroad'.   The water supply for the farm derives principally from Loch Coulter, two miles south of the fishery.   Sir James was particularly keen to secure the best quality fish and while he selected specimen brood stock from all of the best-known trout fisheries, his speciality was Loch Leven trout.   So careful was he with his brood stock that he even designed special silk suits to be worn by his men when handling them, lest they damage the skin or eyes of the fish when taking eggs or milt.   Howietoun has provided most of the trout fisheries of the world with their foundation stock and anglers in New Zealand, Australia, South and Central Africa and Asia, as well as British reservoir trout fisheries have appreciated the qualities of stock of Howietoun lineage.

The coarse fisheries of central Scotland have much to offer the angler and whilst as yet under exploited, they represent a resource which may be particularly valuable in future, especially in those waters where they do not conflict with the interests of salmonid fisheries. The river Forth provides the all-time Scottish record for Scottish coarse fish.   In five hours a party of five anglers took 532lbs of roach, the best individual catch being 140lbs including a specimen of 1¾lbs.   Catches of this calibre are not common but it does indicate the potential of the area.

Eels (*Anguilla anguilla*), our only truly catadromous species, are abundant throughout the area.   Although they enter and travel up the Forth, they succeed in migrating from it into a wide variety of ponds and lochs with no apparent direct access to the river.

Pike (*Esox lucius*) and perch (*Perca fluviatilis*) are generally distributed throughout the region. Large pike are regularly caught and perch of two pounds and more are not uncommon.

A full listing of the freshwater species known to occur in the region is as follows.

Check List of Freshwater Fish Species
known to occur in the Stirling Area

Order	Family	Specific Name	Common Name	Known localities
Isospondylii	Salmonidae	Salmo salar	Atlantic salmon	Restricted to the Forth, Teith and Allan and certain intermediary lochs.
		Salmo trutta	Sea trout, Brown trout	Forth, Teith and Allan rivers. Widespread throughout the area in virtually all waters.
		Salmo gairdneri	Rainbow trout	An introduced species restricted to managed fisheries such as Lake of Menteith and Airthrey Loch There is an established certificated disease-free stock at Howietoun.
		Salvelinus alpinus	Char	Limited to local lochs, notably Loch Lubnaig.
	Osmeridae	Osmerus operlanus	Smelt	Recorded in Lower reaches of Forth, believed strayed from estuary.
Ostariophysi	Cyprinidae	Phoxinus phoxinus	Minnow	Widespread, especially in clean stoney areas of lochs and rivers. Abundant in Forth and Teith systems and also certain hill lochs, especially Ochil hills.
		Rutilis rutilis	Roach	Localized mainly to the Forth, and lower Forth.
	Cobitidae	Naemacheilus barbatulus	Stone Loach	Present in some stoney streams, but records poor.
Taplomi	Esocidae	Esox lucius	Pike	Common in most lochs (e.g. Lubnaig, Chon, Ard, Venacher) and their interconnecting waters.
Percomorphi	Percidae	Perca fluciatilis	Perch	Common. Distribution similar to pike.
Thora costia	Gasterostidae	Gasterosteus aculeatus	Three-spined Stickleback	Present in most of the water-courses

Order	Family	Specific Name	Common Name	Known localities
Apodes	*Anguillidae*	*Anguilla anguilla*	Eel	Probably reaches most waters in the area. Very abundant in main Forth system.
Heterosomata	*Pleuronectidae*	*Platichithyes flesus*	Flounder	Very abundant in the Forth, especially tidal region.

FURTHER   READING

1   Sir James Maitland, 1887.   *The History of Howietoun*.   Privately produced.

2   Augustus Grimble   1899   *The Salmon Rivers of Scotland.*   London: Routledge, Kegan Paul, Trench and Trubner.

3   'A key for the identification of the freshwater fishes of the British Isles'.*Scient. Publ.* Freshwater Biol. Assoc. Windermere. (1972)

4   Scottish Tourist Board, Annual publication.   *Scotland for Fishing* and *Scotland for Coarse Fishing.*

PART THREE

SETTLEMENT AND ECONOMY

INTRODUCTION

SETTLEMENT AND ECONOMY – INTRODUCTION

The varied physical and biological environment of the Stirling Region has provided a rich matrix for human settlement. In addition, the central location of the area, 'at the cross-roads of Scotland', has led to its playing a crucial role in the development of the nation. It may not be claiming too much indeed to suggest that the Stirling Region has been the crucible in which the Scottish identity has been forged.

The Scottish nation emerged from the union of several distinct ethnic groups which came to occupy the area of Central Scotland during the Dark Ages. The oldest inhabitants to contribute to the union were an ancient Celtic people known as the Picts. They were joined by Romanized Britons from the south-west, by Angles pushing up through the Lothians from Northumbria, and by the Scottii, invaders from Ireland via Dalriada (modern Argyll). The contact between the groups varied between the bloody and the co-operative. Much of the contact must have taken place around Stirling, then, as now, existing on the fringe of power bases to east and west and guarding the routes to the north. Each group spoke a distinct language and, as T Martin points out in his chapter on the development of the settlement pattern, has left a permanent memorial in the place-names of the region.

From the earliest days of the unification under Malcolm Canmore, the slayer of Mac-Beth, there was a constant tension between Highlands and Lowlands. As Smout (1969, p 26) remarks: 'the truth of the matter was that even knights and castles, the effective teeth of feudalism, could do no more than grip the fringe of this wild country for the king'. In this context, few castles matched the strategic importance of Stirling. From the time of Alexander I, who died there in 1124, Stirling became a 'principal and favourite resort' of the Scottish court. The Castle and the surrounding countryside provided the locale for many of the battles and intrigues which characterised the history of Scotland for the next 600 years. In the Wars of Independence, major battles were fought at Stirling Bridge, at Falkirk and, most famously, at Bannockburn. James II was overthrown in a battle just south of Stirling in 1488 and murdered at Beaton's Mill, Whins of Milton. James VI was crowned at Stirling in 1567. His accession to the English throne, as James I in 1603, brought to an end Stirling's role as a royal residence. Battles at Sheriffmuir, in 1715, and at Falkirk, in 1745, were the last occasions on which the area figured actively in military strategy.

In the eighteenth and nineteenth centuries the importance of the Stirling Region lay in its contribution to the changing economy of Scotland. In chapter 10, T R B Dicks outlines the agricultural and industrial developments which characterised the region during the period. In the Highland areas the processes of improvement, enclosure and clearance altered not just the economy but also the population geography and the whole social structure. Scarcely less dramatic effects were produced by the reclamation of the carse lands in the Carse o: Stirling, by the burgeoning of heavy industry around Falkirk and by the growth of coal-mining.

The industrial development of the Stirling Region was closely paralleled by the growth of its urban settlements. In chapter 11 G Gordon traces the developing morphology of the major urban centres, contrasting the slow and long-continued growth of Stirling with the more mercurial developments in Falkirk and Grangemouth. He concludes by noting that the Region 'encompasses the interface between the urban Central Lowlands and the rural settlement pattern of the Highlands and as such provides a fascinating field laboratory for the student of settlement geography'.

The contemporary agricultural and industrial economies of the Stirling Region provide the raw materials for chapters 12 and 13 of the Survey. In his analysis of the agricultural scene, S Matthews emphasises the importance of improved varieties of crops and of animals in determining the patterning of agricultural land use. He points out that the region con-tains all three agricultural land uses: arable, typical of eastern Scotland, permanent pasture, typical of the south-west, and upland grazings, typical of the highland north. The agricul-tural diversity is overlain by industrial diversity. Taking a wide economic perspective, J Hughes distinguishes between the service-oriented, small-town north of the region around Stirling, and the major concentration of heavy industry centred on Falkirk and Grangemouth. In contrast to most parts of Scotland both sub-regions have seen considerable recent growth. In large measure this reflects the growth of new industries in the region: petrochemicals in Falkirk/Grangemouth and professional and scientific services in the Stirling district. The point may have been reached where the image of the region as being a centre for growth may have become, in effect, a self-fulfilling prophecy. In addition, the location of the region close to the newly-dynamic east of Scotland and its combination of good access and a desir-able residential environment promise well for a continuation of economic prosperity.

It should come as no surprise, in view of the diversity of economic, physical and bio-logical characteristics of the area, to discover that the Stirling Region presents a highly-variegated social fabric. Differences in the social characteristics of the thirteen burghs which fall within the newly-constituted Central Region provide the raw material for the concluding chapter of the Stirling Region Survey. A wide range of permutations is played, some burghs combining high social rank with old populations, others with young, and so on. The vari-ation in social characteristics is closely correlated with a variation in the nature of local politics. The results of the first elections for the new local authority areas, held in May 1974, produced a series of knife-edge situations which serve as eloquent testimony to the variegated nature of the Stirling Region.

CHAPTER 9

THE DEVELOPMENT OF THE SETTLEMENT PATTERN

Introduction

Human settlement throughout history has been both stimulated and constrained by the relationship between man and his environment. The physical environment has provided man with basic resources, but has also imposed limitations on human activities. The fact that early communities depended upon the resources of the immediate locality in which they lived is evident, although in some cases trade was used to supplement local deficiencies. In attempting to understand the patterns of life of prehistoric communities, the character of the landscape they inhabited is important. On the other hand, man has created, within the limitations of his environment and his technological development, various cultural, organisational and institutional forms and structures to suit the mode of life of a particular era. The settlements that he built attempted to meet the requirements of the economic and social structures into which he was organised. These elements of the cultural landscape form an interwoven mesh of influences within which human groups have operated, both in space and in time, and they have undergone change as human society has developed. The landscape has been gradually transformed by human activity at a pace which quickened with the levels of technology, population pressures and changes of emphasis within the economy.

The Stirling Region in Prehistory

The end of the Pleistocene glacial epoch was a complex period during which the overall retreat of the ice sheets from Scotland was interrupted by local readvances that caused valley glaciers to persist locally until about 8,000 B.C. (see chapter 63). The final retreat and melting of the ice produced a rise in sea level and also readjustments of the land surface in response to the removal of the weight of the ice. The resultant balance of these two processes produced raised beaches at various heights above sea level, of which the 25 foot beach is the most significant for our present purposes, having produced some of the oldest evidences of human activity in Scotland.

The 25 foot raised beach represents an encroachment of the sea on the land during the period 5,500 – 3,000 B.C., when the sea extended considerably further inland up the valley of the Forth than at present. The upper limit of this shoreline is particularly conspicuous in the landscape and has yielded abundant evidence of the first inhabitants of the region, the fishers and hunters of Mesolithic times. Below the shoreline lie the carselands of Stirling and Falkirk, where the remains of implements worked in bone and antler have been found, attesting to the nature of the way of life followed by this cultural group. After submer-

Fig 9.1   THE STIRLING REGION IN PRE-HISTORY

gence, the land recovered slowly to reach the present shoreline by the beginning of the Christian era, giving rise to the dichotomy between carseland and dry field that was to be an important subdivision of land potential and utilisation in the region throughout history despite the land reclamation work of the eighteenth and nineteenth centuries.

The juxtaposition of land and sea was only one factor however in the prehistoric settlement of the area.   Climatic fluctuations produced differences in vegetation cover and influenced soil forming processes which in turn moulded the pattern of life of prehistoric man.   The forest cover approached its maximum extent in Boreal times and was followed by a degeneration which has been dated to the period immediately prior to the formation of the 25 foot raised beach.   This degeneration fostered a rapid extension of peat deposits which began to encroach on the forests as the warm, dry climatic conditions of the Boreal gave way to the mild, damp conditions of Atlantic times, the period during which both upland and lowland peats were formed.

Soil variations were mirrored by differences in the type and density of the forests. Clay soils supported dense oakwood whereas the lighter sands and gravels supported a more open vegetation cover that attracted the first farmers during Neolithic times.   The lower slopes of the hills with better drainage supported a lighter forest cover than the heavy lowland clays and consequently most of the prehistoric settlement in the region is found within a narrow band of countryside situated between the 90m (300ft) and 230m (750ft) contours.   It was not until population increased and the advent of the heavy plough in Iron Age times that the better soils with thick woodland cover below 100m (330ft) were opened up. Similarly, the early settlers appeared to have shunned the carse areas of the middle Forth valley and the exposed highland areas above 230m (750ft).

The location of an area with respect to trade and migration routes was also a very important factor in explaining the distribution of prehistoric population.   Throughout prehistory, the Forth valley appears to have been an area of transit, permitting cultural influences with an easterly distribution in Scotland to penetrate westwards and those of the west to be diffused eastwards.   In Mesolithic times, Baltic influences penetrated inland to Balmaha, Luss and beyond, whilst in the Neolithic and later in history the area received a certain intermingling of cultural traits from the east and the west.

During Mesolithic times a cultural group, akin to the Baltic forest cultures of similar date, eked out a strandlooping existence around the tidal mudflats of the Forth basin.   Evidence from the kitchen-middens found along the 25 foot raised shoreline, and the antler and bone implements from the carse clays suggests a small population living by fishing, hunting and food-gathering.   It represents the first human occupation of the virgin landscape conditions that were both warmer and wetter than those of today.

Sites dated to the Mesolithic are concentrated in two main areas: around Falkirk and on the carse clays around Stirling. The kitchen-middens of the Falkirk area, notably one discovered at Polmonthill, have been dated just subsequent to the period of maximum submergence. The kitchen-middens are composed mainly of oyster shells, but also yield limited amounts of mussels, cockle, periwinkle and whelk, attesting to the remains of countless meals of a small group of strandloopers.

The implements of bone and antler recovered from the carse clays around Stirling leave no room for doubt that Baltic strains penetrated the Forth valley. All but one of the finds were found in association with whalebone, but whales caught by the falling tide could have been only one component of a diet also including crustaceans, fish, wildfowl and animals of the forest. There appears to be no great disparity in age between these finds and the kitchen-middens further east, both showing close affinities to the Erteboille culture of Denmark.

The first agriculturalists appeared on the local scene about 3,000 B.C. The primary colonisation was effected by both the west coast and North Sea routes, whilst a later, secondary colonisation is also in evidence with origins in England and from native Scottish sources. The western colonisation is represented by chambered tombs of the Clyde — Carlington type, such as those at Stockiemuir and Rottenreoch, just beyond the bounds of the region. The eastern influence is present in the long barrows of the Blair Drummond group. These sites represent two divergent and distinct cultural traditions. It would appear from other evidence that the western culture was somewhat earlier than that of the east coast.

The advent of the first metalworkers, the Beaker people of the Bronze Age, about 1,700 B.C. is evidenced by changes in ritual sites and by a demand for new raw materials. The local region possessed limited amounts of gold in the Loch Tay — Loch Earn area and of copper in the Ochils, but was forced to rely on tin imported from Cornwall, a trade that introduced exotic items to the region in the form of grave goods. To a certain extent the initial impact of the new culture coincided with a survival of secondary Neolithic culture, but later cup and ring markings depict sites of metalworking. The Bronze Age colonisation with its marked easterly distribution began with the onset of the drier conditions of the Sub-Boreal climatic phase and terminated contemporaneously with the changes to the damper, cooler climate of Sub-Atlantic times about 500 B.C. It is during this period of prehistory that settlement reaches its highest limits, although there was still a preference for the drier, lighter soils within the region.

Bronze Age sites are mainly confined to the eastern half of the region. The cairn at

Hill of Airthrey included finds of both the earlier, Beaker period and the middle Bronze Age or Food Vessel period. Similar finds have been made at Cairnhill and Todholes. There is a group of standing stones in the upper part of the valley of Machany Water and a smaller group near Airthrey Castle. The most significant site dating to this period in the region is King's Park, Stirling, where a single cup and ring marking was found in association with several Bronze Age burials and pottery finds. Whereas all the sites mentioned above are of a ritual nature, there can be no doubt that both bronzesmiths and primitive farmers were active in close proximity to them.

Although there is no well defined termination of the Scottish Bronze Age, a sparse occurrence of foreign objects indicates that the local population was being augmented from about 500 B.C. onwards. The increased population after this date indicates the arrival of a Celtic population that developed an Iron Age culture upon which the later Roman occupation of the region was superimposed. The main evidence for the archaeology of this period derives from both settlements and fortifications. In the highland zone these were generally built of stone, whereas those of the lowland areas were of timber construction. The Stirling region was one of intermixture between a more northerly cultural province, based on the broch, and the hill-forts and settlements of the central area of the country.

Most of the fortifications of the Iron Age were forts of the timber-laced variety, many of them subsequently becoming vitrified such as those at Abbey Craig, Stirling and at Braes. Some like that at Castle Craig may be post-Roman in date since the fort is situated within the protection of additional defensive works, designed to provide defence in depth against a more sophisticated range of weapons. Other forts display a citadel surrounded by outworks of the order of strength of the ramparts of an early Iron Age fort, but with the whole structure occupying a hitherto barren site unlike most of those selected by the earlier fort builders. Dumyat and Myot Hill fall into this category and have been ascribed by Feachem to the *Maeatae* of Dio Cassius. Myot Hill would appear to have been dismantled by the Romans due to its closeness to the Antonine Wall in a similar way to the fort situated at Bochastle, near Callander. A group of six small, oval or D-shaped structures of the dun class have been identified in the upper reaches of the Bannockburn, among them Castlehill Wood and Sauchie Craig. These are placed on a rocky eminence and gain defensive strength from the cliffs around them. Their proximity to the Roman frontier again suggests that they are either pre-Roman or post-Roman in date, but since Roman finds of first and second century date have been discovered at Castlehill Wood, they must be pre-Antonine structures.

Brochs or fortified dwelling houses were generally located adjacent to areas of good arable land and were normally therefore confined to the river valleys of the eastern lowlands. Their origin is open to dispute, but it may be said that, although they belong to the period during which the people eventually to be known as the historic Picts had not yet emerged

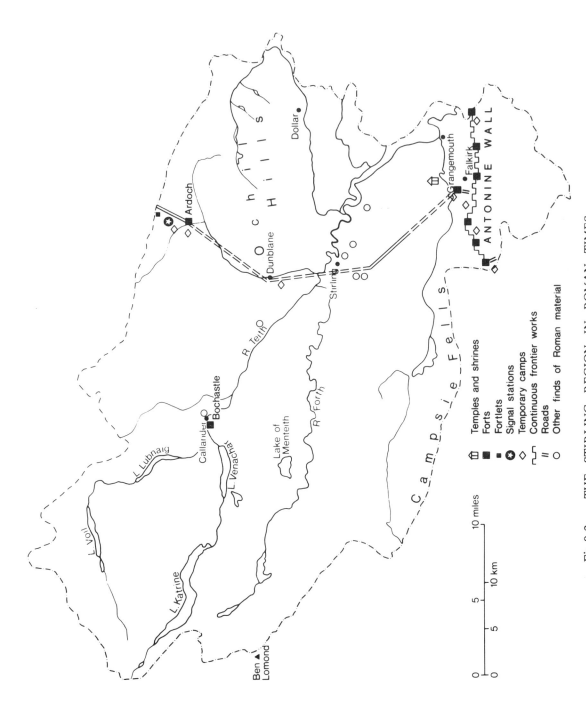

Fig 9.2   THE STIRLING REGION IN ROMAN TIMES

from the welding together of separate Iron Age population groups, it is very likely that the broch builders were an important element among these groups. Only two brochs are known in the region, those at Coldoch and Torwood, which are members of the Tay — Tweed group of brochs situated athwart the southern boundary of the area later to become Pictland. They, like the duns, may possibly be ascribed to the *Maeatae* of Dio Cassius.

Homesteads of an early Iron Age date have been discovered at Keir Hill of Gargunnock and at West Plean, giving the first direct evidence of settlement as opposed to ritual and other sites. The former was occupied in pre-Roman times and into the first century A.D. The West Plean settlement is one of the most important early Iron Age sites in North Britain and the archaeological evidence points to an occupation that began in the late Bronze Age and continues during the early period of the Iron Age into the first century of the Christian era.

The main elements of these varying cultural streams were slowly unified and welded into recognisable regional cultures during and immediately after the Roman occupation of Scotland and were eventually transmitted through to the British kingdom of Manau Goddodin and the Pictish kingdom of the Dark Ages.

The Region in Roman Times

Ptolemy's *Geography* indicates that by Roman times a people called the *Votadini* occupied the eastern part of Scotland, south of the Forth, while the *Damnonii* are seen to occupy the region situated athwart the Clyde. The inhabitants of Fife were given the name *Venicones* although this appears to have been changed to *Maeatae* later in the Roman period of occupation. These peoples were Iron Age in culture and Celtic in speech. They had established themselves in their homesteads and forts during the turbulent years just prior to the Roman occupation of Britain and at least some of the later immigrants have been seen by archaeologists as a type of refugee from Roman advances and military successes in Gaul.

Agricola arrived in Britain as Roman governor in 78 A.D. and was almost immediately engaged in extending the frontiers of the Roman province. He pushed the northern frontier of the province forward so that within three years he had reached the Tay estuary and estab lished a temporary frontier across the narrowest part of the country, the Forth — Clyde isthmus. The native tribes of the frontier zone, who had previously been independent or hostile, were kept in check by a chain of forts commanding the main lines of communication from the south. The battle of *Mons Graupius* in 84 A.D. left the Highlands tamed and the legions mounted what was essentially a holding operation along the edge of the Highland fastness of the Caledonians.

The military strategy of the Flavian period was based on the road from Inveresk which crossed the Forth – Clyde defences at Camelon and from here linked the forts at Ardoch and Strageath to the legionary fortress at Inchtuthil near Dunkeld.   To the west of this road to the north, frontier posts were erected at points where the river valleys left the Highlands and entered the eastern lowlands.   The forts at Bochastle, Dalginross and Fendoch served this function of keeping the Highlands policed at a distance north of what Agricola appears to have considered a temporary frontier which he could later use as a base for the occupation of Northern Scotland.   However, after the withdrawal of Agricola and the Second Legion from Britain, this plan was shelved and these isolated forts were abandoned.   In the general reorganisation that followed, Roman positions appear to have been held as far north as Ardoch but the centre of operations was moved from Inchtuthil to Newstead in the Borders.

In the interval between the end of the Flavian occupation of Scotland about 100 A.D and the Antonine campaigns of 142 – 4 which culminated in the construction of the Antonine Wall between the Forth and the Clyde, there appears to have been continued trade between the native inhabitants and the Roman province since coins, pottery and other Roman goods have been discovered at West Plean and Castlehill Wood.   These have been dated to both during and after the Flavian period.

It has also been suggested that during the early part of the second century population shift occurred in the lowlands which may have given rise to Hadrian's decision to concentrate on the Tyne – Solway frontier after 122 A.D.   The lowland tribes responded to this decision with aggression, culminating in the construction of the Antonine frontier works by Lollius Urbicus in 142 A.D. together with the reoccupation of Ardoch as a forward post. The Antonine system was maintained, despite the raids of 155 and 180 – 1, until 196 A.D. when it was abandoned in favour of the Hadrianic frontier.

The years 209 – 11 saw an attempt by Severus to contain the Caledonians and the Maeatae by a punitive campaign north of the Forth, but it is doubtful if the Antonine Wall was occupied at this time.   The net result appears to have been the development of a Roman protectorate system in the area between the walls which lasted until the final withdrawal of Roman troops from Britain in the early fifth century.

The impact of the Roman occupation on the region is difficult to assess, but there can be no doubt that it went deeper than a mere relationship of conqueror to a heterogenous group of vanquished tribes.   Scotland received a steady stream of Roman coins, pottery and manufactured articles and there is evidence to suggest that the Civil Zone in Southern Britain obtained raw materials, particularly wool, from the Iron Age societies of the north.   On the other hand, the size of the granaries at Roman forts suggests that this basic commodity was imported via the Forth from the villas of the south, pointing to the largely pastoral nature of the regional economy.   The addition of civilian settlements to many of the Antonine forts and the discovery of native objects within their bounds similarly suggests that the influence was not confined to a one-way traffic.

The Region during the Dark Ages

The period between the withdrawal of the Roman troops from the region and the Union of Scotland in the eleventh century is aptly termed the Dark Ages.   The evidence for this formative phase in the development of the rural settlement pattern of the region must rest on archaeological material and linguistic evidence preserved in the local place-names. The region lay at the cross-roads of four different cultural streams — Britain, Anglian, Pictish and Scots, all of which have left, to varying degrees, an indelible imprint on the landscape.

A glance at the topographical maps of the region shows that the settlement pattern of the area is dominated by place-names of British or Gaelic origin with the occasional Pictish element also being in evidence.   These names however, are overlain by many English elements which derive from the twelfth and thirteenth centuries when Anglo — Norman feudalism was introduced, but which in general are much later in date.

The immediate post Roman period saw the establishment of the British kingdoms of Strathclyde in the west and Manau Goddodin across the upper reaches of the Forth estuary. This latter area has given rise to the present names of Slamannan and Clackmannan, "Stone of Manan", possibly the centre of this kingdom.   To the north of the Ochils the kingdom of Pictland developed, giving rise to P — Celtic names prefixed by *pit, aber, pert,* and *lanerc* elements.   The Scots of Dalriada had extended into the upper Forth valley by the sixth century bringing with them the influence of the Celtic church and establishing early monastic sites at Aberfoyle and Dunblane.   Gaelic place-names with *bal* as in Balfron and Balquhidder, *auch* as in Auchterarder and *kil* as in Killearn and Kilmadock are also indicative of Scottish influence in the region.   By the ninth century, Scots and Picts were united, an historical fact mirrored linguistically in amalgam place-names with both Pictish and Gaelic roots.

The Angles of the Lothians appear to have had only a marginal impact on the region, for despite the fact that they reached Stirling and eventually annexed the area covered by Manau Goddodin, the western frontier of Lothian appears to have run through the country between the rivers Carron and Avon and the *—ing, —ham,* and *—ton* suffixes of the Lothians are absent.   The fact that the region was located on the southern frontier of Pictland is reflected in the thin scatter of *pit* elements across Clackmannanshire and Strathearn and the groups of other P — Celtic elements such as *carden, lanerc, pert, pevr* and *aber* distributed up the valleys of the Forth and Teith.

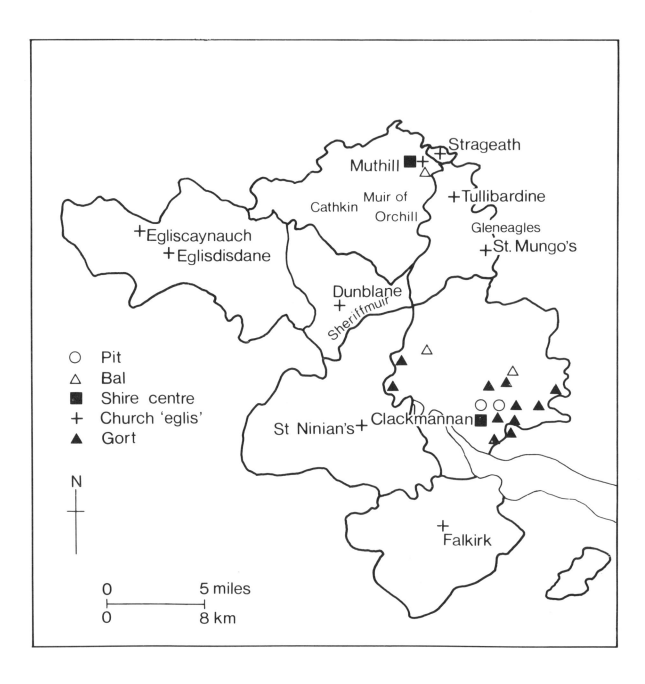

Fig 9.3   THE STIRLING REGION IN THE DARK AGES

In many respects the pattern of these cultural influences becomes clearer when one examines the work completed by Barrow on certain documentary sources of the eleventh and twelfth centuries which afford an insight into the evolution of the rural settlement pattern as well as the agrarian and territorial organisation of pre-feudal Scotland.

In early medieval Scotland an important link has been found to exist between the *shire*, the unit of royal lordship, and the *thanage* who administered these units of terrirotial organisation. The existence of a shire system has been proven in the cases of Stirling, Callander and Clackmannan and postulated in the instances of Dunblane or Lecropt, Muthill, Kilmadock and Catherlauenach.

The lordship of Callander was royal demesne in the twelfth century and lay between the Carron and the Avon, stretching back from the Forth to include much of the present parishes of Grangemouth, Falkirk, Muiravonside and Slamannan. The ecclesiastical centre of this area was at Egglesbrec or Falkirk and prior to 1165 a number of dependent chapels were already in existence. The original shire of Stirling appears to have had a similar type of organisation and indeed the ancient shire later became the nucleus of a much larger royal sheriffdom. The main church was sited at St Ninians, then known as Eccles, and its parochial territory, including that of its dependent chapels, stretched from Cambusbarron and Cornton in the north to Dunipace and Larbert in the south and to the boundary of Airth and Bothkennar in the east.

On the other side of the Forth, the shire of Clackmannan does not appear to have had this *egles* element within its bounds, a trait also evident in the postulated shire of Dunblane or Lecropt and Muthill. On the other hand, the smaller areas of Kilmadock, centred on Egliscaynauch and Eglisdisdane, and Catherlavenach centred on Gleneagles possess this early ecclesiastical element. The basic difference between these and the shires of Stirling and Callander appears to be in areal extent. The fact that the more northerly areas are smaller than those in South-east Scotland is claimed by Barrow to indicate a poorer and more sparsely populated countryside.

The common moor and the mill to which the tenants of these lordships were thirled appear also as essential ingredients of the shire system. It has also been shown that when feudal barons replaced the thanes in the twelfth and thirteenth centuries and were granted jurisdiction over these areas on behalf of the king, the shire became the unit for the assessment of goods and services. Of these basic elements of the shire a definable area of common pasture may be seen as an essential, perhaps fairly primitive, characteristic of the shire system and is certainly that most apparent in the present landscape. Slamannan Muir can be linked to Callander and Sheriffmuir to the possible shire of Dunblane, whereas the Muir of Orchill, otherwise known as Cotken (Coitcheann — common in Gaelic) may have fulfilled a similar role for the vanished shire of Cathermothel or Muthill and perhaps also for Catherlavenach or Blackford, just beyond the region towards Perth.

From the link which has been established between the early church or egles element and the shire, it is evident that the shire system determined the pattern of lordship and land distribution over a long period of time before it appeared in the documents of the twelfth century. Although it could be argued that the apparent coincidence of ecclesiastical and secular organisation suggests that the shire was merely an early form of the parish, the evidence points to the contrary. In the first place, several shires were either smaller or larger than a parish and took their names from non-ecclesiastical sites, and secondly many of the shires bear Brittonic names. They therefore predate the widespread use of Gaelic in the east, that is to say they are earlier than the ninth century and many are likely to be much older than this since they refer to topographical features.

The place name evidence is helpful in another context as the relative balance between the Pictish *pit* element and the Gaelic *baile* element is important in deciding the cultural influences at this formative stage. Many Pictish names were influenced if not changed completely by the eastward diffusion of Gaelic and this may account for the relatively few instances cited on the map depicting the shire boundaries. The *egles* element is Brittonic and some of these, for example those in Kilmadock appear to have been converted to the Gaelic *kil* type due to the same process. Other P − Gaelic elements, such as *aber, pol* and *pert* contain hybrid names from a similar bilingual phase and, like the other evidence, point to a surplanting of older names by the incoming Gaelic forms after the union of the kingdoms of Picts and Scots in the ninth century.

In the light of such evidence, it can hardly be claimed that the shire system was invented by the Celtic church no matter what date one gives for its inception. The Church merely adapted itself to the existing social structure and territorial organisation. Many of the egles churches appear to have been founded on a shire basis and were often located close to its centre. The high ratio of lost names and places, many of them without clerical foundations, also suggests antiquity so that the survival of old English names, like *gort,* could denote a persistent but unmeasured Anglian influence within peripheral Pictish areas.

The Medieval Period

In medieval times the regional dichotomy between highland and lowland was as marked as it is in contemporary Scotland. The highland areas were dominated by scattered townships, small compact holdings and the shielings located on the unimproved summer pastures beyond the head-dyke which separated them from the lower areas of more intensive use. The lowland areas had a completely different form of agrarian and social organisation founded on larger settlements, fermtouns with a greater agricultural potential and larger areas of arable land.

Nucleated villages were undoubtedly a reality in the lower lying areas south of the Forth. Many of them had parochial status at an early date or were associated with baronial ownership by the twelfth and thirteenth centuries. Frequently they were linked to outlying settlements to form a shire unit, the unity of which was expressed not so much in the resident population as in the shire centre and the landowner, usually the king, the church or some feudal baron. It was also expressed in the thane, the officer who administered the shire and yet at the same time was virtually its hereditary tenant. The earliest documentary evidence indicates that the arable land lay open in a large tract around the nucleus of the settlement and that individual holdings consisted of a number of rigs dispersed across the fields. Areas of meadowland, common pasture and often hill grazing were assigned to most of the settlements. There is no indication in early documents of any system of infield — outfield cultivations, although the texts are not incompatible with the existence of such a system. The twelfth and thirteenth centuries were a period of growing population with pressure on available land, a factor which explains the steady process of extending the arable into the waste that can be discerned in land charters.

North of the Forth, the main social unit was the relatively widely dispersed township, often with no obvious nucleus and sometimes with the church located at a site bearing relevance to any other major feature in the parish. Each of these townships had for its support a small amount of arable land, the infield, in close proximity to the settlement that was cultivated annually on a communal basis. Arable situated at a distance from the settlement was more limited and was confined to the periodic cultivation of small plots in the outfield which was normally used for grazing. The larger extent of grazing land around the townships indicates that the main emphasis of the agricultural economy was on pastoralism. With the introduction of Anglo — Norman feudalism to these areas during the reigns of David I (1124 — 53) and subsequent kings, the barony, a new unit of organisation was introduced. These were often centred on a motte and baile type of castle which eventually was replaced by the stone built castle or peel, but they also gave rise to a type of estate which might include many fermtouns, including a 'milton', a 'kirkton' and 'the mains', the fermtoun of the lord's demesne or home-farm.

In the highland areas the main settlement unit was the clachan, a small closely knit community huddled close to the limited amount of arable land where small amounts of oats and bere could be cultivated. The main wealth of these townships accrued from the cattle which they owned and which during the summer were taken to the mountain pastures beyond the head-dyke where the shieling or summer residences were located.

It is evident from medieval as well as from later sources, that the basic pattern of rural settlement and agrarian society remained virtually unchanged until the improvements in agriculture and the enclosures of the eighteenth century. The distinctive features of the rural settlements were the result of the different background of legislation relating to the

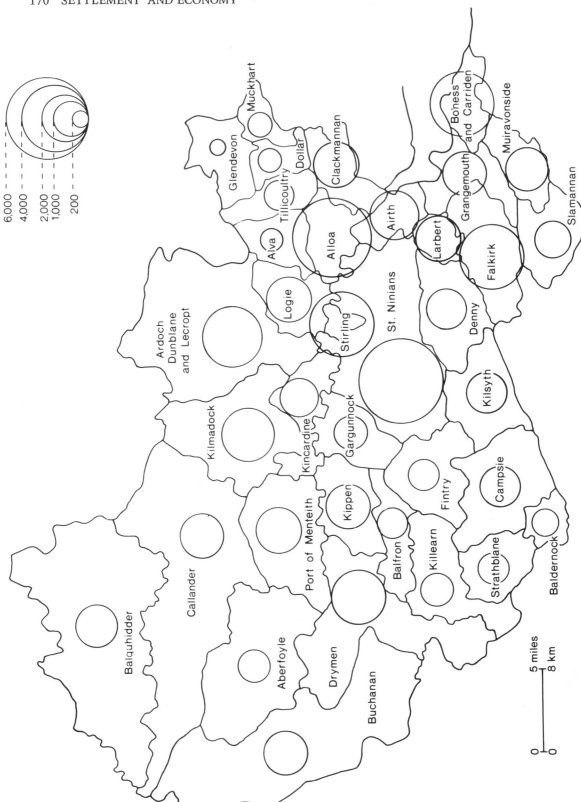

Fig 9.4   POPULATION OF THE STIRLING REGION IN 1755

land and the organisation of the burghs in Scotland compared with that in England. It also reflects a different form of social organisation. The exclusive marketing monopoly of the Scottish burgh until the sixteenth century is largely responsible for the absence of true villages in Scotland in all areas save the anglicised Lothians and for the belated development of rural industries and the provision in rural areas of any form of services apart from those of a basic agricultural nature.

Rural Settlement in the Eighteenth and Nineteenth Centuries

One of the most fundamental features affecting the pattern of rural settlement and agrarian organisation was the enclosure and consolidation of land holding which prefaced the improvements in agriculture during the course of the eighteenth century. Land consolidation meant the end of the fermtoun and clachan and the general dispersal of these nucleations into the surrounding fields. The general reorganisation and improvement of agriculture also gave impetus for the dispossessed and landless to migrate to the growing towns or the industrial and planned villages which were developing in response to changes and developments in the industrial and transport sectors of the economy.

The progress of enclosure and improvement varied widely according to land potential, but the pioneers of the agricultural revolution were of necessity the landowners because of the poverty and general lack of knowledge about the new methods on the part of the tenants. The general trend of enclosure in the region was therefore similar to that in most parts of the country. The first part of the eighteenth century was characterised by a few enclosures carried out by prominent landowners whereas the bulk of enclosures can be dated to the second half of the century. The estates of Sir John Erskine at Alva and the estate of Callander House are mentioned by Sibbald in 1707 as being enclosed. On the other hand, the parish minister of Muiravonside, writing in the Statistical Account in the 1790's, claimed that "a considerable part of the parish has been inclosed within these last few years". The changes in a parish like Kippen appear to have begun after the completion of the military road from Stirling to Dumbarton along the northern edge of the Campsies. After a very uneven start at the beginning of the century, considerable improvements and landscape changes had been made during the course of the eighteenth century, but in most cases these changes were in evidence in the lowland areas several decades prior to their appearance in the highland areas of the region. There were however some notable exceptions in the lowlands, like Slamannan where the old system of run-rig persisted quite late. New areas were also opened up for agriculture, notably the carselands of the Forth valley where the carse reclamation schemes of landowners like Lord Kames at Blair Drummond completely changed the face of a formerly negative area.

In the Highlands, the clearances and evictions, together with the introduction of sheep in place of black cattle as the mainstay of the pastoral economy, had a dramatic effect on both the social fabric and the settlement pattern of the region. The relationship of clachan to shieling was broken down, the former often becoming either deserted or replaced by a single sheep farm and the latter falling into disuse and decay. The net result was depopulation of many highland glens and the subsequent migration of the displaced population to the improved agricultural areas of the Carse of Stirling and the eastern lowlands, or to the developing industrial areas in the east of the region.

The century after 1745 may be described as the era of the planned village. The general economic and social changes in Scotland during this period led to the development of planned village units, related to the stimulation of trade and industry in rural areas, and to estate planning. The economic changes pointed to the need for a village society to stimulate trade and industry in areas where an unfavourable environment required employment to supplement agriculture or, where it was essential, to erect villages to absorb the surplus rural population that resulted from the agricultural changes of the eighteenth century. If one excludes the mining villages of the coalfields, it can be seen that many planned villages fulfilled several of these aims.

Prior to 1780 agricultural activities predominated the erection of new villages, notably the estate villages associated with the improvement of private estates. The village of Braco, for example, was built on feus on the estate of the same name and was developed after the completion of the church in 1780. Callander was also developed on feus held by the Perth family although it also contained plots associated with a soldier's settlement developed after the rising of 1745.

In the period 1770 — 1800 village planning reached its peak largely due to the rapid growth of the textile industry. Balfron was greatly enlarged in the 1790's by the Dunmore family in Ballindalloch and Ballikinrain. Here the original settlement was located close to the church and the planned element lying between the church and the Endrick was associated with the rising cotton industry, a feature still in evidence in present day street names like Cotton Street, Printer's Row and Spoker's Loan. Fintry was erected to house workers employed in a cotton factory started by the Speirs family and Deanston was erected in 1785 for a similar purpose.

After 1800 the movement was more closely associated with the highlands where the later enclosures and the social implications of the agricultural changes and clearances for sheep farming were the major forces influencing village development. In this area too, the development of transport links led to a concentration of a widely scattered population into the developing service centres at nodal points in the communications network.

In the industrial areas in the east of the region, coal and ironstone mining led to the development of the grid-iron plan of large mining settlements like Coalsnaughton, Maddiston,

Redding, Devonside and similar settlements on the Stirlingshire and Clackmannanshire coalfields.

The result of these changes are reflected in the settlement pattern of the present day. Around the mountain core lies an upland fringe of widely scattered farmsteads and clachan remnants whilst recent developments have led to the formation of valley clusters. In the lowland areas with its more favourable agriculture environment one enters a region of plentiful farmsteads, hamlets and later planned villages with market towns and small burghs liberally sprinkled throughout the area. In the industrial belt of the east are situated the urban areas and mining and industrial villages but these still retain a girdle of fields with scattered farm units.

REFERENCES

Barrow, G W S   1973   *The Kingdom of the Scots*, London.

Barrow, G W S   1962   'Rural settlement in central and eastern Scotland', *Scottish Studies*, 6, Pt. 2.

Cadell, H M   1913   *The Story of the Forth*, Glasgow.

Caird, J B   1964   'The making of the Scottish rural landscape', *Scottish Geographical Magazine*, 80.

Chadwick, H M   1949   *Early Scotland*, Cambridge.

Fairhurst, H   1954   'The geography of Scotland in prehistoric times', *Trans. Archaeological Soc.*, Glasgow 13.

Fairhurst, H   1960   'Scottish clachans', *Scottish Geographical Magazine*, 76.

Feachem, R   1963   *A Guide to Prehistoric Scotland*, Edinburgh.

Graham, P   1812   *A General View of The Agriculture of the County of Stirling*, Edinburgh.

Grant, I F   1930   *The Social and Economic Development of Scotland before 1603*, Edinburgh.

Houston, J M   1948   'Village planning in Scotland, 1745 – 1845', *Advancement of Science,* 5.

Jackson, K   1956   *Language and History in Early Britain,* Edinburgh.

Kirk, W   1957   'The primary agricultural colonisation of Scotland', *Scottish Geographical Magazine,* 73.

Lacaille, A D   1954   *The Stone Age in Scotland,* London.

MacDonald, Sir G   1934   *The Roman Wall in Scotland,* Oxford.

Nimmo, W   1817   *History of Stirlingshire,* edited and revised by W M Stirling, Stirling.

Piggott, S   1962   *The Prehistoric Peoples of Scotland,* Edinburgh.

Richmond, I A   1958   *Roman and Native in Roman Britain,* Edinburgh.

Robertson, A S   1963   *The Antonine Wall,* Glasgow.

Robertson, I M   1949   'The head-dyke – a fundamental line in Scottish geography', *Scottish Geographical Magazine,* 65.

Sibbald, R   1707   *A History and Description of Stirlingshire,* reprinted Edinburgh, 1892.

Wainwright, F T   1955   *The Problem of the Picts,* Edinburgh.

Watson, W J   1926   *History of the Celtic Place-Names of Scotland,* Edinburgh.

The relevant volumes of the *Old* and *New Statistical Accounts of Scotland* also contain valuable information.

CHAPTER 10

THE REGION IN THE EIGHTEENTH AND NINETEENTH CENTURIES

It is not possible, within the space of a short chapter, to do justice to the significant role the Stirling Region played in the economic development of modern Scotland. Although following in general the major phases of Scotland's economic and social development the region was often in the forefront of innovation and change and acted as a laboratory from which ideas and improvements spread to other parts of the country. Many would agree that the Carse of Stirling, stretching along the Forth from Menteith to Falkirk, was the scene of the great awakening of Scottish agriculture in the eighteenth century. Improvements by the large landowners, including enclosure, reclamation and drainage, were technical advances that were followed in other parts of the country and the names of Lord Kames of Blair Drummond, the Duke of Montrose, William Forbes of Callander and John Ramsay of Ochtertyre, etc., survive in the annals as some of the main exponents of agricultural innovation in Scotland.

The region played no less a prominent part in Scotland's industrial and manufacturing progress. The famous Carron Iron Company, established in the parish of Larbert in 1759, made manufacturing history with its use of coke as a fuel in the iron industry. The success of the Company heralded the modern phase of Scottish iron production and Carron developed as one of the foremost producers in Britain. The significance of the region's early iron and other industries is revealed in the wide variety of industrial remains scattered throughout almost every parish. These are of exceptional interest to the industrial archaeologist as are the remnants of past transport systems — drove roads, turnpikes, canals, tramways and railways — on which economic progress depended (see Butt, 1967).

In view of the complexities of the region's economic history, this essay can present only a general commentary on the major developments and changes that have taken place since c. 1750. In total, however, these have produced a composite agricultural and industrial landscape which provides some insight and understanding to the region's modern economic character and development problems.

A Landscape of Improvement

The rural landscape of the Stirling Region, like that of much of Scotland, is one of agricultural improvement. So drastic and widespread were the changes in the period 1750 to 1850 that few signs of previous settlement and land-use systems are visible today and the patterns then established in respect to farm sizes, field boundaries and even farm buildings,

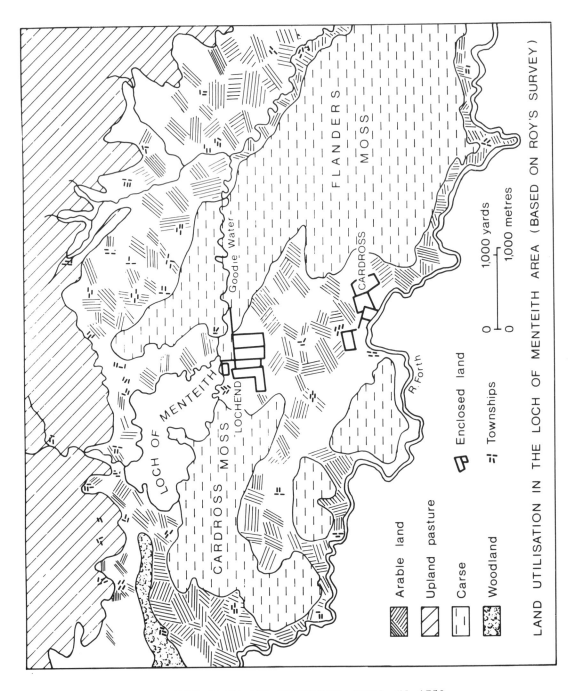

Fig 10.1   THE   LAKE   OF   MENTEITH   AREA   IN   1750

have persisted with relatively little change into the present (Kay, 1962). Caird (1964) has termed Scotland's rural landscape as one of 'revolution' rather than one of slow evolution, 'a landscape deliberately created' and one that reveals 'the total impact of human decision, mainly laird's decisions in the eighteenth and nineteenth centuries'.

A general picture of the Region's rural landscape prior to general improvement may be gained from the valuable map produced by William Roy in 1747 − 55. Primarily a military survey on a scale of 1,000 yards to 1 inch, it covers the whole of mainland Scotland at a time when the major part of the country still followed the old ways of agriculture. The map, of which Figure 10.1 is a part, shows the relief by hachuring, the rivers, the ridges of the run-rig system of agriculture in a generalised form, the wasteland (distinguishing between heathland and peat moss and marsh), the woods and forests, the enclosures and plantations, and gives information on settlements and communications.

The agriculture of the Stirling Region followed the standard Scottish pattern where the farmed lands were subdivided into infields and outfields and the cultivated fields were partitioned into rigs or ridges, usually held alternately by different tenants (for an enlightened view on infield − outfield see Dodghson, 1973). The infield was the ground nearest to the farmsteads and usually comprised about one-fifth of the arable land of the township. It was kept in permanent tillage and with few exceptions was divided into three equal parts which carried a rotation of grains. The terms infield and outfield were descriptive not of separate field areas but of types of ground (Smout, 1973, p112). The infield portion of the arable land usually occupied the best and most conveniently situated land of the settlement. The rest was termed outfield and was intermittently cropped, that is, it was cropped year after year until its fertility declined. Thereafter it was abandoned until nature and the dung of grazing animals restored enough fertility to justify the resumption of cropping.

The division between the land in permanent use and the moorland was usually marked by the head-dyke which ran along the hillside separating the arable land, meadows, woodland and rough grazing from the higher slopes which were used less often. The head-dyke has been regarded as a fundamental line in Scottish Geography for it marked not the limits of land utilisation but the distinction between intensive and extensive agriculture. The moor above the head-dyke was used for pasturing horses and sheep and, if of good quality, cattle during the summer months. This practice involved the daily or seasonal transference of flocks and herds from lowland to highland.

For the Stirling Region ample evidence for charting the break up of infield − outfield and for measuring the progress of agricultural improvement is afforded in the *First* and *Second Statistical Account,* in the varied collections of estate papers and documents, and the works of numerous contemporary writers. Credit for improvement is mainly assigned to the landowners who alone were in a position to initiate them. 'It was only when the landlord found it convenient to do the work at his own expense', writes Nimmo (1880, pp243 − 4), 'that any progress in this direction was made, for however willing the tenant might be to have his ground improved it was rare that he could command the funds thus to be sunk'. The point is reiterated by Tait (1884, p162) who comments that 'farmers . . . . had not the skill, the capital, or the enterprise which they subsequently acquired, and which transformed them into active and successful improvers of land'. But there were exceptions. There is record of one tenant on the Ochtertyre estate in Perthshire who limed a single ridge in what had evidently been enclosed run-rig land (Symon, 1959, p114). The resultant crop was so luxuriant that the laird offered to take the produce in payment of the rent of the whole farm. Other enterprising tenants followed this example and there is evidence of extensive liming on the lands of the Tullibody estate in Clackmannanshire. For the most part, however, agricultural improvements was the result of the local landowners' initiative and some of the modest first steps are made clear on Roy's map where the limited consolidation and enclosure of scattered rigs is associated with the country houses (Fig. 10.1).

Notwithstanding the improvements introduced by the landowners towards the conclusion of the eighteenth century, it is interesting to note that the Stirling Region, in comparison with other parts of Scotland, had few large estates. In Stirlingshire only the Duke of Montrose and Forbes of Callander held more than 10,000 acres, the former estate centred on Buchanan Castle in the parish of Drymen, comprising 68,878 acres and the latter located in the Falkirk area, 13,041 acres. In addition there were 41 estates of 1,000 acres and upwards, a large number of proprietors with less than 100 acres and many small farmers feuing from a subject superior. With the unsettled conditions during the early years of the eighteenth century and the decline in the value of property it was common for landowners to parcel out properties among their retainers at rents equivalent to little more than moderate feu duties. Large sections of the estate of the Duke of Montrose and the Earls of Mar, Menteith and Glencairn were disposed of in this way. The Earl of Wigtown, who opposed the Union with England and believed that it would be ruinous to Scotland, divided his estate among his tenants on the condition that they would continue to pay the rents of the time. This accounted for the large number of small proprietors in the parishes of St Ninians, Denny, Campsie, Slamannan and areas of the Carse (Tait, 1884, p151).

William Forbes of Callander was justly acclaimed as one of the principal agricultural improvers of the Region. 'In his operations in various departments of agriculture', states Graham (1812, p123), 'especially in that of inclosing he furnishes a distinguished example'. Forbes purchased his estate in 1783 and the first stages in its improvement included the enclosure of 4,000 acres and the subdivision of the lands around Falkirk into fields of six or seven acres. These were surrounded by hedges or ditches and limed at the rate of 100 bushels an acre. After a crop of oats, which was sowed along with clover and rye grass, the lands leased and tenants throughout the estate were encouraged to improve after the example of the proprietor.

As on estates throughout Scotland, the plantation of woodlands went hand in hand with enclosure. This was done partly from recognition of the commercial value of timber, partly to embellish the appearance of property. According to Graham (1812, p124) the construction of fences on the Callendar estate required 'not less than six million thorns' and the trees of various kinds, planted in hedge-rows, amounted to above 200,000, 'forming alone a forest'. The planted woodlands of Callendar covered several hundred acres, but in no way could they compete with the large-scale afforestation undertaken on the lands of the Duke of Montrose. In addition to the valuable coppice wood of natural oak, ash, birch and alder that clothed the sides of Loch Lomond, the policy of the estate was to plant annually an average of 60 acres with deciduous and coniferous species. Between 1792 and 1812, 1,200 acres were planted in Buchanan parish alone, which was equivalent to 1,200,000 oaks and ashes and two million larches and Scots firs. These woodlands were divided into 24 portions or hags, one of which was cut down annually for sale and then replanted.

The plantation of woodlands received praise from the agricultural writers of the time, especially where the presence of trees contrasted with the flat and monotonous areas of the Region's carselands. The Carse of Stirling, however, had its own agricultural revolution and its landscape changes were as dramatic as anywhere in Scotland. In Stirlingshire the Carse covered an area of over 36,000 acres, but extensive areas were also found north of the Forth in Perthshire where Lord Kames' achievements in drainage and reclamation became legendary. Within his Blair Drummond estate was the extensive Moss of Kincardine which, under a deposit of 8 or 9 feet of peat, had a subsoil of much the same nature as that of the alluvial clay soils on adjoining farms. Kames conceived the plan of cutting the peat into pieces and floating it down to the Forth (Symon, 1959, p143). Part of the waters of the Teith, one of the Forth's tributaries, was raised 17ft by means of a water wheel and stored in reservoirs. At given times it was released and the velocity of the freed waters carried the cut peat into the Forth.

The success of the reclamation depended on cheap labour and the moss was let out in lots of eight Scots acres on improving leases of 38 years. The first colonists came in 1767 and by 1774, 13 tenants had reclaimed 104 acres of what was known as the Low Moss. Each tenant was supplied with sufficient timber for a house and was provided with two bolls of oatmeal while employed in its construction. The walls were usually of turf taken from the moss. During Kames' lifetime about one-third of the 1,800 acres of moss was reclaimed and other landlords of the Stirlingshire carselands had also joined the band waggon. Lord Dundas began a process of reclamation in 1788 and in 20 years had improved 174 acres of land. The Earl of Dunmore, about the same time, was responsible for reclaiming

170 acres in the parish of Airth. Cottars were given small patches of moss and were allowed to retain the produce once the lands were drained and cultivated. John Crasson's map of Stirlingshire, published in 1817, illustrated some of the progress achieved in drainage and reclamation. Large areas of moss, however, still existed in the upper Forth Valley where the great Flanders Moss extended three miles from west to east and averaged a mile in width. To the south-east of Stirling unreclaimed moss occupied between 2,000 and 2,500 acres.

The large-scale reclamation of the carselands came to an end in the middle of the nineteenth century when the method of peat floating developed by Kames was declared a public nuisance; it polluted the Forth and its tributaries and destroyed the salmon and oyster beds. Although this terminated the most singular and considerable agricultural reclamation yet accomplished in Scotland, improvement in the carse areas contained throughout the nineteenth century in the form of ground drainage, fertilisation and improved crop rotations (see Drysdale, 1909). Elsewhere in the Region the widespread increase in turnip and potato production, together with improvements in livestock and the development of dairying, revolutionised farming and provided the necessary produce for the expanding urban and industrial areas. Dairying was particularly important in the parishes to the west of Menteith where milk, butter and cheese were sent regularly to Glasgow. Other important dairying areas were the parishes of south and south-west Stirlingshire.

The Cattle Trade

As well as leading in many aspects of agricultural improvement, the Stirling region also played a vital role in the development and organisation of Scotland's cattle trade. The droving of black cattle and other livestock from the Highlands and Islands to the fairs and markets of the south was the natural outcome of primitive farming methods which made a reduction of stock with the approach of autumn a matter of economic necessity (for a history of Scotland's cattle trade and the social and economic implications of droving see Haldane, 1952 and Bower, 1970); 'The central situation of Stirlingshire', writes Graham (1812, pp 332 − 3), 'with regard to the breeders of cattle in the northern and western counties on the one hand and the buyers and dealers from the southern and eastern parts of the island on the other, has for a long period rendered it the theatre of the principal fairs or cattle markets in Scotland'. Up until the middle of the eighteenth century Crieff, which acquired statutory market rights in 1672, was the great centre for cattle trade from the Highlands. From 1750 onwards a number of factors combined to undermine its importance and led ultimately to the transference of the main trade to Falkirk, which developed as the greatest Scottish cattle market and collecting centre of all time. Falkirk was better situated for tapping the breeding grounds of Argyllshire and was also more attractive to the English buyers, few of whom had ventured as far north as the borders of the Highlands. On Falkirk, drove roads converged from all parts of northern and western Scotland and the greater part of the livestock continued their journey south through the Southern Uplands to the Borders and then to the fairs of Northumberland and Westmorland.

The Falkirk Tryst, a Scots term signifying a preconcerted meeting of buyers and sellers of cattle, trace their origin to the years immediately following 1707 when the Union of the English and Scottish Parliaments and the resultant common market brought a great expansion in the south-bound trade in cattle. From their original position at Polmont, to the west of Falkirk, the Trysts were moved to Roughcastle and then to an extensive site of over 200 acres at Stenhousemuir in the parish of Larbert. The dealers met tri-annually in August, September and October and the latter meeting was associated with a Tryst at Hawick, inaugurated in 1785. According to Miller, (1936) 'all the cattle that were driven from Falkirk to Newcastle or Carlisle were driven through Hawick or within twelve miles of it' (18). The October Tryst was the largest and busiest of the three and its commercial significance made lasting impressions on contemporary visitors to the area. In 1772, Thomas Pennant's description of Falkirk was that of 'a large ill-built town, supported by the great fairs of black cattle from the Highlands, it being computed that 24,000 head are annually sold there' (1790, p 229). By 1812, Graham (1812, p 333) estimated that the number of cattle sold at the October Tryst varied between 25,000 and 40,000 and there were sales of some 25,000 sheep as well as many thousands of horses. Gisborne (1854, p 15) describes how Letters of Credit were operated by the large Scottish banks who erected temporary premises on the Tryst site at Stenhousemuir. In 1844 one bank alone had honoured bills to the extent of £150,000 and Graham estimated that the total value of cattle bought and sold at the Tryst amounted to half-a-million pounds sterling.

Although the greater part of the livestock sold at the Trysts continued their journey to England, there is also evidence of buying by Scots graziers who fattened the animals in Stirlingshire and Dunbartonshire. The rise of industry and the expansion of towns throughout central Scotland led to an increase in the demand for beef. Within the Region, the Stirlingshire parishes of Campsie, Fintry, Kilsyth and Strathblane were important grazing and fattening areas as were the Ochil parishes of Clackmannanshire and the parishes of southern Perthshire.

The local livestock industry continued to prosper throughout the nineteenth century, but after 1859 the importance of the Falkirk Trysts began to decline. The great advance in agricultural knowledge which spread over Scotland was ultimately detrimental to droving. With turnip cultivation and the improvement of pasture came a change from stock breeding to stock fattening and the keeping and feeding of cattle during winter was now possible. Also, the restriction of the area given over to cattle grazing pushed the industry farther and farther north and the effects of enclosure and modern communications challenged the drovers' freedom of passage and of wayside grazing. With the decline of the Trysts, however, the eyes of Scotland were still centred on the Falkirk area where the prosperity of its rail had its effects on the fairs and markets, but this was not immediate. Indeed, in the 1860's it was reported in the local press that the Falkirk Trysts were prospering because more buyers were now able to come more easily by rail and this attracted more cattle. But in October 1880 there were only 15,000 cattle and 20,000 sheep at the Tryst and thereafter the great fair had practically ceased (Bower, 1970).

The Rise of Heavy Industry

The beginnings of Scottish modern industry may be said to date from 1759 when the Carron Ironworks was established in the Stirlingshire parish of Larbert. The founders were William Cadell of Cockenzie, near Prestonpans, an importer of iron and timber, Samuel Garbett, a Birmingham manufacturer and John Roebuck of Sheffield, a medical graduate of Edinburgh (see the definitive history by Campbell, 1961). The site of the works, beside the river Carron, possessed all the prerequisites for a successful iron industry — the proximity to iron-stone and coal supplies, water power for working bellows and heavy machinery and the proximity to the port of Borrowstouness (Bo'ness) which was convenient for London and continental markets. From the correspondence which passed between the promotors before the site was finally chosen, it appears that the availability of timber supplies was also taken into account and in its early days the furnaces at Carron were operated entirely with charcoal. There is record of the Company purchasing wood from the Glenmoriston Estate at a cost of £900 and the prospects of planting woods near Carron was also considered. This, however, was never undertaken for Carron pioneered the use of local coal and iron-stone in Scottish iron production and its use of coke as a fuel inaugurated the beginnings of heavy industry in the Central Lowlands.

The original partnership began with a capital of £12,000, but by 1773 this had increased to £150,000 when the Company enjoyed the benefits of joint-stock organisation by virtue of a royal charter of incorporation. The Anglo-Scottish character of the enterprise was responsible for many major technological advances. Prior to his successful partnership with Matthew Boulton at the Soho Works, Birmingham, James Watt came to Carron and his early experiments with the steam engine were supported by Roebuck (Butt, 1967, p 108). William Symington of Leadhills and Carron built the engine for his steamship, *Charlotte Dundas,* and other pioneers of steam navigation, Patrick Miller and James Taylor, were associated with the Carron Company in early steam development. The success of Carron, however, was secured with the introduction of Smeaton's blowing engine which was powerful enough to permit the use of coke in furnaces. In 1768, when Smeaton was engaged on engineering work in Scotland, he was commissioned by Roebuck to develop the engine which not only marked an important stage in the progress of the iron trade but also aided the rapid devlopment of coal-mining.

The reputation of Carron was based on its production of fine-quality castings and armaments. John Adam, the eldest of three famous brothers, designed elegant Carron fireplaces for stately country homes and town houses. More humble stoves for the houses of American pioneers were also virtually mass-produced. By the end of the American War of Independence the Company had the largest foundry in the world and enjoyed the highest reputation for the 'Carronade', a large-bore cannon of relatively short length. Its invention remains shrouded in mystery although it seems likely that Patrick Millar was responsible for its design. Carronades were used by the navies on both sides in the French Revolutionary and Napoleonic Wars when 5,000 cannons were turned out annually, together with cannon balls and, later, shrapnel. Nelson had carronades on the *Victory* and they were successfully employed by Wellington in the Battle of Waterloo. In addition to armaments and fireplaces Carron produced all kinds of cast iron goods as well as domestic utensils and agricultural implements which were exported to America and Europe. A direct service of vessels to transport wares to London was inaugurated and the navigability of the Carron river was improved for this purpose.

Although its example was not quickly followed the success of Carron marked the decline of the small charcoal-based furnaces that had been widely dispersed throughout Scotland and whose remains are particularly plentiful in the Stirlingshire parish of Buchanan. It was not until extensive developments had been made in transportation, particularly in canal development, that other iron works were established. In 1819, workers from Carron were responsible for founding the Falkirk Iron Works (Nimmo, 1880). It was situated to the south of the Forth-Clyde Canal to which it was connected by a basin. Falkirk became the second largest iron works in Scotland and, like Carron, became dependent on war demand. It prospered during the Crimean War when it supplied 16,000 tons of shot and shell and guns of all sizes. Happily, the Company was also devoted to the arts of peace and developed an extensive trade in ornamental and artistic castings, including iron stairs, verandahs, stoves, garden-seats, hat and umbrella stands, mirror frames and statues. Among its products were castings for some of the principal iron bridges in India, Italy, and Spain, and foreign contracts also extended to the Americas and the West Indies.

Between 1854 and 1877 nineteen other iron works were founded in south-eastern Stirlingshire (Table 10.1) and access to the Forth-Clyde Canal was critical in their siting, particularly in the cases of Burnbank, Gowanbank, Grahamston, Parkhouse and Camelon. The other principal siting factor was proximity to the branch line of the North British Railway. Many of the companies, however, were small, employing less than 100 workers and specialised in nail-making which was also a traditional industry of St Ninians (Stirling).

TABLE 10.1

STIRLINGSHIRE IRON WORKS IN 1880

(after Nimmo)

	Foundation	Number of Workers
Carron Iron Works	1759	2,500
Falkirk Iron Works	1819	900
Union Foundry	1854	100
Abbot's Foundry	1856	120
Burnbank Foundry	1860	140
Carron Bank Foundry	1860	30
Bpnnybridge Stove Works	1860	250
Bonnybridge Foundry	1860	400
Gowanbank Iron Works	1864	300
Grahamston Iron Works	1868	350
Denny Iron Works	1870	90
Larbert Foundry	1870	150
Camelon Iron Company	1872	180
Parkhouse Iron Company	1875	100
Gael Foundry	1875	40
Port Downie Iron Works	1875	100
Forth and Clyde Iron Works	1876	80
Springfield Iron Works	1876	20
Etna Foundry	1877	120
Callendar Iron Company	1877	80
Bonnybridge Malleable Iron Works	1877	8
		Total Workers 6,058

The expansion in coalmining was concomitant with the technical progress in iron production and both industries were responsible for the development of the region's 'black
country'. Throughout most of the eighteenth century coalmining was largely organised as
incidental to estate management, but its increased importance to iron production let to its
development as a major industry. As early as 1623 there is record of drift mines in operation
near Alloa and during the eighteenth century the county of Clackmannan developed as a
significant coal producing region, largely because of the possibilities of coastwise traffic to
Leith (Butt, 1967). Conditions, however, were primitive and miners were little better than
slaves. Under a law passed by the Scottish Parliament in 1606, every man who was employed in a coal mine, was legally bound to labour in it for the rest of his life as a 'necessary servant' Although the Act was repealed in 1775 it was not until the end of the century that this form of serfdom was completely abolished. Colliers often bound over their
infant children to coal-masters and in Alloa colliery in 1780 there were 103 children under
seven years of age at work.

Progress in coal-mining was related to the expanding needs of the iron industry and advances were made with drainage, ventilation and new machinery.   In 1793 the Carron Company held coal mines in the parish of Polmont at an annual rent of £1,200 and the initial stages in Watt's experiments with the steam engine were associated with Roebuck's new pit at Kinneil which suffered from flooding.   By the turn of the century Graham (1812, p.49) considered coal to be 'the basis of national improvement and of arts.   Wherever this fuel abounds comfort prevails and manufacturing increases'.   In Stirlingshire the chief coal producing districts were Bannockburn, Auchenbowie, Kilsyth, St Ninians, Denny, Lennoxtown, Kinnaird, Falkirk, Redding, and Slamannan.   In 1793, 20,000 tons were raised from the Bannockburn pits alone.   As well as supplying the iron works and local needs, coal was exported to Glasgow and to other expanding centres of Scotland.   From the Dundas pits 30,000 tons were carried by an iron railway for shipment at Carronshore. Throughout the nineteenth century coal production increased and Nimmo gives the Stirlingshire output for 1879 as 967,855 tons.   This came from 34 pits which employed a total of 1,800 miners.   The production of ironstone was also significant with an output of 108,766 tons, chiefly from the parishes of Kilsyth, Campsie, Denny, Baldernock and Muiravonside.

Of the Region's other industries in the eighteenth and nineteenth centuries textiles were of considerable importance.   In Stirlingshire, yarn and woollen manufacturers were largely confined to Alva, Stirling and Bannockburn.   Historically, however, the Tillicoultry woollen trade ranks among the first in Scotland and its products were known throughout the country as 'Tillicoultry serge'.   The industry reached its lowest ebb in 1792 — 5 when its woollen trade was transferred to Alva.   Around 1824 Tillicoultry's tradition in textiles was continued with the introduction of tartan manufactures which received royal patronage. Within the parish twelve factories employed upwards of 2,000 workers and a further nine establishments employed an equal number of handloom weavers.   Other industries included calico-printing at Campsie, Blanefield and Denny and a cotton mill at Fintry.   The latter was founded by Peter Spiers of Culcreuch in 1795.   At the time of the *New Statistical Account* the mill contained 20,000 spindles and employed 260 people.   It was closed in 1896.

Another important branch of industry was more directly linked with agriculture.   Distilling and brewing were common industries in many Stirlingshire and Clackmannanshire parishes (Butt, 1967, pp 44 — 53).   The Carsebridge Distillery was built at Alloa in 1799 by John Bald and by 1866 produced over 1 million gallons of whisky.   In Clackmannan itself the Kilbagie and Kennetpane Distilleries were owned by the Steins family who were important entrepreneurs in the early nineteenth century.   In Stirlingshire there were distilleries in the parishes of Strathblane, Denny and Falkirk and the Bankier (1828) and Rosebank (1794) distilleries in the latter two parishes, respectively, offer clear examples of the influence of the Forth and Clyde Canal on industrial location.   Four breweries also existed in Falkirk parish and quantities of beer were sent to London. Alloa, however, developed as the major centre of the brewing trade. George Younger founded a brewery firm c. 1745 which, by 1889, was the most important of the town's eight breweries employing 150 workers.

Improvements in Transport

No less significant than the landscape changes associated with agriculture and industry were the major developments and improvements in transport from 1750 onwards. The Drove roads, as already stated, were a vital means of communication between the Region and Highland Scotland, as indeed were the military roads constructed by Wade and others which focussed on Stirling, Perth and Dumbarton. Road improvement was long promised by the Scottish Parliament and Privy Council but made little headway until the second half of the eighteenth century. By 1800, however, the Stirling Region was adequately served by Turnpike roads although the country roads remained indifferent and unsuited to wheeled traffic during certain months of the year.

The fact that heavy traffic, such as coal, ironstone and timber could not be carried on the eighteenth century roads gave impetus to canal construction and the success of Brindley's Bridgewater Canal led to similar plans throughout central Scotland. The Forth and Clyde Canal envisaged in the seventeenth century and later by Defoe, was the subject of several reports before its construction. In 1764 John Smeaton was consulted on its development and his plan for a 38 miles long canal from the Clyde to Grangemouth on the Forth was authorised by an Act of 1768. Operations were suspended for financial reasons between 1775 and 1784 and the Canal was completed in 1790. It was of commercial success and utility for half a century and as traffic increased new industries, especially brewing, distilling, chemicals, saw milling and metallurgy were attracted to its banks and basins in Falkirk and Grangemouth. A direct link with Edinburgh was provided by the construction of the Union Canal (1817 − 22) which joined it at Falkirk. Although this was never a success in terms of the goods it carried it was much used by passengers until superseded by the railways. Grangemouth's importance dates from its becoming the terminus of the Forth and Clyde Canal. In 1836 the Company opened a wet dock, in 1859 a second dock, and in 1860 a railway to connect the growing port with the Edinburgh and Glasgow Railway at Falkirk. Grangemouth developed an extensive trade with England and northern Europe and became the outlet for the iron goods of Carron and other works. By 1882 the Carron Company operated steamers three times a week to and from London and important trade linked Grangemouth with Rotterdam and Hamburg. In the same year the number of vessels entering and leaving the port was 1,616, carrying a total cargo of 860,000 tons.

The great revolution in transport came with the railway era. Horse-drawn railways were first associated with the coal and iron producing areas where short lines linked them with water transport. By 1800 iron railways, including the Alloa wagon-way (1765), had been introduced on a large scale in Clackmannanshire, but Graham (1812, p 326) laments their slow development in Stirlingshire: 'Though it is certain that the Carron Company, by establishing railways throughout the vicinity of their important works, would make an immense savings, whilst they could, at the same time, construct them at a much cheaper rate than others, they have hitherto done nothing in this way'. At the time of his writing the only railways were those that led from Lord Dundas' coal-pits to Carronshore and from the Banton Colliery in Kilsyth parish to the Forth — Clyde Canal, though Carron and other iron works were to follow the Clackmannanshire example.

As railways were increasingly and successfully tested against stern economic criteria, entrepeneurs became enthusiastic about longer lines. There were numerous proposals for railways throughout central Scotland connecting with the Forth and Clyde Canal and hence linking Glasgow, Edinburgh and Grangemouth. The Edinburgh — Glasgow line, later amalgamated with the North British, was completed in 1842 and passed through the parish of Falkirk. Extensions quickly followed, including the Greenhill — Stirling line (1848), the South Alloa branch (1850), the Polmont Junction (1852), the Denny Branch (1858) and the Grangemouth branch (1861) (see Nimmo, 1880, pp 34 — 5). The other public railways wholly or in part in the Region were the Forth and Clyde Junction, the Milngavie branch and the Blane Valley and the Stirling and Dunfermline, all of which were owned or leased by the Caledonian and North British Companies. The story of further extensions, rival companies and amalgamations is complex and serves to emphasise the significance or railways to the expanding economy of central Scotland. For the Stirling Region the improved system of transport had major effects on its agricultural and industrial structure, tying both farming and manufacturing to the major markets of Scotland and Britain. The era of railway construction marked the breakdown of local parochialism and self-sufficiency and paved the way for the continued success of the Stirling Region within the Scottish economy.

REFERENCES

Bonser, K J — 1970 — *The Drovers,* London.

Butt, J — 1967 — *Industrial Archaeology of Scotland,* Newton Abbot.

Caird, J B — 1964 — 'The Making of the Scottish Rural Landscape', *Scottish Geographical Magazine,* Vol. 80.

Campbell, R H — 1961 — *Carron Company,* London.

Dodghson, R A — 1973 — The nature and development of infield – outfield in Scotland. *Institute of British Geographers (Transaction)* Vol. 59.

Drysdale, J — 1909 — Carse Farming in Stirlingshire. *Trans. Highland and Agric. Soc. of Scotland,* 5th Series, Vol. 221.

Gisborne, T jnr — 1854 — *Essays on Agriculture.* Reprinted from the Ouarterly Review, London.

Graham, P — 1812 — *General view of the Agriculture of Stirlingshire.* Edinburgh.

Haldane, A R B — 1952 — *The Drove Roads of Scotland,* Edinburgh.

Kay, G — 1962 — 'The Landscape of Improvement, a case study of agricultural change in north-east Scotland.' *Scottish Geographical Magazine,* Vol. 78.

Miller, T — 1936 — Origin of the Falkirk Trysts, *Proc. Falkirk Archaeol. and Nat. Hist. Soc.* Vol. 1.

Nimmo, W — 1880 — *The History of Stirlingshire,* London.

Pennant, T — 1790 — *A Tour in Scotland and Voyage to the Hebrides 1773,* 3 vols – Vol. II

Smout, T C   1973   *A History of the Scottish People* 1560 - 1830, London.

Symon, J A   1959   *Scottish Farming Past and Present,* Edinburgh.

Tait, J   1884   The Agriculture of the County of Stirling.   *Trans. Highland and Agric. Soc. of Scotland,* 4th Series, Vol. 16.

See also the *Old* and *New Statistical Accounts of Scotland* and British Museum Ms K XLVIII 25 — 8 'General Roy's Map of Scotland 1747 — 55'.

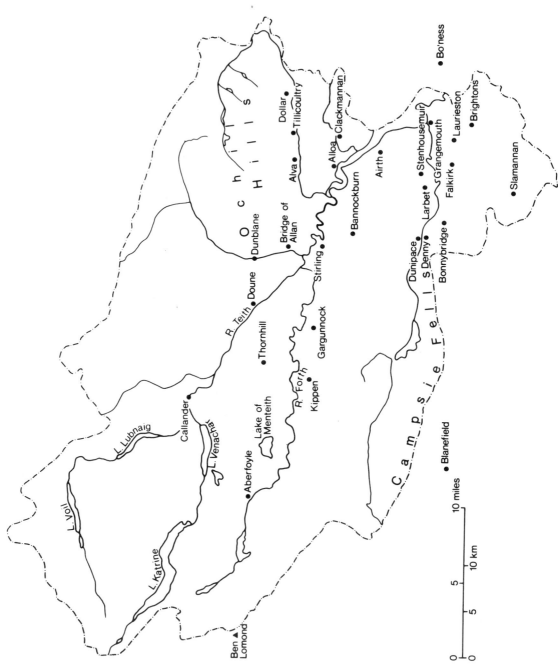

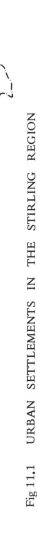

Fig 11.1 URBAN SETTLEMENTS IN THE STIRLING REGION

CHAPTER 11

URBAN SETTLEMENT

Introduction

The urban settlements of the Stirling Region present many contrasts in terms of origin, growth, structure and function. Stirling and Falkirk are the main towns but the region lacks a major city or indeed a major town. Instead, there is a sprawling urbanised area on the southern margin stretching from Bonnybridge to Grangemouth and smaller urban zones around Stirling and Alloa. Much of the western part of the region is almost devoid of urban settlements, partly due to the rugged terrain, but also resulting from the predominantly rural character of the upper Forth Valley.

This chapter will attempt to outline the principal facets of the urban settlements in the region.

Stirling

Opinions vary about the exact origin of Stirling, but the settlement was created a burgh in 1226 by the Royal Charter of Alexander II. There are obvious similarities of site between Stirling and the Old Town of Edinburgh, both crowned by a castle on the summit of a volcanic plug and with a sloping eastern ridge which formed the basis of the civil settlement. In both cases the land slopes northwards down to the River Forth, although the distance and intervening topographic variation differs, and also in both cases the land rises southwards, although again with very significant differences.

The Castle Ridge of Stirling stands out sharply above the low lying carselands to the west, north and east and even on the southern side there is a pronounced valley before the land rises steadily towards Torbrex and the prominent rise of Coxit Hill.

The situation of Stirling has also been compared with that of Perth at a convergence of routes beside what, in earlier times, was the lowest bridging point of the River Forth.

Fig. 11.2, based on a map by Mears (1936), gives some impression of the morphology of the medieval burgh of Stirling. Around the broad Market Place, each house occupied a long, narrow toft or plot with the gardens stretching down the ribs of the slope. Gradually the settlement spread eastwards down the slope and then with continued growth infilling of the tofts occurred, creating wynds and alleys leading to the interior properties, and infilling of the main street occurred, firstly in the old Market Place and then in the narrow eastern

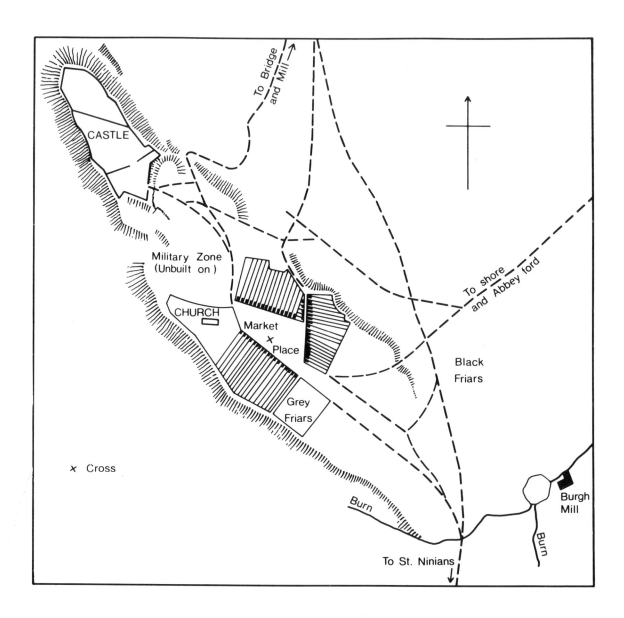

Fig 11.2   THE MORPHOLOGY OF STIRLING IN THE MIDDLE AGES

extension. Thus Broad Street and Flesh Market or St John's Street occupied the original Market Place and Baker Street and Spittal Street the eastern extension, with the narrowest portion forming Meal Market, later known as King Street. The ports or town gates also reflect this expansion and by the early sixteenth century they were sited in Meal Market, in Barrasyet (the road south to St Ninians), in Dirt Row (the road to the Burgh Mill), in Friar's Wynd (the road to Cambuskenneth Abbey) and in Mary Wynd (the road to the old bridge). Thus medieval Stirling had a morphological evolution closely reminiscent of that of Edinburgh. Both displayed the classic medieval elements of the Castle, Wall, Market and Church and indeed in both instances other ecclesiastical foundations further influenced the morphological pattern. Moreover, there were obvious similarities in their respective functional developments. Like Edinburgh, Stirling was a place of residence of the monarch and the court. As in the Canongate in Edinburgh, the Castle Wynd and Vennel in Stirling became the site of several noblemen's town houses or lodgings. Nimmo (1877) lists the residents as including the Earls of Morton, Glencairn, Cassilis, Eglinton, Linlithgow, Lennox, Montrose, Buchan, Argyle and Mar; also Lords Semphill, Cathcart, Ochiltree, Glammis, Ruthven and Methven.

Maritime trade for the burgh was transacted through the Port of Airth which also enjoyed a notable phase in the sixteenth century as the royal shipbuilding yard. At this time, the principal manufactures of Stirling were worsted cloth, shallon, stockings, thread and serge, much of which went to the markets of Europe, notably Bruges. Stirling, however, was soon to experience trading competition as a number of neighbouring settlements attained burgh status in the sixteenth and seventeenth centuries. Moreover, the departure of the Court to London removed some of the glitter of fashionable and noble life which had long been an integral part of the social fabric of the settlement.

Although the burgh exercised royalty over a large area in the seventeenth century, the actual settlement remained predominantly confined to the slopes of the Castle Ridge and this situation prevailed into the eighteenth century as Fig 11.3 reveals.

The old core was now intensively developed; the old tofts were mostly infilled and many of the streets narrow and congested. To the west lay the King's Park, the old hunting lands of the monarch and to the south were a series of lands and crofts. During the eighteenth century and the early decades of the nineteenth century, Spittal's Hospital acquired several of these crofts, including Parkfield, Rude's croft, Justinflats, Busbir's orchard and South Brae. This large landholding later formed the base for a substantial Victorian villa development in the nineteenth century.

Even at the time of John Wood's survey in 1820, Stirling still focussed upon the old town with only minor accretions. To the north there was a ribbon of houses in Upper and

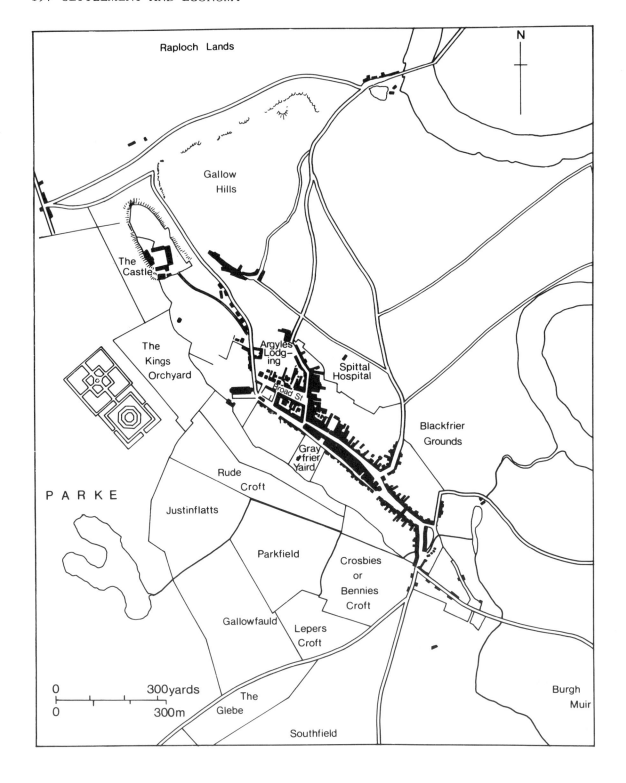

Fig 11.3   STIRLING IN THE EIGHTEENTH CENTURY

Lower Bridge Street, on the north-east side of Cowane Street and also a few houses in Queen Street and Irvine Place, whilst a similar linear spread followed Short Road. Barrasyet was now named The Port and was lined with buildings and from it a small knot of properties led eastwards in The Craigs. To the south a few Georgian villas now adjoined Melville Place and faced the mansions of Viewforth, Springbank and Annfield.

During the first half of the nineteenth century Stirling experienced quite rapid population growth; increasing from 5,271 in 1801 to 10,006 by 1851, but scarcely commensurate urban expansion. Nonetheless, urban growth did occur, notably after the arrival of the railway in 1848 and by 1866 much of the area between the old nucleus and the railway had been developed. In the process, the new main street of Murray Place and Barnton Place was constructed, heralding the functional eclipse of Broad Street and the old urban core. Ribbon development southward had now almost linked Stirling with the village of St Ninians, a small nail-making and tanning centre and an old ecclesiastical hamlet (see Fig 11.4). This phase of growth transformed the predominantly north-west — south-east alignment of the medieval burgh into the north — south arrangement of the nineteenth and twentieth century settlement.

The Boundary Commission Report on Stirling in 1832 listed the chief manufactures as tartans, shawls, carpets, yarns, dyeing, cotton goods, malt, leather, soap, candles and ropes and this pattern remained throughout the nineteenth century with the subsequent addition of agricultural machinery and coachbuilding. These industries were mostly located to the east of the old town on the low-lying carse lands near the railway, although a small weaving village had developed at Raploch at the beginning of the nineteenth century.

By 1901 Stirling had 18,403 inhabitants and the major urban accretion in the second half of the nineteenth century was the development of a Victorian suburb on the lands acquired earlier by Spittal's Hospital. All of the eastern side of Glasgow Road was also developed whilst an expanding urban node had emerged at St Ninians. To the north, all of the land between the Old Town and the bridge was now occupied and development had spread along the Shore Road to Riverside.

Between 1881 and 1921 small terraced houses and two-storey tenements were constructed in the area between Shore Road and Dean Crescent at Riverside, whilst the southern extension continued with the feuing of the estate of Wester Livilands and Williamfield producing the villas and terraced houses at Clifford Road, Randolph Road and Lennox Avenue. Infilling also occurred between Dumbarton Road and Park Terrace with the forming of Glebe Crescent and Windsor Place. To the east of the Rochvale Mills, a small working class development included Nelson Place, Burghmuir and Colquhoun Street. Western expansion was restricted by the presence of the Crown property of the King's Park whilst the abrupt

0   500 yards

0   500 metres

Fig 11.4   STIRLING   IN   1860

change of slope to the east of the mansions of Annfield, Brentham Park and Wester Livilands tended to discourage growth in the south-eastern sector of the burgh. To the south-west much of the land was still farmed but some urban incursions were penetrating the area, such as the nurseries near Laurelhill and the cricket ground at Williamfield. On the northern fringe, villas now lined the road from the bridge to the old settlement of Causewayhead, possibly encourages by the extension of the horse-tramway.

Between 1901 and 1971 Stirling has grown from 18,403 to 29,776 inhabitants, a larger absolute and relative increase than Falkirk over the corresponding period. In addition the burgh boundary has been extended to incorporate the lands of Cornton and Causewayhead north of the River Forth and a broad fringe of land all around the old nineteenth century boundary to the south of the river (see Fig 11.5).

Since 1919 the local authority has assumed an important role in the creation of the residential pattern, building 5,234 dwellings in total, about two-fifths being constructed prior to 1945. The largest inter-war development occurred at Raploch between the castle and the River Forth but smaller estates were also built at Riverside, Linden Avenue, Bannockburn Road and Alloa Road. In addition the local authority undertook the redevelopment of a few blocks in the old core.

Causewayhead was one of the few sites of inter-war private housing although a few additions also sought sites along Glasgow Road. In the immediate post-war period, new developments were almost entirely confined to the local authority sector and the Scottish Special Housing Association. The former extended the schemes at Raploch and Linden Avenue and also initiated projects at Cornton Road, St Ninians and Coxithill Road whilst the latter concentrated upon two ventures at Cornton and Borestone. Most of the 51 private houses built between 1945 and 1952 were situated at Causewayhead or were on individual plots scattered throughout the sparsely developed southern fringe.

Since 1953 two large local authority estates have been constructed at Coxithill on the south-western margin of the burgh and between Glasgow Road and Bannockburn Road on the south-eastern edge. East of the by-pass road the Linden Avenue area has been extended southwards on the carse lands whilst north of the river the Cornton estate has been completed. Additions have also been made at Raploch and central redevelopments at Broad Street and St John Street and at Cowane Street. Substantial private housing developments have also occurred, notably at Torbrex, Easter Cornton, Borestone Brae and Easter Livilands. Additionally, vacant sites have been infilled by small developments and some of the larger mansions have had parts of their gardens converted into tiny estates of bungalows and villas.

During this century many centrally sited land users such as the County Offices, the

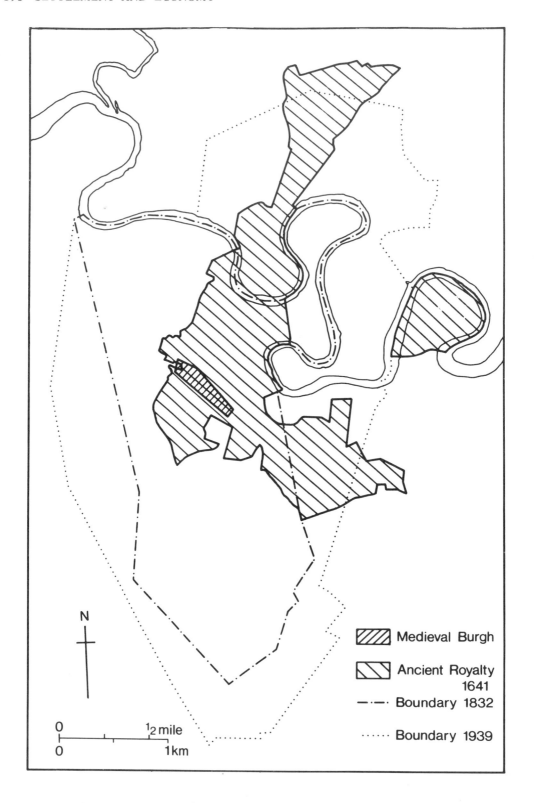

N

0           $\frac{1}{2}$ mile

0   1km

Medieval Burgh

Ancient Royalty 1641

—·— Boundary 1832

········· Boundary 1939

Fig 11.5   THE EXTENSION OF THE BURGH'S BOUNDARIES

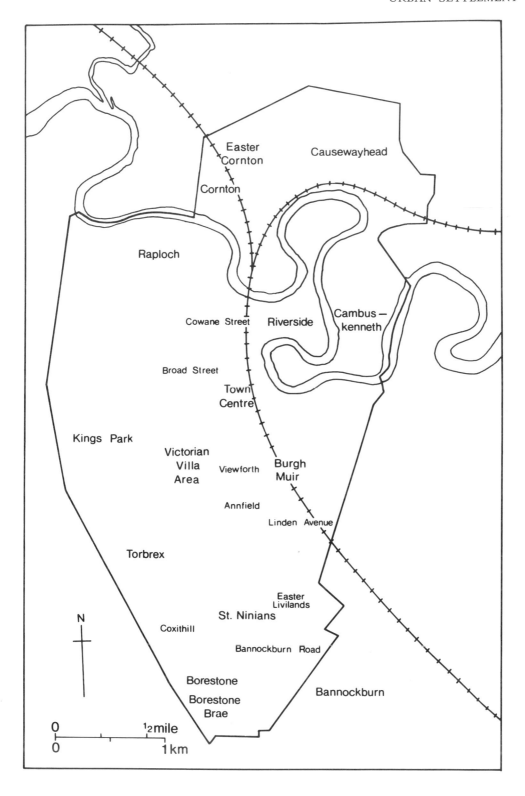

Fig 11.6   DISTRICTS IN MODERN STIRLING

High School and the Royal Infirmary have moved to southern surburban locations, and the old core has experienced a number of functional changes. By the end of the nineteenth century, the shops and offices of the central area were deserting Baker Street in favour of King Street and Murray Place. Indeed Upper Craigs, Port Street and Barnton Street were gradually being colonised by central area land users.

In the twentieth century the Port Street, Murray Place, Barnton Place axis has clearly emerged as the main shopping street with a major node at the King Street junction, and a substantial extension of the office area has incorporated much of the Victorian area to the south of the Old Town.

Thus Levein (1973) concludes that the central area grew substantially between 1880 and 1966 with the most marked expansion being to the south and the main area of discard involving the older street on Castle Hill.

Functionally, Stirling is not an important industrial town although textiles and tobacco manufacturing are important employers. Instead the burgh performs an important role as an administrative centre and a market focus, traits reflected in the large percentages employed in local government, distribution and miscellaneous services and office services. More than two-thirds of the economically active population are engaged in tertiary activities and the University has merely served to strengthen this employment character (see chapter 13). Industry is still mainly situated beside the railway and the river with minor departures at Burghmuir and twentieth century extensions at Shore, Cornton and alongside the branch railway line at Causewayhead. Although coal mining has never occurred within Stirling, the large Polmaise mine was located to the east on Kerse Road and at one time about one thousand inhabitants of the burgh were engaged in coal mining.

Gillespie and Parnell (1967) claimed that Stirling served an intensive retail hinterland of 40,000 people and a larger extensive zone of about 60,000 inhabitants. Proposals emerging from that study recommended the construction of a new inner relief road, which is now in existence beside the railway station, and the development of a new shopping precinct between Goosecroft Road and Murray Place which has not yet materialised. The latter proposal largely stems from the twin problems of traffic congestion in the principal shopping thoroughfare and a complex land use pattern created by the mainly unstructured growth of the area since 1880 in respense to varied stimuli such as new transport termini, changes in the distribution of population, the removal of some central land users to more peripheral sites and the progressive adaptation, and often intensification, of usage of the existing sites. Despite this competition, however, residences still occur on the upper floors of buildings fronting the principal shopping thoroughfare.

In contrast to the anticipated growth of the Falkirk — Grangemouth area, current planning proposals only project minor expansion in the Stirling district, principally at Bannockburn and Bridge of Allan. Indeed the overall strategy would appear to favour growth in already developed industrial areas but containment or only modest increase in the less industrial and rural areas of the County. The main exception to that generalisation is south-west Stirlingshire which will become part of the Strathclyde Region and has increasingly experienced the pressures of suburban growth on the periphery of that city-region.

Small Burghs in the Stirling District

In the immediate vicinity of Stirling is the burgh of Bridge of Allan, the urban concentration of Bannockburn and a series of smaller agricultural and mining foci such as Gargunnock, Plean and Cowie and the old seaport of Airth. To the south, Denny and Dunipace and Larbert/Stenhousemuir mark the transition to the Falkirk hinterland but to the west lies the heart of rural Stirlingshire and a succession of small central places such as Aberfoyle, Buchlyvie, Balfron, Killearn and Blanefield. Those in the Forth Valley remain preponderantly agricultural foci with only minor dormitory accretions but Blanefield and to a lesser extent Killearn have been progressively incorporated into the expanding residential hinterland of Glasgow.

Nimmo (1877) described Bridge of Allan as a romantic and fashionable spa and it was the waters from Westerton Hill which stimulated a phase of villa development in the Victorian era which transformed the settlement from a tiny village into a flourishing resort and retirement town. The wooded slopes of Westerton Hill became lined with villas while mills and a bleaching works were located by the Allan Water. The demise of the spa was more than compensated by the emergence of a dormitory function for Stirling. Bridge of Allan has successfully retained this attractive residential image whilst the main street is increasingly devoted to hotels revealing a continuing link with tourism.

Bannockburn, to the south-east of Stirling, stands in sharp contrast to Bridge of Allan. Blossoming during the nineteenth century as a centre of carpet-making and woollen mills, the settlement subsequently housed many miners working in the adjoining coalfield. With many of the old houses now demolished Bannockburn consists overwhelmingly of twentieth century local authority houses which, in places, merge indistinguishably with similar estates in adjoining portions of Stirling Burgh.

Three Perthshire burghs lie within the Stirling District of the Central Region, namely Callander, Dunblane and Doune. All three are small settlements, notably Doune which had a population in 1971 of 741 and even Dunblane, the largest of the three, had only 4,497 inhabitants at that date.

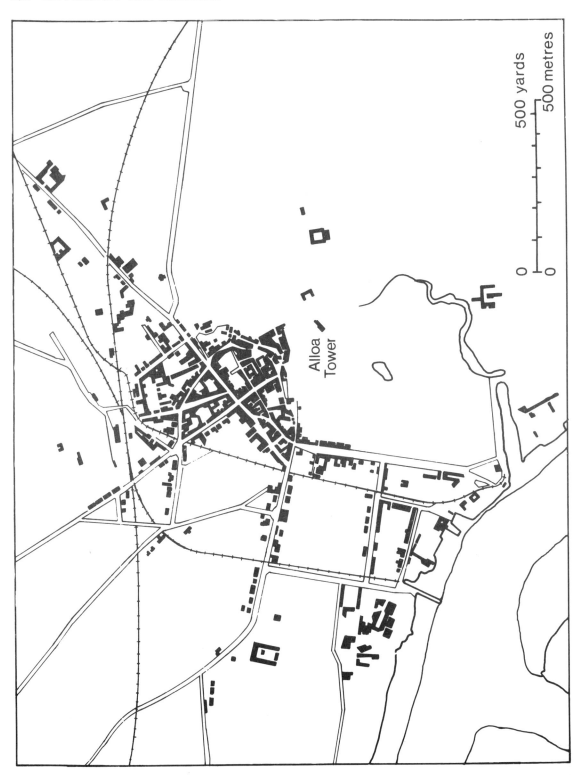

Fig 11.7 ALLOA IN 1863

They were all small market towns but subsequently Callander and Dunblane acquired additional functions. In the case of Callander this was tourism, possibly dating from the early nineteenth century and the strategic location it occupied on an important route to the Western Highlands, but certainly from the arrival of the railway which encouraged a phase of villa construction in the Victorian era. Dunblane also benefited from the railway but in this instance the Victorian villas housed commuters many of whom worked in Glasgow. This dormitory role has been maintained and, in fact, extended, and within the last decade large new housing estates have been added on some of the steep slopes overlooking the old nucleus around the Cathedral. In addition Dunblane developed a small textile industry based upon the Allan Water at the Springbank Mills. Meanwhile Doune has declined in population and remains a small compact village but with an increasing dormitory function. Dunblane and Doune clearly lie within the Stirling catchment area for shopping but Callander is more peripheral, although there are no obvious competing centres or intervening choices.

These settlements are not significantly different in population size from places such as Thronhill or Kippen which merely lack burgh status, although their dormitory function is of some importance to an understanding of the spatial patterns of the Stirling Region.

Alloa

For many years the largest settlement in the County of Clackmannan, Alloa is the principal burgh within the Stirling Region to be situated on the north bank of the River Forth.

Towards the end of the seventeenth century it was a small settlement in the shadow of Alloa Tower with a traditional market function and a thriving textile industry based upon local wool. Coal had been worked in the area for some time but commercial development did not occur until the seventeenth century. As in the case of Grangemouth, the feudal superior, the Mar and Kellie house, were influential in the development of the burgh, by sponsoring the introduction of glassmaking, in the eighteenth century. Brewing also commenced at this time, the Meadow Brewery opening in 1762, and by the end of the eighteenth century, Alloa had a flourishing base. Abundant local supplies of coal continued to foster this development in the nineteenth century and Alloa acquired iron founding and copper working to add to the now established textile, distilling, brewing and glassmaking industries. Nonetheless, Wood's Plan of 1820 reveals that Alloa was a small settlement bounded by Broad Street and Stripe Head on the west, Shilling Hill and Bridge Street on the east, Mar Street and Primrose Street on the north and Old Market Place and Alloa Tower on the south. There were, however, extra-mural industrial extensions with Alloa Brewery and Hutton's Brewery on the east flank, the Grange Distillery on the west, and the Shore Brewery and Shipyards beside the river.

The construction of the railway from Stirling to Dunfermline in 1850, with a harbour branch line at Alloa, provided a vital stimulus to the town and, in particular, to the shore area and the port. The extent of the town, in 1866, is shown in Fig 11.7, and from this it can be seen that a wide array of industries had been attracted to riverside sites. Some ribbon suburban development had commenced, notably along Grange Place, Mar Place and Whins Road but most of the settlement was located to the south and east of the railway.

Between 1861 and 1901 the population of Alloa increased from 6,425 to 11,421 inhabitants but the urban area still remained compact with minor extensions to the north at Greenfield, and the east at Springfield, and with an intensification of the usage of the area between the settlement core and the harbour including an expansion westwards along the riverside.

To the north-east a struggling agglomeration of small rows of houses adjoining the rapidly expanding Carsebridge Distillery but to the south-east Alloa House and Park formed a major barrier to urban expansion and distorted the pattern of urban growth in Alloa.

Between 1900 and 1924 only minor accretions were added to the urban area, principally in the vicinity of Tullibody Road, but one interesting development was that of the Caudron Aeroplane Factory beside the Forthbank Shipbuilding Yard to the south of Alloa Park.

Alloa Harbour, which had always encountered problems because of mudbanks, entered a sharp period of decline in 1951 culminating in closure in 1962. Even before this closure, however, one area of post-war housing was located immediately to the north of the Wet Dock, whilst another new housing area was located to the north of Clackmannan Road. During the 1950's a further estate was constructed to the south of that thoroughfare whilst in the 1960's much of the expansion occurred alongside Tullibody Road.

Alloa has managed to retain a varied and prosperous industrial structure although local coal-mining has suffered a serious decline and many of the traditional industries have only survived by changing their product or specialising in certain goods.

By 1961 almost half of the houses in the burgh had been built by the local authority and this proportion is increasing as some of the older stone terraces and tenements are demolished. Major new housing areas have been developed at Hawkhill, Fairyburn, Fairyfield and Inglewood.

Immediately to the north-east of Alloa lies the urbanised district of Sauchie which has experienced substantial population growth in this century with the erection of large housing areas at Beechwood, Williamwood and Posthill. Until 1960 mining was the major source of employment but now many of the inhabitants travel to Alloa, Alva and Tillicoultry or work in the Carsebridge Distillery or at a local knitwear factory.

Clackmannan County Council were forced to concentrate large housing developments at Sauchie and also, to the north-west of Alloa, at Tullibody because of the extensive tracts which are liable to mining subsidence.

The opening in 1952 of the short-lived Glenochil Mine transformed Tullibody from a small village into an extensive local authority housing area. From a population of only a few hundred in 1951 Tullibody district mushroomed to 6,620 inhabitants at the latest census.

The Small Burghs of Clackmannanshire

The Clackmannan District of the Central Region contains several other urban concentrations as well as Alloa. Three settlements, Alva, Tillicoultry and Dollar, possess small burgh status, while a further significant concentration occurs at Clackmannan itself.

In 1690, the feudal superior of Alva, Sir John Erskine, laid out two sides of Green Square and effectively initiated the transformation of the morphology of the town, from that of a small clachan into a regularly structured burgh. During the early part of the nineteenth century the waters of the local burn and the coal from the neighbouring mines supplied the base which produced a thriving textile industry. With the construction of the new hillfoot road from Stirling, replacing the old toll road, the focus of the settlement moved from Green Square beside the burn to Stirling Street. Most of the houses were located on the west bank of the burn, with the east bank devoted to several woollen mills. At the middle of the nineteenth century, most of the inhabitants lived in three streets of regular houses to the north of Stirling Street (Silver Street, Nether Row and Back Row) or in Green Square. More than a century later this basic urban form remains although some local authority houses have been constructed to the south of Stirling Street and at the western and eastern edges of the burgh. Since 1901 Alva has actually experienced a decline of population largely reflecting diminishing employment opportunities in the textile industry and the coal mines.

Clackmannan presents something of a contrast. In 1866 it really consisted of one street, the combined High Street which widened eastwards into Main Street and from which wynds led to the north and south with a classic back lane represented in Back Street. Some growth has taken place during the ensuing period but Clackmannan remains a small settlement within the shopping and service hinterland of Alloa.

Fig 11.8   FALKIRK IN 1832

Dollar is sometimes described in local historical sources as the Classic Burgh because of John McNabb's School, Dollar Academy.   Apart from the school, the settlement was associated in the nineteenth century with the textile industry but Dollar is primarily a nucleated residential area.   The opening of the railway station in 1869 doubtless assisted in the acquisition of this functional role although in addition to a commuting element the town has also traditionally had a retired colonial component in the population.

Tillicoultry, however, is more closely akin to Alva, being another textile settlement which expanded during the nineteenth century beside the Tillicoultry Burn.   In 1866 most of the town lay on the east bank and to the north of High Street, the main hillfoot road. Much of the textile industry which supplied a flourishing industrial base has now departed and only diversification into paper-coating and colour-printing had sustained employment opportunities.   Nonetheless, there was a sharp decline in population between 1951 and 1961 caused largely by the demise of the mining industry which particularly affected the village of Coalsnaughton which forms part of the burgh.

Collectively these Clackmannanshire settlements present considerable development problems with a pressing need for industrial expansion and diversification.   They lie on the extensive periphery of the Stirling catchment area and are separated from the Falkirk — Grangemouth growth node by the obvious obstacle of the River Forth.   As a result much of the immediate future prosperity must be associated with the fortunes of the principal settlement, Alloa and with a development of their commuting roles.

Falkirk

In the thirteenth and fourteenth centuries this district consisted of two great estates, those of Kerse and Callander.   The latter was owned by the Livingstone family and the small village of Falkirk was situated close to the march between the two estates.   In the fifteenth century, the feudal superior attempted to stimulate settlement by feuing the plots on the High Street and gradually a small agricultural settlement emerged.   Records show the presence of a market cross in 1566 and of various trades by 1584.   In 1600 the settlement was created a Burgh of Barony.   Soon afterwards it became a Burgh of Regality.   This progressive functional development was presumably accompanied by population growth and urban expansion although, as Fig 11.8 reveals, in 1832 Falkirk was a compact linear settlement consisting mainly of High Street and a series of wynds leading to the north and south with minor ramifications in New Market Road and Bank Street on the northern fringe and Howgate on the southern periphery.   To the north lay the suburbs of Bainsford and Grahamston, which had developed because of the Forth and Clyde Canal and nearby Carron Iron Works.   At that time Falkirk was largely renowned for leather and cattle trysts although a number of industries including corn mills, a foundry, a distillery and a boatyard, had clustered alongside the Forth and Clyde Canal.

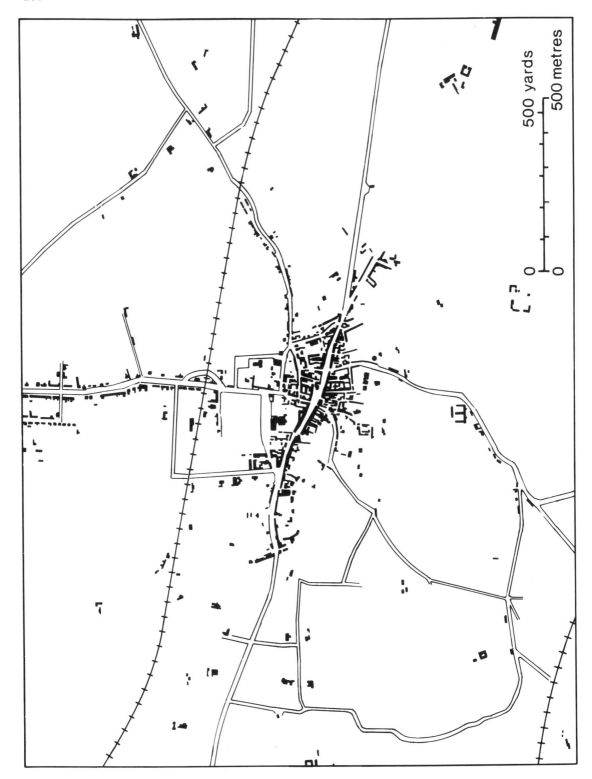

Fig 11.9   FALKIRK IN 1860

During this period Falkirk was governed by Stentmasters and Feuars, a situation instigated by the loss of power of the Livingstone family following the Jacobite Rebellion of 1745. The town became a Parliamentary Burgh in 1832 and the boundary was extended substantially, but by 1851 it only housed 8,752 inhabitants. Thus, although the founding of the Carron Iron Works in 1759 by John Roebuck, Samuel Garbett and William Cadell was of fundamental importance for the district, the impact was cumulative rather than instantaneous. Indeed it could be argued that the opening of the Grahamston branch of the railway line between Edinburgh and Glasgow, in 1850, was at least of equal significance. Certainly Falkirk experienced rapid growth during the second half of the nineteenth century, gaining more than 20,000 inhabitants and enjoying a simultaneous phase of urban extension.

In 1866 Falkirk, as can be seen from Fig. 11.9, was still a compact settlement, experiencing some growth to the south towards Rose Hall and to the north towards the railway and Grahamston. Ribbon development along Graham's Road linked the settlements and a small node had developed at the centre of Grahamston which, in turn, was separated from Bainsford by the Canal. The remaining area of settlement occurred to the west where the small village of Camelon adjoined the Glasgow Road. Here, a small industrial focus had begun to emerge beside the canal with the distillery at Rosebank as the principal component. There were a number of large houses to the south of Glasgow Road, such as Bantaskine House, and this southern portion of the burgh also included some fringe land uses such as a nursery, pleasure gardens and the Poorhouse.

In 1890 the burgh boundaries were extended to include Mungal Head Road to the north, Arnot Hill to the west and Gartcows and, in 1900, to incorporate Camelon. Considerable building had occurred between New Market Street near the town centre and the canal on the northern margins although some villa clusters had spread westwards to Arnot Hill and southwards to Woodlands. A major industrial zone now lined the canal and the Grahamston railway line, although the only major sites in central Falkirk were a large brewery beside the railway station and a tannery to the south of West Bridge Street.

Between 1901 and 1971 there has been a limited amount of population growth but the urban area has mushroomed with the development of a girdle of residential areas, largely built by the local authority, encircling the nineteenth century core. Between 1926 and 1960 a substantial area of local authority houses was erected at Carmuirs on the western margin of the burgh between the Canal and Glasgow Road. On the northern periphery large local authority estates were constructed in the inter-war period at Bainsford and during the 1950's at Langlees, whilst to the east similar developments occurred at Ladysmill and Middlefield. In addition, smaller pockets of development have occurred, such as the flats at Callander Park and various estates of private houses, notably in the south-western sector of the burgh. Between 1919 and 1971 a total of 7,852 local authority houses were constructed in Falkirk.

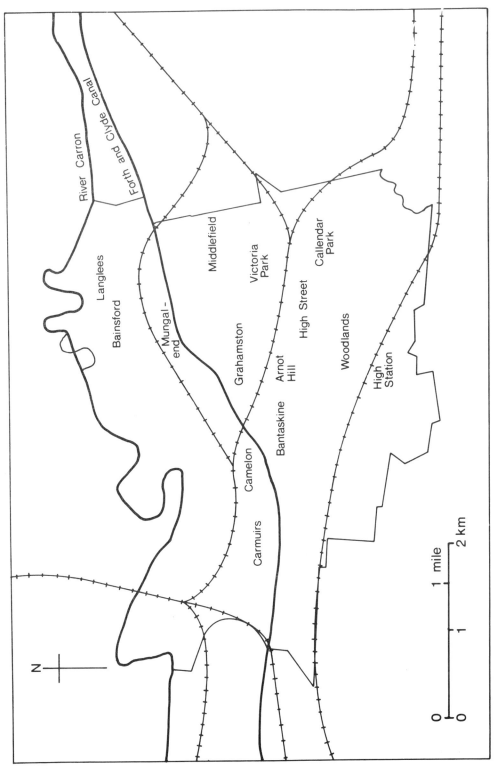

Fig 11.10 DISTRICTS IN MODERN FALKIRK

Nevertheless, in 1961, the burgh had over 3,000 nineteenth century stone cottages and tenements, many of which had only two rooms and were over-crowded and substandard. Surprisingly, however, the main high density residential areas are inter-war local authority developments at Bainsford and Easter Carmuirs.

Falkirk occupies a topographically varied site with the land rising from the river to almost 100m (330ft) on the southern periphery, but further complexity is added by ice-moulded ridges and adjoining hollows. The town centre stands on one of these ridges. Throughout the history of the settlement the site has influenced the structure and direction of urban growth, encouraging the early concentration on the High Street ridge and equally fostering the neglect of the southern slopes across steep declivity adjoining the old urban nucleus until the second half of the nineteenth century. Indeed two hospitals were amongst the first major land uses to colonise the southernmost margins despite the existence for more than a century of the potential magnet of Falkirk High railway station.

Sissons (1973) identified eight districts in Falkirk: Callendar, Ladysmill, the town centre, the southwestern sector around Bantaskine, the middleward or Grahamston, Langlees, Bainsford and Camelon. Apart from Callendar, which is mainly composed of local authority houses, and the southwestern sector, the principal middle class district, the other areas are all characterised by admixtures of land use, particularly the intermixing of housing and industry. The middle ward is particularly complex lying to the north of the town centre and consequently including many of the old working-class houses, but also some small cottages and villas, more recent local authority houses, Grahamston railway station, several iron foundries and industrial premises and some derelict areas.

During the twentieth century the iron industry has experienced some decline, but it is still the dominant industry although the construction of the aluminium rolling mills at Langlees in 1944 provided a valuable new large employer. The burgh, however, has a wide range of industries although nothing remains from the brief phase of linen and muslin weaving which immediately preceded the ironfounding era in the eighteenth century. There are now four industrial estates at Middlefield, Lochlands, Glasgow Road Camelon, and Carron Road, and additional sites are being created during the redevelopment of the old inner fringe of the burgh.

Falkirk has on several occasions attempted to introduce a boundary extension to incorporate Larbert, most recently in 1950, but this has always proved unsuccessful. On each occasion minor extensions have been granted, that of 1950 producing Lochlands and the Callendar policies. Another extension produced lands south of the main railway line at Hallglen and Princes Park which are scheduled for residential development.

Although more than one third of the labour force in 1965 were engaged in metal manufacturing there has been an element of convergence between the occupational structures of Stirling and Falkirk with the increases in female employment in the latter in the new light industries and the expansion of the white collar sector with the growth of the Technical College, Callendar Park College of Education, the Burgh Offices and a general growth of tertiary activity.

Although High Street has always been the main shopping street, the overall structure of the Central Business District has altered during the last one hundred years as Levein (1973) has revealed. During the later decades of the nineteenth century, New Market Street, Kirk Wynd, Vicker Street, Wooler Street and Manor Street were all part of the central area. Thereafter, however, expansion has been to the north towards Grahamston Station and eastwards towards the Callander Riggs Bus Station. Levein (1973) concludes that Falkirk's central area has grown substantially since 1880 with a marked period of expansion in the interwar years. More recently there has been a tendency towards western invasion illustrated most strikingly by the relocation of the Municipal Offices to a site in West Bridge Street. Given the early concentration of working-class residential areas to the north of High Street it was perhaps inevitable that the Central Business District would be extended in that direction but the steep-sided southern slope of High Street ridge may well have acted as a powerful negative barried further distorting the direction of growth.

A shopping survey by Donaldson & Sons (1972) revealed a number of interesting features of the retail geography of Falkirk. From a pedestrian flow count it emerged that the southern side of the High Street formed the principal activity area, with Boots the Chemist as the focal point, although high flows occurred at a number of other points to the east of this, but always on the southern side of the street. A supermarket seemed to be the principal magnet in the new Callander Riggs shopping centre at the extreme eastern end of High Street whilst pedestrian flows declined appreciably in the adjoining streets presumably reflecting the number of entry points to the main shopping focus.

This survey also established, perhaps re-assuringly for the planners, that 90% of all home based shoppers came from within the Falkirk – Grangemouth growth area. Just under half of all the shoppers interviewed lived in Falkirk, most of the remainder travelling from the girdle of urban settlements between Bonnybridge and Polmont. The survey provides some evidence of the limited linkage with Bo'ness, however, for only 3% of the home based Saturday shoppers came from the Bo'ness area compared with 10% from the Laurieston – Brightons district which is of similar population size. Significantly, although the overwhelming majority of shoppers listed food purchases as their primary trip purpose, quite large percentages of Saturday shoppers also referred to clothing and household goods. Thus Falkirk can lay reasonable claim to the regional shopping role envisaged in the

Grangemouth — Falkirk Survey (Robertson, 1968), although the intensity of contact with all parts of the hinterland is almost certainly unequal and an extensive hinterland zone of varying dimension would seem to exist reflecting distance, travel facilities and intervening or competing choices.   As can be seen from Table 11.1 Falkirk occupies premier position in the Stirling Region in terms of gross retail floorspace.   Moreover, the town is sufficiently large to have an internal pattern of district centres at Grahamston, Bainsford and Camelon, in addition to minor ribbons and shopping clusters.   Nonetheless the town centre clearly constitutes the principal node, as Table 11.2 illustrates, notably in terms of non-food goods. Current plans for the town centre which include the construction of a ring road, the pedestrianisation of the main shopping streets and the comprehensive redevelopment of the Garrison area, including the old brewery site immediately to the south of Grahamston Station, should all serve to enhance the shopping and service appeal of the regional central place.   In addition, the town has a large service hinterland notably in terms of hospitals and schools.   A recent indicator of the scale of the catchment area is the South of Scotland Electricity Board's decision to move their regional offices from Stirling to Falkirk.

TABLE 11.1

Gross Retail Floorspace in Selected Urban Areas (in sq ft)

	Food	Non-Food
Falkirk	186,077	615,692
Stirling	150,006	595,375
Grangemouth	63,678	120,719
Larbert — Stenhousemuir	38,420	51,504
Denny and Dunipace	29,828	40,194
Bonnybridge	20,912	22,650
Bridge of Allan	17,966	24,024
Brightons	13,439	9,585
Laurieston — Westquarter	11,263	8,363
Bannockburn	17,735	1,339

Source: Stirling and Clackmannan joint valuation Authority 1973:
Falkirk Planning Department Study 1971.

TABLE 11.2

Gross Retail Floorspace in Falkirk (in sq ft)

District	Food	Non-Food
Town Centre	92,012	547,429
Fringe of Centre	13,729	12,699
Grahamston	19,070	21,361
Bainsford	32,555	16,641
Camelon	29,711	17,562

Source: Falkirk Planning Department Study 1971.

Thus the fabric and structure of Falkirk has witnessed considerable change within the last few decades.

Other Settlements in the Falkirk area.

To the north and west of Falkirk an expanding urban zone incorporates the settlements of Denny and Dunipace, Bonnybridge, Larbert, Stenhousemuir and Carronshore. All of these settlements have experienced population growth during the present century. Between 1901 and 1971 the burgh of Denny and Dunipace grew from 4,161 to 9,841 inhabitants. The principal industries in the burgh are iron founding and papermaking although the linen industry and calico printing both enjoyed a flourishing phase during the nineteenth century. Stirling Street, the central thoroughfare of the burgh, is the principal shopping street and the location of a district shopping centre. The Grangemouth – Falkirk Survey (Robertson, 1968) predicted substantial growth for the Denny and Dunipace district with a target population in 1986 of 29,750 largely resulting from a major area of residential expansion at Dales Wood but this has not, as yet, materialised.

Larbert and Stenhousemuir, formerly independent settlements, now constitute an expanding urban zone which also includes Carronshore and is sufficiently developed to rank fourth in Table 11 in terms of gross retail floorspace. The Carron Iron Works supplied the initial growth catalyst transforming an established cattle tryst at Stenhousemuir and two quiet villages into a growing industrial area. However, it is only in recent decades that major residential extensions have linked the settlements into a rather amorphous, largely linear, urban mass, consisting of several minor nodes. Industry is largely concentrated at Larbert Cross and Carron Iron Works, whereas shopping facilities are mainly at Main Street, Stenhousemuir with a smaller grouping in Larbert. Carronshore and the area to the south of Main Street consists predominantly of local authority houses but two substantial private estates have recently built on the northern margins of the settlements. In addition, a large area of open space to the north of Main Street contains a cricket ground and a golf course whilst these in turn adjoin extensive hospital properties.

The Larbert – Stenhousemuir area was programmed for massive population growth in the Grangemouth – Falkirk Survey (Robertson, 1968) with a target population by 1986 of 51,750, an increase of some 33,000 people. The intention was to extend the present built up areas to the north, east and north-west to include major new residential areas at Carronshore, Glenbervie, Kinnaird, Torwood and Antonshill. With the substantial reduction in the planned growth of the whole region, however, much of this development will probably not now occur within the specified period and the emergence of what would have been the equivalent of a substantial town seems unlikely, at least during the next decade.

The rash of mining and industrial settlements in a southern arc between Bonnybridge and Brightons provide a number of small urban nodes. In 1871 the Bonnybridge area had a population of less than 1,000, but by 1971 the number had swollen to some 11,000. Iron founding and brickmaking form the twin foci of the industrial base dispersed in a scattered pattern of industrial areas. Indeed, the settlement is characterised by an inter-mixture of land uses and a poorly structured urban layout.

A number of small settlements developed towards the end of the nineteenth century on the moorland area to the south of Falkirk, attracted to the upland slopes by local coal reserves. With the collapse of the local mining industry, these settlements are now strongly linked to Falkirk for shopping and employment and some have developed small private estates during the last decade, e.g. Wallacestone.

The Laurieston — Brightons area consists of a number of partly linked settlements on the eastern margins of Falkirk, with a total population in excess of 12,000 inhabitants. Mining also formed the industrial base in this area and there are now very few manufacturing industries in these settlements.

Laurieston was a planned village in 1756 astride the main route leading east from Falkirk but most of the other settlements are of more recent origin, notably Westquarter, an inter-war local authority estate on the site of an old country estate. Despite the incursions by mining and settlement much of the land to the south and south-east of Falkirk is still predominantly rural, at least in part a function of the altitude and topography of the area, and it is intended that this rural character should be retained and growth largely channelled to the north and west of Falkirk.

Bo'ness

Bo'ness or Borrowstounness forms the easternmost settlement in the Stirling Region and is almost an outlier lying to the east of the River Avon and to the north of Linlithgow. For many purposes it has more in common with the Lothians Region than it does with that centred on Stirling and Falkirk.

Originally the settlement clung to the foreshore area beneath the steep slopes of the raised shoreline but gradually settlement has ascended the slope and spread southwards on to the clifftop. From the medieval period coal was mined in the area and exported through the small port at Bo'ness. It became a burgh of regality in 1668 but the completion of the Forth and Clyde Canal precipitated the eclipse of the port by its western neighbour, Grangemouth. In the nineteenth century the flourishing industries included ironfounding, timberyards and mining and this encouraged a phase of rapid population growth. Much of the apparent growth in the present century resulted from a boundary extension in the 1950's and the construction of some new housing areas in the southern portions of the burgh. Diamond (1968) calculated the shopping centre at Bo'ness to be approximately equal in area and structure to that of Camelon, in Falkirk. Swift (1968) found that just over half the houses were local authority properties but significantly nearly one third were old dwellings rented from private landlords. This compared strikingly with Denny and Dunipace where 80% of the dwellings had been constructed by the local authority and only one tenth were rented from private landlords. Bo'ness, therefore, has a substantial number of old houses, many of them substandard and in a poor state of repair and largely located in the old nucleus at the foreshore. It is scarcely surprising, therefore, that some of the main areas of high density (more than 60 persons per acre) identified in the Grangemouth — Falkirk survey (Robertson, 1968) were at Corbiehall and Castle Loan, Bo'ness. It is proposed to re-locate the town centre at Douglas Park on the southern higher land and effectively re-arrange the focus of Bo'ness so that the settlement turns its back on the foreshore area. The Falkirk — Grangemouth survey (Robertson, 1968) also recommended that Bo'ness should almost double in population size by 1986 mainly by a southward expansion of the residential area from Kinneil to Muirhouse. Since only limited industrial development was anticipated, principally along the foreshore, many of the new residents would inevitably have to commute to work in Falkirk and Grangemouth. However, this would have the advantage of strengthening the functional linkages with this eastern outpost, although the present physical isolation would also be progressively reduced by the eastwards expansion of Grangemouth towards the River Avon.

Grangemouth

The founding of the town of Grangemouth is normally linked with the construction between 1768 and 1790 of the Forth and Clyde Canal. However, Thorn (1966) claims that there is evidence of a port at an earlier date and, indeed, of a whaling factory.

The creation and early growth of Grangemouth was closely linked with the initiative of the feudal superiors of these lands, the Dundas family. It was Sir Laurence Dundas who removed the first sod from the Forth and Clyde Canal on 10 July 1768, and the family controlled the fortunes of Grangemouth until the Lindsay Act in 1872 made the seaport a Burgh administered by nine commissioners. In effect, the feudal superior acted as a form of planning authority directing the rate and form of urban development and many Scottish settlements illustrate the part played by these landowners in shaping the morphology, and sometimes the functional character. of their properties. Carter (1970) has documented similar evidence for Welsh settlements.

The object at Grangemouth was to provide a sea link for the Canal and the mouth of the Grange Burn provided a suitable harbour. At first, the urban development was restricted to a small neck of land between the River Carron and the Canal but by the beginning of the nineteenth century additional land was required and the settlement spread beyond the canal towards the Grange Burn. This was structured growth however, based upon carefully designed plans approved by the Dundas family and each feu-charter included this clause:

'The said householder shall keep the street opposite their house free from any nuisance and allow no dung or other nauseous matter, or do, or act any other thing which may be deemed nauseous or dirty or which shall anyways encumber the said street or land'. (Porteous, 1970).

Although many of the buildings in the urban nucleus were associated with maritime functions there were also some very large houses. In Canal Street, for example, Porteous (1970) records that the houses ranged from ten to fourteen rooms and that several of them were let as whole houses, although some were subdivided into apartments. Thus, within a decade of the founding of the settlement, families of some substance were making this their place of residence, particularly in the attractive dwellings adjoining the Canal Basin. As the trade and prosperity of the port increased, many of the houses were deserted in the nineteenth century and converted to offices and other uses.

The original tidal harbour was of limited dimensions and after some years of debate and delay, a Wet Dock was opened in 1843. Shortly afterwards an additional large timber basin was constructed and a succession of harbour improvements followed during the Victorian period. Despite some urban growth, the town was clearly focussed upon the docks and the old core around Middle Street and in 1861 the still compact settlement only contained 2,000 inhabitants.

The dock improvements allowed Grangemouth to capture an increasing share of trade and this, in turn, encouraged a phase of quite rapid growth. By 1880 the population numbered 4,560 and by 1901 it had increased to 8,386. The large influx of working-class population stimulated a phase of house-building resulting in the erection of the Dundas Street and Lumley Street area of small substandard dwellings in the last quarter of the nineteenth century.

During the nineteenth century most industries were associated with the maritime role of the settlement and included rope-works, shipbuilding, timberyards and sawmills and graneries, although brickmaking was also a flourishing industry and some of the inhabitants found employment in the coal pits of the surrounding area. In 1897, the Scottish Co-operative Wholesale Society opened a soap factory and this can be claimed as the original representative of the subsequently predominant industry, the chemical industry. However, in this field the significant developments occurred after the First World War with the opening of Scottish Dye Works at Earl's Road in 1919 and the incorporation, in 1928, of that company into the expanding Imperial Chemical Industries group.

An additional dock, the Grange Dock, was opened in 1906 and featured a large area of railway sidings and large oil tanks which were built for the Anglo-American Oil Company. Although they later moved their base of operations to Bowling on the Clyde, other oil storage depots developed at Grangemouth, notably an Admiralty oil fuel depot. Draining and reclamation of the marshy shoreline provide further land for industrial development.

In 1924, Scottish Oils Ltd., a part of the Anglo-Persian Company, opened a refinery at Grangemouth which became the foundation stone of the now vast British Petroleum refinery, on a large flat site adjoining the river. Processing output increased from 350,000 tons in 1938 to more than 2,500,000 tons by 1952. Much of the crude oil is now delivered by a pipeline, built in 1954, from the terminal on Loch Finnart and the refinery produces a large range of chemical products and feedstocks. In addition it has acted as a catalyst attracting a wide array of oil and chemical industries, which transformed Grangemouth from a prosperous and expanding seaport into a vital growth node in the Scottish economy.

The population increased by almost 300% between 1901 and 1971 and as a result considerable areas have now been developed to house these new inhabitants, consuming much of the land which separated the seaport from Falkirk. Between 1919 — 1971 almost 6,000 local authority houses were erected in Grangemouth and about two-thirds of the inhabitants live in these new houses. Indeed, with the gradual clearance of old properties in the original core the local authority sector is responsible for an increasing share of the housing market. Few new private housing developments have occurred and many white-collar workers have elected to live in other settlements in the Stirling Region and commute to Grangemouth. Robertson et al (1968) found that the main high density residential areas lay around the Old Dock and in the core of the settlement although some of the early local authority projects were built to quite high densities.

In the substantially expanded and altered fabric of the settlement, industry is now a major land use and the centre of gravity of the residential areas has progressively moved southwards. Diamond (1968) estimated that the shopping hinterland population by 1986 would number 38,000 people but the projections for the whole survey region have subsequently been reduced and the Grangemouth total may also be affected. On the basis of shopping floorspace Grangemouth ranks third in Table 11.1 and the large amount of non-food space suggests that it is quite a powerful district centre, predominantly serving its own population.

In the short-term the continued economic prosperity of Grangemouth would seem assured, but continued industrial expansion will present problems given the limited availability of land in the vicinity of the settlement and one solution may be an increased proportion of commuting from other parts of the Region, notably the eastern portions of the 'dispersed city', the Falkirk — Grangemouth area.

Conclusions

Despite the differences in site, situation, development and functional composition, many of the urban settlements in the Stirling Region have been similarly influenced by the general urban trends of suburban growth, physical extension and internal renewal during the present century. There has also been a certain amount of functional convergence although the settlements retain quite distinctive individual characteristics.

In terms of spatial relationships the Region contains two major hinterlands or activity systems, those of Falkirk and Stirling, with a number of minor sub-systems, especially that based upon Alloa, and a series of minor urban nodes serving local tributary areas. This pattern of interlinking spheres of influences describes much of the movement for shopping purchases but the system in not self-contained and for specialised purchases and urban services people within the Region travel to Glasgow and Edinburgh.

Whilst some similarities recur in the pattern of employment hinterlands, variations are introduced by the distribution of employment opportunities and also the location of the major dormitory residential areas.

There are substantial variations in the pattern of urbanisation with the loosely-structured urban southern zone contrasting with the rural western and northern segments both in terms of extant occupance and also developmental trends. In fact, the Region encompasses the interface between the urban Central Lowlands and the rural settlement pattern of the Highlands and as such provides a fascinating field laboratory for the student of settlement geography.

REFERENCES

Burgh Architects Department, Stirling   1954   *Royal Burgh of Stirling. First Development Plan.* Stirling

Carter, H   1970   'A decision-making approach to town plan analysis: A case study of Llnadudno' in Carter, H and Davies, W K D., *Urban Essays: Studies in the Geography of Wales.* London Methuen.

Diamond, D R	1968	'Provision of commercial facilities' in Robertson, D J. *Grangemouth Falkirk – Regional Survey and Plan,* Vol. 1, H.M.S.O., Edinburgh.
Donaldson and Sons	1972	*Falkirk Shopping Study,* Parts I and II. London, Donaldson.
Gillespie, W H and Parnell, B K	1967	*C.D.A. No. 1 Survey Analysis and Policy.* Stirling Planning Department.
Levein, C P A	1973	*Delimitation and Comparative Analysis of the Central Areas of Medium Sized Towns in Central Scotland.* Unpublished PhD. Thesis, University of Edinburgh.
Morris, D B	1926	*Stirling 1820 – 1920.*
Nimmo, W	1877	*History of Stirlingshire.* Volume. 1.
Porteous, R	1970	*Grangemouth's Modern History.*
Rennie, R C and Crouther Gordon, T	1966	*The Third Statistical Account of Scotland. The Counties of Stirling and Clackmannan.* Glasgow, Collins.
Robertson, D J	1968	*Grangemouth Falkirk – Regional Survey and Plan.* 2 Volumes. H.M.S.O., Edinburgh.
Sissons, P L	1973	*The Social Significance of Church Membership in Falkirk.* Unpublished PhD. Thesis, University of Edinburgh.
Swift, B M	1968	'Housing' in Robertson, D J. *Grangemouth Falkirk – Regional Survey and Plan.* Volume 1. H.M.S.O., Edinburgh.
Thom, H R	1966	'Parish of Grangemouth' in Rennie, R C and Crouther Gordon, T. *The Third Statistical Account of Scotland. The Counties of Stirling and Clackmannan.* Glasgow, Collins.

CHAPTER 12

THE AGRICULTURAL ECONOMY

Introduction

The appearance of the British countryside has been greatly influenced by man and, despite the fact that the effect of industrial activities is both readily recognised and highly publicised, it is agriculture that has had the greatest influence. But for agriculture much of Britain would be covered by woodlands and even though this is a crowded and heavily industrialised island nearly three quarters of the land is under the influence of some form of agriculture. A description of the agriculture in an area like the Stirling region is therefore, to a large extent, synonymous with a description of the "natural" setting, and what is thought to be natural is, in reality, the outcome of many centuries of human influence.

In any region the agricultural activities are influenced by several interacting factors chief among which are climate, soil, topography and economic and social circumstances. In the last ten years the most significant force for change in the agriculture of Scotland, and Britain for that matter, has been a biological factor, the availability of new varieties of crops whose successful interaction with their environment, both physical and economic, has brought about a striking change. The agriculture of the Stirling region will be presented with these factors in mind, two of which, soil and climate, are dealt with in detail elsewhere in this book.

Agricultural Land use in the Stirling Region

Any visitor to the area around Stirling would see that there is a variety of agricultural activities in the region, which encompasses the mixed arable and livestock farming of the Carse of Stirling and the upland sheep grazings of the Ochil and Fintry Hills. The Agricultural Census data for Scotland enables a quantitative description to be made which confirms the immediate impression of diversity (Table 12.1).

In 1973 most (66%) of the 426,000 acres of agricultural land in the region were rough grazings, 14% were under permanent grass, that is grass that had been down for 7 years or more, and 20% were under temporary grass or crops; the last mentioned area is usually referred to as arable land. This is a smaller proportion of rough grazings than is found in Scotland as a whole, there being more permanent grass and a similar proportion of arable land in the region compared with the country. This illustrates that the region contains all three agricultural land uses: arable, typical of the east of Scotland, permanent grass, typical of the south-west and upland grazings, characteristic of the north.

TABLE 12.1

Changes in agricultural land use in the Stirling Region and Scotland as a whole, 1938 — 1973, expressed in 1,000's of acres; figures in parentheses show the areas as a % of total agricultural land.

		1938	1943	1953	1963	1973
Rough grazings	Scotland	10,448	10,825	10,896	12,400	11,179
		(70)	(71)	(71)	(74)	(73)
	Stirling	307	306	295	297	280
		(64)	(65)	(64)	(65)	(66)
Permanent grass	Scotland	1,577	1,056	1,165	870	1,015
		(10)	(7)	(8)	(5)	(7)
	Stirling	92	61	71	50	59
		(19)	(13)	(15)	(11)	(14)
Temporary grass and crops	Scotland	2,983	3,371	3,222	3,435	3,098
		(20)	(22)	(21)	(21)	(20)
	Stirling	77	104	86	108	87
		(16)	(22)	(19)	(24)	(20)

The changes in agricultural land use in the region from before the Second World War to the present day follow similar trends to Scotland as a whole (Table 12.1). There was a rise in the amount of arable land during the war and a fall in the acreage of permanent grass. Indeed, the move to arable during this time was more marked in the Stirling Region. The apparent fall in permanent grass and accompanying increase in the arable acres between 1953 and 1963 in both the country and the region resulted largely from a change in the classification of some permanent grass which had been referred to as permanent until the 1960 census when the label permanent became reserved for grass of 7 years or older. The apparent rise in rough grazings from 1953 to 1963 was also caused by a census change, namely, the inclusion, from 1959, of all deer forests in the rough grazings. Agricultural statistics are valuable but can be misleading!

The diversity of the agricultural activities within the region reflects a wide range in topography, climate and soils. About 40% of the land is below 120m and about 10% is above 300m (Fig 3.3). Most of the high ground is in the north-west and the lower ground lies along the Forth and its major tributaries, largely in the south-east of the region. This altitude difference accentuates the east-west rainfall gradient resulting in a considerable range in mean annual rainfall from as little as 890mm in the east to more than 2,000mm in the west (Fig 3.3).

For most of the region the mean daily seasonal temperature in the winter months lies between 3.5 and 4.0°C and in the summer months it is between 14.5 and 15°C (Booth, 1969).   The south-east corner of the region has one of the highest mean daily seasonal summer temperatures, over 15°C, to be found in Scotland (Booth, 1969).   Except for the highest ground the region has, in common with the eastern seaboard and the south-west of Scotland, between 7 and 8 months when the mean monthly temperature is high enough to allow plant growth, that is, greater than 6°C (Gregory, 1954).

The south-eastern part of the region enjoys a higher mean daily sunshine duration, 3.72 hours at Stirling, than any other part where recordings are made, for example Gleneagles where the mean is 3.56 hours (Chapter 3).   As a result of the higher temperature, greater sunshine duration and lower rainfall the south-east of the region can suffer a slight soil moisture deficit in the early months of the summer (Birse and Dry, 1970).   The rainfall in the later and wetter months of the summer, August and September, is such that even in the east of the region the climate is not entirely suitable for the ripening and harvesting of cereals but otherwise the climate of the lower ground, particularly in the east, favours successful cropping.

The climatological diversity of the region is matched by a wide-ranging variety of soils (Chapter 4), from the finely structural gley soils of the Forth Valley to the acidic podzols in the north-west.   The land use capability classification of the soils is equally wide ranging from land in the Carse of Stirling with moderate limitations on cultivation in the form of a relatively high rainfall at sowing and harvesting, coupled with a finely structured heavy clay soil, to the higher ground (over 700m) of the north-west, where extreme limitations on land usage are to be found (Chapter 4).

Arable land

The arable areas within the region are concentrated on the lower ground alongside the Forth, and its major tributaries, the Teith and the Allan.   This concentration is illustrated by the distribution of cereal crops (Fig 12.1).   At the June Census in 1973, over 50% (47,390 acres) of the 87,340 acres of arable land were under grass (Table 12.2) and nearly 40% (33,300 acres) were under cereals, principally barley (22,320 acres).   The next two most important crops were root crops for stock feeding – rape (1,840 acres) and turnips, which with swedes occupied 1,670 acres – followed by potatoes (1,560 acres).   This presents a picture of arable cropping linked to livestock production.

The changes in the native proportions of crops in the Stirling Region since 1938 have been considerable (Table 12.2) and, although similar to the trends for Scotland, show some interesting differences to the changes seen in the country as a whole.   The war-time need for greater self-sufficiency in food led to increases in the area under cereals, particularly wheat, and in potatoes and several other crops (Table 12.2).   Since 1943 there has been a pro-

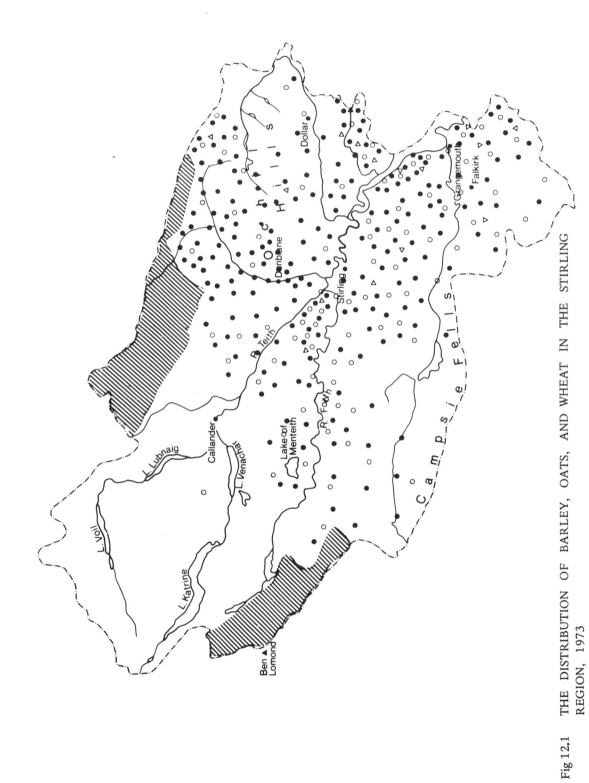

Fig 12.1 THE DISTRIBUTION OF BARLEY, OATS, AND WHEAT IN THE STIRLING REGION, 1973

Barley is shown by solid dots, oats by circles and wheat by triangles. Each symbol represents 100 acres under the crop concerned.

gressive decline in the popularity of all crops except barley.   The area of land under oats fell spectacularly from 77% (30,830 acres) of the cereal acreage in 1943 to 27% (9,100 acres) in 1973 (Tables 12.2 and 12.3).

Since the war one of the most dramatic changes in farming in Scotland, and indeed in Britain, has been the switch from oats to barley. This has been especially rapid, for instance, there was more than twice as much oats grown as barley in 1963 but by 1973 the position had been reversed.   And yet the change from oats to barley has been less marked in the Stirling Region than in Scotland.   In 1973, the country as a whole grew more than four times as much barley as oats.

This difference is due to a traditionally higher proportion of oats being grown around Stirling than in the rest of Scotland (Table 12.3) and to a slower decline in the oats acreage, both before and after 1963 (Table 12.3).   Oats yield well in the area, particularly in the Carse, which, combined with a higher government subsidy for oats than barley, has made oats more popular around Stirling than in many other areas.   This explains the relative reluctance within the region to move out of oats and into barley.   There may also be a tendency to retain the more traditional oats among the local farmers than elsewhere.

The distribution of the three cereal crops within the region in 1973 (Fig 12.1) is also revealing.   The ratio of barley to oats is low in the Carse of Stirling.   The areas around Gargunnock, Port of Menteith, Blair Drummond, Kippen, Grangemouth and Falkirk grew a similar acreage of oats and barley.   In contrast, around Dunblane the acreage under barley was 18 times greater than that under oats, which may reflect the influence of a large estate enterprise in the area.

The move out of oats and into barley resulted, for the most part, from an interaction of economic considerations and new crop varieties.

In any enterprise a farmer is ultimately interested in the financial gain relative to both the effort and the money he has invested.   The economic improvement in farming since the war has resulted from considerable improvements in the yield of nearly all crops (Ministry of Agriculture, 1968) brought about by increased fertilizer application, improved weed control and the growing of more productive varieties, against a background of stable prices.

The varieties of barley that became available to the farmer after 1950 had greater yield potential than did the oat varieties of the time.   Comparisons of estimated average yields of oats and barley in Scotland (Table 12.4) illustrate the yield advantage enjoyed by barley.   Furthermore, the possibility of selling barley at a premium price for malting to the

TABLE 12.2

Changes in the use of arable land in the Stirling Region, 1938 — 1973; areas are expressed in 1000's of acres.

	1938	1943	1953	1963	1973
Total arable land	77.29	104.00	90.70	107.95	87.34
Cereals	30.89	47.83	37.37	30.87	33.30
Wheat	4.10	8.57	3.99	2.66	1.88
Barley	0.47	2.33	1.56	8.74	22.32
Oats	26.32	36.83	31.82	19.47	9.10
Rape	0.70	2.72	2.37	1.64	1.84
Turnips and Swedes	5.55	5.85	5.01	3.08	1.67
All Potatoes	5.00	9.43	6.23	4.61	1.56
Beans and Vetches	1.66	4.61	1.79	0.50	0.40
Kale and Cabbage	0.28	0.52	1.36	0.39	0.15
Vegetables (human consumption)	*	*	0.15	0.10	0.07
Bare fallow	1.01	0.83	0.92	0.99	0.57
Temporary grass	32.19	37.31	35.50	65.76	47.42

* Not noted

TABLE 12.3

Changes in the percentage of the cereal acreage under barley and oats in the Stirling Region and Scotland, 1938 — 1973.

		1938	1943	1953	1963	1973
Stirling	Oats	85	77	85	63	27
	Barley	2	5	4	28	67
Scotland	Oats	81	72	77	51	17
	Barley	10	15	17	40	76

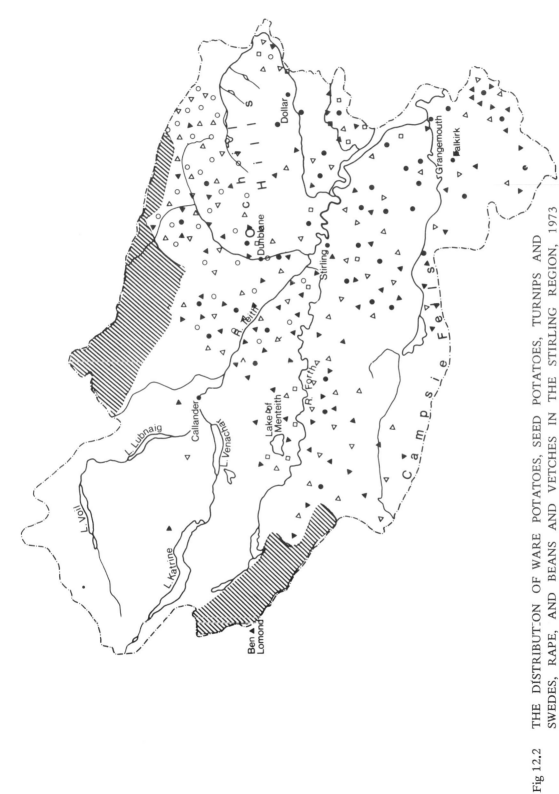

Fig 12.2   THE DISTRIBUTION OF WARE POTATOES, SEED POTATOES, TURNIPS AND SWEDES, RAPE, AND BEANS AND VETCHES IN THE STIRLING REGION, 1973

Ware potatoes are shown by solid dots, seed potatoes by circles, turnips and swedes by open triangles, rape by solid triangles, and beans and vetches by boxes. Each symbol represents 20 acres.

brewing and distilling industries existed, provided the grain was of suitable quality. The new, shorter and stiffer-strawed varieties of barley lent themselves more readily to combine harvesting than did the older oat varieties, which was important during a time when the labour force was dwindling. There was also a greater stock-feeding value in barley than oats and, lastly and for some sadly, the replacement on farms of horses by tractors meant a reduced demand for oat straw. All in all barley was, and still is, a more economically attractive crop than oats.

TABLE 12.4

Means of estimated average yields of barley, oats, potatoes and turnips in Scotland, 1950 – 1971 (Source: D.A.F.S, statistics).

	1950 – 54	1955 – 59	1960 – 64	1965 – 69	1970 & 1971
Barley (cwts/acre)	23.6	27.0	28.6	30.1	33.7
Oats (cwt/acre)	17.7	19.4	20.8	23.3	27.2
Potatoes (tons/acre)	7.7	7.6	8.5	9.4	11.4
Turnips and swedes (tons/acre)	18.1	17.4	19.9	21.7	24.8

The barley variety Ymer which made the initial incursion into cereal acreages in Scotland, was of Swedish origin and was particularly suited to Scottish conditions. More recently, Ymer has been replaced by an English bred variety, Golden Promise, which is particularly favoured by maltsters. In 1967, 70% of the barley acreage inspected by the Department of Agriculture for Scotland for seed certification was Ymer and only 2% was Golden Promise (Davies, 1973). A survey of growers (Davies, 1973) showed that by 1972 only 20% of the barley acreage was sown with Ymer whilst nearly 40% was under Golden Promise. By 1974 the area of Golden Promise had probably increased to more than 60% of the barley acreage.

Such a predominance of one variety carries with it the possibility of fungal disease epidemics. Golden Promise is especially susceptible to powdery mildew, a disease of little importance in Scotland before the advent of this variety and, but for the disease control afforded by the new systemic fungicides, the variety would probably not be grown on such a large scale. However, the vulnerability of a single variety barley crop to diseases still exists and epidemics would be particularly serious in an area like the Stirling Region where the crop is concentrated. Over-simplification in crop production has many attendant hazards.

Since the war there has been a decline in the importance in the arable acreage of the stock feeding crops – turnips, swedes, rape, kale and cabbage – both in the Stirling Region and in Scotland (Table 12.5). This has arisen because, although average yields have increased, by about a third in the case of turnips (Table 12.4), barley yields have increased more; no new high yielding varieties of turnips were developed during this time. Moreover, the post-war development of selective weed killers for cereals reduced the need for a weed cleaning crop in the rotation, and the relatively high labour demands of these root crops have been difficult to meet.

TABLE 12.5

Percentage of total arable land growing various named crops in Scotland and the Stirling Region, 1938 — 1973.

		1938	1943	1953	1963	1973
Turnips and swedes	Stirling	7.0	5.5	5.5	3.0	2.0
	Scotland	11.0	10.0	9.0	6.0	4.5
Potatoes	Stirling	6.5	9.0	7.0	4.5	2.0
	Scotland	4.5	7.0	5.5	4.5	3.0
Rape	Stirling	1.0	2.5	2.5	1.5	2.0
	Scotland	0.5	1.0	1.0	1.0	1.0
Beans and vetches	Stirling	2.0	4.5	2.0	0.5	0.5
	Scotland	0.5	1.0	0.5	0.5	0.5
Kale and cabbage	Stirling	0.5	0.5	1.5	0.5	0.5
	Scotland	0.5	0.5	0.5	0.5	0.5

Turnips and swedes have never been popular crops in the Stirling Region, possibly because in the heavy clays of the Carse of Stirling it is difficult to produce a satisfactory seed bed for these small-seeded crops (Table 12.5). The distribution of these crops (Fig 12.2) illustrates that they are less popular in the Carse than in the arable areas of Perthshire.

The Carse of Stirling was once famous for its Carse beans, a type of field bean (*Vicia faba*) used for stock feeding. In 1943 the crop occupied, along with vetches, about 4.5% of the arable acreage in the region (Table 12.5). But the crop has fallen out of favour, so much so that now it is no more common in the Stirling Region than in Scotland as a whole. (Table 12.5) and is not particularly common in the Carse (Fig 12.2). The present world shortage of protein might see an improvement in its status.

Since the 1940's the area of arable land in Scotland devoted to potatoes has fallen (Tables 12.2 and 12.5). Once again, the development of new varieties has been crucial. In 1964 the maincrop varieties grown in Scotland were largely Majestic (31% of the potato acreage), Redskin (20%), King Edward (14%) and Kerrs Pink (14%). Since 1965 two new varieties, Pentland Crown and Pentland Dell, both of which originated at the Scottish Plant Breeding Station near Edinburgh have come into prominence, both in Scotland and in the rest of Britain. By 1972 these two varieties together accounted for about a third of the maincrop acreage in Scotland (Wytcher, 1973).

These two varieties have been major contributors to the increase in average yields seen in the late 1960's and early 70's (Table 12.4). The fact that this improved productivity led to a decrease and not an increase in the potato acreage results from attempts to curb a problem peculiar to agriculture, over-production.

The demand for potatoes is inelastic, people can have enough of them. Therefore, simply put, in a free market situation once national production has equalled demand there is a fall in price. Because of this some restrictions, in the form of quotas of potato acreages, are put on potato production by the Potato Marketing Board. As the average yields increased in Scotland, and Britain, the area needed to grow our potato requirements diminished and quotas were therefore reduced.

There are two components to the potato acreage in Scotland, ware potatoes for consumption and seed potatoes for sale south of the border. Seed potato production is a major item in Scottish agriculture. In 1974, 53,500 acres of seed potatoes were grown compared with 42,000 acres of maincrop ware potatoes and 4,100 acres of earlies (D.A.F.S., 1972). The decline in Scotland and the region in recent years has been in both ware and seed potatoes.

In the Stirling Region the Forth provides a clear dividing line with respect to potatoes, seed potatoes are only produced north of the river in Perthshire (Fig 12.2). The reason for this is biological. Seed potatoes are produced only in areas such as Perthshire where, for climatic reasons, populations of the virus transmitting aphid *Myzus persicae* are at a low level. The accumulation of virus infections in ware potatoes grown for several years in an aphid area, like most of England, reduces yields sharply. An additional factor in the decline in seed potato acreages has been the relative resistance of Pentland Crown to some viruses which has led to a longer retention of seed stocks by English growers and consequently a fall in the demand for Scotch seed of Pentland Crown. As in many things one man's gain has turned out to be another man's loss.

The use of bare fallow in the rotations of the region did not decline until the last 10 years (Table 12.2) and has been particularly persistent on the Carse. In Scotland the fallow acreage showed an earlier decline which was particularly sharp during the war. This may be another example of a more traditional attitude on the part of growers around Stirling.

The most important crop in the region is the grass crop, especially the grass which is in the rotation, now classified for census purposes as grass under 7 years old. This temporary grass constitutes over half of the arable acreage (Table 12.2) indicating a long interlude, up to 6 years, of grass between other crops In the Stirling region not only is this grass produced for consumption by livestock on the farm but it is also an important cash crop.

Timothy (*Phleum pratense*) hay from the Carse of Stirling is famous throughout Scotland and has long been an export to the north west.

Some idea of the importance of the hay crop is given by the fact that, in 1973, 48% of the area of temporary grass was mown in the Stirling region compared with 41% in Scotland as a whole.   Although silage has increased in importance in recent years most of the mown grass is conserved as hay, which is especially the case in Stirlingshire (D. A. F. S., 1972). In some of the parishes on the Carse — Kincardine (Near Blair Drummond), Clackmannan, Airth, St Ninians and Larbert — the total percentage of temporary grass that was mown was about 65% which underlines the importance of the hay crop on the Carse land.

The grass on the Carse which is classified as permanent consists, for the most part, of Timothy and may really represent a prolonged grass interlude in a rotation.   On the higher ground the permanent grass is dominated by Common bent-grass (*Agrostis tenuis*) and Sheep's Fescue (*Festuca ovina* agg) with, in some places, small proportions of perennial rye-grass (Chapter 5).   The acreage of permanent grass has risen in the last 10 years at the expense of the temporary grass.   The permanent grassland is nearly all grazed and makes a major contribution to livestock production in the region.   This is particularly the case where the rainfall is high such as west Stirlingshire and to a lesser extent the Slamannan plateau (Chapter 3).

Horticultural Crops

Horticultural crops are not very important in the region.   Vegetables produced for human consumption, mostly cabbages, turnips and lettuce, amounted to only about 70 acres in 1973 most of which was grown close to the urban areas of Grangemouth and Falkirk in the drier and warmer eastern part of the region.   Only about 30 acres of soft fruits, strawberries and raspberries, were being grown in the region in June 1973.   Some horticultural produce is grown under glass, mostly tomatoes and cut flowers, again close to the built-up areas in the east, especially near Larbert.

Livestock Production

The eventual product of much of the agriculture of the region is livestock, which is in keeping with the status of Scotland as a major livestock producer.   In the 10 years up until 1973 increases were seen in Scotland in all types of livestock; the numbers of cattle rose by 29%, pigs by 52% and poultry by 72% (Table 12.6).   Increases in cattle and pigs, but not poultry, also occurred in the Stirling Region (Table 12.6).   These increases were, in part, associated with improvements in the yields of barley and oats which resulted in an increase in the national production of these cereals from 1,075,000 tons in 1961 (M.A.F.F. and D.A.F.S., 1968) to 1,744,000 tons in 1971 (D.A.F.S., 1972), 80% of which was used for stock-feed. These production increases coupled with more efficient use of grassland enabled a large livestock population to be supported by the agricultural land.

The increase in the total number of cattle was accompanied by a shift in emphasis away from dairying and into beef production. Although there was a greater fall in dairy cattle numbers in the region than in the country, there was a less pronounced increase in beef cattle (Table 12.6). However, contrary to the national trend the region showed an increase of 8% in sheep numbers. Apparently, the dairy herd in the region has been replaced by both beef and sheep. This may be a sign of reluctance on the part of local farmers to substitute entirely with beef, which requires a higher capital investment than do sheep.

TABLE 12.6

Changes in livestock numbers in the Stirling Region, 1938 — 1973. (1,000's of acres) and % change 1963 — 73 for the region and Scotland

| | 1938 | 1943 | 1953 | 1963 | 1973 | % Change 1963 – 1973 | |
						Stirling	Scotland
Cattle	52.57	57.00	64.14	78.35	87.29	+11	+29
Dairy	*	38.04	36.59	31.00	17.72	- 36	- 11
Beef	*	18.96	27.55	47.35	67.57	- 43	+52
Sheep	269.31	233.15	249.19	294.78	319.34	+ 8	- 11
Pigs	7.99	7.38	15.10	14.38	15.38	+ 9	+52
Poultry	*	158.81	246.89	294.04	243.93	- 17	+72
				* not noted			

The dairy herd has declined in nearly all parts of the region. One exception has been the area around Dunblane where there has been a rise which may be associated with an increased local demand for milk, following the rapid expansion of the population in the area. The 1973 distribution of dairy cattle in the region (Fig 12.3) also shows the influence of urban areas on the location of milk production, dairy cattle being relatively concentrated around Falkirk and in west Stirlingshire close to the Glasgow conurbation. In the latter area, around Drymen, Balfron and Killearn, which is traditionally a dairying area, there has been a pronounced move out of dairy cattle and into beef and sheep.

In the fields of west Stirlingshire, the Ayrshires and Freisians have been partially replaced by a variety of crossbred beef cattle. Popular beef cattle are the offspring from crosses of Hereford or Aberdeen Angus bulls and either crossbred Highland or 'Blue-Grey' cows. The statistics for the same area show that between 1963 and 1973 dairy cattle numbers fell by 32%, beef numbers rose by 62% and sheep by 41%.

The reasons for the decline in the popularity of dairying are both economic and social. Although milk production gave a steady and regular income, the returns for milk remained static and became insufficient recompense for the arduous daily routine demanded of farmers

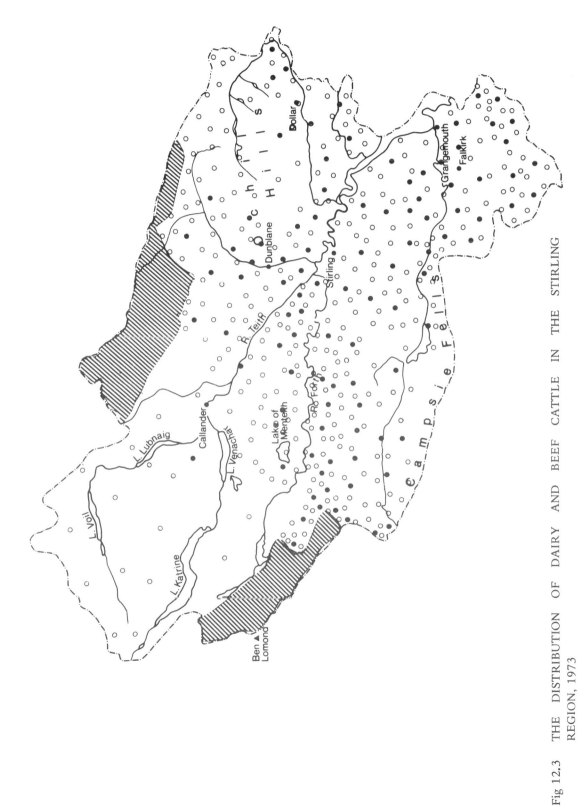

Fig 12.3 THE DISTRIBUTION OF DAIRY AND BEEF CATTLE IN THE STIRLING REGION, 1973

Dairy cattle are shown by solid dots, beef cattle by circles. Each symbol represents 200 beasts.

and their workers at a time when the working week in industry was shortening. The change may also have been assisted by the fact that cattle were being replaced on a relatively large scale in the drive to obtain herds free of *Brucellosis*, a bacterial disease which can infect humans.

The traditional location of dairy farming close to urban areas underlines the important influence that production outlets can have on agricultural activities. This is also exemplified in the existence for many years of a livestock market at Stirling, which has no doubt assisted in the development of the area as a livestock producer.

In 1966 two new markets were formed out of the old market, both on new premises: the Caledonian Market, to the south of Stirling and Kildean Market, the larger of the two, a few miles to the north. This expansion was an outward sign of an increasingly active livestock industry.

The total livestock sales of cattle and sheep for slaughter at the Kildean Market actually fell by 7% between 1971 and 1973, largely through a decline in sheep sales. But the value of these sales rose during that time by about 65%. This reflects what we were all aware of in 1973, an increase in the price of beef.

The consequences of this 1973 price rise are still being felt by beef producers themselves. The period between 1971 and 1973 was a marked increase at Kildean in the sales of cattle and sheep for further feeding, cattle by 24% and sheep by 7% but, more importantly, the value of these sales rose by 100%.

This increase in total value resulted, in part, from an increase in the proportion of sales that were beef, but was mostly caused by an increase in the price paid by farmers for young stock. Over the last year, because of a world shortage of cereals, the price of livestock feed has doubled. The combination of expensive stock, costly feed and a less bouyant market in 1974 has led to serious economic difficulties for beef producers, one consequence of which will be a fall in the national beef herd. This is a good, but unfortunate, illustration of the impace that economic factors can have on agricultural activities.

So far the agricultural activities of the whole of the region have been examined but the upland grazings and the Carse of Stirling which represent the greatest contrast to be found in the Stirling Region merit special attention. Both are important in the region, the grazings because of the amount of land they occupy (65%) and the Carse by virtue of its productivity and history.

Upland Grazings

There are three separate areas of upland grazings in the region: an area in the north-west, the Ochils, and an area in the south consisting of the Fintry Hills and the Campsie Fells. All the areas are predominantly mountain grassland consisting of various combinations of *Argostis spp, Festuca ovina, F. rubra, Deschampsia flecuosa, Nardus stricta* and *Milinia caetulea* (Chapter 5).   Differences in productivity between these areas are illustrated by comparisons of stocking rates in 1973 in three parishes.   In Aberfoyle (north-west), Glendevon (Ochils) and Fintry the sheep stocking rates were, respectively,0.65, 1.21 and 1.23 per acre of agricultural land, including rough grazings which comprised more than 93% of the area in all three parishes.   The upland areas have seen little change in sheep numbers over the last ten years.   There is no clear evidence of a decline in the numbers of upland sheep because of increased afforestation, which has been a feature of many upland grazings in other parts of Scotland in recent years.

The harsher climate (Chapter 3) of the upland areas demands a hardy breed of sheep like the Scotch Blackface. The north-west area produces pure Blackface lambs whereas the Ochils and the southern uplands produce lambs from Scotch Blackface ewes and Border Leicester rams, an indication of a greater productivity and a less harsh climate.

The Carse of Stirling

There is no better illustration in Britain of the impact that the pursuit of agricultural productivity can have on the landscape than the Carse of Stirling.   The truly natural vegetation of the Forth Valley is blanket bog; Flanders Moss is one of the few remaining areas (Chapter 5). The Carse itself has been produced by the large scale removal of between 3 and 12 feet of peat to expose the fertile clay deposits beneath.

This agricultural improvement was instigated in the late 18th century around the Vale of Menteith by Lord Kames when he 'retired' to the Blair Drummond Estate near Doune. Special leases were drawn up to induce the tenants to clear the peat. The method employed was simple and arduous.   Channels were dug in the bog which drained into the Forth and after removal by hand the peat was floated down the channels into the river.   In the flatter arcas water wheels were used to create a flow of water down the channels. These improvements went on until the mid 19th century and the result was the low lying and productive Carse that we see today.

The most renowned crop of the Carse is Timothy hay. Yields of up to 4 tons per acre, double that in most other parts of Scotland, are possible without particularly high inputs of fertilizer.   Until the last few years traditional methods were used for this crop; the pick-up baler has only recently taken the place of the 'rucking' machine which used to produce the cone-shaped 'rucks' of hay that were once a feature of the Carse land in July.

The strain of Timothy which has been selected over the years in the Carse and proved so productive, has enabled the development of a Scots Timothy grass seed industry. This enterprise has grown, albeit unsteadily, since 1962, until in 1973, 140 tons worth £50,000 were produced on 715 acres.

In several respects, some of which have been illustrated in this survey, Carse land farming appears to cling to traditional ways. However, working the clay soil to produce a usable seed-bed requires skill and fine timing. This serves to exemplify that no matter what the circumstances, economic or physical, the personal preferences and skills of individual farmers can greatly influence the agricultural activities in any area.

This survey has been an attempt to produce more than a description. In the belief that comparisons are an important means of detecting influences, many comparisons have been made. Hopefully, this approach has drawn attention to the factors that can influence the agricultural activities in any area and not just the Stirling Region.

Acknowledgements

The help of the Scottish Records Office and the Economics and Statistics Unit of the Department of Agriculture and Fisheries for Scotland in providing Agricultural Census data as recent as June 1973, is gratefully acknowledged. All the data for the region was a compilation of the Parish Summaries available and the distribution maps (Figs 12.1, 12.2, and 12.3) were also produced from Parish census data.

I would like to thank Mr W Lyons of the West of Scotland Agricultural College and Mr A Watson and his colleagues of Livestock Marts Ltd. for information and helpful discussions. My thanks also to Dr J Proctor for valuable comments on the manuscript.

REFERENCES

Birse, E L and
Dry, F T
1970 *Assessment of climatic Conditions in Scotland.* Based on Accumulated Temperature and Potential Water Deficit. Map and Explanatory Pamphlet. The Macaulay Institute for Soil Research, Craigiebuckler, Aberdeen.

Booth, R E (Ed.)
1969 *Climatological Memorandum 43A 1931-60.* Monthly seasonal and annual maps of mean maximum, mean daily minimum, mean temperature and mean temperature range over the British Isles. Meteorological Office, Climatological Services (Met.03), Bracknell, England.

Davies, D H K
1973 *Physical and economic optima in sowing densities of spring barley in Scotland.* Unpublished Ph.D. thesis, University of Stirling.

Department of Agriculture and Fisheries for Scotland
1972 *Agricultural Statistics 1971 Scotland,* Edinburgh H.M.S.O.

Gregory, S
1964 *Climate* in British Isles: *A Systematic Geography.* Ed by J W Watson and J B Sissons,Edinburgh, Nelson.

Ministry of Agriculture, Fisheries and Food and Department of Agriculture and Fisheries for Scotland
1968 *A Century of Agricultural Statistics,* London, H.M.S.O.

Witcher, B
1973 Private communication based on calculations on Potato Marketing Board statistics.

CHAPTER 13

THE INDUSTRIAL ECONOMY OF THE CENTRAL REGION

Economically, the region is divided into two distinct parts. The greater part of the region in the north and west and immediately around Stirling itself is rural, dominated by the market towns of Stirling, Dunblane, Dollar, Callander and the more industrialised Alloa. Industrial enterprises are by size and type these which fit into a small town economy. By contrast in the south-east there is a major industrial area centred on Falkirk and Grangemouth, comprising also Polmont, Larbert, Bonnybridge and Denny. To some extent Alloa, in Clackmannanshire, and Kilsyth, in the narrow strip of Stirlingshire to the south of the Campsie Hills may be regarded as outposts of industrialisation. The south-east area (which we shall call the Grangemouth-Falkirk sub-region) is separated, however, from the rest of the region by the coalfield around Airth and Plean. Department of Employment statistics of insured employees enable the two sub-regions to be analysed separately: the Grangemouth-Falkirk sub-region extending to include the Denny and Bo'ness Local Exchange Areas while the Stirling — Alloa sub-region consists of the Alloa and Stirling Local Exchange Areas including the local offices at Callander and Doune.

The Central Region as a whole has over the last decade been one of the few areas in Scotland which has not experienced economic decline. As measured by the number of insured employees employment in the Region showed a marginal increase of 400 employees or 0.4 per cent over the period 1961 - 1971. The comparable increase in Great Britain for the same period was 0.7 per cent. Table 10.1 gives the composition of the increase. Clearly a most important influence has been the establishment of the University of Stirling, reflected in the increase of almost 5,000 in Professional Services.

There are two sets of reasons to explain why employment in a local economy might grow at a different rate from the national or regional average or why the economic performance of two local economics might diverge significantly from each other. On the one hand, the industrial composition of the area will contain differing proportions of growing stagnant or declining industries. The pattern of industrial growth will, therefore, be a major determinant of local economic growth. On the other hand, there may be a considerable variation in the extent to which an area may share in the growth or decline of industries during any period of time. The reasons may be that the area has general locational advantages or disadvantages which make it a more or less favoured site for employment growth; alternatively there may be highly specific reasons for an area's economic performance. For example, the growth of an industry in a local area may be heavily dependent upon the particular fortunes of one or a few establishments. These units may be subjected to more or less random shocks, such as the failure of one contract, which do not necessarily have any

TABLE 13.1

Region — Total Actual Change by Industrial Grouping

Grouping	Change Persons	
Professional and scientific services		+ 4,956
Clothing and footwear		+ 1,351
Mechanical engineering (MLH 331 − 349)		+ 1,295
Electrical engineering (MLH 361 − 369)		+ 1,070
Bricks		+ 971
Miscellaneous services		+ 966
Wholesale distribution (MLH 810)		+ 497
Public administration		+ 489
Insurance, banking and finance		+ 434
Chemical and Allied (coal and petrol) (MLH 261 − 263)		+ 348
Food, drink and tobacco		+ 130
Chemical and allied (other) (MLH 271 − 277)		+ 117
Timber, furniture, etc		+ 113
Other manufacturing		+ 112
Vehicles		+ 90
Other distribution (MLH 831 − 832)		+ 65
Instrument engineering (MLH 351 − 352)		+ 60
Leather, leather goods and fur	− 74	
Shipbuilding and Marine Engineering	− 91	
Gas, electricity and water	− 95	
Retail distribution (MLH 820)	− 332	
Construction	− 386	
Paper, printing and publishing	− 463	
Metal goods	− 702	
Transport and communication	− 914	
Textiles	− 1,281	
Agriculture	− 1,302	
Metal manufacture	− 2,853	
Mining and Quarrying	− 4,165	
	12,658	+ 13,064
	Net Change	+406

long run significance. In order to assess the relative importance of each factor and the likely economic future of the Central Region it is necessary to examine the existing industrial structure.

*Principal industries in the Central Region**

The industrial structure of the region is laid out in Table 13.2 with the aid of location quotients. This statistic is defined as the percentage of the employed labour force in a given category in the area concerned divided by the corresponding percentage in Great Britain as a whole. Industries relatively underrepresented in the local area have location quotients of less than unity; industries which are relatively over-represented have location quotients of more than unity. The location quotient has a number of inadequacies as an analytical device, but in this case it is used simply as a measure of the deviation of the local employment structure from the national average.

The most significant specialisation is that of oil refining and petrochemicals at Grangemouth. The origins of the oil refining industry lie in the nineteenth century when 'Paraffin' Young established a process to refine the oil extracted from the shale deposits in the Lothians. In 1924 Scottish Oils built a refinery at Grangemouth to rationalise its production of oil products. After the Second World War the Forth was no longer capable of taking the tankers which were by then bringing crude oil from abroad, but since 1954 crude oil has been pumped through a 57 mile pipeline from the deep-water terminal at Finnart on Loch Long. The Forth terminal jetty continues to be used for the transportation of feedstock for petrochemicals and other partly refined products. Although the ownership of the petrochemical industry has involved British Petroleum, Distillers and ICI, the basic ownership of petrochemicals is now in the hands of British Petroleum; their ownership includes Border Chemicals. Independent firms have also gathered round the complex at Grangemouth, including Bakelite Xylonite (a subsidiary of Union Carbide of the USA), International Synthetic Rubber (I.S.R.), and Marbon Chemicals (owned by Borg-Warner) in the production of plastics and resins. Their presence reflects in part the influence of the refinery but also the plentiful supplies of pure water available to the Grangemouth area. Chemicals, outside Grangemouth, have been reduced by the closure of an ICI factory in Falkirk but Scottish Tar Distillers and Scottish Enamelling remain.

In Grangemouth-Falkirk the other outstanding high location quotient is in SIC Order 5, Metal Manufacture. This reflects the declining but still significant dependence on light iron castings. There are approximately fifteen firms classified in iron castings located in Falkirk, Denny, Bonnybridge and Larbert. Their size is typically modest, only five employ-

In preparing this section I have had the help of the listing of firms in the Region compiled for the Scottish Council (Development and Industry) and prepared by my colleague, Mr John R Firn, Department of Social and Economic Research, University of Glasgow.

TABLE 13.2

Location Quotients by Industry 1971

		Central Region	Grangemouth/ Falkirk	Stirling
1	Agriculture, forestry and fishing	1.0	—	1.8
2	Mining and quarrying	1.9	0.9	3.2
3	Food, drink and tobacco	1.1	0.9	1.5
4	Chemical and allied industries			
	(a) MLH 261 – 263	7.0	12.5	—
	(b) MLH 271 – 277	2.9	4.9	—
5	Metal manufacture	3.0	5.1	—
6	Engineering and electrical goods			
	(a) MLH 331 – 349	0.6	0.4	0.8
	(b) MLH 351 – 352	—	—	—
	(c) MLH 361 – 369	0.3	0.5	—
7	Shipbuilding and marine engineering	—	—	—
8	Vehicles	0.3	0.5	—
9	Metal goods	0.6	—	—
10	Textiles	1.4	—	3.3
11	Leather, leather goods and fur	—	—	—
12	Clothing and footwear	0.6	1.1	—
13	Bricks	3.2	2.9	3.7
14	Timber, furniture, etc.	1.7	2.5	—
15	Paper, printing and publishing	1.0	1.0	1.2
16	Other manufacturing	—	—	—
17	Construction	1.4	1.4	1.4
18	Gas, electricity and water	0.9	—	1.6
19	Transport and communication	0.8	0.9	0.7
20	Distributive trades			
	(a) MLH 810	—	—	-
	(b) MLH 820	1.0	0.9	1.1
	(c) MLH 831, 832	—	—	—
21	Insurance, banking and finance	0.3	—	—
22	Professional scientific services	1.0	0.8	1.2
23	Miscellaneous services	1.0	0.8	1.3
24	Public administration	0.9	0.7	1.1

Note: No Location Quotient is calculated where employment in the local economy is less than 1,000.

ing more than 200 employees; the exception is Glynwed's (formerly Allied Ironfounders) foundry in Falkirk which is the result of many years of local rationalisation and is almost ten times as large, in employment terms, as the next largest establishment. The modern development of metal manufacture in the area on a large scale may be dated from the establishment of the Carron Ironworks by Dr John Roebuck and his associates in 1760. The evolution of the industry was not closely associated with the engineering industry, although at least one firm, Cruikshanks of Denny, produced casting for heavy engineering. Light castings remained wedded to finished products based on 'grey' iron castings. The names of local firms can be seen on street manhole covers, lamp-posts, stoves, boilers and letter-boxes thoughout the British Isles. As the use of cast iron dwindles in face of competition from concrete in general construction, the fortunes of the industry were dictated by the house buidling industry through the production of baths, rainwater goods and solid fuel stoves. The post-war period brought cyclical problems from housebuilding cycles and a steady retreat before the use of plastics and the decline, after an initial success, of solid-fuel stoves. However, further diversification and the introduction of new management following some major closure in the rationalisation of Allied Ironfounders establishments and of firms such as R. and A. Main (producing cookers) prevented further decline after the mid-1960's. Such is the diversity of the associated industries that most of the well-known names are classified in the 'miscellaneous' industrial groupings, such as Carron in 'Other metal manufacture' and Smith and Wellstood in 'Other mechanical engineering'.

Textiles in the Stirling sub-region are concentrated mainly in Clackmannan at the foothills of the Ochil Hills in Alva, Tillicoultry and Alloa. The dozen or so establishments in that area typically employ less than 200 people except Donbros and Paton and Baldwin both in Alloa. Some fewer textiles establishments have settled in and to the east of Kilsyth to absorb the available supply of female labour.

Brickmaking is the main specialism in the manufacture of non-metalliferous materials (bricks, pottery, glass, cement, etc.) in the Grangemouth/Falkirk sub-region. Although there is manufacture of ordinary bricks, a major part of the industry (notably G. R. -Stein) produces refractory bricks from the seam of fireclay which is accessible in the area and in areas to the east. Since refractory bricks are used to line furnaces, this part of the industry is very sensitive to the cycles in the level of general industrial activity. In the Stirling area the activities of firms in this Order tend to be more varied but the principal employer is United Glass at Alloa. The last noteworthy specialisation in manufacturing, which is revealed in Table 13.2, is that of the Grangemouth/Falkirk area in timber and woodworking industries. To a large extent the specialisation is a consequence of the dominance of Grangemouth as a port for importing wood from Scandinavia and latterly from farther afield. A major firm in the industry is Muirhead at Grangemouth itself but other major employers are at Falkirk and Larbert.

TABLE 13.3

Components of Change Analysis of Employment Change in Central Region 1961 — 71
(SIC — 1958 Classification)

	ORDER	Actual Change	National Growth Component $E\bar{N}+(n\frac{E}{N})\,(\bar{n}-\bar{N})$	Structural Component $\angle\bar{e}-(n\frac{E}{N})\,7(\bar{n}-\bar{N})$	Differential Component (Regional Relative) $e(\bar{e}-\bar{n}) - (\bar{n}-\bar{N})$ $=e(\bar{e}-\bar{n})$
		No	No	No	No
1	Agriculture, forestry and fishing	- 1,302	- 1,070	- 18	- 213
2	Mining and quarrying	- 4,165	- 1,370	- 1,915	- 880
	Total primary (sum of MLHs)	- 5,467	- 2,440	- 1,933	- 1,093
3	Food, drink and tobacco	+ 130	+ 187	+ 18	- 76
4	Chemicals and allied industries				
	(a) MLH 261 — 263)	+ 348	- 31	- 107	+ 486
	(b) MLH 271 — 277	+ 117	+ 111	+ 125	- 119
5	Metal manufacture	- 2,853	- 213	- 761	- 1,878
6	Engineering and electrical goods				
	(a) MLH 331 — 349	+ 1,295	+ 316	- 195	+ 1,173
	(b) MLH 351 — 352	+ 60	+ 37	- 37	+ 60
	(c) MLH 361 — 369	+ 1,070	+ 397	- 372	+ 1,044
7	Shipbuilding and marine engineering	- 91	- 237	+ 103	+ 43
8	Vehicles	+ 90	- 297	+ 230	+ 156
9	Metal goods	- 702	- 21	+ 3	- 683
10	Textiles	- 1,281	- 922	- 394	+ 35
11	Leather, leather goods and fur	- 74	- 44	+ 32	- 62
12	Clothing and footwear	+ 1,351	- 428	+ 419	+ 1,360
13	Bricks	+ 971	- 35	- 85	+ 1,092
14	Timber, furniture, etc.	+ 113	+ 61	+ 30	+ 23
15	Paper, printing and publishing	- 463	+ 72	+ 10	- 545
16	Other manufacturing	+ 112	+ 200	- 157	+ 68
	Total manufacturing (sum of MLHs)	+ 189	- 848	- 1,138	+ 2,178
17	Construction	- 386	- 629	- 220	+ 463
18	Gas, electricity and water	- 95	- 21	+ 3	- 77
19	Transport and communication	- 914	- 242	+ 30	- 701
20	Distributive trades				
	(a) MLH 810	+ 497	3 29	- 21	+ 488
	(b) MLH 820	- 332	- 738	+ 57	+ 349
	(c) MLH 831, 832	+ 65	- 124	3 82	+ 107
21	Insurance, banking and finance	+ 434	+ 1,890	- 1,012	- 444
22	Professional scientific services	+ 4,956	+ 3,834	- 595	+ 1,717
23	Miscellaneous services	+ 966	- 720	+ 162	+ 1,523
24	Public administration	+ 489	+ 745	- 51	- 205
	Total services (sum of MLHs)	+ 5,680	+ 4,024	- 1,565	+ 3,220
	TOTAL	+ 406	+ 736	- 4,636	+ 4,305

Source: *This material has been prepared by the Planning Department, Stirling County Council. I am grateful for permission to use their work.*

Since the service industries tend to vary geographically less than manufacturing, their location quotients seldom differ widely from unity. The values in Table 13.2 underline the relatively greater importance of the service sector in the Stirling sub-region, partly because of Stirling's position as a market town and regional centre. The high location quotient for the public utilities, gas, electricity and water, reflects the electrical generating stations in the Kincardine and Longannet areas, a 'spin-off' from the coal industry. Conversely Grangemouth/Falkirk looks relatively 'deprived' in most service sectors.

Shift-share Analysis

An analytical technique which facilitates a broad distinction to be drawn between the 'structural' effects — i.e. the effects of the industrial composition — and the 'competitive advantage' — i.e. the extent to which industrial growth in an area deviates from the national average — is shift-share analysis. Despite its widespread use in regional economics, there is no Ultimate Truth revealed in its results. Its main usefulness is to provide a framework which facilitates understanding of the factors which together have shaped the employment trends in the Central Region. We shall examine the employment trends in the Region in terms of shift-share analysis and follow up the results in the light of more general information about the local economy. The results of a shift-share analysis are presented in Table 13.3.

In manufacturing, the most suitable declines have taken place in Order 5 (Metal manufacture) and 9 (Metal production). There has been a major contraction of the light iron castings industry in Falkirk, Larbert and Bonnybridge. The industry in these places was closely related to the housebuilding industry by the production of baths, rainwater roods and solid-fuel stoves. It suffered from the cycles of housebuilding up to 1971 and also from a long-run trend of the replacement of thin-wall iron castings by plastics and from a shift in heating systems to more automatic central heating systems using electricity, gas and oil. The high differential loss attributable to castings in this area is explained by the fact that other areas which specialised in castings were producing engineering castings with higher quality metal which could be machined for use in engineering industries. A number of firms in the castings industry investigated the possibility of supplying castings to the new factories of the British Motor Corporation and Rootes when they established their plants at Bathgate and Linwood in the early 1960's. Their lack of success on any scale was a reflection of the wide differences between the local industry and the motor industry's traditional suppliers from the Midlands and elsewhere in metallurgical requirements and entrepreneurial response. The differential loss of Order 9 (Metal goods production) is associated with the fortunes of the light castings industry.

In services a surprisingly large differential loss occurs in Transport and communication (Order 19). The loss has been concentrated in the Grangemouth/Falkirk sub-region and seems to have occurred in railway and port employment. In the primary sector, coalmining in the Central Region has declined more rapidly than the industry in Britain as a whole as production has concentrated upon the newer and more economic deposits in the East Midlands and South Yorkshire coalfields.

On the other hand, whereas there was a modest, structural and differential loss in the primary sector, a structural loss but differential gain in manufacturing, the service sector as a whole displays a massive differential gain. This large gain is more than twice the loss which was caused by structural factors and occurs mainly in Professional and Scientific services and in Miscellaneous services. The location of this increase is fairly evenly distributed between parts of the Region and between males and females, as may be seen in Table 13.4. The distribution of this increase of employment suggests that the University of Stirling is not the only influence; also an increase in higher-grade services entails a consequent increase in supporting female employment.

TABLE 13.4

Actual increase in employment in selected service industries
Central Region, 1961 - 71

Order 22 Professional and Scientific Services		
	Grangemouth/Falkirk	*Stirling*
Males	+ 579	+ 745
Females	+ 1,716	+ 1.907

Order 23 Miscellaneous services		
	Grangemouth/Falkirk	*Stirling*
Males	+ 110	- 41
Females	+ 246	+ 551

In manufacturing there has been a large increase in Mechanical engineering (MLH 331 — 349), Electrical engineering (MLH 361 — 369) which has had the effect of establishing these engineering trades as a major industry in the Region, 4.2% of the Grangemouth/Falkirk and 4.7% of the Stirling sub-regions' employment. Of the two other industries with a large differential gain, one has been long-established in the Region and the other is a newcomer. The first comprises the category bricks, pottery, glass, etc: and the second clothing and footwear. Brickmaking has increased despite quite large cycles in the 1960's on the basis of its specialisation of refractory bricks. The manufacture of glass bottles and containers, also included in this Order, has been expanded in the Alloa district although the brewery industry, with which it was once closely associated, has not expanded. Clothing and footwear has risen from an insignificant level in the Region to over 1,300 employees in the Grangemouth/Falkirk area. This increase has been caused mainly by the establishment of largely female-employing plants in areas where there has been a low rate of female participation in the workforce and where women have been put out of work by the contraction of the castings industry. No less than 95% of the workers in clothing and footwear in Grangemouth/Falkirk at 1971 were female.

A divided region

There is a limit to which the foregoing analysis can convey an understanding of the Region's economy and its future development. During a substantial part of the post-war period, there was a continuation of the decline of the staple manufacturing industries without substantial growth of new industries (see Appendix-Table 13.1). However, during the 1960's the Region's economic performance not only surpassed that of Scotland, but when allowance is made for its industrial structure, the performance shows competitive gains compared to the UK economy. In other words, a significant number of industries grew faster or declined more slowly than the national average. There are indications that this period of improved economic fortunes is based upon the growth of new industries. In Grangemouth/Falkirk these industries were in the manufacturing sector and in Stirling in Professional and Scientific services. However, in order to clarify the economic trends within the Region, it will be more useful to look in turn at the two separate parts. They have different economic structures and they appear to have experienced changing economic fortunes during the 1960's. In the Grangemouth/Falkirk sub-region, total employment increased by about 1,700 whereas in the Stirling sub-region total employment dropped by 1,300. The economic health of an area is also reflected in the prevailing unemployment rates. The Stirling area has experienced a steady deterioration in unemployment conditions from a situation in which unemployment was markedly lower than the Scottish average to one of near-average unemployment in 1973. Grangemouth/Falkirk, on the other hand, has improved steadily since 1965 to an unemployment rate below both the Stirling area rate and the Scottish average. The divergence in economic fortunes is reason enough for a closer examination of the Region (see Appendix-Table 13.2); a further reason lies in examining the effects of regional policy during the 1960's.

From 1961 to 1971 both areas suffered from the universal decline in the primary sector although in the Stirling area this decline of 3,785 employees had a relatively greater effect. The comparatively under-represented manufacturing sector in Stirling lost a further 950 employees (textiles – 1,000; paper etc. – 350; metal goods – 250; mechanical engineering +450; bricks etc +700). Manufacturing in Grangemouth/Falkirk shows a net

TABLE 13.5

Unemployment rates in the Central Region and in Scotland

	Stirling Sub-region	Grangemouth/ Falkirk Sub-region	Scotland
August, 1963	—	4.1	4.3
August, 1964	—	3.5	3.4
August, 1965	—	3.3	2.9
August, 1966	1.6	3.0	2.7
August, 1967	2.8	3.6	3.8
August, 1968	2.4	2.9	3.8
August, 1969	2.4	2.6	3.8
August, 1970	3.2	3.6	4.5
August, 1971	4.9	5.8	6.3
August, 1972	6.5	5.8	6.6
August, 1973	4.1	3.5	4.4

Note: Unemployment rates are total registered unemployed as a percent of total employees (employed and unemployed). Both the Stirling and Grangemouth/Falkirk area correspond to the areas used for the employment analysis. The Stirling area was not included in the statistics of local employment until 1966; previously only development districts and principal cities were included.

Source: (annually) Ministry of Labour Gazette, Employment and Productivity Gazette, Department of Employment Gazette.

absolute gain of 1,150 employees which appears to be the result of a process whereby a large loss of nearly 2,200 in industries with a location quotient of 1 in 1961 was more than compensated by a gain of 3,300 in industries new to the area or with a share in total Grangemouth/Falkirk employment less than the national average.

The tertiary sector in the Stirling sub-region increased by 16 percent or from 50.6 to 60.2 percent of total employees. Services in Grangemouth/Falkirk increased by only 9 percent, less than the national average, but in large measure this is accounted for by a fall of over 700 in Construction, a normally highly variable industry. The principal change in the Stirling economy was the 71 percent increase in professional and scientific services. This increase does not entirely depend upon the growth of Stirling University, but certainly the establishment of the University explains the extent to which the increase exceeds the national average rate of growth.

Although the reasons for the divergence in economic trends are not easy to identify definitively, one powerful underlying force has been a gradual reduction in the relative geographical isolation of the Grangemouth/Falkirk area in the light of a general need to seek space to restructure the industrial central belt of Scotland. Historically there have been strong links between the Grangemouth/Falkirk area and the rest of Stirlingshire and counties to the north (which could, in any case, be reached only through Stirling); one example is Falkirk Tryst, a distribution point for agricultural products from the north to Central Scotland. Increasingly the spatial links have integrated the area more closely with the Central Belt. The Glasgow–Edinburgh rail link is now almost exclusively through the area; Cumbernauld New Town has been sited mid-way between the outskirts of Glasgow and Falkirk; residential development on the eastern fringe of the area is in large measure overspill demand from the Edinburgh housing market. In its planning of Central Scotland, the Grangemouth/Falkirk sub-region was identified by the Scottish Development Department as a 'growth area', an area capable of sustaining an above-average rate of population growth. It was intended that the area would be able to accept immigration of Glasgow 'overspill' population In order to achieve this goal it was necessary to project a much higher rate of employment growth than had been obtained for more than a quarter of a century (see Appendix-Table 13.1). Following the 1963 White Paper (Central Scotland : A Programme for Growth) the Grangemouth/Falkirk area was the subject of a two year economic and planning study carried out by the Universities of Edinburgh and Glasgow under the direction of Professor Percy Johnson-Marshall (Edinburgh) and Professor Donald J Robertson (University of Glasgow). There was another aim of the study, to rationalise and improve the existing urban structure of the area. Although heavily industrialised, the Grangemouth/Falkirk area is a loosely polynucleated urban area as a direct result of the growth of the principal industries in separate centres. It was intended that an extended period of growth would provide the opportunity not only to stimulate regional development but also to improve the existing, somewhat decayed environment with its legacy of derelict works, spoiled land and poor social facilities in relation to a total population in the area in 1961 of 125,000.

One question which inevitably arises is the extent to which the changed economic climate in the Central Region and Grangemouth/Falkirk in particular can be explained by regional development policies.   By 1971 it would be too early to expect a marked improvement as a result of the growth area policy in that, following acceptance of the sub-regional plan, the immigration of population and housing programme had not developed on a large scale.   It would appear that there was a favourable combination of circumstances which in part resulted from the early developments of the sub-region plan.   The other elements in the economic changes have been a reduction in the rate of contraction of traditional industries which has been a feature of employment change since 1931 (see Appendix-Table 13.1), and the introduction of new industries on a large enough scale to have a significant effect upon total employment.   The growth of petrochemicals at Grangemouth was a major new industry which, being highly capital-intensive, did not have a dramatic effect on total employment in the whole Grangemouth/Falkirk area.   That industry and the promotion of new industrial sites on the former Grangemouth airfield did, however, create a reputation of 'growth' without which the area would have had the appearance of almost unrelieved decline and dereliction.   The latter part of the 1960's witnessed a spread of growth from Grangemouth, which at the time of its application for large burgh status, had a rateable value higher than most existing large burghs.

If it is unclear whether growth antedated regional development or vice-versa, it follows that the projection of future development in the region is difficult.   Although the Grangemouth/Falkirk Plan projected a population in 1985 of around 250,000 people and the plan has been broadly accepted by regional and local government, the speed of development is largely dependent upon public investment programmes.   The Grangemouth/Falkirk area is well placed in relation to transport improvements and new infrastructure developments to continue its favourable rate of economic growth.   The most specific of future plans is the expansion of the Grangemouth refinery as crude oil from BP's Forties field is piped to it. As yet the expansion of the associated petrochemicals industries has not been foreshadowed; the shortage of land and proximity to residential development are major constraints.   The remainder of the Region will probably benefit from the widening of residential choice in Central Scotland and includes some of the most attractive housing sites, considering environment and distance from major employment centres, in Central Scotland.

REFERENCE

Robertson, D J ed   1968   *Grangemouth/Falkirk Regional Survey and Plan Vol. 1.*
                                  Edinburgh: H.M.S.O.

APPENDIX TABLE 13.1

Employment in principal industries in the Central Region
(Counties of Stirling and Clackmannan) 1931 — 61

	1931	%	1951	%	1961	%
Agriculture, forestry and fishing	4,354	4.91	3,914	3.99	2,910	2.96
Mining and quarrying	11,952	13.46	8,177	8.33	5,570	5.67
Bricks, pottery, glass, etc.	1,981	2.23	3,179	3.24	3,810	3.88
Chemicals	2,380	2.68	4,395	4.48	7,210	7.34
Textiles, clothes, leather, etc.	5,786	6.52	4,929	5.02	4,410	4.49
Metal and engineering	15,329	17.27	21,827	22.23	16,210	16.50
Timber, furniture	1,848	2.08	2,187	2.23	1,980	2.02
Food, drink, tobacco	2,630	2.97	3,784	3.85	3,290	3.55
Paper and printing	1,570	1.77	2,847	2.90	3,110	3.17
Other manufacturing	290	0.33	343	0.35	350	0.36
Construction	3,731	4.21	6,378	6.50	8,140	8.28
Gas, water, electricity	602	0.68	1,066	1.09	1,450	1.48
Transport and communication	6,938	7.82	7,220	7.35	6,520	6.64
Financial and distributive services	12,055	13.58	10,134	10.32	12,230	12.45
Professional, personal and miscellaneous services	10,630	11.88	12,938	12.97	15,630	15.91
Public administration and defence	5,727	6.45	5,000	5.09	5,310	5.40
Total	88,810		98,170		98,250	

Sources: Census of Population Scotland, 1931, 1951 and 1961

Note: Industry groups are not directly comparable owing to changes in the Standard Industrial Classification.

APPENDIX TABLE 13.2

Structure of Employment in the Central Region 1961 – 1971

		Central Region						Grangemouth/Falkirk				Stirling			
		1961		GB	1971		GB	1961		1971		1961		1971	
	SIC Order	No.	%	%	No.	%	%	No	%	No.	%	No.	%	No.	%
1	Agriculture, forestry and fishing	2,712	2.8	2.6	1,410	1.4	1.4	732	1.3	333	0.6	1,978	4.5	1,077	2.5
2	Mining and quarrying	7,697	7.6	3.2	3,532	3.5	1.8	2,294	4.1	1,013	1.7	5,403	12.3	2,519	5.9
	Total Primary Sector	10,409	10.4	5.9	4,942	4.9	3.4	3,029	5.4	1,346	2.3	7,381	16.8	3,596	8.4
3	Food, drink and tobacco	4,042	4.0	3.6	4,172	4.1	3.7	1,473	2.6	1,843	3.2	2,569	5.8	2,329	5.4
4	Chemical and Allied Industries														
	(a) MLH 261 – 263	1,125	1.1	0.2	1,473	1.4	0.2	1,102	2.0	1,471	2.5	23	–	2	–
	(b) MLH 271 – 277	5,936	5.9	2.0	6,053	6.0	2.1	5,918	10.5	5,954	10.3	18	–	99	0.2
5	Metal manufacture	10,303	10.2	2.8	7,450	7.4	2.5	10,290	18.3	7,437	12.8	13	–	13	–
6	Engineering and electrical goods														
	(a) MLH 331 – 349 Mechanical	1,875	1.8	5.2	3,170	3.1	5.5	367	0.6	1,208	2.1	1,508	3.4	1,962	4.6
	(b) MLH 351, 352 Instrument	4	–	0.6	64	–	0.7	–	–	2	–	4	–	62	0.1
	(c) MLH 361 – 369 Electrical	220	0.2	3.5	1,290	1.2	3.9	135	0.2	1,233	2.1	85	0.2	57	0.1
7	Shipbuilding and marine engineering	646	0.6	1.1	555	0.5	0.8	629	1.1	554	0.9	17	–	1	–
8	Vehicles	965	1.0	3.9	1,055	1.0	3.6	876	1.5	1,012	1.7	89	0.2	43	0.1
9	Metal goods	2,299	2.3	2.5	1,597	1.5	2.4	1,080	1.9	648	1.1	1,219	2.8	949	2.2
10	Textiles	5,296	5.3	3.7	4,015	3.9	2.7	540	1.0	272	0.5	4,756	10.8	3,743	8.6
11	Leather, leather goods and fur	81	–	0.2	7	–	0.2					81	0.2	7	–
12	Clothing and footwear	55	–	2.5	1,406	1.3	2.1	–	–	1,377	2.4	55	0.1	29	–
13	Bricks	3,640	3.6	1.5	4,611	4.5	1.4	2,146	3.8	2,390	4.1	1,494	3.4	2,221	5.2
14	Timber, furniture, etc.	2,146	2.1	1.2	2,259	2.2	1.3	1,720	3.1	1,921	3.3	426	1.0	338	0.8
15	Paper, printing and publishing	3,343	3.3	2.7	2,880	2.8	2.7	1,590	2.8	1,492	2.6	1,753	4.0	1,388	3.2
16	Other manufacturing	287	0.3	1.3	399	0.3	1.5	32	0.0	232	0.4	255	0.6	167	0.4
	Total Manufacturing Sector	42,266	42.3	39.4	42,455	42.2	38.2	27,900	50.0	29,045	50.2	14,366	32.6	13,410	31.4
17	Construction	8,862	8.9	6.7	8,476	8.4	6.0	5,685	10.1	4,959	8.6	3,177	7.2	3,417	8.2
18	Gas, electricity and water	1,566	1.6	1.6	1,471	1.4	1.6	634	1.1	376	0.6	932	2.1	1,095	2.6
19	Transport and communication	6,611	6.6	7.3	5,697	5.6	7.0	4,427	7.9	3,612	6.2	2,184	5.0	2,085	4.9
20	Distribution														
	(a) MLH 810 Wholesale	456	0.5	2.3	953	0.9	2.3	253	0.4	824	1.4	203	0.5	129	0.3
	(b) MLH 820 Retail	8,323	8.3	8.9	7,991	7.9	8.1	4,346	7.7	4,232	7.3	3,977	9.0	3,759	8.8
	(c) MLH 831 – 832 Other	462	0.5	1.2	527	0.5	1.1	189	0.3	208	0.3	273	0.6	319	0.7
21	Insurance, banking and finance	1,153	1.1	2.4	1,587	1.5	4.3	534	0.9	669	1.1	619	1.4	918	2.1
22	Professional and scientific services	7,730	7.7	9.1	12,686	12.6	12.9	3,965	7.0	6,260	10.8	3,765	8.5	6,426	15.0
23	Miscellaneous services	7,063	7.1	8.9	8,029	7.9	8.1	3,171	5.6	3,627	6.3	3,892	8.8	4,402	10.3
24	Public administration	5,282	5.3	5.6	5,771	5.7	6.3	2,049	3.6	2,703	4.7	3,233	7.3	3,068	7.2
	Total Services	47,508	47.5	54.6	53,188	52.8	58.2	25,253	44.9	27,470	47.5	22,255	50.6	25,718	60.2
	TOTAL	100,180			100,586			56,181		57,863		44,001		42,724	

CHAPTER 14

SOCIAL CHARACTERISTICS OF THE CENTRAL REGION BURGHS

The Central Region is pre-eminently an area of small communities. The largest town, Falkirk, has a population of less than 40,000 and only 57 percent of the total population of the region live in places officially designated burghs. Two-thirds of the regional population live in settlements containing fewer than 15,000 and approximately half live in settlements of less than 5,000. Small size does not, however, indicate uniformity and the Central Region burghs exhibit a wide range of demographic, socio-economic and political contrasts.

Demographic Characteristics

The demographic history of the Central Region burghs is illustrated by Table 14.1 which gives population totals for successive censuses between 1851 and 1971.

The background to the fluctuating fortunes of the thirteen burghs is given in Chapter 11 It suffices here to note a few of the more general formal characteristics revealed in the historical data. A comparison of 1971 population totals with those for 1871 reveals a general pattern of slight change. Most of the smaller centres have recorded increases which are proportionately rather less than that characteristic of Scotland as a whole during the same period. The 1971 Scottish population is some one and a half times as great as that for 1871. Six of the Central Region burghs have increased at a slower rate. Alva, Tillicoultry and Dollar have only recently re-attained the sizes they achieved in the middle of the nineteenth century; Doune is little more than half its previous size, having experienced an almost constant decline in numbers since the early decades of the nineteenth century. Several of the smaller centres have undergone a recent spurt in growth following the development of private housing estates aimed at the developing commuter and university markets. This is particularly noticeable in the case of Dunblane, but is also characteristic of Bridge of Allan and Dollar. By the time of the 1976 Census it is also likely that the figures for Doune will show a dramatic turn-round reflecting the influence of speculative private building. Bo'ness and Denny have approximately tripled in size between 1871 and 1971 and share a pattern in which nineteenth century growth leads to a population plateau in the early decades of the twentieth century and a more recent period in which growth is renewed as the result of over-spill development. In contrast to the irregular pattern exhibited by Bo'ness and Denny, Alloa has experienced a slow but steady increase throughout the period, its 1971 population being rather less than twice that achieved one hundred years earlier. A somewhat similar pattern, albeit at a higher rate of increase, is characteristic of Stirling. The growth of both towns seems to have reflected the general prosperity of their service hinterlands rather than

TABLE 14.1

Population of Central Region Burghs, 1851 – 1971

	1851	1861	1871	1881	1891	1901	1911	1921	1931	1951	1961	1971	1971 as % of 1871
Falkirk	8752	9030	9547	13170	19312	29280	33574	33308	36566	37535	38044	37579	394
Stirling	9361	10277	10873	16012	16781	18403	21200	21345	22593	26962	27551	29776	274
Grangemouth		2000	2569	4560	6345	8386	10219	9723	11799	15432	18857	24569	956
Alloa	6676	6425	7637	8822	10754	11421	11893	12420	13323	13436	13898	14100	185
Bo'ness	2645	3893	4256	5284	5866	9306	10862	10162	10095	9950	10195	12853	302
Denny & Dunipace	2446	3435	3623	4080	4161	5158	5164	5130	5512	6756	7760	9841	272
Dunblane	1816	1718	1921	2186	2186	2516	2978	2931	2692	2985	2932	4497	234
Bridge of Allan		1803	3036	3005	3207	3240	3121	3579	2897	3173	3318	4314	142
Alva	3058	3147	4096	4961	5225	4624	4332	4107	3820	4106	3957	4180	102
Tillicoultry	3217	3584	3745	3732	3939	3338	3105	3100	2953	3819	3963	4026	108
Dollar	1079	1540	2090	2014	1807	1619	1497	1584	1485	1386	1955	2280	109
Callander		884	1271	1522	1538	1458	1504	1874	1572	1728	1655	1786	141
Doune	1459	1256	1262	996	940	930	893	865	822	834	786	741	59

any specific industrial developments. The growth of Falkirk and, even more so, of Grangemouth has been much more spectacular, Falkirk increasing almost four-fold in the hundred years 1871 — 1971 and Grangemouth increasing almost tenfold in the same period. The growth of Falkirk was most rapid at the turn of the century, the population more than doubling between 1881 and 1901, reflecting the prosperity of the town's metal manufacture and its attraction to migrants. Much of the more recent growth connected with the town's industry has occurred outside its legal boundaries and is not reflected in the burgh statistics. In large measure the growth of Grangemouth may be seen as a more recent manifestation of the continued prosperity of the Falkirk/Grangemouth sub-region and, in particular, of the growing importance of oil-based industries in the regional and national economies.

Details of the population changes which have characterised the Central Region burghs in the period 1951 — 1971 are given in Table 14.2. As a whole the Region has been an

TABLE 14.2

Annual Percentage Change in Population 1951 — 1971

| | Total 1951 — 61 | 1961 — 1971 | | |
		Total	By Births and Deaths	Balance
Alloa	0.27	0.14	0.71	- 0.60
Alva	- 0.33	0.49	0.43	0.07
Dollar	3.46	1.55	- 0.03	1.58
Tillicoultry	0.22	0.16	0.63	- 0.50
Bo'ness	- 1.58	1.61	1.61	- 0.00
Callander	- 0.50	0.23	- 0.28	0.49
Doune	- 0.50	- 0.59	- 0.01	- 0.57
Dunblane	- 0.31	4.40	0.36	4.15
Falkirk	0.13	-0.13	0.53	- 0.69
Stirling	0.15	0.78	0.68	0.11
Bridge of Allan	0.45	2.66	0.42	2.32
Denny	1.39	2.40	1.17	1.35
Grangemouth	2.02	2.66	1.15	1.67

area of relative growth, easily exceeding the aggregate Scottish growth rates of 0.16 percent per annum in the 1951 — 61 decade and 0.09 percent per annum in the 1961 — 71 decade. In contrast to the national figures the Central Region exhibits a swing towards more rapid growth in the latter period. Perhaps the most notable characteristic of the recent demographic history of the Region, however, is the variability in growth patterns. Five of the Central Region burghs experienced a net decline in population during the 1950's, in the 1961 — 71 decade only two burghs show an overall decrease. The swing from decline to growth is especially marked in the case of Dunblane and, to a lesser extent, Bo'ness. Dunblane experienced a net decline of 0.31 percent per annum in the 1951 – 61 decade but in the 1961 – 71 period has grown at an average annual rate of 4.4 percent, fifty times the national figure. The equivalent Bo'ness rates are -1.58 percent per annum in 1951 – 61 and 1.61 percent per annum in 1961 – 71. Throughout the period Grangemouth has kept up a relatively constant and high rate of growth.

Changes in population reflect the balance of births and deaths and the effects of migration. The low rate of overall growth in the Scottish population has long reflected a relatively high rate of natural increase allied with a similarly high rate of emigration. In the 1061 – 71 decade Scotland experienced a rate of natural increase averaging 0.67 percent per annum compared with a rate for England and Wales of 0.59 percent per annum. In the same years Scotland experienced a rate of emigration averaging 0.52 percent per annum compared with an English and Welsh figure of 0.06 percent per annum. The Central Region exhibits a highly variegated pattern. High rates of natural increase, approximately twice the national average, are characteristic of Bo'ness, Denny and Grangemouth. Three burghs: Callander, Dollar and Doune have negative rates of natural increase, deaths outnumbering births. High rates of net immigration are characteristic of Dunblane, Bridge of Allan, Grangemouth, Dollar and Denny. Several burghs on the other hand, notably Falkirk, Alloa, Doune and Tillicoultry have experienced significant rates of emigration, although it is doubtful whether much of this has actually been out of the area especially in the case of Falkirk.

The crude birth and death rates which yield the rate of natural increase are greatly affected by variations in the age and sex characteristics of the population. Standardisation to take account of the differences between local and national demographic structures helps to reduce the variation in the vital statistics of the Central Region burghs but also reveals interesting differences in 'natural propensities'. Details are given in Table 14.3 based on the reports of the Registrar General for Scotland for 1966–70 inclusive.

The crude birth rate for Scotland as a whole during the five years 1966 – 70 averages 174 per 1,000 population. Standardising to the national age and sex structure yields an aggregate Central Region birth rate which is almost identical to the national figure. The major exceptions to the general similarity with the national picture are the relatively low birth rates in Tillicoultry, Bo'ness and Dollar and the exceptionally high rate in Dunblane.

In Scotland as a whole some seven percent of all live births are classified as illegitimate. Only two of the Central Region burghs, Callander and Alloa, exceed the national figure and most of the burghs exhibit relatively low rates of illegitimacy. It is generally found that illegitimacy is a large city or resort phenomenon and the low figures for the Central Region burghs, as well as the relatively high figure for Callander, with its important tourist industry, appear to conform with the general pattern.

TABLE 14.3

Births, Deaths and Illegitimacy 1966 — 70

	Standardised Birth Rate per 1000	Percent Live Birth Illegitimate	Standardised Death Rate per 1000	Infant Mortality per 1000 Live Births
Alloa	18.0	9.9	13.7	21
Alva	16.8	5.4	12.3	22
Dollar	14.3	3.9	9.0	41
Tillicoultry	13.2	6.9	11.5	11
Bo'ness	14.3	3.9	11.3	22
Callander	18.0	10.2	12.4	38
Doune	18.0	*	16.9	15
Dunblane	24.1	2.8	10.7	19
Falkirk	16.9	5.7	12.4	25
Stirling	19.6	6.7	12.2	26
Bridge of Allan	17.7	5.3	8.7	23
Denny	19.0	4.6	12.0	13
Grangemouth	17.6	4.3	11.1	21

NOTE: 'births, still births and deaths have been allocated to the usual place of residence if it is in
Scotland, otherwise to the place of occurrence'

Annual Report of the Registrar for Scotland 1966, p XV

* Only one illegitimate birth, in 1966, was recorded in Doune during the 1961 — 70 decade.

Standardised death rates provide an indication of the overall health of the population.
The crude death rate in Scotland as a whole during the five years of the study period
averages 12.3 per thousand of the population.   This figure is exceeded by only four of the
Central Region burghs, Doune, Alloa, Callander and Falkirk, while notably low standardised
death rates are characteristic of Bridge of Allan and Dollar.   Both towns clearly live up to
their reputations as healthy places in which to retire.

The final column in Table 14.3 gives data on infant mortality in the Central Region
burghs.   Scottish figures for deaths in the first year of life are consistently some fifteen percent above the rate for England and Wales at an average of 21.1 per thousand live births in
the 1966 — 70 period.   In his report for 1970 the Registrar General makes the point that
there is an urban to rural trend in infant mortality with cities having the higher rates.   There
is little sign of an equivalent trend in the Central Region where the highest rates of infant
mortality, approximately twice the national average, are found in Dollar and Callander and
the lowest rates in Tillicoultry and Denny.   Variations in infant mortality are difficult to

explain in the absence of more detailed knowledge of the circumstances involved in each case but the Central Region data appear consistent with an explanation in terms of the age structure of women bearing children.

TABLE 14.4

Population by Country of Birth, 1971

	Scotland	England and Wales	Ireland	New Commonwealth	Other
Alloa	92.4	5.1	.7	.3	1.5
Alva	91.3	6.5	.9	.1	1.3
Dollar	74.1	18.0	.6	4.4	2.9
Tillicoultry	92.7	5.2	.6	.2	1.3
Bo'ness	94.5	3.8	.7	.2	.9
Callander	87.3	9.3	1.1	.6	1.7
Doune	87.2	8.8	1.4	1.4	1.4
Dunblane	81.6	14.3	1.0	.7	2.4
Falkirk	93.2	4.1	1.2	.2	1.3
Stirling	90.5	6.5	.9	.6	1.6
Bridge of Allan	80.8	14.3	.8	1.6	2.6
Denny	95.0	3.1	.7	.1	1.1
Grangemouth	91.4	5.1	1.1	.5	1.9

Just as variations in age structure are related to differences in 'vital propensities' so differences in the migration experiences of the Central Region burghs find expression in the variation of their population by country of origin. As Table 14.4 shows all the burgh are overwhelmingly Scottish-born. The aggregate distribution of the population according to birth place is similar to that for Scotland as a whole. Within the general pattern, however, a clear distinction exists between Dollar, Bridge of Allan and Dunblane, each with relatively large non-Scots populations, more than twice the national proportions, and the remaining burghs. A more detailed break-down of the immigrant populations serves simply to explicate the division. In Dollar almost one-in-five and in Bridge of Allan and Dunblane one-in-seven of the population were born in England and Wales. By contrast less than one-in-thirty of the population of Denny, and one-in-twenty-six of that of Bo'ness are from 'south of the border'. In Scotland as a whole approximately one-in-nineteen of the population are of English and Welsh birth. The numbers from other birth-place categories in the Central Region are small and the only remarkable datum is the 4.4 percent of the population of Dollar with 'New Commonwealth' birth-places. On the whole, however, with the exception of the enclaves of English settlers in Dollar, Dunblane and Bridge of Allan, the population of the Central Region burghs is homogeneously Scottish.

TABLE 14.5

Age Structure, 1971

	Percent of Population Aged				Dependency Rates
	0 – 4	5 – 14	15 – 64	65 and over	
Alloa	9.3	17.3	60.8	12.6	730
Alva	8.9	17.1	61.4	12.7	718
Dollar	5.9	24.6	57.0	12.5	818
Tillicoultry	8.8	17.4	62.0	11.8	698
Bo'ness	7.4	16.8	62.7	13.1	699
Callander	6.8	14.1	60.2	18.9	673
Doune	7.4	14.9	61.5	16.2	764
Dunblane	9.6	17.9	56.6	15.9	876
Falkirk	7.9	16.0	63.0	13.1	675
Stirling	9.1	17.7	61.2	12.1	724
Bridge of Allan	7.8	16.2	60.8	15.2	724
Denny	11.1	19.2	61.6	8.1	686
Grangemouth	9.5	20.0	62.6	7.9	656

The combination of fertility, mortality and migration patterns yields characteristic age structures.   Details are given in Table 14.5.   In the most general terms Denny and Grangemouth may be characterised as being essentially 'young' in age structure while Callander is essentially old and the other burghs have structures relatively similar to the national pattern. In addition to Denny and Grangemouth, high figures for the under five year age group are recorded in Dunblane, Alloa and Stirling.   The very low figure in Dollar reflects the distortion to the town's age structure which results from the inclusion of Dollar Academy in its census returns.   At the opposite end of the age continuum high proportions of the 65 years and over age group are found in Callander, Doune, Dunblane and Bridge of Allan, reflecting their status as retirement centres.

Variations in age structures are summarised in the figures for the dependency ratio, here defined as the ratio of those aged 0 – 14 years and those of retirement age (60 years in the case of women, 65 years in that of men) to the remainder of the population.   In Scotland as a whole there are 669 'dependents' for every 1000 'producers'.   In the Central Region only Grangemouth has a lower figure.   The highest proportion of dependents is in Dunblane which has a high figure of both the elderly, reflecting its traditional retirement role, and the young, reflecting its recent rapid growth as a commuter settlement.   Dollar, also, exhibits a high dependency ratio, in this case reflecting the high proportion of school-age children in its population.

TABLE 14.6

Marital Status, 1971

	Percent females 20—24 ever married	Percent females never married	Percent males never married	Percent females ever married now divorced
Alloa	69.3	21.6	25.3	1.7
Alva	71.0	19.1	21.0	1.1
Dollar	57.1	22.0	33.0	1.6
Tillicoultry	69.0	21.6	22.6	0.8
Bo'ness	61.8	21.1	27.5	0.9
Callander	55.6	24.2	23.6	2.5
Doune	60.0	24.1	22.6	2.1
Dunblane	61.3	20.8	18.5	1.1
Falkirk	59.9	21.3	25.3	1.3
Stirling	57.6	23.7	25.6	1.4
Bridge of Allan	40.7	26.7	21.5	1.1
Denny	67.1	19.8	26.1	1.1
Grangemouth	75.0	17.2	22.3	0.8

Data on the marital status of the population both reflect and help to explain the variations in fertility and age structures. In aggregate terms marriage is not as 'popular' in Scotland as it is in England and Wales. Thus, whereas in England and Wales 59.6 percent of women aged 20 — 24 years and 79.8 percent of all women aged 15 years and over are or have been married, the equivalent figures for Scotland are 57.3 percent and 75.9 percent. In the Central Region marriage reaches its peak of popularity in Grangemouth, with 74 percent of the 20 — 24 year old females married, and its trough in Bridge of Allan, where only 41 percent of the equivalent group are married. Below-national figures for the proportion married are also found in Callander and Dollar. The percent of spinsters varies inversely with the figures for marriage amongst the 20 — 24 year olds, although only Bridge of Allan has a significantly higher proportion of never-married women than Scotland as a whole. Figures for the percent of men never-married reveal a rather different pattern. Only Dollar, with one-third of its males aged 15 years and over never married, exceeds the Scottish aggregate figure of 27.8 percent. The Dollar figure is a further indication of the influence of Dollar Academy on the town's demography. Elsewhere the figures range from 18 percent in Dunblane to 27 percent in Bo'ness. Rates of divorce are relatively low throughout the Region with only Callander, Doune and Alloa exceeding the Scottish national rate.

Housing Characteristics

On the basis of the returns from the 1951 Census, Moser and Scott (1961, p 153) state that 'housing is the Scottish lament'. Comparative national figures for 1971 are unobtainable at the time of writing but it is clear from the 1966 sample census that there is still a considerable discrepancy between housing standards north and south of the border. In the 1966 data it is revealed that 40.0 percent of occupied dwellings in Scotland have 1 – 3 rooms as compared with 12.3 percent in England and Wales. Twenty-nine percent of the Scottish population live at a residential density of more than one person per room and 9.9 percent live at a density of more than 1½ persons per room. The equivalent figures for England and Wales are 11 percent and 2.5 percent. The average number of persons per room in England and Wales is 0.57; in Scotland it is 0.61. Only in terms of the standard household amenities, (hot water, an internal WC and a fixed bath or shower), is Scotland relatively favoured, with 78 percent of all Scottish households having exclusive use of all three amenities compared with 72 percent of English and Welsh households.

TABLE 14.7

Housing Characteristics

	Percent of dwellings 1 - 3 rooms	Percent of persons at >1 per room	Percent of persons at >1½ per room	Persons per room	Percent of dwellings with all amenities
Alloa	52.5	32.4	10.8	.80	93.3
Alva	47.2	28.5	6.5	.76	94.7
Dollar	23.4	9.7	1.7	.58	98.0
Tillicoultry	39.3	25.0	6.8	.74	98.1
Bo'ness	43.8	33.2	9.9	.80	89.9
Callander	30.3	18.3	6.7	.56	93.7
Doune	35.2	19.4	4.9	.62	93.8
Dunblane	28.4	15.1	5.0	.61	96.5
Falkirk	47.7	30.1	9.2	.77	88.5
Stirling	32.6	26.6	7.8	.72	93.8
Bridge of Allan	23.0	13.0	2.3	.58	94.4
Denny	29.3	30.9	8.1	.82	98.1
Grangemouth	53.0	38.4	9.5	.88	97.2

The Central Region is relatively well endowed in terms of Scottish housing standards yet the 1971 data given in Table 14.7 presents a picture which is strikingly different from that considered acceptable south of the border. More than half the dwellings in Alloa and Grangemouth have less than four rooms for eating, living and sleeping. Even the apparently spacious villas of Dollar and Bridge of Allan yield a large number of one-to three-room dwellings, almost a quarter of the total in each case. Not surprisingly the burghs exhibit what by

U.K. standards are relatively high degrees of overcrowding.   The problem is more severe in Alloa and Bo'ness which have approximately one-third of their population living in households with a residential density of one or more persons per room and a tenth of their population living at more than one-and-a-half persons per room.   Only Dollar and Bridge of Allan approach the average residential densities found in England and Wales.   Figures for the average number of persons per room simply underline the difference in housing standards. The 1971 figure for Great Britain as a whole is 0.60 persons per room.   In the Central Region only Dollar, Bridge of Allan and, somewhat surprisingly, Callander exhibit a lower average density.   The low Callander figure is a function of the relatively large number of single-person households in the burgh.   In contrast to the three favoured communities, Grangemouth, Denny, Alloa and Bo'ness have average occupancy rates some 30 − 45 percent above the Great Britain figures.   Variation in the percent of dwellings with exclusive access to hot water, internal WC's and baths is less pronounced than is the case with the other housing characteristics and all the Central Region burghs have figures comfortably above the 1966 national average.

Analyses of urban social structure in Britain have pointed to the importance of housing tenure in the patterning of social differences.   This again is an area in which the Scottish situation is quite unlike that in England and Wales.   The majority of the Scottish population rent their accommodation from local authorities or from the Scottish Special Housing Association.   Approximately a quarter of the Scottish population live in owner-occupied dwellings, about half the equivalent proportion for England and Wales.   Although the percentage of owner-occupiers in Scotland shows signs of increase, the general domination of the housing market by the public sector is evidenced by the fact that 80 percent of the new building completed in 1970 and 70 percent of that in 1971 was in the public sector.

As Table 13.8 shows the dominance of public housing is not a uniform characteristic of the Scottish scene.   Variations in tenure and in the associated types of housing form one of the most obvious bases of differentiation in the Central Region.   In Bridge of Allan, Dunblane and Dollar more than three-fifths of the population live in owner-occupied dwellings; in Denny only one-fifteenth of the population are owner-occupiers.   Conversely, while in Denny nine-tenths and in Bo'ness and Grangemouth almost four-fifths of the population rent their accommodation from the local authority or the Scottish Special Housing Association, in Bridge of Allan and Dunblane little more than a quarter of the population live in dwellings rented in the public sector.   A clear three-fold differentiation exists: Bridge of Allan, Dunblane and Dollar are largely owner-occupied; Callander and Doune have roughly equal proportions of owner-occupiers and public housing tenants; the population of Alloa, Alva, Stirling, Falkirk, Tillicoultry, Bo'ness, Grangemouth and, above all, Denny are largely local authority and Scottish Special Housing Association tenants.   Given the dominating influence of the public rental section it is little surprise to find that the private rental sector, and especially that for furnished property, is insignificant throughout the Region.

TABLE 14.8

Housing Tenure

	Percent of persons in Accommodation occupied by —		
	Owner	Council or SSHA tenant	Tenant of private landlord (furnished property)
Alloa	18.2	73.0	1.3
Alva	24.2	68.6	1.3
Dollar	60.9	30.3	2.5
Tillicoultry	18.9	74.3	.9
Bo'ness	16.0	78.0	.3
Callander	45.4	38.7	3.0
Doune	43.0	45.0	1.4
Dunblane	61.8	27.5	2.8
Falkirk	23.0	70.8	.9
Stirling	26.2	65.4	2.1
Bridge of Allan	62.6	27.6	3.1
Denny	6.7	89.7	.3
Grangemouth	14.5	77.6	.6

A summary measure of the desirability of housing is provided by data on rateable values. Rateable values are derived from assessed gross values: 'the rent at which the heredi-tament might reasonably be expected to let from year to year if the tenant undertook to pay all usual tenant's rates and taxes and the landlord undertook to bear the cost of the repairs and insurance and the expenses, if any, necessary to maintain the hereditament in a state to command that rent'. The responsibility for calculating gross values rests with local Assessors (the Scottish equivalent of local valuation officers). In detail, the process necessarily involves individual judgement and a considerable degree of arbitrariness. In general, how-ever, the resulting values provide a reasonable approximation to the rental value of property: the higher the rateable value the higher the rent the property can attract. Table 14.9 gives data on the average rateable value of private houses in the Central Region burghs and the *per capita* value of all residential property.

Average rateable values for private houses vary between £72 per annum in Bo'ness and Doune and £118 – 119 per annum in Dollar and Dunblane. Relatively high rateable values are also found amongst the private houses of Dunblane and Alloa while low values characte-rise that in Alva and Tillicoultry. It is difficult to place much reliance on the significance of the figures, however, outside those burghs in which a major percent of the population are owner-occupiers. A more sensitive measure of overall housing standards is supplied by the data on residential rateable values *per capita.*   These include material on public as well as private housing and 'provide proxies .. for .. income characteristics — proxies that are superior to the socio-economic and occupational groups ordinarily used' (Sarks and Firestone, 1972, pp 238 — 239).   By far the highest rateable value *per capita* is found in Bridge of Allan, nearly £38.   The next highest are Dunblane, £35, and Dollar £32.   The lowest are in Bo'ness, Denny and Grangemouth, approximately £26 *per capita.*

TABLE 14.9

Rateable Value of Housing, 1971 — 72

	Average Rateable Value of Private Houses	Residential Rateable Value *per capita*
	£	£
Alloa	107	27.6
Alva	76	27.8
Dollar	118	32.2
Tillicoultry	78	27.4
Bo'ness	72	26.6
Callander	83	30.8
Doune	72	27.1
Dunblane	112	34.9
Falkirk	87	29.0
Stirling	94	29.5
Bridge of Allan	119	27.9
Denny	94	26.5
Grangemouth	86	26.5

Source: Scottish Development Department

Occupational Characteristics

In a seminal work on the classification of communities, Shevky and Bell (1955, p 10) assert that 'just as occupation has so much meaning in regard to individual position or rank, no single set of closely related facts tells us so much about a total society as do the statistics describing its working population'.   The differentiation of the Central Region burghs in terms of their occupational characteristics is perhaps the most important single indicator of the variation in their overall social characteristics.

Differences in the economic functions of the Central Region burghs have been dealt with previously (see Chapter 13).   The present concern is with variations in the occupational characteristic of their work-forces.   As Table 14.10 shows, these are very considerable.

TABLE 14.10

Occupational Characteristics

	Percent Economically Active Males:			Percent Women
	Out of Employment	Professional/ Managerial Workers 1966	Manual Workers	15 — 59 years in workforce 1071
Alloa	8.2	9.1	69.8	54.4
Alva	3.7	11.3	66.9	58.3
Dollar	2.6	27.1	39.6	46.6
Tillicoultry	4.8	8.0	71.4	56.9
Bo'ness	7.5	6.4	75.3	55.9
Callander	3.1	20.7	49.0	59.6
Doune	2.4	33.3	66.7	51.2
Dunblane	2.2	33.0	36.0	47.3
Falkirk	7.2	10.6	67.9	55.2
Stirling	7.7	15.6	58.8	54.0
Bridge of Allan	3.0	35.6	36.6	45.0
Denny	5.7	7.1	72.2	52.8
Grangemouth	5.3	11.3	66.0	49.3

At the time of the 1971 Census 8.2 percent of the economically active males in Scotland were out of work, either through unemployment, sickness or transfer.   The relative economic disadvantage of Scotland is illustrated by the difference between the Scottish figure for percent out of work and the 5.1 percent registered in England and Wales.   At the same time, the relative prosperity of the Central Region is highlighted by the fact that only one burgh, Alloa, approaches the aggregate Scottish figure for non-employment, and that more than half the burghs have better employment figures even than the aggregate English and Welsh data.   Three categories may be distinguished in terms of the out-of-employment figures: four communities, Alloa, Stirling, Bo'ness and Falkirk have more than seven percent of their male workforce out of work; Denny, Grangemouth and Tillicoultry have around five percent out of employment, and the remaining six small burghs have well under four percent in the non-working category.

Perhaps of even greater importance for the social character of the thirteen Central Region burghs is the difference in the proportions of their workforce following professional, technical and managerial occupations, on the one hand, and manual occupations on the other. In the returns for the 1966 Sample Census, Dunblane and Bridge of Allan have almost equal numbers of their male workforce in each category; Bo'ness and Denny have ten times as many manual workers as they do professional, technical and managerial workers. In relative terms Dunblane, Bridge of Allan, Doune and Dollar have approximately three times as many professional, technical and managerial workers as does Scotland as a whole; Bo'ness, Denny, Tillicoultry and Alloa have less than the national proportion. Conversely, Dunblane, Bridge of Allan and Dollar have little more than half the national proportion of manual workers while Bo'ness, Denny and Tillicoultry easily exceed the national figure (62 percent). A basic division exists between Bridge of Allan, Dunblane and Dollar, in each of which more than three-fifths of economically active males are classified as non-manual workers, and Bo'ness, Denny, Tillicoultry, Alloa, Alva, Falkirk and Grangemouth, each of which has two-thirds of its male workforce in manual occupations. Doune, Callander and Stirling appear to occupy an intermediate position, although the Doune figures probably contain a high degree of sampling error. With the exception of these three, however, the Central Region burghs divide naturally into manual and non-manual communities.

Approximately a third of the British workforce is female. Along with the shift from manual to non-manual employment — and closely associated with it — the increase in female participation in the workforce has been the major structural change in the occupational system during the twentieth century. Differences in the occupational characteristics of gainfully employed women tend to follow those of gainfully employed men. Perhaps of greater import is the variation in the proportion of women who are economically active. In Scotland as a whole 54.6 percent of women aged 15 − 59 years are in the workforce, approximately one percent fewer than in England and Wales. In the Central Region the figure varies between 45 percent in Bridge of Allan and 60 percent in Callander. Five burghs, Callander, Alva, Bo'ness, Tillicoultry and Falkirk have figures which are higher than the Scottish average. On the other hand, Bridge of Allan, Dollar, Dunblane and Grangemouth have less than half of their women gainfully employed. Variations in the figures are not simply a reflection of women choosing between careers and children since both the group of burghs with higher-than-average proportions of working women and that with lower-than-average proportions contain burghs having both high and low fertility rates and high and low marriage rates.

Dimensions of Social Differentiation

Communities differ from one another in a multitude of ways. Even if attention is confined to the differences in their social characteristics it is still possible to conceive of an almost limitless set of variables which could be used in a discussion of their variation. In practice, however, the task is simplified by the high degree of inter-correlation which exists among the variables describing social differentiation. Large numbers of variables can be conceptualised as being the manifest indicators of underlying and more general latent properties. Thus, for example, data on such highly inter-correlated variables as percent professional and managerial workers, house values and educational characteristics may be subsumed under the more general construct of social rank. A parsimonious description of social differentiation will be one phrased in terms of those basic constructs which tell us most about the total phenomenon. In traditional statistical terms the analytical power of a construct is measured in terms of its correlation with other variables and those properties are most admired which institute 'natural divisions', that is divisions which in Kaplan's terms (1964, p 50) allow 'the discovery of many more, and more important, resemblances than those originally recognised'. In well-developed sciences the search for basic properties is likely to stress deductive reasoning; in the social sciences much greater stress is likely to be placed on inductive reasoning and on techniques of analysis which stay 'close to the data'. In the search for 'basic properties' under these conditions particular reliance is placed on that set of techniques which is collectively known as factor analysis.

In the words of Harman (1960, p4): 'The principal concern of factor analysis is the resolution of a set of variables linearly in terms of (usually) a small number of categories or 'factors'. This resolution can be accomplished by the analysis of the correlation among the variables. A satisfactory solution will yield factors which convey all the essential information of the original set of variables. Thus, the chief aim is to obtain scientific parsimony or economy of description'. According to Sweetser (1956, p 219) 'Modern factor analysis, using factor structure as a model for ecological structure, is the method *par excellence* for comparing cross-nationally (and intra-nationally) the ecological differentiation of residential areas'.

Most of the theory relating to factorial ecology — and the great majority of empricial applications of the techniques — has been concerned with differentiation within large urban areas (see Timms 1971 for a general discussion). The method is, however, applicable to the study of differentiation at any scale. In the present case the techniques of factorial ecology are used in an attempt to uncover the bases of social differentiation between the thirteen burghs of the Central Region. Given the general absence of detailed theory at the inter-community level, the approach used is 'blind' — that is factor analysis is used simply to search the data matrix for that set of latent dimensions which most satisfactorily accounts for the observed patterns. The particular algorithm employed uses the principal components technique followed by rotation to orthogonal simple structure according to the varimax criterion (see Harman 1960 for a definitive statement of the method). The principal components technique is so defined that each component extracted at any stage of the analysis consists of that linear combination of indicants which accounts for the maximum possible amount of variance existing in the data matrix. A set of principal components accounts for the maximum possible proportion of original variance. Rotation to simple structure is a procedure used to aid the interpretation of factors and has the important aspect that the resulting pattern of indicant-factor correlations tends to be in variant under changes in the composition of the data matrix

The output of any factor analysis is dependent on the input. The initial data matrix for the present analysis is formed by 23 variables, chosen in terms of their substantive significance and computational independence. A full listing of the variables, with their definitions, is given in Table 14.11.

TABLE 14.11

Variables Used in the Factor Analysis of Central Region Burghs

Abbreviation	Definition
POP	Total population, 1971
NAT	Average rate of increase per annum, births minus deaths, 1961 – 71.
DEN	Gross density (population: area), 1971
CHI	Percent of population aged 0 – 14 years, 1971
AGE	Percent of population of 'pensionable' age, 1971
DEP	Ratio of children 0 – 14 years and those of pensionable age to remainder of population, 1971
FER	Ratio of children 0 – 4 years to women 15 – 44 years, 1971
DIV	Percent of ever-married women now divorced, 1971
NMF	Percent of women aged 15 years and over never-married, 1971
SCO	Percent of population Scottish-born, 1971
NCO	Percent of overseas-born U.K. residents born in New Commonwealth, 1971
MIG	Average rate of increase per annum not due to births-deaths, 1961 – 71
NAW	Percent of economically active males not at work, 1971
SCK	Percent of economically active males off work and sick, 1971
STU	Ratio of students aged 15 years and over to population aged 15 – 20 years, 1971
WWF	Percent of women aged 15 – 59 years economically active, 1971
OOC	Percent of population in owner-occupied dwellings, 1971
CRO	Percent of population in dwellings with more than one person per room, 1971
AME	Percent of population in dwellings with exclusive use of standard amenities, 1971
PRO	Percent of economically active males in professional, managerial and technical occupations (S.E.G. 1, 2, 3, 4), 1966
MAN	Percent of economically active males in manual occupation (S.E.G. 9, 10, 11), 1966
VAL	Residential rateable value per capita, 1971
PRI	Average rateable value of private dwellings, 1971

Sources:	all 1971 data, with the exception of VAL and PRI, is from 1971 Census County Reports. NAW, SCK, STU, and WWF are based on unpublished versions of County Report tables.
	PRO and MAN are based on the County Reports of the 1966 Census.
	VAL and PRI are based on data supplied by the Scottish Development Department.

The input to the principal components analysis consists of the matrix of correlations between the 23 variables over the thirteen burghs (see Appendix). The correlation matrix indicates the degree of similarity between the variables and the variation in their 'diagnostic power'. Several variables, notably the percent Scottish-born, the percent owner-occupiers, the percent overcrowded, the percent professional and managerial workers, and the percent manual workers, exhibit a large number of high correlation coefficients (over .71). In six pairs, correlation coefficients of more than .90 are exhibited. On the other hand, two variables, percent of women never married, and percent with exclusive use of all household amenities, have no correlations greater than .66.

It is a characteristic of the principal components technique that as many components are extracted in the analysis as there are initial variables. The majority of the components are, however, generally trivial, accounting for a very small proportion of original variance. The decision 'when to stop factoring' is essentially arbitrary, but reflects both substantive and statistical considerations. In the present case three components, accounting for approximately 80 percent of initial variance, have been retained. Table 14.13 shows the pattern of factor loadings, correlations between variables and factors, obtained after a varimax rotation of the three components.

The interpretation of factors always involves an intuitive leap – a leap guided, however, by the pattern of variable-factor correlations and by the existing body of theory, however loosely-articulated, which relates to the problem at hand. The interpretation of two of the three factors identified in the Central Region burghs is relatively straightforward, but the third is more problematic. Factor I is highly saturated with variables relating to the socio-economic composition of the population. Its highest correlations are with the percent of 15 to 20 year olds categorised as students (negative), with the percent of manual workers and of Scots-born (positive), with three variables relating to housing, the average rateable value of private houses, the percent of owner-occupiers and residential rateable value *per capita* (all negative), and with the percent of women in the work force. The factor may be identified as one of 'social rank', high on the factor reflecting low rank scores Factor II, on the other hand, relates to the demographic structure of the population and may be interpreted as indexing variations in 'family life cycle' characteristics. The highest correlations are with the percent aged 0 – 14 years (negative), the percent over retirement age, and the percent of the ever-married now divorced (positive) and the rate of natural increase (negative). Factor III exhibited high correlations with three variables only: the percent of the economically-active not at work, population size, and the percent reporting 'sick'. It may, perhaps, be interpreted as a 'social deprivation' factor, confidence in this interpretation being enhanced by the moderate positive correlations with overcrowding and gross density and the moderate negative correlations with household amenities, professional and managerial workers and growth resulting from migration.

TABLE 14.12

Varimax Three-Factor Solution for Central Region Burghs

Variable	Factor I	Factor II	Factor III	h^2
	I	II	III	
STU	-94			90
MAN	89			89
SCO	88			94
PRI	-88			85
OOC	-85			99
VAL	-83			80
WWF	81			74
CRO	75			89
NCO	-72	43		74
PRO	-72	40		88
DEP	-70			62
MIG	-66	-41	-41	78
CHI		-91		88
AGE		85		87
DIV		79		66
NAT		-78		86
NMF		72		65
AME		-66	-53	72
FER	40	-65		59
DEN		-59	54	86
NAW	46		83	91
POP			82	70
SCK			78	78
Percent Variance	37.7	24.8	17.3	79.7

Decimal points are omitted and only coefficients of ⩾.40 shown

The differentiation of communities is a reflection of differentiation in the encompassing society. An analysis of the dimensions of community differentiation provides a key to the understanding of social structure. The relationship between residential differentiation and the underlying characteristics of society is complex and, in its details, little understood. Most theoretical speculation is, moreover, implicitly concerned with residential differentiation within urban areas rather than between them. Nonetheless, the discovery of 'basic properties' demands an attempt at their understanding for every classification implies a set of underlying propositions.

Community characteristics reflect a combination of history and of individual or institutional choice. At the level of history are such factors as existing housing stock, economic background and urban functions. At the level of choice are such factors as immigration and emigration, decisions about additions to the housing stock, and variations in preferred life style. In their turn these reflect some of the basic characteristics of the society, economy, and culture in question. Differences between communities rest on the fundamental beliefs and practices of the population. 'We might therefore postulate that the manifest similarities of cities are due to certain fundamental "latent" traits, tendencies, or progenitors like social status, resulting from basic cultural traits and processes, such as the aggressive pursuit of economic achievement and related "success"? (Berry, 1972, p 11). Variations in the patterning of the 'latent traits' provide clues to the nature of the more basic processes.

Factorial ecology is a development of an earlier concern of a group of American sociologists led by Esref Shevky with the theory and method of social area analysis (Shevky and Bell, 1955). According to its proponents social area analysis represents an attempt to link residential differentiation with a general theory of social change. The argument is complex and controversial (e.g. see Timms 1971, pp 138 – 49) but, in essence, states that the process of urban-industrial development leads to a differentiation of the population along three major dimensions: social rank, family life style and ethnicity. The categorisation of people in terms of social rank, family life style and ethnicity provides a basis for their differential treatment. In turn, this is reflected in their differential access to opportunities in the housing market. Spatial differences thus come to parallel social differences and factor structure can serve as an indicator of social structure as well as indicating ecological structure. The full emergence of the three social area constructs of social rank, family life style and ethnicity demands both a heterogeneous population and a relatively advanced degree of modernisation. For ethnicity to emerge as a separate basis of differentiation at the community level there must not only be a relatively large 'ethnic' population but also a situation in which discrimination on grounds of ethnicity is independent of evaluation according to social rank and differentiation according to family life cycle characteristics. Where these conditions are not met ethnicity is likely to become part of the more general social rank factor: ethnically distinct groups rarely share equal access to the opportunity structures enjoyed or endured by the native population. The imputation of casuality is hazardous, but in the Central Region it is noticeable that the higher the proportion of non-Scots in a community the higher is its social rank.

In the development of modern urban-industrial society particular interest attaches to the relationship between social rank and family life cycle variables. Eisenstadt (1966, p3) has suggested that perhaps the most important aspect of the differentiation which has characterised the development of modern society 'is the separation between the different roles held by an individual ... This separation has taken place first, and perhaps most dramatically, between family and economic occupational roles during the industrial revolution'. At the community level the process of modernisation is accompanied by a differentiation of populations along social rank and family life cycle dimensions (see Timms, 1970). In the most modern societies (e.g. Scandinavia, West Coast U.S.A. and Australasia) social rank and family life cycle variables are fully independent: knowledge of a community's characteristics in terms of one set does not predict to its characteristics on the other. Fertility, marriage patterns and the participation of women in the labour force provide a particularly sensitive indicator of the degree of independence between social rank and family life cycle dimensions: in the most modern societies they show little if any relationship with social rank, in more traditional societies they may become a sub-set of social rank (cf Abu-Lughod's description of Cairo, 1969). It is apparent from the pattern of item-factor loadings in Table 14.12 that, at the burgh level, Central Scotland occupies an intermediate position: the percent of women in the workforce is closely correlated with social rank, fertility relates to both factors while marriage patterns relate primarily to the family life cycle dimension. The separation of family life cycle characteristics from social rank is by no means as complete in the Central Region as appears to be the case in, say, New Zealand or Sweden. Whether the Central Region resembles other areas of the United Kingdom in this respect remains a question pending further study. A similar remark applies to the salience of social deprivation as a separate basis of differentiation.

Apart from any light which it may throw on overall social structure, factorial ecology provides the basis for a simplified classification of communities. In the Central Region a three-dimensional classification, according to the dimensions of social rank, family life cycle and social deprivation, captures almost all the information contained in the initial 23-variable matrix. For present purposes it suffices to present the rough outlines of the classification, to begin with, one dimension at a time.

The social rank dimension is signed negatively. Communities which score highly on the factor possess low rank: few students or professional workers, many manual workers, Scots-born, and working women, few owner-occupiers, low house values and much over-crowding They are also communities which have experienced either net emigration or at best a very low rate of increase resulting from immigration. Burghs scoring highest on the factor are, in order, Bo'ness, Tillicoultry, Denny and Alva; burghs scoring lowest (i.e. having the highest social rank) are Bridge of Allan, Dunblane and Dollar, followed by Callander and Doune.

The family life cycle factor distinguishes between burghs with a young population, few unmarrieds and high fertility, and those with an old population, relatively high proportions of single and divorced women, and low fertility. Burghs scoring highly on the factor (i.e. with young family populations) are, again in order, Denny, Grangemouth and Tillicoultry; burghs which have low scores include Callander, Doune, Bridge of Allan, Falkirk and Bo'ness. Dollar and Dunblane have rather anomalous patterns on the family life cycle dimension. In overall terms they present as relatively young and familistic, but they also contain large percentages of the elderly and the unmarried. The explanation appears to lie in their dual role as retirement centres and as commuter settlements. The Dollar situation is made even more complex by the inclusion of Dollar Academy. In the future, as their commuting role increases, it seems likely that both burghs will move further in the direction of young familism.

The social deprivation factor indexes variation in employment and sickness but is also highly saturated with population size. The most deprived burghs are Alloa and Bo'ness followed by Falkirk and Stirling; the least deprived are Dunblane, Doune, Dollar, Bridge of Allan and Callander. Information on other aspects of deprivation is lacking but it seems likely that those living in the burghs which score highest in terms of the social deprivation factor are likely to be those with the least favourable life chances.

TABLE 14.13

A Classification of Central Region Burghs based on Social Rank and Family Life Cycle

Social Rank	Family Life Cycle		
	Young/Family		Old/Non-Family
High	Dollar	Dunblane	Bridge of Allan
			Callander
	Grangemouth	Stirling	Doune
		Alva	Falkirk
Low	Tillicoultry Denny	Alloa	Bo'ness

Burghs underlined fall into the highest third on the social deprivation factor

By definition, each of the dimensions extracted in an orthogonal factor analysis is independent of all others.   Variation in terms of social rank is analytically distinct from that in terms of family life cycle or social deprivation.   To extract maximum information it is necessary to consider the variation along each dimension simultaneously.   The combination of social rank, family life cycle and social deprivation yields a three-dimensional attribute space in which the location of communities describes their overall social characteristics.

Table 14.13 gives a general outline of the combined effects of variation in terms of social rank, family life cycle and social deprivation.   The social profile of each community is summarised by its location.   Communities which are close together in the three-dimensional attribute space are similar in their overall social characteristics;   those that are far apart are dissimilar.   The number of observation units is too small to justify the use of any sophisticated clustering techniques but Table 14.13 serves to illustrate the relative positioning of the burghs.

Bridge of Allan is a unique combination of high social rank, low social deprivation and a population which includes many elderly and relatively large numbers of the unmarried.   In conventional terms it may be described as an established commuter suburb, but one in which familism is played down.   Callander and Doune are somewhat similar to Bridge of Allan in overall characteristics but have lower social rank and a greater preponderance of the elderly.   Retirement plays a more important role, and commuting less, than in Bridge of Allan.   Dollar and Dunblane, on the other hand, combine high social rank commuters with relatively young populations and a considerable emphasis on familism.   The recent nature of their suburban explosion is highlighted by their anomalous combination of many young and many old.

Just as Bridge of Allan is a unique high rank burgh, so is Bo'ness unique at the opposite end of the social rank continuum.   It combines low social rank with a relatively old and non-family population and has the highest score on social deprivation of any of the thirteen burghs.   Denny and Tillicoultry, on the other hand, combine low social rank with young families and little social deprivation.   Both towns have been greatly affected by SSHA and local authority building which has served to attract a young and able workforce.

The four largest settlements in the Central Region, Falkirk, Stirling, Grangemouth and Alloa, occupy positions towards the middle of the attribute space.   Stirling is almost in the centre, combining middling social rank and a middle-aged population with rather higher-than-average deprivation.   Falkirk and Grangemouth have a similar location in terms of middling social rank but differ radically from each other and from Stirling in terms of their family cycle characteristics: Grangemouth has a young family population, Falkirk has a relatively old non-family population.   To the extent that they form a single functional unit their combined characteristics are similar to those of Stirling.   Alloa (and Alva) also fall into the middling category, combining middle social rank with middling life cycle characteristics.

The overall impression of the Central Region burghs which is yielded by an analysis of their factorial ecology is one of variation. There is little evidence of clustering; instead a wide range of permutations is played on the three classificatory dimensions. How the burghs compare with other communities in Scotland is as yet unclear, but it is abundantly apparent that within the Central Region itself there is a great range of social characteristics.

Political Characteristics

The Central Region has been called into existence as the result of a concern with the reform of local government in Scotland. The reform is presented in terms of four objectives: power, effectiveness, local democracy and local involvement. According to the White Paper introducing the formal proposals (Cmnd 4583, p 5): 'local authorities form a vital part of the nation's democracy, and a modern and effective system of local government is essential to achieve the Government's aim of freedom and responsibility at all levels of society'. The proposals 'aim to ensure that local authorities shall be strong enough to carry the burden of responsibility for local affairs and at the same time shall be responsive to local opinion' (Cmnd 4583, p7). To ensure the proper exercise of this responsibility and responsiveness, local government councillors have to appeal to the electorate. 'Local interest and attention will then be engaged, and the citizen will know that he has a stake in an authority which is concerned about his needs' (Cmnd 4583, p 7). The arena of local politics represents a stage on which the interests and desires of the population are caught up in political action. Given the varied nature of their social characteristics, it may be anticipated that there will be just as much variation in the patterns of political activity which characterise the thirteen burghs now to be absorbed into the Central Region.

To many inhabitants of the Central Region it seems that 'politics' is something which relates to the national but not the local level of government. A local government officer in one of the small burghs speaks for many when he claims in April 1974 that 'you won't find politics here'. By politics, in this context, is meant parties — nationally organised and recognised, with 'official' programmes. In the past, a majority of local councillors in the Central Region have eschewed party labels, standing and being returned instead as 'independents'. Prior to the Second World War, Stirling itself had a burgh council exclusively composed of Independents. Although national party labels have since been used at all local elections in the burgh there remains a considerable body of opinion which avers that party politics is inappropriate at the local level. Indeed, a dislike for the introduction of parties has been a potent source of dissatisfaction with the local government reforms being introduced in 1974 and 1975.

The cleavage between 'pro-party' and 'anti-party' factions has been found in several other parts of Britain, especially in the more rural areas (see Bulpitt 1967, pp 1 -- 10). In general, the pro-party group emphasise the heterogeneity of the community and the need for individuals to band together for protection and for the enhancement of their interests. The anti-party group, on the other hand, emphasise homogeneity and consensus. The conflict between the views can readily be illustrated in the report of a pilot study of local influentials in Stirling (Brooke 1974). The study is exploratory in nature but serves to illustrate the positions adopted by proponents of the two perspectives.

The analysis is based on a series of relatively unstructured interviews with seventeen respondents chosen in snowball fashion. The respondents included past and present councillors of all shades of political opinion, party activists and local government officials. Two main categories of response were elicited. On the one hand, one group maintain that Stirling is an integrated community, that party politics are unnecessary and that power in the burgh rests with the formal organs of government. The second group, on the other hand, see cleavages and conflict, believe that formal representation for different interests is essential, and feel that considerable power is exercised not just by the local government agencies but also by business interests, trade unions and other extra-governmental organisations. The division between the two groups roughly corresponds to that between those who label themselves as 'Independents' and those willing to accept the label of 'Labour'. 'Scottish Nationalists' tend to hold an intermediate view.

Prior to the Second World War, Stirling burgh council was made up of 'Moderates' and 'Independents'. Most were substantial shopkeepers and tradesmen among whom the Guilds were still an important social bond. The same individuals were prominent in the social life of the burgh and in its voluntary organisations. As in nineteenth century Glossop (Birch, 1959 , p 34) 'this common leadership of business, social and political affairs served to unify the community'. Since the War the unified elite has become fragmented. The 'old families' have lost influence and high rates of migration, both in and out of the burgh, have let to their partial replacement. Of the 21 council members in 1974 only four are said to be natives of Stirling, only three are members of the Guilds, and only one is both. Outside control of the economy has increased, the major industrial employers being parts of national, even multinational, combines. National chain stores have appeared on the retail front challenging the hegemony enjoyed by local concerns. Unlike the old shopkeepers and industrialists, the new managers are perceived as taking an active part in local politics only when their own — or their firms' — interests are directly involved. The breakdown of the old integrated system creates a situation where party labels may become a more effective means of identification than personal knowledge based on acquaintance. The growing scale of society seems inimical to a continuation of individualistic appeals to the electorate. In the burgh council which is due to disappear in 1975, five councillors wear the label of Independent   In the May

1974 elections to the Stirling District Council, none of the candidates for the eight wards within the burgh stood as an Independent and those returned included four Scottish Nationalists, three Labour Party representatives and one Conservative. A similar pattern is repeated at the Regional Council level, those returned for the four Stirling divisions being two Scottish Nationalists, one Labour and one Conservative.

The salience of the Scottish National Party in Stirling, although in its modern guise dating only from the 1960's, represents the continuation of a long nationalist tradition, which may in its turn derive at least symbolic support from the ancient history of the burgh as the Scottish capital. The nineteenth century Wallace monument campaign and the 1930's New Covenant provide precursors to the more recent revival of Nationalist sentiment and the development of a strong local organisation. For three terms the provost of Stirling has been a nationally prominent member of the S.N.P. and for a considerable period in the 1960's Stirling served as the centre for Nationalist activity in Scotland.

The Labour Party in Stirling appears to have gained its initial momentum from the industrial changes of the 1930's, with the concomitant development of trades unions and a trades council, and from the concentration of manual workers in council estates following slum clearance. Party support has remained strongly localised, even though in total percentage terms Labour Party support (38.3 percent of the total in the May 1974 elections) is almost identical with that for the S.N.P. at District level.

The Conservative Party, overtly at least, is the most recent of the national parties to attempt to gain power at the local level in Stirling burgh. In previous local elections the Chairman of the local Conservative Association has not only stood as an Independent but has been at pains to distance himself from party assistance. In the May 1974 elections, the 21.9 percent of the votes cast for Conservative candidates in Stirling burgh were sufficient to return a single councillor.

The political changes which have characterised the recent history of Stirling burgh are repeated *mutatis mutandis*, in the rest of the Central Region. The demise of Independents in local government is characteristic at both District and Regional levels throughout Central Scotland. The increase in party representation in the Central Region has not, however, yielded a simple political pattern. As a result of the May 1974 elections the Central Regional Council is delicately balanced. The Labour Party have the greatest number of seats – 17 out of 34 – but have to depend on an Independent Labour Councillor for a majority. The S.N.P. have nine seats, the Conservatives have four, there are three Independents and one Independent Labour. A similar knife-edge situation exists in each of the three Districts of the Region. In the Stirling District the Conservatives have the largest number of Councillors – 8 out of 20 – followed by the Labour Party with seven seats, the S.N.P. with four, and one Independent.   In the Clackmannan District the S.N.P. have maintained the momentum of their Parliamentary success in the Clackmannan and East Stirling Constituency, emerging as the largest single party with six seats out of 12; the Labour Party have five and there is a single Independent.   In the Falkirk District the Labour Party have the greatest number of seats — 17 out of 36 — followed by the S.N.P. with 11, Independents with six, and one each Conservative and Independent Labour.   Heterogeneity in social characterists is parallelled by pluralism at the political level.

It used to be one of the cherished beliefs of British political sociology that the percentage of votes cast for the Labour Party is a sensitive indicator of social class.   The equation may well have been true in an era of two-party politics, but appears much less applicable in one where three or more parties are vying for political favour.   In the Central Region the equation of Labour representation with low social rank and Independents with high social rank seems to have been broadly valid in the local government system prior to reorganisation.

TABLE 14.4

Voting Patterns in the District Council Elections, May 1974

	Percentage of Votes Cast for:				Turnout
	S.N.P.	Labour	Conservative	Other	
Alloa	46	44		11	n.a.
Alva	44	26		30	57
Dollar				100	63
Tillicoultry		Unopposed			No election
Bo'ness	48	52			58
Callander	29		48	23	56
Doune	42		58		43
Dunblane	35		46	19	52
Falkirk	42	42	6	10	55
Stirling	38	38	22	2	61
Bridge of Allan	27	12	61	21	60
Denny		43	36	21	54
Grangemouth	23	46		31	57

The four burghs with highest social rank — Bridge of Allan, Dunblane, Dollar and Callander — had local councils entirely composed of Independents.   Those with lowest social rank had overwhelmingly Labour councils.   At the same time, those burghs returning Independents frequently did so unopposed: over the five years 1966 — 70 inclusive less than two-fifths of the seats in Bridge of Allan and less than half of those in Dunblane and Doune were contested.   At the other end of the scale, Alloa, Alva and Grangemouth had 100 percent of their seats contested.   Contested elections and party identification seem to have varied together.

Table 14.4 shows the percentage of votes cast in the 1974 District Council elections for each of the major parties and 'others' in the wards corresponding to the thirteen Central Region burghs.   The total picture is complex.   Of the national parties the most consistent showing is that of the S.N.P., which fielded candidates in all except Dollar, Tillicoultry and Denny, and took more than two-fifths of the votes cast in Alloa, Alva, Bo'ness, Doune and Falkirk.   The Labour Party achieved its greatest successes in Tillicoultry, where its candidate was unopposed, and in Bo'ness, Grangemouth, Denny, Alloa and Falkirk, where its candidates took at least two-fifths of the votes cast.   The successes of the Conservative Party were strongly localised, mainly in the Stirling District.   Bridge of Allan, Callander, Doune, and Dunblane each saw Conservative victories.   The continued saliance of political independence at the local level is evidenced in the high turn-out in Dollar, which was contested by two 'Independent' candidates.   The equation of Independent candidates and low turn-outs, strongly supported in previous elections, receives little support in the 1974 data.   In terms of the traditional links with social rank the nexus between Conservative votes and high rank seems to have withstood the change in local government organisation.   The traditional connection between Labour Party votes and low social rank is much less clear.   In several of the burghs which rank towards the bottom of the social rank scale the dominance of the Labour Party is under considerable Nationalist challange.   Whether or not this reflects a more general 're-alignment' of political allegiance only time will tell.

Conclusion

The Central Region is the smallest in area of the nine regional authorities which comprise the new pattern of local government in Scotland. Such are its links with other areas, however, and its pattern of internal diversity that 'of all the regions this one has at present the least degree of conscious identity' (Cmnd 4583, p 16).

Variation is a constant theme in the discussion of the Central Region. Only in terms of their moderate size do the Central Region burghs display much similarity one to another. In economic function, demography, social rank and political characteristics the burghs present a highly variegated picture. Common identity may indeed be in their diversity. Rather than being a series of discrete and 'well balanced' communities the Central Region burghs approximate to a series of specialised sub-communities, each catering to a particular segment of the population. Within the confines of the Region is found everything from the mining village to the high rank commuter settlement, from the Highland service centre to the high technology industrial town, from the retirement resort to the employment centre. In terms of social rank is found variation between communities which are numerically dominated by high-income professionals and those which consist almost wholly of unskilled and semi-skilled manual workers. Some communities have large numbers of the elderly, the widowed and the single. Others have few but the young and the married. Some burghs are Conservative in politics, others are Labour or S.N.P. In few is the political scene one of boring homogeneity. What was true of the physical characteristics of the Region is also true of the social and political: in few other parts of Britain can such variety be encompassed in so small an area and population.

REFERENCES

Abu-Lughod, J	1969	'Testing the theory of social area analysis: the ecology of Cairo, Egypt.' *American Sociological Review,* 34: 198 – 212.
Bell, C and Newby, H	1971	*Community Studies,* London.
Berry, B J L	1972	*City Classification Handbook : Methods and Applications,* New York: Wiley.
Birch, A H	1959	*Small Town Politics. A Study of Political Life in Glossop.* Oxford: Oxford University Press.

Brand, J   1968   'These are the Scotnats'. *New Statesman, 17 May, 1968.*

Brooke, J   1974   *Party and Politics : Some aspects of government in Stirling and the Central Region.* Unpublished Research Paper, University of Stirling.

Brownrigg, M   1971   *A study of The Impact of The University of Stirling on the local economy.* Unpublished PhD. Thesis, University of Stirling.

Bulpitt, J G   1967   *Party Politics in English Local Government.* London, Longmans.

Central Statistical Office   1973   *Annual Abstract of Statistics.* London, H.M.S.O.

Craig, F W S   1969   *British Parliamentary Election Results, 1918 – 48.* Glasgow.

Eisenstadt, S N   1966   *Modernisation : Protest and Change.* New Jersey, Prentice Hall

Evans, E J   1972   *Tillicoultry. A Centenary History.* Tillicoultry.

General Register Office   1971   Census (Scotland) County Reports. for Perth, Stirling, Clackmannan. Edinburgh.

General Register Officer   1971   Census (Scotland) Second Preliminary Report. Advance Analysis of Computer – Read Data. Edinburgh.

General Register Office   1966   Sample census (Scotland) Economic Activity. County Tables for Perth; Stirling; Clackmannan.

Hanham, H J   1969   *Scottish Nationalism.* London.

Harman, H H   1960   *Modern Factor Analysis.* Chicago, Chicago University Press.

H.M.S.O. (Cmnd 4583)   1971   *Reform of Local Government in Scotland,* Edinburgh.

International Encyclopaedia of The Social Sciences, 1968.
'Politics' Vol 12. New York, MacMillan.

Kaplan, A   1964   *The Conduct of Inquiry,* San Francisco.

Kellas, J G   1973   *The Scottish Political System.* Cambridge, Cambridge University Press.

Mackintosh, J   1970   'The Royal Commission on Local Government in Scotland 1966 — 69'. *Public Administration,* 1970; 49 — 56.

Maclean, E   1970   *Bridge of Allan: The Rise of a village.* Alloa.

Moser, C A and Scott, W   1961   *British Towns.* Edinburgh, Oliver and Boyd.

New Statistical Account of Scotland, 1845.
Edinburgh, Blackwood.

Registrar General   1966   *Annual Reports,* Edinburgh, H.M.S.O.
for Scotland   et seq

Rennie, R C and   1966   *Third Statistical Account of Scotland.* Glasgow, Collins.
Grouther Gordon, T

Sacks, S and   1972   'Dimensions and classification of british towns on the
Firestone, R   basis of new data' in BJL Berry (ed) *City Classification Handbook : Methods and Applications.* New York, Wiley.

Scottish Development   1972   *Rating Report.* Manuscript.
Department

Scottish Development   1968   *The Grangemouth/Falkirk Regional Survey and Plan.*
Department   2 Vols. Edinburgh, H.M.S.O.

Scotsman 9 May, 1974   Regional Election Results.

Scotsman 2 March, 1974   General Election Supplement.

Shevky, E and Bell, W   1955   *Social Area Analysis : Theory, Illustrative Application and Computational Procedures.*   Stanford University Press.

Sinclair, Sir J   1791– 99   *The Statistical Account of Scotland.*

Stacey, M   1960   *Tradition and Change.   A study of Banbury.*   Oxford, Oxford University Press.

Stirling Observer,   15 May, 1974
     Regional and District Election Results.

Sweetser, F L   1965   'Factor structure as ecological structure in Helsinki and Boston'.   *Acta Sociologica,*   8, 202 – 225.

The Times   1954 et seq   *Guide to the House of Commons.*   London, Times Newspapers.

Timms, D W G   1970   'Modernisation and the factional ecology of the Cook Islands, Brisbane and Auckland.'   *Australian and New Zealand Journal of Sociology.*   6.   139 – 49.

Timms, D W G   1971   *The Urban Mosaic : Towards a Theory of Residential Differentiation.*   Cambridge, Cambridge University Press.

Wheatley, J   1969   *Royal Commission on Local Government in Scotland, 1966 – 69.*   Report and Appendices presented to Parliament, September, 1969.   London, H.M.S.O. (Cmnd. 4150).

Woolfe, J N (ed)   1969   *Government and Nationalism in Scotland.*   Edinburgh Edinburgh University Press.

Appendix 14.1

Product – moment Correlation Coefficients for the 13 Central Region Burghs.

Decimal points omitted

	POP	NAT	DEN	CHI	AGE	DEP	FER	DIV	NMF	SCO	NCO	MIG	NAW	SCK	STU	WWF	OOC	CRO	AME	PRO	MAN	VAL	PRI
POP	100																						
NAT	51	100																					
DEN	35	62	100																				
CHI	10	57	60	100																			
AGE	-39	-85	-67	-82	100																		
DEP	-40	-40	-16	21	33	100																	
FER	09	71	52	40	-43	-02	100																
DIV	-25	-73	-45	-61	71	07	-43	100															
NMF	-27	-57	-50	-63	65	11	-49	51	100														
SCO	50	58	41	-12	-35	-74	52	-18	-36	100													
NCO	-38	-69	-43	-12	46	61	-67	46	57	-86	100												
MIG	-25	02	-23	39	00	59	15	-34	-09	-61	18	100											
NAW	71	58	61	08	-45	-54	33	-14	-09	75	-55	-58	100										
SCK	54	52	77	30	-56	-37	27	-34	-15	56	-41	-51	86	100									
STU	-22	-40	-22	33	11	70	-01	-47	22	-90	73	63	-53	-31	100								
WWF	11	-05	-38	11	-57	72	13	23	-12	69	-53	40	37	-74	-74	100							
OOC	-46	-70	-59	-19	61	72	-56	27	53	69	-53	58	-76	-64	81	-61	100						
CRO	57	74	51	18	-61	-69	51	-32	-58	-93	82	-46	78	59	-74	47	-94	100					
AME	-53	23	11	66	-46	20	-44	-40	-29	-25	-85	41	-32	-08	19	-27	-01	-08	100				
PRO	-47	-63	-75	-29	63	-44	44	35	59	76	00	54	-71	-69	66	-66	91	-82	-00	100			
MAN	35	53	46	01	-44	-64	44	-09	-44	89	-75	66	53	-84	62	-75	83	-93	-10	-80	100		
VAL	-22	-50	-46	-25	53	53	-50	03	55	-75	59	56	-52	-43	69	-54	89	-75	-15	76	-91	100	
PRI	-08	-02	12	59	-05	55	-10	-19	24	-66	45	64	-18	-07	78	-73	59	-50	14	-72	-80	65	100
Number of r's ⩾ ±0.71	1	4	2	1	3	2	1	2	0	9	5	1	6	2	7	2	9	9	0	8	8	5	3